ISBN 978-7-5495-7902-0
9 787549 579020 >
定價：1800.00元（全3冊）

Treasures for Scholars Worldwide

哈佛燕京圖書館文獻叢刊第十五種
Harvard-Yenching Library Reprint Series, No. 15

美國哈佛大學
哈佛燕京圖書館藏
鋼和泰未刊往來書信集

The Unpublished Correspondence of Alexander von Staël-Holstein in the Harvard-Yenching Library, Harvard University

鄒新明　編

上

GUANGXI NORMAL UNIVERSITY PRESS
广西师范大学出版社
· 桂林 ·

北京大学出版社
PEKING UNIVERSITY PRESS
· 北京 ·

圖書在版編目（CIP）數據

美國哈佛大學哈佛燕京圖書館藏鋼和泰未刊往來書信集：全3册：漢文、英文 / 鄒新明編．—桂林：廣西師範大學出版社，2016.3
ISBN 978-7-5495-7902-0

Ⅰ．①美… Ⅱ．①鄒… Ⅲ．①鋼和泰（1877～1937）－書信集－漢、英 Ⅳ．①K835.116.55

中國版本圖書館CIP數據核字（2016）第036131號

廣西師範大學出版社
北京大學出版社 出版
廣西師範大學出版社發行
（廣西桂林市中華路22號 郵政編碼：541001
網址：http://www.bbtpress.com）
出版人：何林夏
全國新華書店經銷
廣西大華印刷有限公司印刷
(廣西南寧市高新區科園大道62號 郵政編碼：530007)
開本：880 mm ×1 240 mm 1/16
印張：119.5 字數：1912千字
2016年3月第1版 2016年3月第1次印刷
定價：1800.00元（全3册）

前 言

鋼和泰（Alexander von Staël-Holstein，1877—1937），著名佛學家、藏學家、梵文學家。大約在1917年，鋼和泰來到北京，此後直到去世，後半生主要在北京（1928年改稱北平）度過。但也許由於研究過於專門，鋼和泰其人其學在現在國内學界不大爲人所知。

國内較早系統介紹鋼和泰生平學術的文字當屬錢文忠教授發表的《男爵及其幻想：紀念鋼和泰》[1]一文。錢教授此文主要依據的材料是哈佛燕京學社第一任社長葉理綏（Serge Elisséeff，1889—1975）回憶鋼和泰的一篇文章[2]和胡適日記中關於鋼和泰的記載。此後，國内主要系統研究和介紹鋼和泰生平及學術者當首推曾供職於清華大學的王啓龍和鄧小詠夫婦，王啓龍教授編有《鋼和泰學術年譜簡編》，王啓龍、鄧小詠合著有《鋼和泰學術評傳》，并撰寫論文數篇。此外，還有上海社會科學院歷史研究所研究員馬軍先生翻譯的德國學者謝禮士（Ernst Schierlitz）的《悼念鋼和泰男爵》[3]一文，文後附有鋼和泰著述和有關研究目録甚詳。

編者對藏學和佛學所知甚少，這裏僅對鋼和泰的生平略作介紹，有興趣的讀者可以參閱上述文獻資料。

鋼和泰出生於俄屬愛沙尼亞一個貴族家庭，祖先是德國人。少年時代接受良好的教育，通曉俄文、德文、法文、拉丁文、希臘文。1894年在多爾帕特帝國大學（Dorpat Imperial University）學習，1896年到德國柏林大學研究梵文和印地文文獻，三年半後轉到哈勒－威登伯格大學，1900年獲哲學博士學位。在伯恩大學和牛津大學短暫游學之後，鋼和泰回到俄國，在外交部門擔任翻譯。1903—1904年，曾任俄國駐孟買總領館文化參贊。1909年任聖彼得堡大學梵文和印度哲學助理教授。1916年隨聖彼德堡科學院科學使團訪問日本，次年到北京，因十月革命爆發而滯留中國。1918年受聘在北京大學講授梵文和古印度宗教史。1926年前後，在北京創辦中印研究所。1928—1929年，到哈佛大學訪問講學。1929年，被聘爲哈佛大學中亞語文學教授，同時中印研究所并入哈佛燕京學社，被任命爲所長，同年回北平。此後在北平主持中印研究所，組織相關學習和研究。1937年因病在北平去世。鋼和泰還曾兼任北京大學國學門導師、中央研究院史語所特約研究員、故宫博物院委員會委員、《燕京學報》編委、《華裔學志》副主編等職。主要著作有《大寶積經迦葉品梵藏漢六種合刊》等。

哈佛燕京圖書館收藏的鋼和泰檔案資料，很明顯多年前有人整理過，書信部分一律用牛皮紙信封

---

[1] 發表於《讀書》，1997年第1期。

[2] Serge Elisséeff. *Staël-Holstein's Contribution to Asiatic Studies. Harvard Journal of Asiatic Studies*, Vol. 3, No. 1, 1938

[3] Ernst Schierlitz. *In Memory of Alexander Wihelm Baron von Staël-Holstein. Monumenta Serica Journal of Oriental Studies*（《華裔學志》），Vol. III, Fasc. I, 1938. 馬軍先生的譯文收入《漢學研究》第十四集，學苑出版社，2002年。

按書信人分别存放。據《鋼和泰學術年譜簡編》(以下簡稱《年譜簡編》),鋼和泰去世後,1937年7月1日,葉理綏在北平召集了一次會議,專門討論中印研究所後續事宜,備忘録於11月8日向學社理事會提交。備忘録第七條"德·斯太爾先生的酬勞"中記載:"一致同意,從1937年3月15日起,由哈佛燕京學社每月支付德·斯太爾250美元,作爲他照看中印研究所圖書資料和財産、圖書目録整理以及對故男爵的文件和著述進行整理和分類的酬勞。"[4] 德·斯太爾是鋼和泰的侄子,哈佛畢業生,鋼和泰去世後被聘請爲中印研究所的秘書和圖書館員,其中一項工作就是整理鋼和泰的文件和著述。從上述牛皮紙信封上的工整漂亮的毛筆小楷來看,這項整理工作應該是得到某位中國人的幫助,具體不詳。

至於鋼和泰檔案資料是如何最終入藏哈佛燕京圖書館的,編者没有查到具體的記載。鋼和泰去世後,中印研究所曾由來華進修的柯立夫(Francis Cleaves)主持,太平洋戰爭爆發後停辦,抗戰勝利後恢復,更名爲"美國亞洲學研究所",1951年從北京撤出。[5] 編者推測,鋼和泰檔案資料至遲在1951年"美國亞洲學研究所"撤出時被運到哈佛。至於是否直接入藏哈佛燕京圖書館,有待進一步考證。

現存哈佛燕京圖書館的這批鋼和泰檔案資料,最主要的部分就是鋼和泰往來書信。前面提到的王啓龍教授所編《年譜簡編》主要依據的就是這些書信資料。將哈佛燕京圖書館藏鋼和泰書信與《年譜簡編》比對,編者遺憾地發現,後者并没有全部參考前者,所利用的比例不到三分之一,具體來説,前者收藏的840餘封書信中,後者衹參考了大約不到250封。從比對的情况看,似乎王啓龍教授過於匆忙,没有全部查閱或者掌握這些書信資料,衹是按照鋼和泰檔案原整理的字母順序,拍下了從A到F的書信資料,而且F部分的傅涇波(Philip Fugh)和福克司(Walter Fuchs)書信也没有來得及拍攝。我想這應該是在《年譜簡編》公布鋼和泰書信之後整理出版鋼和泰往來書信集的最重要的原因。

其次,正如有學者指出的,《年譜簡編》衹有書信譯文,没有原文,學術參考價值便打了折扣。而且,已經有一些研究者指出,《年譜簡編》存在不少辨識和翻譯上的錯誤。[6] 因此,編者認爲,有必要把鋼和泰的書信影印出版,爲研究者提供原汁原味的參考資料。

據編者粗略統計,本書收集的鋼和泰往來書信共計852封,算上信件所附論文等資料,共計1753頁,涉及書信往來個人、單位164個。這些與鋼和泰書信往來的人物,多爲大名鼎鼎的學者或文化界人士,真可謂"談笑有鴻儒,往來無白丁"。這其中所涉及的中國學者有:胡適、陳寅恪、趙元任、傅斯年、丁文江、翁文灝、陳大齊、蔣夢麟、洪煨蓮、俞同奎、馬衡、聞宥、容庚、顧頡剛、黄文弼、張歆海等。與鋼和泰書信往來的當時長期在華的外國學者和文化界人士有:美國的司徒雷登(John Leighton Stuart)、顧臨(Roger S. Greene)、索克思(George E. Sokolsky)、博晨光(Lucius C. Porter)、恒慕義(Arthur Willian Hummel)、費正清(John King Fairbank)、顧立雅(Herrlee Glessner Creel)、義理壽(Irvin V. Gillis)等;法國的普意雅(Bouillard Georges)、沙海昂(Antoine Henry Charignon);德國

[4] Ernst Schierlitz. *In Memory of Alexander Wihelm Baron von Staël-Holstein. Monumenta Serica Journal of Oriental Studies*(《華裔學志》), Vol. III, Fasc. I, 1938. 馬軍先生的譯文收入《漢學研究》第十四集,學苑出版社,2002年。

[5] 參閲聶崇歧《簡述"哈佛燕京學社"》,《文史資料選輯》第二十五輯,中華書局,1981年。

[6] 如高杉杉《鋼和泰年譜訂誤》,初刊於《東方早報·上海書評》2008年5月25日試刊號,後收入高杉杉文集《佛書料簡》,浙江大學出版社,2012年。此外,網上"布衣書局"的"布衣論壇"2008年4月19日開始有不少討論。儘管如此,《年譜簡編》作爲第一本系統研究鋼和泰生平學術的著作,其開創之功還是應該給予充分肯定的。

的艾鍔風(Emil Wilhelm Gustav Ecke)、福克司、雷興(Ferdinand Diedrich Lessing)、米和伯(Herbert Mueller)等;比利時的田清波(Father Antoine Mostaert);瑞典的安特生(J. G. Andersson)、斯文・赫定(Sven Hedin)、喜仁龍(Osvald Sirén)等;前蘇聯的伊鳳閣(Aleksei Lvanovich Lvanov);英國的裴麗珠(Madame Lauru)等。哈佛大學和哈佛燕京學社方面,與鋼和泰書信交往最多的有學社首任社長葉理綏、哈佛文理研究生院院長 George Henry Chase、哈佛大學印度哲學教授 James H. Woods 等。與鋼和泰交往的其他外國學者,主要爲東方學、印度學、佛學、藏學、漢學、梵文等領域的著名人物,如法國的烈維(Sylvain Lévi)、伯希和(Paul Pelliot)、戴密微(Paul Demiéville)、戴何都(Robert des Rotours)、戈鷺波(V. Goloubew)等;德國的 Max Walleser、Heinrich Lüders、Ernst Leumann、Friedrich Weller、Siegfried Behrsing、Helmuth von Glasenapp 等;比利時的 Louis de La Vallée Poussin;美國的 Walter Eugene Clark、Alice Getty、Clarence H. Hamilton、Charles R. Lanman、賴德烈(Kenneth Scott Latourette)、Owen Lattimore、Berthold Laufer、普愛倫(Alan Priest)等;挪威的 Sten Konow;日本的白鳥庫吉、荻原雲來等;意大利的 Giuseppe Tucci;印度的 V. Bhattacharya、Kshiti Mohan Sen 等;英國的 Charles Eliot、E. Denison Ross、Frederick William Thomas 等。這一長串的著名人物名單,足以證明鋼和泰學術交游之廣,在學術界的影響之大。

讀鋼和泰的往來書信,不僅可以深入了解鋼和泰的學術研究和學術造詣,而且可以全面瞭解鋼和泰的爲人處世,讓這位有點兒神秘的男爵變得有血有肉。如從鋼和泰 1936 年 4 月 8 日寫給胡適的信中,我們可以瞭解到鋼和泰對於民主、獨裁與科學發展的關係很有自己的思考,可見鋼和泰并不衹是獨坐書齋,衹關心自己的藏學、佛教研究。又如,爲了擴大自己的學術影響,争取哈佛燕京學社的支持,鋼和泰曾給 Louis de La Vallée Poussin、Charles Eliot、Howard Coonley Hollis 等人寫信,請他們在有關報刊上發表對自己學術研究的評論。再如鋼和泰 1933 年 12 月 24 日給博晨光的信中説,自己最近收到一些信上有些郵票,博晨光的小兒子可能會感興趣,所以寄給對方。由此可見,鋼和泰是一個心思細密,并且很注意與人交往的人。至於鋼和泰書信中很多參加或邀請别人參加家庭聚會的書信,更是透露出鋼和泰對於自己學術文化交際圈的刻意經營。

鋼和泰的一些書信也揭示出一些不太爲人知的往事。如從袁同禮、馬衡 1930 年 3 月 7 日寫給鋼和泰的書信,和鋼和泰 1930 年 2 月 18 日寫給 George Henry Chase 的書信,我們可以瞭解到,大約在 1930 前不久,經 James H. Woods 的介紹,鋼和泰通過 Woods 的兄弟,從小洛克菲勒那裏争取到一筆經費,用於修復故宫中的喇嘛廟,由洛克菲勒基金會方面的美國建築師負責監督施工。此項捐贈帶動了相關的捐贈,爲北平古建築文物的保護做出了貢獻。又如,鋼和泰在商務印書館出版《大寶積經迦葉品梵藏漢六種合刊》,中文序言爲梁啓超所作,這中間與商務印書館和梁啓超的聯繫是通過誰的幫助呢?我們很容易想到與鋼和泰交往頗多,與商務印書館關係密切,且與梁啓超熟稔的胡適。然而,讀鋼和泰與丁文江的書信,編者才知道,這位幕後英雄原來是丁文江。再如,著名藏學家于道泉,當年不顧家人反對和父親斷絶經濟支持的聲明,放棄已經考取的山東官費留美,决心到印度學習梵文和佛教,後經泰戈爾推薦,擔任鋼和泰的梵文課翻譯,并隨其學習梵文,到雍和宫學習藏文。從本書收録的兩封于道泉寫給鋼和泰的書信看,也許由於没有家庭經濟的資助,于道泉當時經濟上處於相當困窘的狀態,讀後讓人對這位一心向學、矢志不移的學者肅然起敬。

鋼和泰的往來書信還可以幫助我們確定他本人的一些重大事件的時間。如鋼和泰的結婚時間,《年譜簡編》認爲是 1929 年 9 月。據《北華正報》(*North China Standard*) 1929 年 6 月 18 日關於鋼和泰婚禮的報道，鋼和泰應是在 6 月結婚的。至於具體日期，司徒雷登 1929 年 6 月 13 日寫給鋼和泰的信中提到，鋼和泰將於“下個周一”結婚，查萬年曆，可以確定爲 1929 年 6 月 16 日。

以上是編者在整理過程中的一管之見。可以想見，有關研究者將從鋼和泰書信中得到豐富的資源和意想不到的收獲。

2013 年，編者有幸在哈佛燕京圖書館訪問交流一年，其中一項工作就是整理鋼和泰檔案資料。蒙鄭炯文館長信任，鋼和泰往來書信的編輯出版作爲整理的後續工作，由編者回國後完成。

編者對鋼和泰的研究領域——佛學、藏學，幾乎完全陌生，之所以敢於斗膽接下這項任務，主要出於以下考慮：

第一，本書采取影印出版的方式，主要整理編輯工作爲書信年代的編排和書信人的簡單介紹。編者有此前整理胡適藏書、手稿等所積纍的知識與經驗可資借鑒。

第二，這批鋼和泰書信之前已經有了簡單的整理，省去了不少在書信人辨識方面的功夫。

第三，鑒於《年譜簡編》存在大量未收書信，以及其他遺憾，編者認爲有必要盡快將這批書信整理公布，這無論是對於研究者，還是《年譜簡編》編者，都將是一件好事。

對於鋼和泰，編者在去哈佛之前，主要是在讀《胡適日記全集》時零星瞭解到一些情况。由於整理胡適藏書的關係，到哈佛燕京圖書館時，我最主要的興趣點仍然是胡適。我對鋼和泰的關注，是因爲之前從北大東語系王邦維教授的一篇介紹文章中瞭解到，胡適與鋼和泰有書信往來。還記得前年第一次接觸鋼和泰檔案原始資料的情形，當時出乎我意料的有兩點，一是鋼和泰給胡適的書信有不少底稿留存，且不見於《年譜簡編》；一是鋼和泰交游之廣，留下往來書信數量之多。

一般來説，整理一個人的往來書信有三方面的困難，一是手寫書信和書信人簽名的辨識，這需要很高的字體辨識能力和豐富的經驗積纍；二是没有時間或時間不完整的書信的年代的考證，這需要比較廣博的知識，以及細密的考證推理功夫；三是對於書信人情況的瞭解，這需要豐富的背景知識和較好的人物資料綜合檢索能力。

正如前文指出的，幸運的是，鋼和泰書信在編者整理之前，已經有了初步的整理，基本上按照書信人分放於信封中，并按字母順序排列。所以第一點要解决的困難，就是遇到日期不確定的書信，需要查閲原文。好在編者在整理胡適藏書中接觸到不少西文題記，有一定的經驗，且當時身在哈佛，可以非常方便地向以英語等西方語言爲母語的學者請教。

書信年代的考證是編者整理過程中最感困難，也最感興趣，且最費時間的部分。從鋼和泰留下的書信來看，他非常注重個人檔案的保存，留下了大量的寫給他人書信的底稿，但這些底稿往往没有寫明年代，或者衹寫月日，没有年。在編者看來，整理這些書信，頗有點兒像偵探斷案，需要從書信中需找蛛絲馬迹，進行推理判斷，有時候又是環環相扣，因此，雖然非常勞神費時，却也是趣味盎然。這部分工作主要是編者在哈佛燕京期間完成，回國後進一步整理時，又做了補充和修正。據編者的粗略統計，鋼和泰 850 餘封往來書信中，經編者考證年代的有 190 封之多，當然，因爲受資料等限制，有的衹能是大致年代範圍的推斷，無法具體到年月日。編者推理查考這些書信年代的主要方法爲：

一、直接根據書信原件補充底稿缺失的年代。

這方面主要是參考了哈佛燕京學社“鋼和泰檔案”和中國社科院近代史所“胡適檔案”中的鋼和泰書信原件。

二、根據往來書信提供的綫索，確定書信年代。

往來書信不僅會討論同一件事情，而且往往會在信開頭提到收到對方某月某日的來信。如鋼和泰寫給商務印書館的一封信，提到收到對方 1922 年 4 月 20 日和 5 月 6 日兩封信，并且隨信寄給商務 18—59 頁的簽名校樣，商務印書館 1922 年 6 月 14 日給鋼和泰的信中提到，此信是對鋼和泰上月 18 日書信的回復，并且已經修改了 18—59 頁的第二次校樣。故可大致斷定，鋼和泰此信寫於 1922 年 5 月 18 日。

三、根據書信中提到的有確定時間的事件，推斷書信年代。

如鋼和泰一封寫給戴密微的信，第一頁說自己的助手黃建（黃樹因）大約兩個月前去世。據《北大日刊》，黃建 1923 年 6 月 15 日去世，故大致可推定此信寫於 1923 年 8 月。

四、根據書信中提到的某月某日對應的星期，推斷書信年代。

主要根據萬年曆查某月某日對應爲星期幾的爲哪一年，有時候會有不止一個年代，需要根據往來書信人的交往年代進行判斷。如鋼和泰寫給畢安祺的一封信，開頭說“我很高興接受您 1 月 7 日周五的晚宴邀請”，哈佛燕京圖書館藏鋼和泰檔案中，鋼和泰與畢安祺書信往來的年代範圍爲 1926—1932，查萬年曆，在此七年中，1927 年 1 月 7 日爲星期五。由此可以大致推定此信寫於 1927 年 1 月。

五、根據信封或明信片上的郵戳日期，大致推斷書信年代。

如雷興寫給鋼和泰的一個明信片，没有寫信日期，郵戳爲 1927 年 4 月 11 日，故可推斷此明信片寫於 1927 年 4 月。

六、根據寫在同一頁紙上的不同書信推斷書信年代。

鋼和泰的書信草稿中，有的同一張信紙上寫有好幾封信，這幾封信的年代應該相近，因此，衹要大致知道其中一封書信的年代，其他書信的年代就比較容易推斷了。

關於書信人的簡介方面，雖然與鋼和泰交往者多爲著名學人，但由於他們的研究多爲藏學、印度學、東方學等專門領域，相關資料不易獲得。此外，由中國人物的英文名字還原爲中文，也頗不易，除了要瞭解當時的韋氏拼音之外，有的人物本身也略嫌冷僻。如 Kungpah T. King、Sohtsu G. King 即金鞏伯、金紹基兄弟，Wen Yu 即聞宥。

此外，鋼和泰往來書信涉及英文、法文、德文、俄文、日文、中文等文字，這也大大增加了整理的難度。

雖然有種種困難，本書總算如期完成了，行文至此，編者頗有如釋重負之感。

本書的完成，首先要感謝哈佛燕京圖書館館長鄭炯文先生的信任和支持。哈佛燕京圖書館的馬小鶴先生、楊麗瑄老師、王繫老師、宋小惠老師、梁慧芬老師，武漢大學訪問館員汪雁老師，國家圖書館訪問館員劉波兄，哈佛燕京學社李若虹博士、Susan Alpert 女士，國家圖書館彭福英老師，社科院近代史所檔案館的茹静老師，北大圖書館趙飛老師等，在鋼和泰書信整理編輯過程中，都給予了編者很大的幫助，在此一并表示衷心的感謝。

如果說到哈佛燕京學社訪問交流一年對編者來說多少是個意外，那麼整理編輯鋼和泰往來書信就更是出乎編者的意料了，但細思之後，又彷彿是冥冥之中的注定。書稿的整理編輯從編者去年一月初回國至今，恰好整整一年的時間，幾乎主要業餘時間都用在上面。在北京陋室電腦前辛苦忙碌的不經意間，前年編者幾乎每個上班日都要往返的 Brattle Street 上已是花開花謝，而我曾經在那條街上留下的足迹也早已被風吹雨打去。想起胡適常給人題寫的那句話："要怎麼收穫，先那麼栽。"一年的努力栽種，我希望收穫的是什麼呢？我想也許是給前年的鋼和泰書信整理一個讓自己心安的交代，也許是對在波士頓風輕雲淡、充實從容的一年異域生活的最好紀念吧。

受時間和編者知識所限，本書難免會有錯誤疏漏之處，敬請指正。

鄒新明

2015 年 12 月 5 日於北京

編輯體例

一、爲給研究者提供原始可靠的參考資料，本書采取影印的方式出版。

二、書信西文、俄文部分統一按照書信人姓的字母順序排列，不能辨識書信人姓名的書信，統一以“Letters Unidentified”爲名集中於本部分最後。中文和日文書信各按照書信人的中文和日文姓氏拼音排序。

三、同一書信人的往來書信按照年代排列，年代不詳者列於最後。

四、原存放於某一書信人信封内，不屬於書信人的書信，能辨識出姓名者，單獨列出，名字不能辨識或僅有先生、教授之類稱呼者，作爲附録列於該書信人的書信之後。書信人親屬的書信，如無具體姓名，也列於書信人的書信之後。

五、對於没有書信年代，或者年代不完整的書信，能推斷確切年代者，給出確切年代，并在信件擬目中説明推斷依據。衹能確定大致時間範圍者，在推斷時間後用“？”存疑，同時在信件擬目中説明推斷依據。不能推斷年代者，直接在信件擬目中説明此信“日期不詳”。

六、對於往來書信涉及的書信人，在書信前給予簡單的介紹，不能提供介紹者，以“生平不詳”標出。

七、書信人簡介部分，對於不確定的機構、職務等譯文，用括號提供原文。有著述題名原文者，在譯名之後用括號提供原文。

目　録

序號	書信人	信件擬目	頁碼
001	Mr. Acton	01 Alexander von Staël-Holstein to Mr. Acton, Sept.?, 1934–1935 此信無日期，開頭説："It is indeed kind of you to enquire about my diet." 鋼和泰 1934 年 10 月 10 日給 Priest 的信中説："Many thanks for your letter. I fear that Mr. 陳 's diet is just as strict as mine……"，Chase 1935 年 4 月 17 日給鋼和泰的信中説："I was very sorry to hear that you have to be on such a strict diet"，故此信的時間應該大致在 1934 年或 1935 年。此信原置於 "Priest 回發" 信封内。	1
002	J. G. Andersson	01 J. G. Andersson to Alexander von Staël-Holstein, Apr. 2, 1927	3
		02 J. G. Andersson to Alexander von Staël-Holstein, May 6, 1927	4
		03 Alexander von Staël-Holstein to J. G. Andersson, May 6, 1927 此信爲鋼和泰致安特生草稿，未具日期。安特生 1927 年 6 月 14 日回復鋼和泰的信開頭説："I have to acknowledge with sincerest thanks your letter of May 26th and also the earlier letter of May 6th." 信中又説："With reference to your earlier letter I am glad to tell you that I will be in Stockholm for the next 12 months at least. Furthermore I hope that all questions raised in your letter of May 6th will be answered in my next communication to you after the receipt of the material." 安特生此信是對鋼和泰 1927 年 5 月 6 日和 5 月 26 日兩封信的回復，這裏的 "earlier letter" 當指 5 月 6 日一信。而鋼和泰在此信第一頁恰恰提到："I fear that you might leave Stockholm for South Africa, North greenland, ……"，綜上可以推定，鋼和泰此信寫於 1927 年 5 月 6 日。而王啓龍所編《鋼和泰學術年譜簡編》（中華書局，2008 年，以下簡稱《年譜簡編》。）將此信定爲七月，似不確。	5

序號	書信人	信件擬目	頁碼
		04 Alexander von Staël-Holstein to J. G. Andersson, May 26, 1927 此信爲鋼和泰致安特生草稿，未具日期。鋼和泰此信中説：“As you will see from the enclosed paper the ‘Calchas’ was scheduled to leave Taku Bar for Hamburg on Monday (yesterday).” 其中的“Calchas”，據信中所説，爲運送鋼和泰收藏的英國貨輪。安特生 1927 年 6 月 14 日的復信説：“We expect to get your collection, as well as our own consignment with the s/s Calchas early next month, ……”，也提到“Calchas”號，應是對鋼和泰此信上引一句的回復，據安特生 6 月 14 日書信開頭内容可知，安特生 6 月 14 日書信是對鋼和泰 5 月 6 日和 26 日兩封信的回復，既然上一封信爲 5 月 6 日無疑，則此信似當爲鋼和泰 5 月 26 日所寫。有一點疑問，信末説“Monday (yesterday)”，則 5 月 26 日當爲星期二，查萬年曆，1927 年 5 月 26 日是星期四。《年譜簡編》將此信定爲 7 月，似不確。從書信内容看，此信在安特生 6 月 14 日書信之前，當無疑問。	7
		05 J. G. Andersson to Alexander von Staël-Holstein, Jun. 14, 1927	8
		06 Alexander von Staël-Holstein to J. G. Andersson, Oct. 1st, 1927 此信第一頁爲他人抄録複寫鋼和泰書信，寫明年代爲 1927 年 10 月 1 日。第二、三頁爲鋼和泰擬的書信草稿，内容與第一頁基本相同。	9
		附 01 Alexander von Staël-Holstein to Comte 此信寫於鋼和泰 1927 年 10 月 1 日致安特生書信的背面，鋼和泰親筆，法文，日期不詳。伯爵（Comte）具體姓名不詳，暫繫於此。	12
003	C. W. Anner	01 C. W. Anner to Alexander von Staël-Holstein, Jul. 17, 1929 此信原置於“Rockefeller (Foundation) 來”文件夾内，附有電報一頁。	13
004	Baldur	01 Alexander von Staël-Holstein to Baldur 此信收信人全名不詳。此信原置於“Mdvani, Prince 回發”信封内。	15
005	Florence T. Bayley	01 Florence T. Bayley to Alexander von Staël-Holstein, Dec. 12, 1931 此信原置於“Clark, Walter 來”文件夾内。	17

序號	書信人	信件擬目	頁碼
006	Siegfried Behrsing	01 Siegfried Behrsing to Alexander von Staël-Holstein 五封電報，無年月，僅有日期。	18
		02 Alexander von Staël-Holstein to Siegfried Behrsing 此信爲鋼和泰手書德文底稿，無日期。	23
007	Bennett	01 Alexander von Staël-Holstein to Bennett, 1926–1927 此信無日期，開頭說：“A Sino-Indian Institute in which I am much interested is being organized in Peking ……”，據鋼和泰與博晨光的往來書信，似乎燕京大學從 1926 年 8 月開始資助鋼和泰辦中印研究所，信中又提到希望到歐洲和美國，此信大致寫於 1926—1927 年。此信原置於“Porter, Lucius 回發”信封内。	25
008	V. Bhattacharya	01 V. Bhattacharya to Alexander von Staël-Holstein, Sept. 30, 1924	26
009	George D. Birkhoff	01 George D. Birkhoff to Alexander von Staël-Holstein, Jun. 4, 1929	27
010	Carl W. Bishop	01 Carl W. Bishop to Alexander von Staël-Holstein, Jan. 21, 1926	29
		02 Alexander von Staël-Holstein to Carl W. Bishop, Jan.?, 1927 此信爲鋼和泰手書底稿，無日期。書信開頭說：“I have much pleasure in accepting your invitation to dinner on Friday January 7th ……”，哈佛燕京圖書館藏鋼和泰檔案中，鋼和泰與畢安祺書信往來的年代範圍爲 1926—1932 年，查萬年曆，在此七年中，1927 年 1 月 7 日爲星期五。由此可以大致推定此信寫於 1927 年 1 月，而鋼和泰的回復應在畢安祺 1 月 7 日宴請之前，則此信大致寫於 1927 年 1 月初。	30
		03 Carl W. Bishop to Alexander von Staël-Holstein, Jan. 28, 1927	32
		04 Carl W. Bishop to Alexander von Staël-Holstein, Mar. 4, 1932	34
		05 Carl W. Bishop to Alexander von Staël-Holstein, Sept. 26, 1932	35

序號	書信人	信件擬目	頁碼
		06 Alexander von Staël-Holstein to Carl W. Bishop, Oct.?, 1932 此信爲鋼和泰手書底稿，無日期。書信開頭說："Mr. Pankratoff, one of my collaborators has seen the Tibetan law book mentioned in your letter ……"，畢安祺是在 1932 年 9 月 26 日給鋼和泰的信中提到請鋼和泰代爲留意藏文法律書籍的，此信應爲對畢安祺 1932 年 9 月 26 日一信的回復，時間大致在 1932 年 10 月前後。	37
		07 Carl W. Bishop to Alexander von Staël-Holstein, Dec. 19, 1932	39
		08 Alexander von Staël-Holstein to Carl W. Bishop, Dec.?, 1932 此信爲鋼和泰手書底稿，無日期。書信開頭說："I am sorry to say that the accompanying block print contains nothing but discussions regarding monastic discipline and that it has nothing to do with temporal jurisprudence." 畢安祺在 1932 年 12 月 19 日給鋼和泰的信說："Recently my assistant, Mr. Tung, turned up with the accompanying work, which he insists is the book in question." 且鋼和泰此信寫於畢安祺 1932 年 12 月 19 日一信的背面，由此可以大致推斷，鋼和泰此信當爲對畢安祺 1932 年 12 月 19 日一信的回復，時間大致在 1932 年 12 月底前後。	40
		09 Alexander von Staël-Holstein to Carl W. Bishop 此信爲鋼和泰手書底稿，日期不詳。	41
011	Robert Pierpont Blake	01 Robert Pierpont Blake to Alexander von Staël-Holstein, Oct. 17–20, 1928	42
		02 Alexander von Staël-Holstein to Robert Pierpont Blake, Dec.?, 1931 此信無日期。開頭說："Many thanks for your letter dated November 20th 1931." 則此信爲對 Blake1931 年 11 月 20 日書信的回復，時間大致推斷爲 1931 年 12 月前後。	43
		03 Alexander von Staël-Holstein to Robert Pierpont Blake, Jul. 25, 1933	44
		04 Robert Pierpont Blake to Alexander von Staël-Holstein, Jan. 23, 1936	46
012	Derk Bodde	01 Derk Bodde to Alexander von Staël-Holstein, Jan. 2, 1934	47

序號	書信人	信件擬目	頁碼
		附 01 Derk Bodde to George H. Chase, Jan. 1, 1934. A Perplexing Passage in the Confucian Analects, by Derk Bodde 此信爲 Derk Bodde1934 年 1 月 2 日致鋼和泰信中的抄送件，另附有其所作 *A Perplexing Passage in the Confucian Analects* 一文。	48
		02 Alexander von Staël-Holstein to Derk Bodde, Jan.?, 1934 此信無日期。Derk Bodde1934 年 1 月 2 日致鋼和泰信中說："I am sending you a copy of a letter which I have just written to Dean Chase in application for a renewal of my fellowship.……if you feel that you could support me again in this matter of a fellowship renewal, I should be extremely grateful." 鋼和泰此信開頭說："I am writing to Cambridge Mass, and I want very much to have a talk with you before posting the letter." 應爲對 Derk Bodde 1934 年 1 月 2 日一信的回復。此信大致寫於 1934 年 1 月。	57
		03 Alexander von Staël-Holstcin to Derk Bodde, Mar. 14, 1935	58
		附 01 Alexander von Staël-Holstein to Baron Plessen, Mar. 11, 1935 此信寫於鋼和泰 1935 年 3 月 14 日致 Derk Bodde 背面，德文。Baron Plesson 生平不詳，暫繫於此。	59
013	Bouillard Georges	01 Bouillard Georges to Alexander von Staël-Holstein, Jul. 4, 1924	60
014	Mr. & Mrs. Boyd-Carpenter	01 Alexander von Staël-Holstein to Mr. & Mrs. Boyd-Carpenter, Sept. 27, 1922 此信寫於鋼和泰 1922 年 12 月致戴何都一信第二頁背面，位於頁面下方三分之一處。	62
015	Mark W. Brown	01 Alexander von Staël-Holstein to Mark W. Brown, Apr.?, 1932 此信寫於鋼和泰 1932 年 4 月 3 日致傅斯年一信同一頁下半頁，無日期，從同頁和背面書信日期均爲 1932 年 4 月 3 日來看，此信大致寫於 1932 年 4 月。	63
		02 Mark W. Brown to Alexander von Staël-Holstein, Dec. 15, 1932	64

序號	書信人	信件擬目	頁碼
016	H. H. Chang	01 H. H. Chang to Alexander von Staël-Holstein 此信僅署 Wednesday，日期不詳。德文。信右上角地址爲 The National University，應即指國立北京大學。張歆海 1923—1926 年任教於北大，此信可能寫於此時期。	67
017	Yuan Ren Chao	01 Alexander von Staël-Holstein to Yuan Ren Chao, May 14, 1935	68
		02 Yuan Ren Chao to Alexander von Staël-Holstein 此信日期不詳。	69
		附 01 Alexander von Staël-Holstein to Someone 此信日期不詳，似缺首頁，原與鋼和泰 1935 年 5 月 14 日致趙元任一信一同存入"Chao Yuan Ren"信封中。據書信内容看，收信人似非趙元任。	70
018	Charignon	01 Alexander von Staël-Holstein to Charignon 此信無結尾，無日期。稱呼爲 "Monsieur et cher collègue"，原整理者在此稱呼上用鉛筆寫明 "Charignon"，且將此信置於 "Charignon 回發" 信封内。	72
019	George H. Chase	01 George H. Chase to Alexander von Staël-Holstein, 1928 此信無日期。開頭説："The Harvard-Yenching Institute is now established, and plans are so far made that I write to ask whether you can come to Cambridge next year as a visiting professor to give one whole course or two half courses in Harvard University on such subjects as you may propose."哈佛燕京學社成立於 1928 年，具體時間有 1 月 4 日和春季等不同説法。此信談及哈佛燕京學社擬邀請鋼和泰赴美講學，《年譜簡編》收録有鋼和泰同年 3 月 16 日接受邀請的復信。綜上，此信當寫於 1928 年 3 月 16 日之前。《年譜簡編》將此信斷定爲 1928 年 1 月，似過早。	73
		02 George H. Chase to Alexander von Staël-Holstein, May 9, 1928	75
		03 George H. Chase to Alexander von Staël-Holstein, Oct. 8, 1928	77
		04 George H. Chase to Alexander von Staël-Holstein, Oct. 10, 1928	78
		05 George H. Chase to Alexander von Staël-Holstein, Jan. 18, 1929	79

序號	書信人	信件擬目	頁碼
		06 George H. Chase to Alexander von Staël-Holstein, Mar. 23, 1929	81
		07 George H. Chase to Alexander von Staël-Holstein, Mar. 30, 1929	82
		08 George H. Chase to Alexander von Staël-Holstein, Jun. 19, 1929	83
		09 Alexander von Staël-Holstein to George H. Chase, Sept. ? 1929 此信無日期。書信開頭説：“Many thanks for your kind letter dated June 19th 1929.” 由此可知，此信爲鋼和泰對 Chase 1929 年 6 月 19 日書信的回復，加之此信最後幾行與鋼和泰同年 9 月 4 日的書信草稿在同一頁（頁面下方三分之一處），推斷時間大致在 1929 年 9 月前後。	86
		附 01 Alexander von Staël-Holstein to the Bursar of Harvard University, Sept. 4, 1929 信件内容位於頁面上方三分之一處。	87
		10 George H. Chase to Alexander von Staël-Holstein, Oct. 8, 1929	88
		11 Alexander von Staël-Holstein to George H. Chase, Oct.? 1929 此信無開頭，無日期，信中説：“During the three or four most expensive months of my life (getting married, organizing a new household, ……”，鋼和泰在 1929 年 6 月結婚，故此信或寫於 1929 年 10 月前後。	90
		12 Alexander von Staël-Holstein to George H. Chase, Dec. 6, 1929 此信無日期，據哈佛燕京學社檔案 “von. Holstein 25_4”，第 68 頁，此信日期爲 1929 年 12 月 6 日。	95
		13 George H. Chase to Alexander von Staël-Holstein, Jan. 11, 1930	98
		14 George H. Chase to Alexander von Staël-Holstein, Apr. 9, 1930	100

序號	書信人	信件擬目	頁碼
		15 Alexander von Staël-Holstein to George H. Chase, Aug. 28, 1930 此信原散亂，前兩頁與後兩頁被分別放入 "Chase, George H. 2" 和 "Chase, George H. 4" 中，據哈佛燕京學社檔案 "von. Holstein 25_4" 第 117—119 頁，將此信合并完整。	103
		16 George H. Chase to Alexander von Staël-Holstein, Oct. 9, 1930	107
		17 George H. Chase to Alexander von Staël-Holstein, Dec. 12, 1930	109
		18 George H. Chase to Alexander von Staël-Holstein, Jan. 5, 1931	110
		19 Alexander von Staël-Holstein to George H. Chase, Feb. 18, 1931	111
		20 George H. Chase to Alexander von Staël-Holstein, Mar. 20, 1931	121
		21 George H. Chase to Alexander von Staël-Holstein, May 12, 1931	122
		22 Alexander von Staël-Holstein to George H. Chase, Sept. 15, 1931	123
		23 Alexander von Staël-Holstein to George H. Chase, Sept. 26, 1931 此信無日期，據哈佛燕京學社檔案 "von.Holstein 25_4" 第 107 頁補。	127
		24 George H. Chase to Alexander von Staël-Holstein, Oct. 17, 1931	129
		25 George H. Chase to Alexander von Staël-Holstein, Nov. 18, 1931	130
		26 Alexander von Staël-Holstein to George H. Chase, Nov. ? 1931 此信無日期，查鋼和泰與 Woods 往來書信，1931 年 11 月 18 日鋼和泰給 Woods 的信中提到要某書出版遲遲不得答復的事情，Woods 同年 12 月 28 日復信也談到出版的事情，以及很長時間不回信的原因。鋼和泰此信中抱怨 Woods 遲遲不回信，	131

序號	書信人	信件擬目	頁碼
		提交手稿一年多不見是否出版答復。并説將給 Woods 的信抄送給 Chase。綜上，此信大致寫於 1931 年 11 月前後。	
		27 Alexander von Staël-Holstein to George H. Chase, Feb. 25, 1932	136
		28 George H. Chase to Alexander von Staël-Holstein, Mar. 29, 1932	140
		29 George H. Chase to Alexander von Staël-Holstein, Apr. 23, 1932	141
		30 George H. Chase to William Hung, Jul. 20, 1932 此爲 Chase 抄送給鋼和泰的致洪煨蓮書信，暫繫於此。	142
		31 Alexander von Staël-Holstein to George H. Chase, Sept. 3, 1932	143
		32 Alexander von Staël-Holstein to George H. Chase, Sept. 4, 1932	145
		33 Alexander von Staël-Holstein to George H. Chase, Sept. 10, 1932	148
		34 Alexander von Staël-Holstein to George H. Chase, Sept. 18, 1932	154
		35 George H. Chase to Alexander von Staël-Holstein, Oct. 14, 1932	165
		36 George H. Chase to Alexander von Staël-Holstein, Nov. 25, 1932	166
		37 Alexander von Staël-Holstein to George H. Chase, Feb. 28, 1933 據哈佛燕京學社檔案 "Von. Holstein 25_4" 第 147 頁，此信最後一頁應置於第八頁中間標有同樣紅色標記之後，即 "Would be of some value" 一句之後。	168
		38 Alexander von Staël-Holstein to George H. Chase, May 3, 1933	180
		39 George H. Chase to Alexander von Staël-Holstein, May. 9, 1933	184

序號	書信人	信件擬目	頁碼
		40 George H. Chase to Alexander von Staël-Holstein, May. 9, 1933	186
		41 George H. Chase to Alexander von Staël-Holstein, Jun. 27, 1933	187
		42 Alexander von Staël-Holstein to George H. Chase, Aug. 29, 1933	188
		43 Alexander von Staël-Holstein to George H. Chase, Oct. 5, 1933	191
		44 Alexander von Staël-Holstein to George H. Chase, Oct. 7, 1933	192
		45 George H. Chase to Alexander von Staël-Holstein, Nov. 27, 1933	196
		46 Alexander von Staël-Holstein to George H. Chase, Feb. 25, 1934	197
		47 Alexander von Staël-Holstein to George H. Chase, Feb. 27, 1934	204
		48 Alexander von Staël-Holstein to George H. Chase, Mar. 3, 1934	223
		49 George H. Chase to Alexander von Staël-Holstein, May 5, 1934	229
		50 Alexander von Staël-Holstein to George H. Chase, Jul. 14, 1934	231
		51 George H. Chase to Alexander von Staël-Holstein, Aug. 23, 1934	241
		52 Alexander von Staël-Holstein to George H. Chase, Autumn ?, 1934 此信無日期，開頭說："During the year 33/34 I received fourteen thousand (14000.00) Mexican dollars from the treasurer of Yenching University." 後面彙報經費使用情況，似是鋼和泰寫的 1933—1934 學年財政報告，據鋼和泰 1933 年 10 月 7 日給 Chase 的書信，學年結束於 6 月 30 日，可以推斷學年財政報告大致寫於秋季，此信大致寫於 1934 年秋季。	244

序號	書信人	信件擬目	頁碼
		53 Alexander von Staël-Holstein to George H. Chase, Oct. 23, 1934 此信爲鋼和泰起草的書信草稿，部分内容重複。	246
		54 George H. Chase to Alexander von Staël-Holstein, Dec.10, 1934	256
		55 Alexander von Staël-Holstein to George H. Chase, 1934 ? 此信無頭無尾，日期不詳。信中說："The only reaction to the copies of my publications (three articles and one book) which I sent to the Harvard Orientalist professors in 1932 and 1933 has been an icy and eventually studied silence." 則此信應似寫於 1934 年，具體月日不詳。	258
		56 Alexander von Staël-Holstein to George H. Chase, Feb. 27, 1935	262
		57 Alexander von Staël-Holstein to George H. Chase, Mar. 3, 1935	266
		58 George H. Chase to Alexander von Staël-Holstein, Apr. 17, 1935	270
		59 Alexander von Staël-Holstein to George H. Chase, 1932–1935 ? 此信無頭無尾，日期不詳。第一頁說："The financial arrangement, under which the first volume of the Series was published is based upon a letter-received here in 1932." 則此信應寫於 1932 年之後。信中希望出版 Harvard Sino-Indian Institute Serics Vol. II 的經費由哈佛燕京學社出，後來第二卷出版於 1935 年，故此信的時間在 1932—1935 之間。	272
		60 Alexander von Staël-Holstein to George H. Chase? 此頁書信無頭無尾，收信人不詳，原置於 "Chase, George H. 回發 4" 信封中，故暫置於鋼和泰與 Chase 往來書信最後。	283
020	Ta-tsi Chen	01 Ta-tsi Chen to Alexander von Staël-Holstein, Jul. 12, 1927	284
		02 陳大齊致鋼和泰，1929 年 10 月 12 日	285

序號	書信人	信件擬目	頁碼
021	Monlin Chiang	01 Monlin Chiang to Alexander von Staël-Holstein, Jul.9, 1926	287
022	Walter E. Clark	01 Walter E. Clark to Alexander von Staël-Holstein, Oct. 13, 1929	289
		02 Alexander von Staël-Holstein to Walter E. Clark, Winter ?, 1930	291
		此信無日期。此信第四頁中說：“He has received nothing on account of the Harvard-Yenching year beginning on July 1st 1930, and he must have some funds before the New Year.” 則此信大致寫於 1930 年 7 月 1 日之後，年底之前。第三頁中又說：“Please ask Woods to accept my best New Year’ s greetings.” 則此信可能寫於 1930 年 11 月底或 12 月初。大致定於 1930 年冬季。	
		03 Walter E. Clark to Alexander von Staël-Holstein, Oct. 4, 1933	296
		04 Alexander von Staël-Holstein to Walter E. Clark, Nov. 28, 1933	297
		05 Alexander von Staël-Holstein to Walter E. Clark, Jul. 24, 1935	301
		06 Walter E. Clark to Alexander von Staël-Holstein, Oct. 26, 1936	303
		07 Alexander von Staël-Holstein to Walter E. Clark, Winter ?, 1936	304
		此信無日期。Clark 1936 年 10 月 26 日給鋼和泰的信中說：“A manuscript of a book on Lamaistic iconography was offered to the Harvard-Yenching Institute for publication by a Mrs. Gordon of New York. ……Professor Pope has heard that you had in view a book on Lamaistic iconography and has asked me to write you……, or if you know anything about Mrs. Gordon.” 鋼和泰在此信中說：“I have a number of articles almost ready for print, some of which deal with Tibetan images, but I never contemplated any work on iconography which could serve as a general work of reference. I am not acquainted with any Mrs. Gordon, who is interested in Tibetan mythology.” 據此，可推斷此信爲對 Clark 1936 年 10 月 26 日一信的回復，時間在此之後，大致定爲 1936 年冬季。	
023	Crane	01 Alexander von Staël-Holstein to Crane, Jun. 16, 1921	305

序號	書信人	信件擬目	頁碼
024	Creel	01 Alexander von Staël-Holstein to Mrs. Creel, Aug.?, 1933 此信寫於鋼和泰大致 1933 年 8 月給袁同禮的書信背面，無日期，草稿劃掉的部分有 “Saturday, August 5th” 等内容，查萬年曆，1933 年 8 月 5 日爲周六，該日期爲 Mrs. Creel 邀請鋼和泰夫婦參加雞尾酒會的日子，故鋼和泰的回信大致應寫於 1933 年 8 月初前後。	307
		02 Alexander von Staël-Holstein to Dr. Creel, Dec. 28, 1933	308
025	Earl H. Cressy	01 Earl H. Cressy to Alexander von Staël-Holstein, Feb. 15, 1924	309
026	The Crown Princess of Sweden	01 The Crown Princess of Sweden to Alexander von Staël-Holstein, Feb. 12 此信日期僅寫明月日，年代不詳。	312
027	De La Vallée Poussin	01 Alexander von Staël-Holstein to De La Vallée Poussin, Jul. 29, 1933 此信無日期，此信第三頁説：“May I ask you to publish a few encouraging words about my edition of the K ā çyapaparivarta commentary, which I am sending you under separate cover, or about my three articles, which appeard in 1932? A few printed words from you would, I am sure, considerably impress the American authorities, upon whose decision my fate depends. The desive meeting of the authorities is to take place in the early spring of 1934.” 鋼和泰請 Poussin 對自己的《大寶積經迦葉品梵藏漢六種合刊》或 1932 年發表的三篇文章寫評論，并説這將對 1934 年美國方面的决策産生影響。則此信應寫於 1933 年，下面 Poussin 的回信説收到鋼和泰 7 月 29 日的來信，則此信當寫於 1933 年 7 月 29 日。	314
		02 De La Vallée Poussin to Alexander von Staël-Holstein, Sept. 18, 1933 此信無日期，從内容看，爲對鋼和泰 1933 年 7 月 29 日一信的回復。第一頁説：“je reçois aujourd’ hui, 18 Septembre” 意即“我在今天，即 9 月 18 日收到”，則此信寫於 1933 年 9 月 18 日。	317
		03 Alexander von Staël-Holstein to De La Vallée Poussin, Oct.?, 1933 此信無日期。Poussin 給鋼和泰的信中提到支那内學院和金陵刻經處，鋼和泰在此信開頭作了回答，故此信當爲對 Poussin 上信的回復，時間大致在 1933 年 10 月前後。	319

序號	書信人	信件擬目	頁碼
028	Ed. H. de Tscharner	01 Alexander von Staël-Holstein to Mnosieur et Madame Ed. H. de Tscharuer, Oct. 8, 1929 此信寫於鋼和泰 1929 年 10 月致 James H. Woods 一信左側。	320
029	P. Demiéville	01 P. Demiéville to Alexander von Staël-Holstein, Jul. 17, 1922	321
		02 Alexander von Staël-Holstein to P. Demiéville, Dec. 10, 1922 此信無日期。第二頁提到："I have several times spoken to Dr. Hu who is now Dean of all the Faculties ……Unfortunately He is ill at the present moment." 胡適 1922 年 4 月當選北大教務長，同年底生病。此信大致寫於 1922 年底。此外，信中還提到 Mr. Cordier' s lithographed Tibetan grammar. 而戴密微 1923 年 1 月 22 日回復鋼和泰的書信開頭説收到鋼和泰 12 月 10 日的信，并且提到試圖爲鋼和泰搞到 Cordier 的藏語語法書，與本信關於此書的内容銜接上了。綜上可推定，此信即戴密微 1923 年 1 月 22 日回復的鋼和泰 1922 年 12 月 10 日所寫的信。	325
		03 P. Demiéville to Alexander von Staël-Holstein, Jan. 22, 1923	327
		04 Alexander von Staël-Holstein to P. Demiéville, Aug.?, 1923 此信無日期。第一頁説鋼和泰的助手黄建（樹因）"died about two months ago"。據《北大日刊》，黄建 1923 年 6 月 15 日去世，故大致推定此信寫於 1923 年 8 月。《年譜簡編》説黄建 8 月去世，并推斷此信寫於 1923 年 10 月，似不確。	335
		05 P. Demiéville to Alexander von Staël-Holstein, Feb. 10, 1924	339
		06 P. Demiéville to Alexander von Staël-Holstein, Mar. 19, 1928	343
		07 Alexander von Staël-Holstein to P. Demiéville, Summer ?, 1929 此信無日期，第一頁的頂部有兩行附記，第一行説："A few days ago, Mr. Lin informed me by telegram that he would arrive at Peking 'in time' ." 此 Mr. Lin 當指林藜光，戴密微 1928 年 3 月 19 日給鋼和泰的信中曾極力向鋼和泰推薦林藜光。另據戴密微追憶林藜光的文章，鋼和泰 1929 年從哈佛回北平主持中印研究所後，請林任助手，林藜光是 1929 年 8 月 7 日到北平的，故此信大致寫於 1929 年 7 月前後，大致是 1929 年夏季。	350

序號	書信人	信件擬目	頁碼
		08 Alexander von Staël-Holstein to P. Demiéville, Aug. 15, 1933	352
030	Robert des Rotours	01 Alexander von Staël-Holstein to Robert des Rotours, Dec. ?, 1922	356
		此信無日期。開頭説："I am very sorry that I was at the last moment prevented from carrying out my intention of seeing you off at the station when you left Peking about a month ago." 鋼和泰很遺憾没有在戴何都離開北京時趕去送行。查戴何都兩次訪華，第一次是 1920 年 12 月 2 日到 1922 年 11 月 4 日，第二次是 1933 年 10 月 14 日從威尼斯乘船到達中國，1934 年 1 月 10 日在穿越西伯利亞後到達巴黎。此信中提到："When you left you were kind enough to say that you would try and get me a copy of the late M. Cordier' s lithographed Tibetan grammar." 而鋼和泰 1922 年 10 月 10 日給戴密微的信中也提到戴何都 "very kindly promised me to send me a copy of the late Mr. Cordier' s lithographed Tibetan grammar"。綜上考慮，此信應寫於戴何都第一次離開中國大約一個月之後，即 1922 年 12 月。 第二頁下方有其他信件草稿。	
031	G. Ecke	01 G. Ecke to Alexander von Staël-Holstein, Aug. 13, 1929	358
032	Editors of the Harvard Journal of Asiatic Studies	01 Alexander von Staël-Holstein to Editors of the Harvard Journal of Asiatic Studies, Jun. 7, 1936	359
		此信原置於 "Elisséeff, Serge 回發 1" 信封中。	
033	Charles Eliot	01 Charles Eliot to Alexander von Staël-Holstein, Dec. 1, 1917	361
		02 Charles Eliot to Alexander von Staël-Holstein, Aug. 18, 1918	363
		03 Charles Eliot to Alexander von Staël-Holstein, Oct. 3, 1918	364
		此信無日期，僅署周四。從信箋上印的年代 "191" 判斷，大致寫於 1910 年代，信箋爲北京飯店，鋼和泰 1917 年到北京，則此信大致寫於 1917—1919 年。另據鋼和泰對此信的回信，提到 10 月 7 日周一，查此三年中，1918 年 10 月 7 日爲周一。故可推定此信寫於 1918 年。鋼和泰的回信説 10 月 7 日周一給 Eliot 的酒店打電話。Eliot 所寫的周四，應該大致是 10 月 7 日所在周的上一周，即 10 月 3 日。故此信應寫於 1918 年 10 月 3 日。	

序號	書信人	信件擬目	頁碼
		04 Alexander von Staël-Holstein to Charles Eliot, Oct.?, 1918 此信無日期，從内容看，應爲 Eliot 寫給鋼和泰僅署周四一信的回復。從 Eliot 寫給鋼和泰一信信箋上印的年代“191”判斷，大致寫於 1910 年代，信箋爲北京飯店，鋼和泰 1917 年到北京，則此信大致寫於 1917—1919 年。此信提到 10 月 7 日周一，查此三年中，1918 年 10 月 7 日爲周一。鋼和泰此信約定 10 月 7 日給 Eliot 下榻的酒店打電話，則此信應寫於 1918 年 10 月 7 日之前，大致在 10 月初。	365
		05 Charles Eliot to Alexander von Staël-Holstein, Sept. 13, 1920	366
		06 Charles Eliot to Alexander von Staël-Holstein, Oct. 23, 1920	369
		07 Charles Eliot to Alexander von Staël-Holstein, Mar. 10, 1921	370
		08 Charles Eliot to Alexander von Staël-Holstein, Dec. 17, 1921	373
		09 Charles Eliot to Alexander von Staël-Holstein, Jul. 23, 1922	376
		10 Alexander von Staël-Holstein to Charles Eliot, Winter, 1922 ? 此信無日期。開頭説：“Many thanks for your kind note and for offering me the loan of Bendall and Rouse’s translation of the Çiksāsamuccaya. I already possess the latter work and so there is no need for me to trouble you about it.” 查 Eliot 1922 年 7 月 23 日寫給鋼和泰的書信，信中説：“Have you seen Bendal & Rouse’s translation of the Çiksāsamuccaya which has recently offered in England? If you would like it, I shall be happy to send it to you.” 綜上，鋼和泰此信當爲對 Eliot1922 年 7 月 23 日一信的回復。另鋼和泰此信提到他在商務印書館出版的《大寶積經迦葉品梵藏漢六種合刊》進展緩慢，“So far 105 pages only have been printed”，王雲五 1922 年 10 月 4 日給鋼和泰的信中提到，將 79—105 頁第二次校樣寄給鋼和泰，則此信似應在此日期之後，大致定爲 1922 年冬季前後。	378
		11 Charles Eliot to Alexander von Staël-Holstein, Jun. 5, 1924	380

序號	書信人	信件擬目	頁碼
		12 Charles Eliot to Alexander von Staël-Holstein, Aug. 14, 1924	383
		13 Charles Eliot to Alexander von Staël-Holstein, Aug. 21, 1924	385
		14 Alexander von Staël-Holstein to Charles Eliot, Jun.?, 1927 此信無日期，信中提到如果沒有權威人士對自己的著作評價的文字發表，鋼和泰主持的中印研究所到 1928 年 6 月 30 截止的那一年的補助將得不到保障。故此信可能寫於 1927 年 6 月 30 日之前。鋼和泰在信中還請 Eliot 幫忙寫評論：“May I ask you to write a few lines on the desirability of editions like the one I have just published?” Eliot 1927 年 8 月 30 日寫給鋼和泰的信開頭說：“I enclose herewith the reply from the Editor of the North China Branch of the R. A. S. from which you will see that my review which I might send would not appear till Sept. 1928.” 表明 Eliot 正在爲發表爲鋼和泰寫的書評而努力。故鋼和泰此信應寫於 1927 年 8 月 30 日之前。綜上，鋼和泰此信可能寫於 1927 年 6 月前後。	386
		15 Charles Eliot to Alexander von Staël-Holstein, Aug. 30, 1927	390
		16 Alexander von Staël-Holstein to Charles Eliot, Dec.?, 1927 此信無日期。信中感謝 Eliot 的賀卡，似爲年底賀卡。信中還提到 “the welcome news concerning the China Journal” 似應指鋼和泰請 Eliot 寫書評之事。Eliot1927 年 8 月 30 日給鋼和泰的信表明還在爲發表書評努力，1928 年 4 月 8 日的信開頭則說：“I am very glad that you like my review of your book & that it has been of some use.” 説明此事已經解决。故可大致推斷，此信寫於 1927 年 12 月前後。	392
		17 Charles Eliot to Alexander von Staël-Holstein, Apr. 8, 1928	395
		18 Charles Eliot to Alexander von Staël-Holstein, Feb. 9, 1930	396
		19 Alexander von Staël-Holstein to Charles Eliot, Mar. 10, 1930 此信無日期。Eliot 1930 年 2 月 9 日寫給鋼和泰的信開頭說：“I dare say that you remember visiting the Daibutsu of Nara with me not very long ago”，鋼和泰此信開頭說：“I do indeed remember	400

序號	書信人	信件擬目	頁碼
		our inspecting the Daibutsu last May”，則鋼和泰此信爲對 Eliot 1930 年 2 月 9 日書信的回復。此信還提到 “I am sorry to say that I have not found any Buddha bearing the Skt name Locana ……”，Eliot 1930 年 3 月 22 日給鋼和泰的信開頭說：“Many thanks for your letter of the 10th March which I have just received on returning to Nara for the Spring.” 從内容看，Eliot 3 月 22 日書信爲對鋼和泰此信的回復，信中說收到鋼和泰 3 月 10 日的來信，故鋼和泰此信的日期可以確定爲 1930 年 3 月 10 日。	
		20 Charles Eliot to Alexander von Staël-Holstein, Mar. 22, 1930	401
		附 01 Charles Eliot to University of Peking, 1918 此信無收信人，從内容看，應爲 Eliot 爲鋼和泰寫給北京大學的推薦信。此信無年代，胡適在 1937 年 3 月 16 日的日記中說：“民國七年，我因 Sir Charles Eliot 的介紹，請他到北大來教梵文，并教印度古宗教史。” 故可大致推定，此信寫於 1918 年。	404
		附 02 Alexander von Staël-Holstein to Someone 此信無開頭，接收人不詳，無日期，原置於 “Eliot, Sir Charles 回發” 信封内，暫繫於此。	408
034	Serge Elisséeff	01 Alexander von Staël-Holstein to Serge Elisséeff, Feb. 20, 1935	409
		02 Alexander von Staël-Holstein to Serge Elisséeff, Feb. 27, 1935	415
		03 Serge Elisséeff to Alexander von Staël-Holstein, Mar. 28, 1935	441
		04 Serge Elisséeff to Alexander von Staël-Holstein, Mar. 28, 1935	443
		05 Alexander von Staël-Holstein to Serge Elisséeff, Apr. 11, 1935	445
		06 Alexander von Staël-Holstein to Serge Elisséeff, May 12, 1935 此信僅署 1935 年 5 月，據哈佛燕京學社檔案 “von. Holstein 25_5” 補充爲 5 月 12 日。	447
		07 Serge Elisséeff to Alexander von Staël-Holstein, Jun. 13, 1935	452

序號	書信人	信件擬目	頁碼
		08 Alexander von Staël-Holstein to Serge Elisséeff, Sept. 29, 1935	453
		09 Serge Elisséeff to Alexander von Staël-Holstein, Oct. 19, 1935	455
		10 Alexander von Staël-Holstein to Serge Elisséeff, Oct. 22, 1935	456
		11 Serge Elisséeff to Alexander von Staël-Holstein, Dec. 11, 1935	460
		12 Alexander von Staël-Holstein to Serge Elisséeff, Jan. 28, 1936	461
		13 Serge Elisséeff to Alexander von Staël-Holstein, Feb. 26, 1936	462
		14 Alexander von Staël-Holstein to Serge Elisséeff, Feb. 27, 1936 此信前 11 頁爲正文，缺第六頁，後六頁爲注釋。	463
		15 Serge Elisséeff to Alexander von Staël-Holstein, Mar. 24, 1936	480
		16 Serge Elisséeff to Alexander von Staël-Holstein, Jun. 30, 1936	482
		17 Alexander von Staël-Holstein to Serge Elisséeff, Jul. 15, 1936 此信書寫的日期爲德文：Mitte Juli，意爲 mid July，年代爲 1936。Elisséeff 是年 8 月 13 日開頭説：Thank you very much for your letter of July 15th. 故此信日期可確定爲 7 月 15 日。	484
		18 Serge Elisséeff to Alexander von Staël-Holstein, Aug. 13, 1936	487
		19 Serge Elisséeff to Alexander von Staël-Holstein, Dec. 1, 1936	488
		20 Serge Elisséeff to Alexander von Staël-Holstein, Dec. 1, 1936	489

序號	書信人	信件擬目	頁碼
		21 Serge Elisséeff to Alexander von Staël-Holstein, Mar. 22 此電報原貼於鋼和泰 1936 年 6 月 7 日致《哈佛亞洲研究》雜誌社編輯一信第二頁上。	491
035	Huger Elliott	01 Huger Elliott to Alexander von Staël-Holstein, Sept. 29, 1928	492
		02 Huger Elliott to Alexander von Staël-Holstein, Oct. 31, 1928	493
		03 Huger Elliott to Alexander von Staël-Holstein, Nov. 2, 1928	494
		04 Huger Elliott to Alexander von Staël-Holstein, Dec. 18, 1928	495
036	Embassies and Legations	01 Russian Embassy, Tokyo to Alexander von Staël-Holstein, Sept. 14, 1917 此信上標注有俄曆和公曆兩种日期，這裏一律采用公曆，以下類似情況不再説明。	496
		02 Russian Embassy, Tokyo to Alexander von Staël-Holstein, Oct. 9, 1917	500
		03 Legation of Denmark, Peking to Alexander von Staël-Holstein, Nov. 16, 1917	504
		04 Swedish Legation, Peking to Alexander von Staël-Holstein, Apr. 3, 1918	506
		05 French Legation, Peking to Alexander von Staël-Holstein, Jul. 6, 1928	508
		06 Embassy of Belgium, Washington to Alexander von Staël-Holstein, Apr. 15, 1929	509
		07 French Legation, Peking to Alexander von Staël-Holstein, Jun. 16, 1929	510
		08 German Embassy, Washington to Alexander von Staël-Holstein, Jan. 25, 1933	511
		09 Embassy of Belgium, Washington to Alexander von Staël-Holstein, Jul. 31, 1934	512

序號	書信人	信件擬目	頁碼
		10 Japanese Legation, Peking to Alexander von Staël-Holstein, Sept. 29 此信無年代。	513
		11 The Minister of Russian, Bangkok to Alexander von Staël-Holstein, Wednesday 此信僅署 “le Mercredi”，法語周三，年月日不詳。	516
		12 Russian Legation, Peking to Alexander von Staël-Holstein 此信無日期。	518
		13 British Legation, Peking to Alexander von Staël-Holstein 此信無日期。	520
037	John King Fairbank	01 John King Fairbank to Alexander von Staël-Holstein, Aug. 24, 1933	521
		附 01 John King Fairbank to John Leighton Stuart, Aug. 24, 1933 此信爲費正清 1933 年 8 月 24 日給鋼和泰書信所附抄送件。	522
		02 John King Fairbank to Alexander von Staël-Holstein, Oct. 10, 1934 此信附有費正清 1934 年 6 月起草的 *Suggestions Regarding the Training of American Students for Research in Chinese Studies* 12 頁。	525
038	John C. Ferguson	01 John C. Ferguson to Alexander von Staël-Holstein, Nov. 5, 1924	538
		02 John C. Ferguson to Alexander von Staël-Holstein, Jun. 13, 1925 此信背面有鋼和泰 1925 年 6 月 19 日致于道泉書信。	539
		03 John C. Ferguson to Alexander von Staël-Holstein, Mar. 21, 1932	540

序號	書信人	信件擬目	頁碼
039	L. Finot	01 L. Finot to Alexander von Staël-Holstein, Oct. 31, 1928	541
		02 Alexander von Staël-Holstein to L. Finot, Winter ?, 1928 此信無日期，從内容看應爲對 Finot 1928 年 10 月 31 日致鋼和泰一信的回復，故大致推斷爲 1928 年冬季。《年譜簡編》定爲 1928 年 11 月。	542
		03 L. Finot to Alexander von Staël-Holstein, 1929 此信無日期，郵戳僅可辨識出年代爲 1929 年。	543
040	Fran	01 Alexander von Staël-Holstein to Fran, May ?, 1930 此信内容位於頁面下半部，無日期，信中提到 5 月 20 日是周二，大致是 1930 年，而這一年 5 月 20 日是周二。故推斷此信寫於 1930 年 5 月。	544
041	Fu Ssû-nien	01 Alexander von Staël-Holstein to Fu Ssû-nien, Mar. 26, 1930 此信在鋼和泰 1930 年 3 月致顧臨夫人的信的背面下半部。信中説：Will you, please, give me the honour of your company at dinner tomorrow (Tuesday, March 27th)，查萬年曆，3 月 27 日是星期四，在 1930 年，且信中説寫信的第二天是 3 月 27 日，故此信寫於 1930 年 3 月 26 日。書信收信人僅署“Mr. Fu”，從信中提及到北海找 Fu，以及 Fu 在北大演講等内容看，此 Mr. Fu 應指傅斯年，當時他任所長的中研院史語所在北海静心齋辦公，且傅斯年還兼任北大教授。	545
		02 Alexander von Staël-Holstein to Fu Ssû-nien, Apr. 3, 1932	546
		03 Alexander von Staël-Holstein to Fu Ssû-nien, Mar. 17, 1935	547
		04 Alexander von Staël-Holstein to Fu Ssû-nien, May. 14, 1935	548
		05 Alexander von Staël-Holstein to Fu Ssû-nien, Apr. 8, 1936 此信收信人爲“Dr. Fu”，信中提到中研院史語所編的《慶祝蔡元培先生六十五歲論文集》，故收信人應爲傅斯年。	549

序號	書信人	信件擬目	頁碼
		06 Alexander von Staël-Holstein to Fu Ssû-nien, Apr. 28, 1936	550
042	Carl Fuchs	01 Carl Fuchs to Alexander von Staël-Holstein, Jun. 17 此電報僅具月日，年代不詳。	551
043	W. Fuchs	01 W. Fuchs to Alexander von Staël-Holstein, Dec.27, 1929	552
		02 W. Fuchs to Alexander von Staël-Holstein, Feb. 28, 1931	554
044	Philip Fugh	01 Philip Fugh to Alexander von Staël-Holstein, Jan. 25, 1932	555
		02 Philip Fugh to Alexander von Staël-Holstein, Feb. 11, 1932	556
		03 Philip Fugh to Alexander von Staël-Holstein, 1932 此信無日期，僅署 "Thursday afternoon"，開頭說："It has been sometimes since our last visit ……"，傅涇波 1932 年 1 月 25 日致鋼和泰的信中說："It was my great pleasure to have a talk with you last week." 如兩信說的是同一次會面，則此信寫於 1932 年，暫將此信繫於 1932 年。	557
045	H. K. Fung	01 H. K. Fung to Alexander von Staël-Holstein, Jan. 12, 1932	558
		02 Alexander von Staël-Holstein to H. K. Fung, May 22, 1932	559
046	T. S. Geshe Lama	01 T. S. Geshe Lama to Alexander von Staël-Holstein, Aug. 18, 1931	560
047	Alice Getty	01 Alice Getty to Alexander von Staël-Holstein, Sep. 15 此信僅署月日，年代不詳。	563
		02 Alexander von Staël-Holstein to Alice Getty 此信日期不詳。信中說："I am very proud to find that you mention me in the preface to the second edition of your splendid	569

序號	書信人	信件擬目	頁碼
		book.” 這裏提到的第二版著作，應即 1928 年出版《北方佛教諸神》修訂版。故可大致推斷此信寫於 1928 年或之後。	
048	John Getty	01 John Getty to Alexander von Staël-Holstein 此信日期不詳。	571

書信人簡介

001 Mr. Acton

全名不詳。鋼和泰此信中說："I hope you will excuse me for behaving on Monday as I always do at dinner parties." 據此可知當時收信人應該也在北平。根據編者判斷此信的時間看，大致可以推斷收信人 1934—1935 年前後生活在北平。查閱相關資料，編者猜測，此 Mr. Acton 或許是英國作家、學者 Harold Acton，Acton 1932—1939 年在北平生活，或許與鋼和泰有所交往。

Harold Acton 全名 Harold Mario Mitchell Acton（1904—1994），生於意大利弗羅倫薩，1918 年入伊頓公學，1923 年入牛津大學。1926 年畢業後去巴黎，1927 年開始創作第一本小説和第三本詩集。1932 年到北平，學習中文、傳統戲劇和詩歌，1939 年返回英國，參加英國皇家空軍。戰後返回弗羅倫薩。在北平期間翻譯出版了《桃花扇》。除詩歌、小説外，還著有《那不勒斯王國》、《波旁王朝》等歷史著作。

002 J. G. Andersson（1874—1960）

全名 Johan Gunnar Andersson, 一譯安特生，又譯作安特森，瑞典考古學家、地質學家。1901 年獲得瑞典烏普薩拉大學地質學博士學位。曾先後參加南極和北極考察，1906 年任瑞典地質調查所所長。1914 年應聘來華，任北洋政府農商部礦政顧問，協助進行地質礦藏調查。後專門收集和研究古生物化石，轉向史前考古。1921 年底在河南澠池縣仰韶村進行大規模發掘，并在後來的著作中首先提出"仰韶文化"命名，被稱爲"仰韶文化之父"。後在中國連續發掘十數處遺址，被高本漢稱爲"中國考古學的創世紀的拓荒者"。1925 年，攜帶數以萬計的文物返國，瑞典政府爲此專門設立遠東文物博物館，安特生任館長。著有《中華遠古之文化》、《甘肅考古記》、《黄土的兒女》、《中國史前史研究》等著作。

003 C. W. Anner

全名、生平不詳，從所收録書信的信箋看，似應爲洛克菲勒設在北平的遠東辦事處下屬建築辦公室的一名建築師。

004 Baldur

全名、生平不詳。

005 Florence T. Bayley

生平不詳。從所收録的這封書信看，曾任哈佛燕京學社秘書。

006 Siegfried Behrsing（1903—1994）

德國漢學家。1921 年至 1929 年先後就讀於格賴夫斯瓦爾德大學、圖賓根大學、萊比錫大學。1929—1930 年曾在北京鋼和泰主持的中印研究所工作。1931 年獲萊比錫大學博士學位。畢業後任萊比錫大學印度學院助理研究員。1945 年在柏林民俗博物館印度與東亞部工作。1951 年任柏林洪堡大學東亞學系教師，1959 年任該校東亞學院現代中國歷史和文學教授，1969 年退休。（據“中國文化海外傳播動態數據庫”）

007 Bennett

全名、生平不詳。

008 V. Bhattacharya（1878—1959）

帕塔恰里亞，印度佛教學者、佛經翻譯家。生於孟加拉邦瑪爾達赫縣。小學畢業後開始學梵文，18 歲在貝拿勒斯學習因明學和吠檀多哲學。1905 年在國際大學教授梵文，同時進修漢文、藏文和巴利文，從事漢學和佛學研究。後任加爾各答大學研究院梵文學部主任。1943 年任國際大學中國學院名譽院長兼研究部主任。1957 年獲加爾各答大學名譽博士稱號。1958 年被印度政府授予國家教授稱號。曾將提婆的《廣百論本》和龍樹的《大乘二十頌》等漢譯本還原爲梵文，校勘《辯中邊論》、《因明入正理論》；著有《從阿育王刻石中所見的經典》、《印度佛教部派史論》等。

009 George D. Birkhoff（1884—1944）

美國著名數學家。早年獲哈佛大學學士、碩士學位。1907 年獲芝加哥大學博士學位。畢業後先後任教於威斯康辛和普林斯頓大學。1912 年起執教哈佛，曾任哈佛文理學院院長。1918 年入選美國國家科學院。1919 年任美國數學學會副主席，1925—1926 年任主席。1923 年被美國數學學會授予博謝紀念獎（Bôcher Memorial Prize）。1926 年獲美國科學促進會獎。1937 年當選美國科學促進會會長。此外，曾入選美國哲學院、美國人文與科學院、哥廷根科學會、法國科學院、丹麥皇家科學與文學院。被布朗大學、哈佛大學、巴黎大學等授予名譽博士學位。

010 Carl W. Bishop（1881—1942）

全名 Carl Whiting Bishop，中文名畢安祺，美國考古學家、人類學家。生於日本東京的一個美國傳教士家庭。1898 年回美國，1912 年獲德堡大學（Depauw University）文學士學位，1913 年獲哥倫比亞大學人類學系碩士學位。1914—1918 年任賓夕法尼亞大學博物館館長助理。1918—1920 年任美國駐華使館海軍副武官。1921—1922 年在哥倫比亞大學進行考古學研究和教學。1922 年任華盛頓弗里爾美術館（Freer Gallery of Art）副館長。曾三度到中國進行考古考察：1915—1917 年代表賓夕法尼亞大學博物館，1923—1927 年、1929—1934 年代表弗里爾美術館。曾撰寫過許多關於中國的考古學論文，著有 *Man from the Farthest Past, The Origin of Far Eastern Civilizations: A Brief Handbook*。

011 Robert Pierpont Blake（1886—1950）

美國拜占庭、亞美尼亞、格魯吉亞文化研究專家。生於三藩市。1908 年獲加州大學學士學位。1909 年獲哈佛大學碩士學位。1910 年遊學德國，次年遊學俄國。1912—1914 年任賓夕法尼亞大學古代史講師。1914 年重返俄國，除了俄語，還學習阿拉伯語、古叙利亞語、亞美尼亞語和格魯吉亞語，繼續研究古代和拜占庭歷史，并開始對格魯吉亞語和亞美尼亞語《聖經》手稿産生興趣。1916 年回哈佛提交博士論文并通過博士學位考試，後重返彼得格勒。1918 年受俄羅斯科學院的派遣到高加索抄寫和校對第比利斯圖書館和博物館收藏的格魯吉亞文《聖經》手稿。因俄國内戰無法返回彼得格勒，在當地教書。格魯吉亞獨立後，任格魯吉亞國立大學教授。1920 年任哈佛大學講師，1928 年升任副教授，1930 年任教授，講授格魯吉亞語、亞美尼亞語、古代和中世紀地中海經濟發展史、拜占庭和奧斯曼帝國等課程。1928—1937 年任哈佛大學圖書館館長，自 1928 年起任哈佛燕京學社董事。1926 年入選美國人文與科學院。1935—1938 年任美國學術團體協會主席，1943 年入選美國哲學學會。1942 年起任敦巴頓橡樹園（Dumbarton Oaks）學者委員會委員。

012 Derk Bodde（1909—2003）

卜德，美國漢學家。十歲時隨父親到上海，三年後回美國。後入哈佛大學。1930 年申請哈佛燕京學社獎學金，在哈佛學習中文一年後，1931 年到北平，直到 1937 年，其間除了學習中文之外，還師從馮友蘭等清華、燕大名師。1938 年起任賓西法尼亞大學中文講師、副教授、教授。珍珠港事件後，先後在美國戰略情報局和美國戰時新聞局服務。1948 年以富布萊特學者身份到北平，一年後返美。1968—1969 年任美國東方學會會長。自賓夕法尼亞大學退休後，1980—1981 年執教於喬治城大學（Georgetown University）。曾任美國哲學學會、美國人文與科學院會員。著有 14 本著作，發表百餘篇論文、90 多篇評論，研究涉及哲學、宗教思想、民俗、歷史、文學、法律等領域。主要著作有《北京日記：革命的一年》（*Peking Diary: A Year of Revolution*）、《托爾斯泰和中國》（*Tolstoy and China*）、《中華帝國的法律》（*Law in Imperial China*）等，曾將馮友蘭的《中國哲學史》譯成英文。

013 Bouillard Georges（1862—1930）[1]

普意雅，法國鐵路工程師，對北京周邊寺廟建築有一定的研究。生於巴黎，畢業於巴黎中央工藝學院。1898 年到中國，幫助建設京漢鐵路，曾任京漢鐵路總工程師，中國政府技術顧問。在中國服務 27 年之後，普意雅在北京定居，研究繪圖技術、地形學和考古學。1930 年因病在北平去世。著有關於北京周邊地區寺廟研究系列著作 15 種，以及《中國鐵路》（*Les Chemins de fer en Chine*）、《中國宗教儀式》（*Notes diverses sur les cultes en Chine*）等。

014 Mr. & Mrs. Boyd-Carpenter

生平不詳。

015 Mark W. Brown

生平不詳，書信地址爲 No. 4 Methodist Mission Peiping，可能是衛理公會在北京的傳教士。

---

[1] 普意雅簡介主要參考《國家圖書館藏普意雅先生（Bouillard Georges）著作考》（收入《國際漢學研究通訊》第 2 期）。此外，本書所收普意雅書信署名僅爲 “Bouillard”，蒙彭福英女士幫助，得以與國家圖書館普意雅藏書上的筆迹進行比對，最終確認此信作者確爲普意雅。在此一并感謝。

016 H. H. Chang（1898—1972）

張歆海，字叔明，浙江海鹽人。早年就讀於上海中國公學。1916 年考入清華學校，1918 年畢業後赴美留學，次年獲約翰·霍普金斯大學文學士學位。後入哈佛大學，1920 年獲文學碩士學位，後師從白璧德攻讀英語文學，1923 年獲哈佛大學博士學位。1921 年曾短期擔任華盛頓會議中國代表團隨員。回國後，先後任北京大學英文系教授兼系主任、清華學校西洋文學教授、國立東南大學外文系主任、上海光華大學副校長兼文學院長、英文學教授等職。1932 年任國民政府外交部歐美司司長。1933 年出任駐葡萄牙公使。1934 年改任駐波蘭大使，兼捷克斯洛伐克公使，1936 年底去職。回國後任上海光華大學英文系教授、中央大學西洋文學教授兼英語文學系主任。1940 年舉家移居美國洛杉磯，擔任新聞電影顧問，并在美國各地演講，宣傳抗日。1943 年，任國民政府外交部長宋子文特別助理。1943—1945 年，先後在美國好萊塢電影中扮演角色。1947 年返滬，任光華大學文學院長。1948 年返美定居。後任紐約私立長島大學研究教授、新澤西州費爾利迪金森大學英文學教授。1972 年到東南亞途徑香港時，應周恩來總理之邀，擬短暫訪問北京，因病在上海去世。著有《蔣介石：亞洲人的命運》、《一位中國外交官的信》、《四海之内》、《美國與中國》等。

017 Yuan Ren Chao（1892—1982）

趙元任，祖籍江蘇武進，生於天津。著名語言學家、音樂家、教育家。1907—1910 年就讀於南京江南高等學堂。1910 年考取清華公費留美，同年入康奈爾大學，1914 年獲文學士學位。1915 年入哈佛大學，1918 年獲哈佛大學物理學博士學位。畢業後在芝加哥和伯克利加州大學學習一年。1919 年任康奈爾大學物理講師。1920 年回國，任教於清華學校，同年擔任來華演講的羅素的翻譯。1921 年赴美，任哈佛大學漢語講師。1924 年離開哈佛，赴歐洲游學。1925 年回國，被聘爲清華國學研究院導師兼哲學系教授。1929 年被聘爲中央研究院歷史語言研究所研究員兼語言組主任。1931 年任留美學生監督，次年歸國。1938 年再度赴美，任教於夏威夷大學，次年任教於耶魯大學。1941 年，受聘哈佛燕京學社，主持漢英詞典的編纂。1943 年任美國海外語言特訓班中文主任。1945 年當選美國語言學會主席。1946 年獲普林斯頓大學名譽文學博士學位。1946—1947 年任密歇根大學語言研究所教授。1947 年當選中央研究院院士，同年改任伯克利加州大學教授，直至退休。1962 年，獲加州大學榮譽博士學位。曾任美國東方學會主席、美國人文與科學院會員。1981 年回國探親，獲北京大學名譽教授稱號。1982 年病逝於美國。

主要著作有《現代吴語的研究》、《音位標音法的多能性》、《湖北方言調查報告》、《國語入門》、《粵語入門》、《中國話的文法》等。譯有《阿麗絲漫游奇境記》、高本漢《中國音韻學研究》（合譯）等。

018 Charignon（1872—1930）

似指 Antoine Henry Charignon，中文名沙海昂，法國里昂人，鐵路技師。1894 年畢業於巴黎中央藝術學校。畢業後到小亞細亞擔任鐵路工程師。1898 年來華，任滇越鐵路工程師，後任正太鐵路、京漢鐵路工程師。曾先後任清郵傳部、北洋政府交通部顧問。清宣統三年（1911）加入中國籍。一戰期間曾回國參戰。戰後回北京任職。1928 年因病辭職。1930 年卒於北京法國醫院。著有《中國鐵路規劃書》。沙海昂在中國長期生活，對中國的歷史地理産生興趣，尤其關注中外文化交流史。主要研究中外文化交流，爲《馬可波羅游記》的法文注譯者。

019 George H. Chase（1874—1952）

全名 George Henry Chase，1896 年畢業於哈佛大學。此後在雅典的美國古典研究學院學習，其間成爲古希臘阿爾戈斯赫拉神廟遺址的主要發掘人。1897 年獲哈佛大學文學碩士學位。1901 年以研究希臘盾牌圖像論文獲哈佛大學博士學位。同年留哈佛任教。1916 年被聘爲考古學教授。1925 年任哈佛文理研究生院院長。二戰期間曾任哈佛代理校長。1945 年獲哈佛榮譽教授稱號。後任波士頓藝術博物館古典藝術執行館長。1952 年在家中突然去世。

020 Ta-tsi Chen（1887—1983）

陳大齊，字百年，浙江海鹽人。心理學家，中國現代心理學的先驅之一。1900 年入江南製造局附設廣方言館學習，次年入浙江求是大學堂。1903 年赴日本留學，先在東京補習學校學習日文，1906 年考取仙臺第二高等學校，學習法律、經濟，1909 年畢業，入東京帝國大學文科哲學門，主修心理學，1912 年畢業，獲文學士學位。同年回國，任浙江高等學校校長，兼浙江私立法政專門學校教授。次年任北京法政專門學校預科教授。1914 年任北京大學教授。1919 年與胡適、馬叙倫等人發起成立北大哲學研究會。1921 年赴德國柏林大學研究西洋哲學，次年歸國，任北京大學哲學系教授兼系主任。1927 年任北京大學教務長。1928 年任國民政府考試院首任秘書長。1929 年初，北京大學改稱國立北平大學北京大學院，任院長。同年七月，北京大學復校，任代理校長，1931 年辭職，仍任考試院秘書長。1932 年任考試院考選委員會副委員長。1934 年升任委員長。1948 年被聘爲總統府國策顧問。同年冬到臺灣，任教於臺灣大學。1954 年起任臺灣政治大學代理校長、校長。1959 年辭去校長職務，專任教授，講授孔孟哲學。1960 年任臺灣孔孟學會理事長。1968 年退休。著有《心理學大綱》、《心理與迷信》、《因明大疏蠡測》、《印度理則學》、《荀子學説》、《孔子學説》、《論語臆解》等，譯有《兒童心理學》、《邏輯大意》等。

021 Monlin Chiang（1886—1964）

蔣夢麟，原名夢熊，字兆賢，號孟鄰，浙江餘姚人。1898 年入上海天主教學堂習英語。1904 年入上海南洋公學。1908 年自費赴美留學，先後入伯克利加州大學、哥倫比亞大學研究院學習，1917 年獲哥倫比亞大學哲學博士學位。同年回國，任上海商務印書館編輯。1919 年任《新教育》月刊主編。1919 年“五四運動”爆發後受蔡元培委託代理北京大學校務，後改任教育學教授兼總務長。1923 年代理北京大學校長。1928 年任國民政府教育部長。1931 年任北京大學校長。抗戰爆發后，1938 年北大、清華、南開組成西南聯合大學，爲校務委員會常委。1945 年任行政院秘書長。1948 年任中國農村復興聯合委員會主任委員。1949 年隨農村復興委員會遷臺灣。1958 年任臺灣石門開發委員會主任。1964 年病故。著有《中國教育原理》、《西潮》(英文)、《新潮》、《過渡時代之思想與教育》等。

022 Walter E. Clark（1881—1960）

全名 Walter Eugene Clark，美國梵文學者。生於加拿大新斯科舍省的迪格比(Digby, Nova Scotia)，1883 年到美國。先後於 1903 年、1904 年、1906 年獲哈佛大學文學學士、文學碩士和博士學位。後到柏林，師從印度學家里夏德・皮舍爾(Richard Pischel)。1915 年任芝加哥大學梵文講師，1923 年升任副教授。1927 年，被聘爲哈佛大學梵文研究威爾斯講座教授(Wales Professor of Sanskrit)，直至 1950 年退休。曾任哈佛東方學叢書第 38—44 卷主編、哈佛燕京學社董事會董事。爲美國東方學會、美國人文與科學院、美國語言學會、英國皇家亞洲學會、法國亞洲學會榮譽會員。曾將鋼和泰送給哈佛的四件喇嘛教諸佛菩薩資料中的兩件整理成爲《兩件喇嘛教衆神譜》(*Two Lamaistic Pantheons*)一書。

023 Crane

全名、生平不詳。

024 Creel（1905—1994）

全名 Herrlee Glessner Creel，中文名顧立雅，美國從事中國古代史專業研究的第一代漢學家，主要研究中國制度史、中國哲學史。生於芝加哥。1926 年獲芝加哥大學學士學位，1927 年獲碩士學位，1929 年獲中國哲學博士學位。1929—1930 年任倫巴德(Lombard)學院英文及心理學助理教授。1930—1932 年獲美國學術團體聯合會獎學金，入哈佛大學進修，從梅光迪學習中文。1932—1935 年受哈佛燕京學社獎助到中國留學，從北平圖書館金石部主任劉節研究中國古文字、甲骨文、金文。1936—1937 年受聘爲芝加哥大學中國語文、哲學及歷史講師。1937—1964 年任該校中國古代文學和制度助理教授、教授。曾於 1939、1940 年兩度訪問中國，采購中文圖書。二戰期間從軍，任國防部陸軍上校情報官，二戰結束後返校任教。1951—1957 年任芝加哥大學遠東研究委員會主任，1954—1962 年任芝加哥大學東方語言文學系及改組的遠東語言及文化學系主任。1964 年被授予馬丁・雷爾森傑出講座教授榮銜，直至 1973 年退休。曾當選美國東方學會會員、亞洲研究協會會員。主要著作有《中國的誕生：中國文明的形成期》（*The Birth of China: A Survey of the Formative Period of Chinese Civilization*）、《孔子：其人與神話》（*Confucius: The Man and the Myth*）、《中國思想：從孔夫子到毛澤東》（*Chinese Thought from Confucius to Mao Tsetung*）、《中國政制的起源：西周王朝卷》（*The Origins of Statecraft of China: Vol. I, Western Chou Empire*）、《申不害：公元前四世紀的中國政治哲學家》（*Shen Pu-Hai: A Chinese Political Philosopher of the Fourth Century B. C.*）等。（主要參考錢存訓《留美雜憶》附録五 師友懷念之"美國漢學家顧立雅教授"）

025 Earl H. Cressy（1883—1979）

全名 Earl Herbert Cressy，中文名葛德基，美國浸禮會傳教士。1910 年來華，曾加入中國基督教大學協會（Council of Christian Colleges in China），中華全國基督教協進會（National Christian Council of China）等教會組織，1916—1923 年任杭州蕙蘭中學校長。曾任華東基督教教育協會總幹事（General Secretary, The East China Christian Educational Association），1923—1929 年任上海滬江大學地理與地質學系主任。著有《基督教高等教育在中國：1925—1926 年的研究》，編有《基督教中學校第六届至第八届統計年報》等。

026 The Crown Princess of Sweden

生平不詳。

027 De La Vallée Poussin（1869—1938）

全名 Louis de La Vallée Poussin，比利時印度學和佛教學家。生於比利時列日（Liège），1884—1888 年就讀於列日大學。1888—1890 年在盧萬大學（University of Louvain）學習巴利文、梵文，1891 年獲東方語言學博士學位。1891 年到巴黎索邦大學師從烈維等。1891—1892 年在列日大學講授梵文。1893 年起任比利時根特大學教授，講授拉丁文和希臘文比較文法，後致力於印度學和佛學研究。一戰期間在英國整理編輯劍橋大學圖書館藏耆那教文獻目録、斯坦因從敦煌盜劫的古藏文文獻目録。1929 年退休。對《中觀論》、《俱舍論》和《唯識論》的校訂和翻譯受到西方學術界的好評。著有《佛教倫理》(*La Morale bouddhique*)、《印度的王朝和歷史：自迦膩色伽到穆斯林入侵》(*Dynasties et histoire de l'Inde depuis Kaniṣka jusqu'aux invasions musulmanes*)、《佛教，教義史論》(*Bouddhisme. Opinions sur l'histoire de la dogmatique*)等。編有《印度事務部圖書館藏敦煌藏文寫本目録》(*Catalogue of the Tibetan Manuscripts from Tun-Huang in the Indian Office Library*)。

028 Ed. H. de Tscharner

生平不詳。

029 P. Demiéville (1894—1979)

全名 Paul Demiéville，中文名戴密微，法國漢學家。生於瑞士洛桑，早年游學慕尼黑、倫敦、愛丁堡、巴黎。1914 年畢業於巴黎大學文學系，獲博士學位。次年入巴黎東方語言學院，師從著名漢學家沙畹和烈維學習漢語和梵文，兼修日文，1919 年畢業。1920 年就職於越南河内法蘭西遠東學校。次年被派往中國考察。1924—1926 年，被聘爲在厦門大學教授。1927 年去日本，1930 年回法國。1931 年起，先後主持巴黎東方語言學院、巴黎大學和高等實驗研究院歷史語言系。馬伯樂去世後，繼任法蘭西學院中國語言文化講座教授，直至 1964 年退休。戴密微治學興趣廣泛，涉及中國哲學、佛教、道教、敦煌學、語言學、中國古典文學等諸多領域，有專著、論文、書評 300 餘種。1956 年起參與《通報》編輯工作，1962 年起主持該刊的編輯工作。主要著譯有《"大乘起信論" 真僞考》、《六祖壇經》、《思想的形象》、《吐蕃僧諍記》、《臨濟語録》等，主編有佛教百科詞典《法寶義林》。

030 Robert des Rotours (1891—1980)

中文名戴何都，法國漢學家。生於里爾，早年在耶穌會讀中學。1909—1910 年在柏林學習政治學。1912 年應徵入伍，一戰期間再度服兵役，期間自學漢語。1920 年畢業於巴黎東方語言學院，同年到中國。1927 年畢業於法國高等研究實驗學院。曾執教於巴黎大學漢學研究所，并於 1945—1959 年主持研究所工作。戴何都主要從事唐史研究，對《新唐書》的《選舉志》、《百官志》和《兵志》做了法文譯注。有《中國唐代各道高官考》、《安禄山事迹譯注》等論文發表。

031 G. Ecke（1896—1971）

全名 Emil Wilhelm Gustav Ecke，中文名艾鍔風，德國漢學家。生於德國波恩，早年在波恩、柏林等地接受中學和大學教育，學習藝術、文學和哲學。1922 年獲德國埃朗根（Erlangen）大學博士學位。1923 年來華，任厦門大學哲學系教授。1928—1933 年任清華大學教授。1933—1934 年到巴黎吉美博物館、盧浮宫學院從事學習和研究。1935—1947 年任輔仁大學教授。1947—1949 年復任厦門大學教授。1949 年到夏威夷，任火奴魯魯博物館中國藝術主任。1950 年任美國夏威夷大學東方美術學教授，1966 年退休。退休後曾到波恩任客座教授。1969 年重返火奴魯魯。1971 年去世。著有《泉州雙塔——中國晚近佛教雕塑研究》（*The Twin Pagodas of Zayton: A Study of Later Buddhist Sculpture in China*）、《陶德曼所藏早期中國青銅器》（*Frühe Chinesisch Bronzen Aus der Sammlung Oskar Truntmann*）、《花梨家俱圖考》（*Chinese Domestic Furniture, One Hundred and Sixty-one Plates Illustrating One Hundred and Twenty-one Pieces of which Twenty-one in Measured Drawings*）、《夏威夷藏中國繪畫》（*Chinese Painting in Hawaii*）等。

032 Editors of the Harvard Journal of Asiatic Studies

生平不詳。

033 Charles Eliot（1862—1931）

全名 Charles Norton Edgcube Eliot, 英國外交官、殖民地官員、東方學家、植物學家。生於英格蘭牛津郡。早年就讀於切爾滕納姆書院和牛津大學。1886 年開始先後在聖彼得堡、君士坦丁堡、摩洛哥、保加利亞、塞爾維亞和華盛頓特區從事外交工作。1901—1904 年任英駐東非保護國專員和總領事(High Commissioner and Commander-in-Chief of the British East African Protectorate)。卸任後任設菲爾德大學（University of Sheffield）校長。1909 年任皇家選舉委員會（Royal Commission on Electoral Systems）委員。1912—1918 年任香港大學校長。1918 年任英國駐西伯利亞專員和總領事。1920 年任英國駐東京大使，1926 年卸任，留居奈良研究佛學。1923 年被授予聖米迦勒及聖喬治爵級大十字勳章，1924 年獲香港大學名譽博士學位，1925 年當選帝國學士院成員。1931 年 3 月死於歸國途中。主要著作有《東非保護國》（*The East African Protectorate*）、《印度教與佛教》（*Hinduism and Buddhism*）、《遠東來信》（*Letters from the Far East*）等。

034 Serge Elisséeff（1889—1975）

葉理綏，日文名英利世夫。俄裔法籍學者，漢學家，西方第一位專業日本學學者。生於聖彼得堡。幼年接受良好的歐洲經典和現代語言訓練。早年在柏林大學開始學習日文，1907 年畢業於 Larinsky College。畢業後入柏林大學，學習日文、中文。1908 年入日本東京帝國大學，學習日本語言、文學、歷史，以及中文，1912 年獲文學士學位。畢業後在東京帝國大學研究生院繼續深造。1915 年通過聖彼得堡大學博士資格考試，被聘爲該校日語無薪教師，不久被聘爲俄羅斯外交部官方翻譯。十月革命後，於 1920 年逃離蘇聯，經芬蘭、瑞典，1921 年到巴黎，任吉美博物館研究助理，并任日本使館翻譯。同時選修伯希和、馬伯樂、梅耶等人的課程，并在巴黎一些院校講授日本文學、歷史等課程。1931 年加入法國國籍。1932—1933 年任哈佛大學訪問教授。1933 年底訪問中國和日本。1934 年，經伯希和推薦，被聘爲哈佛燕京學社首任社長，後兼任哈佛遠東語言學系首任主任。1936 年創辦《哈佛亞洲學報》。二戰期間曾擔任美國戰略服務局顧問，并在哈佛爲美軍開設日語課程。1940 年當選法國遠東學院榮譽會員。1955 年當選英國皇家亞洲學會會員。1946 年被授予法國榮譽騎士勛章。1954—1955 年任美國東方學會主席。1956 年退休。之後繼續在哈佛任教兩年。1957 年回巴黎，任教於巴黎大學高等研究學院。1975 年去世。

035 Huger Elliott（1877—1948）

美國學者。早年先後畢業於哥倫比亞大學建築學院、巴黎美術學院。曾任賓夕法尼亞大學、哈佛大學建築學教師。主要從事博物館教育有關工作，1912—1920 年先後任波士頓美術館教育工作部主任、波士頓美術館設計學院院長。之後的五年任賓夕法尼亞博物館館長、賓西法尼亞工業設計學院院長等職。1925—1941 年任紐約大都會博物館教育工作部主任。

036 Embassies and Legations

本組爲用各國大使館、領事館信箋寫給鋼和泰的信，除個別寫信者姓名能够辨識外，其他不能辨識的信件仍按照原整理者的辦法，以“Embassies and Legations”爲主題集中在一起。

037 John King Fairbank（1907—1991）

費正清，美國著名中國學家。生於美國南達科他州休倫。1925 年考入威斯康辛大學，1927 年轉學到哈佛大學。1929—1931 年以羅兹獎金學者身份赴牛津大學進修。1932 年來華，1933—1935 年任清華大學講師，并師從蔣廷黻。1936 年獲牛津大學博士學位，同年至 1940 年任教於哈佛大學。1942—1943 年任美國駐華大使特别助理，1945—1946 年任美國新聞處主任。1946 年夏回哈佛，1948 年升任教授。1947 年任美國太平洋關係協會理事。1956 年創辦哈佛大學東亞研究中心，并擔任主任。1973 年辭去東亞研究中心主任職務，任新成立的哈佛大學東亞研究委員會主席。1977 年退休。1958 年當選美國亞洲研究協會主席。1973 年任東亞研究理事會主席。費正清的研究涉及中國的各個方面，最大的學術貢獻是創立當代中國學。主要著作《美國與中國》、《現代中國研究中文資料彙編提要》(與劉廣京合編)、《劍橋中國史》、《清代文獻》、《中國對西方的反應：文獻通考》(與鄧嗣禹合編)、《認識中國:中美關係中的形象與政策》、《中國的世界秩序:中國傳統的對外關係》、《中美兩國的相互影響：歷史評述》、《中美關係展望》、《費正清對華回憶録》等。

038 John C. Ferguson (1866—1945)

全名 John Calvin Ferguson，中文名福開森，又名福茂生，美國傳教士、教育家、中國美術研究者、收藏家。生於美國馬薩諸塞州。1886 年畢業於波士頓大學。1888 年被美國美以美會派赴江蘇鎮江傳教，後創辦南京匯文書院(Nanking University)，任第一任監督。1897 年到上海，協助盛宣懷創辦南洋公學，任第一任監院。1899 年收購上海《新聞報》，1907 年在上海創辦英文報紙《上海時報》。1903—1907 年任清商務部外國秘書、政府顧問、郵傳部秘書長等職。曾被清政府授予二品頂戴銜。曾擔任兩江總督劉坤一、湖廣總督張之洞和郵傳部尚書盛宣懷的顧問。1902 年返回波士頓大學攻讀博士學位。民國成立後，先後擔任亞洲文會會長、中國紅十字會副會長、華洋義賑會會長等職。1914 年返回波士頓。1917—1928 年任北洋政府總統府顧問。1936—1938 年，任南京國民政府行政院顧問。1945 年在紐約去世。福開森研究中國美術，并收藏中國古玩。福開森去世後，其女兒根據遺囑將其數十年收藏一萬餘件捐贈金陵大學。著有《中國繪畫》(*Chinese Painting*)、《中國美術大綱》(*Outline of Chinese Art*)、《歷朝瓷器》(*Porcelains of Successive Dynasties*)、《中國藝術巡禮》(*Survey of Chinese Art*)等。編有《歷代著録吉金目》、《歷代著録畫目》等。

039 L. Finot (1864—1935)

全名 Louis Finot，路易・菲諾，法國考古學家。1886 年本科畢業後入法國國立文獻學院(École Nationale des Chartes)，兩年後畢業。畢業後在法國國家圖書館工作，并開始學習梵文。1898 年被任命爲印度支那考古隊負責人，該考古隊於 1900 年成爲法蘭西遠東學院，菲諾任首任院長。1933 年當選法蘭西文學院(Académie des Inscriptions et Belles-Lettres)院士。

040 Fran

生平不詳。

041 Fu Ssû-nien（1896—1950）

傅斯年，字孟真，山東聊城人。1913 年考入北京大學預科乙部，1916 年升入本科國文門。1918 年發起創辦《新潮》雜誌。1919 年“五四”運動被推舉爲學生代表、遊行總指揮。同年畢業，考取山東省官費留學，同年底赴英國倫敦大學研究院學習。1923 年到德國柏林大學學習。1926 年冬歸國，受聘於廣州中山大學。1927 年成立“中山大學語言歷史研究所”。1928 年創辦中央研究院歷史語言研究所，并任所長。1929 年兼任北京大學歷史系教授。抗戰期間兼任北京大學文科研究所所長。抗戰勝利後，任北京大學代理校長。1947 年當選爲中央研究院院士。1948 年被任命爲臺灣大學校長。1950 年在臺北去世。主要著作有《性命古訓辨証》、《夷夏東西説》、《周東封與殷遺民》等。

042 Carl Fuchs

生平不詳。

043 W. Fuchs（1902—1979）

全名 Walter Fuchs, 中文譯名福克司，德國東方學家、中國學家。生於柏林，早年就讀於柏林大學，獲哲學博士學位。1926—1937 年任瀋陽醫學院教授。1937 年任教於北平輔仁大學，1939 年任教授。1940 年兼任北平中德學會會長。1946—1947 年任燕京大學教授。後返德國，1950 年任慕尼黑大學講師。1956—1960 年任柏林大學中文教授。1960 年改任科隆大學中文講座教授，次年在該校創建東亞研究學院，1970 年退休。福克司精通中文、滿文，主要研究清史，對早期中國歷史也有研究，在各種專業雜誌上發表了一些重要學術論文。

044 Philip Fugh（1900—1988）

傅涇波，北京滿族正紅旗人。1912 年就讀於匯文中學，後入北京大學，1918 年結識司徒雷登後，由北京大學轉學燕京大學。1924 年燕京大學畢業後，就職於中國文化經濟協會，曾爲梅蘭芳赴美演出做出努力。1941 年太平洋戰争爆發後，被日軍軟禁家中。1946 年以“大使私人顧問”的名義擔任美國駐華大使司徒雷登的助手。1949 年 8 月與司徒雷登赴美。不久，司徒雷登中風，由傅涇波夫婦照顧其起居。1973 年曾訪問中國大陸，1982 年訪問中國臺灣。1988 年在美國去世。

045 H. K. Fung

疑爲馮慶桂，英文名 Feng Ching-kuei（H. K. Fung），字千里，廣東番禺人，生於廣州。1904 年官費留美，入康奈爾大學學習農業，1908 年獲學士學位，1910 年獲碩士學位，1911 年獲博士學位。爲世界會及美京世界會會員。曾任美國農業部種植局技士、華盛頓國會圖書館中文編目員。1913 年回國，任北京大學生物學教授，兼北京農業專門學校教員、地質研究所教員。1916 年任農業部棉業處技正。後任交通部護路督辦署秘書。爲萬國體育會職員、中國政治社會學會會員。著有《中國棉地氣候考》、《中國文學分類法》等。

046 T. S. Geshe Lama

生平不詳。

047 Alice Getty（1865—1946）

美國東方學家。生於美國密歇根州馬斯基根。早年隨父母多次游歷東西方，主要接受的是家庭教師教育。曾陪伴父親到歐洲和亞洲收集藝術品，其中最主要的是印度諸神像。後定居巴黎，結識烈維、伯希和等著名學者。曾對音樂感興趣，并學習作曲。後在父親的建議下整理父親的收藏，於 1914 年出版《北方佛教諸神》（*The Gods of Northern Buddhism*），由此在西方東方學界知名。一戰期間在巴黎致力於照顧法國致盲傷兵。1920 年父親去世後再度到東方，居住於日本高野山寺院研究真言宗曼荼羅。1928 年出版《北方佛教諸神》修訂版。1936 年出版《伽内什：印度象頭神》（*Ganesha, A Monograph on the Hindu Elephant - faced God*）。1941 年到紐約。1946 年去世。

048 John Getty

生卒不詳。從書信内容看，極可能是 Alice Getty 的父親，他曾多次到遠東游歷，收集藝術品，其中以印度諸神像爲重點。

Dear Mr. Acton,

It is indeed kind of you to ~~ing~~ enquire about my diet. ~~I~~ ~~The other day~~ The other day I replied to a similar enquiry that I could eat absolutely nothing but preserved American peaches in the evening. A tin of such peaches was placed before me and I ~~felt quit~~ took a slice ~~of~~ whenever ~~one~~ a more substantial dish was offered to the other guests and ~~I~~ felt perfectly happy. ~~[illegible]~~ ~~I have Being as dyspeptic as I am I have really not the right to attend dinner parties and~~ whenever I am not asked any questions I simply refrain from eating anything at all and

It is indeed kind of you to take an interest in my dyspeptic condition ~~about~~!

~~I am sorry to learn that a rumour of my dyspeptic condition has reached you~~

Please do not trouble about it. I eat practically nothing in the evening, and ~~the~~ I hope you will excuse me ~~on Monday~~ for behaving on Monday as I always do at dinner parties. I try to improve my mind by listening to the conversation and eat ~~as little~~ just as much as is absolutely necessary to ~~disguise~~ conceal the fact that I have no appetite ~~whatever~~ at all.

Peking, April II, 1927.

Dear Baron Stael Holstein,

I am exceedingly sorry to tell you that I after having thought the matter over very carefully feel convinced that we should agree not to carry on with our plans any further.

Iwill be very glad to offer you all help in supervising the packing of your things, but I now feel perfectly sure that they should be sent to Germany , England or America. I feel sure that it the collection is once in any country outside China you will have to sell it there and Sweden is no good market. Your collection is not archeology and not art. It is a certainly very fine collction of Buddhistic iconography but after having seen the whole today more carefully than before I am sure there will be no means of raising the necessary interest and funds to take it over and we would have only trouble between us.

Dear Baron please make an arrangement with some German, Britisk or American friend. I feel that I cannot do it to your satisfactions.

Yours very truly

J. G. Andersson

Peking, May 6 1927.

Dear Baron Stael Holstein,

My very sincere thanks for the four groups of catalogue and illustration material which you have kindly sent me at different occasions. I have not yet had time to study it but feel sure it ~~is~~ will be of the greatest help for studying your collection.

May I also take this occasion of expressing to you my very hearty thanks for the confidence which you have so kindly shown me in placing your collection in my hands. I sincerely hope that we will be able to represent your interests to your full satisfaction.

Yours very truly

J. G. Andersson

Dear Professor Andersson,

The weak box has been strengthened and the ~~things~~ Buddhas have gone, but there is still one thing which interferes with my nights' rest. I fear that you might leave Stockholm for South America, North Greenland, or other distant parts in quest of prehistoric pottery, and that I might have to deal with a less benevolent party when I come to fetch my collection in 1929.

That less benevolent party might present bills for ~~packing~~ unpacking repacking and strengthening some of the very ancient pictures — and I might be unable to pay ~~those~~ those bills.

~~Please rid me~~

~~That~~ These thoughts cause me much anxiety ~~and if I~~ and have become quite a ~~a sort of~~ nightmare.

Please do relieve me of it by repeating in writing before your departure the promise you made ~~to~~ the other day in the presence of Mr. Ewerlöf: that I shall have to pay nothing to the Swedish museum except the sums specifically mentioned in the ~~treaty~~ agreement (the expenses Hamburg-Stockholm, the money actually advanced by you to me ~~for the port pas~~ plus interest, and possibly ~~insuran~~ certain insurance fees).

I enclose M. Bouillard's article and my own "Remarks on an XVIII Century Lamaist document." These papers are referred to in my lists which I trust you have received.

Dear Professor Anderson,

Everything is O.K. Three men worked more than half a day and made a wonderfully (strong) cage ~~[illegible]~~ for the (heavy) box which caused me a sleepless night.

They finished their work late ~~at night~~ in the evening ~~after the coolies~~ and kept the coolies who came (diplomatic safety (which ~~was~~ in this case ~~[illegible]~~ ~~station~~ was merely a euphemism for the station)) to remove the boxes to ~~the station~~ waiting for a long time. ~~some hours~~ ~~I learned from Mr. F. that all the customs formalities.~~

This morning I learned from our friend ~~the doctor~~ "F." that (after passing through the) customs ~~had been [illegible] passed~~ without difficulty (on Saturday ~~[illegible]~~ have been taken on board the British steamer "Calchas" on Sunday.) ~~and that~~ the things ~~left Pann Bar for Hamburg on Monday (yesterday) on board the steamer "Calchas".~~

As you will see from the enclosed paper the "Calchas" was scheduled to leave Pann Bar for Hamburg on Monday (yesterday).

Stockholm June 14th 1927.

Baron A. Stael Holstein,
Peking Club,
PEKING.

Dear Baron Stael Holstein,

I have to acknowledge with sincerest thanks your letter of May 26th and also the earlier letter of May 6th.

We expect to get your collection, as well as our own consigment with the s/s Calchas early next month, and immediately after receipt of the material I will write you in full detail and give order for payment to you of the sum agreed upon.

With reference to your earlier letter I am glad to tell you that I will be in Stockholm for the next 12 months at least. Furthermore I hope that all questions raised in your letter of May 6th will be answered in my next communication to you after the receipt of the material.

Many of my friends have already seen your illustrated catalogue and take the greatest interest in your beautiful collection. We have not so far framed any difinite plan for the exibition of your collection, but I hope in the near future to be able to write you more definitely on this point.

Yours very truly

J. G. Andersson

c/o the Peking Club, Peking, October 1st 1921.

Dear Professor Andersson,

Many thanks for your kind note. I hear with much pleasure that the things have safely arrived, and I am very much obliged to you for keeping them in your Museum. The latter is about the safest place imaginable.

I am also very grateful to you for your readiness to lend me a sum not exceeding 2500 Mex. dollars (§ 5 of our agreement), but my financial position has changed for the better, and I need not take advantage of your generosity.

On Sept. 23rd I dined with Dr Grabau who is as energetic as ever and who has quite a number of irons in the fire. V. K. Ting was here a few days ago, but he has returned to Dairen since. He lives there not so much for fear of Bolshevistic bullets, as in order to avoid the friendly dinners which he has to attend here and at Tientsin.

I have read with much interest your article on Dr. Hedin's difficulties which appeared in the "Neue Freie Presse" a few months ago.

May I ask to be kindly remembered to Mrs. Andersson?

Believe me yours sincerely and gratefully A. Staël-Holstein.

Dear Professor Anderson,

Many thanks for your kind note.
I ~~am very glad to~~ hear with much pleasure that the
~~the boxes have~~ things have safely arrived and
I am very much obliged to you for keeping
~~it~~ them in your museum. The latter is
about the safest place imaginable.
I am ~~very~~ also very ~~much~~ grateful to
you for your ~~offer~~ readiness to lend me
a sum not exceeding $2500 Mex. dollars
(§5 of our agreement), but my financial
position ~~having~~ has ~~but~~ changed for the better and I
need not take advantage of your generosity.
~~The treaty agreement must does, of course, remain in full force, unless changed by unless changed with the consent of both parties.~~

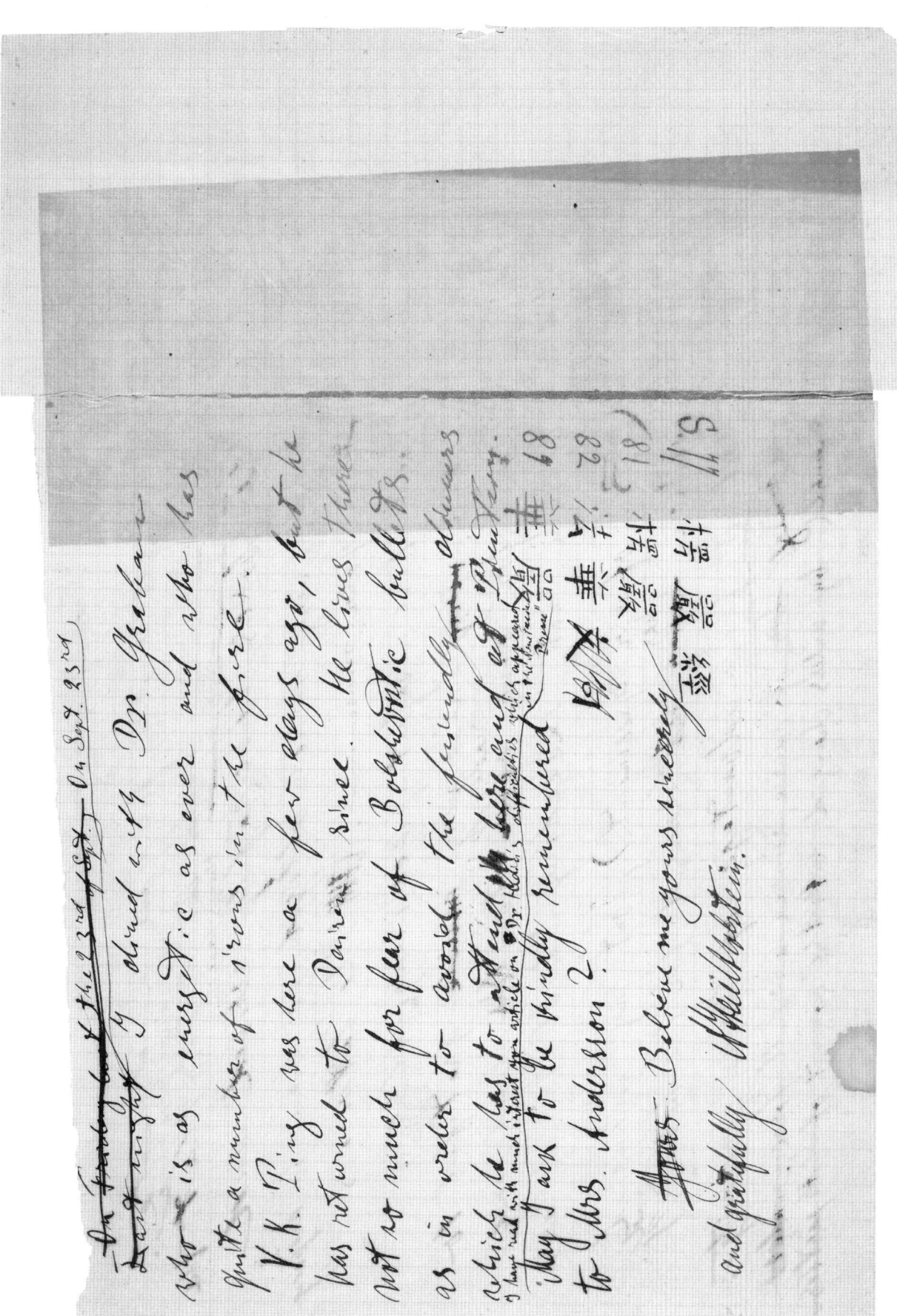

~~On Friday last the 23rd of Sept.~~ On Sept. 23rd ~~Last night~~ I dined with Dr. Grabau who is as energetic as ever and who has quite a number of irons in the fire.

V. K. Ting was here a few days ago, but he has returned to Dairen since. He lives there not so much for fear of Bolshevistic bullets as in order to avoid the friendly dinners which he has to attend here and at Tientsin.

I have read with much interest your article on Dr. Hedin's difficulties which appeared in the [illegible] "Press"

May I ask to be kindly remembered to Mrs. Andersson?

~~Yours~~ Believe me yours sincerely and gratefully
A. Staël Holstein.

68
28
(18)
S 11

Mon cher Comte

C'est avec le plus grand plaisir que j'accepte votre aimable invitation.

J'irai ~~Je viendrai~~ donc ~~~~ vous voir le 29 vers 7 heures.

Croyez, mon cher Comte, à l'expression de mes sentiments distingués.

in spite of the active influence which during

~~almost a~~ he his eight years' were in Peking

THE ROCKEFELLER FOUNDATION
FAR EASTERN OFFICE
PEPING, CHINA

ARCHITECTURAL BUREAU

C. W. ANNER
ARCHITECT

July 17th, 1929

My dear Baron,

According to the arrangement made at the conference on the 15th inst. I have pleasure in sending herewith check for M.$ 200 in payment of photographic work done at the Imperial Palace.

Sincerely yours,

C.W. Anner

Baron A. von Staël-Holstein
ex-Austrian Legation
P e p i n g.

Encl.
CWA:B

FORM 337

THE ROCKEFELLER FOUNDATION

PEKING, CHINA

TO
Baron von Stael Holstein,
ex Austrian Legation,
Peking.

VOUCHER No. 33010
DATE July 16, 1929

THE CHECK ENCLOSED HEREWITH, IS TENDERED IN FULL PAYMENT OF THE FOLLOWING:

Photographic records made for the Committee of the
Palace Museum $200.00

DOLLARS TWO HUNDRED ONLY.

N. G. G.

NO ACKNOWLEDGMENT REQUIRED. KEEP THIS VOUCHER FOR REFERENCE.

Lieber Baldur,

Horvaths Memoiren sind ~~leider~~ noch nicht erschienen, und ~~und werden wohl kaum~~ Korovtzoffs Memoiren sind leider nicht zu haben. In einem besonderen Packet schicke ~~ich~~ Dir aber # Lord Karnocks ~~Memoiren~~ (Sir Arthur Nicolson's) Memoiren als ein ebenso verspätetes wie bescheidenes Geburtstagsgeschenk.

Ich habe in den Zeitungen mit viel Interesse davon gelesen, dass die "Ex-Eunuchen nach der neuen Hauptstadt strömen, um ihren Dienst bei Hofe wieder aufzunehmen. Ob es wohl nötig sein wird neue Operationen vorzunehmen, um aus den Ex-Eunuchen wieder richtige (active oder vielmehr inactive) Eunuchen zu machen? Einfacher wäre es vielleicht, frisch operierte Eunuchen, von denen es jetzt dank den Bemühungen ~~des …~~ Hitlers in Deutschland wimmeln muss, aus Europa kommen zu lassen.

~~Herr~~ H. Keyserling wird ~~a~~ von Otto Reichl als ~~Auslä~~
Emigrant, der sich unbefugterweise in die Angelegenheiten
des Reichs mischt, öffentlich (in Zeitungen) ~~ange~~griffen und wegen ~~seines~~
seiner Stellungnahme gegenüber der Kriegsschuld-
lüge getadelt. Neulich war ein früherer Staatssecretär (unter Schleicher) ~~war~~ Dr. Planck, hier.
Er kennt H. Keyserling sehr gut und ist von ihm
gezwungen worden in Friedrichsruh (bei Bismarcks)
von 12 – 5 Uhr morgens à deux Sekt zu trinken.
Planck ~~ist~~ hat jetzt kein Amt und bedauert
sehr zu einer verrückt gewordenen Rasse zu gehören.
Der Reichsbauernführer hat, wie der Völkische Beobachter
~~berichtet,~~ meldet, den Titel Rittergutsbesitzer abgeschafft.

HARVARD-YENCHING INSTITUTE

17 BOYLSTON HALL
CAMBRIDGE, MASSACHUSETTS

December 12, 1931

Professor von Stael-Holstein,
ex-Austrian Legation,
Peiping, China.

Dear Sir:-

I enclose a card which I have received from the American Express Company in regard to the shipment of an ancient Tibetan book which I had boxed and forwarded to you at Mr. Ware's request.

The charges were as follows:-

American Express Co.	$17.57
Packing, Harvard University interdepartmental charge,	8.83
	$26.40

If you will send a check to the order of the Institute, I will send it to the Bursar of Harvard University, who paid the charges temporarily, at my request.

Yours very truly,
Florence T. Bayley
Secretary

Enclosure

來報紙 RECEIVING

中國電報局

本局號數 JOURNAL NO. 2120

THE CHINESE TELEGRAPH ADMINISTRATION

PEKING 局 OFFICE

21

由 From	CFO 3/8	附註 —REMARKS—	交 To	
時刻 Time	點 H 分 M	LCD EX	時刻 Time	點 H 分 M
簽名 By	PIEN		簽名 By	

原來號數 TELEGRAM NO.	EP10	等第 CLASS		字數 WORDS	11
發報局 Office from	LEIPZIG	日期 Date	8	點 H 12	分 M 45

LCD

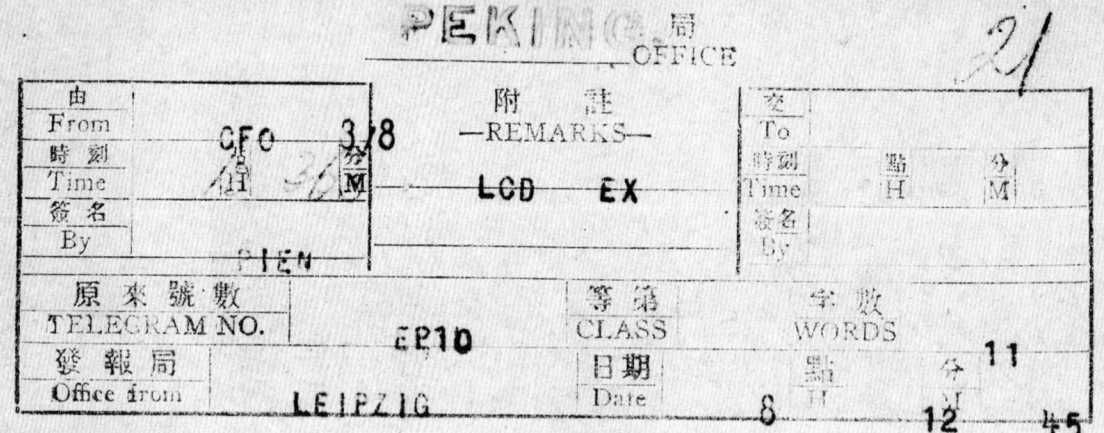

STAELHOLSTEIN PEKING CLUB

PEPING

PLEASE WIRE HUNDREDFIFTY USADOLLARS PEIPZIG

BEHRSING

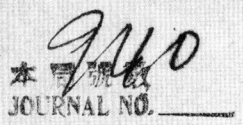

來報紙 RECEIVING

中國電報局

本局號數 JOURNAL NO. 9110

THE CHINESE TELEGRAPH ADMINISTRATION

PEKING 局 OFFICE

6

由 From	CFO 4/3	附註 —REMARKS—	交 To
時刻 Time	7 點 H 分 M		時刻 Time 點 H 分 M
簽名 By	CHANG.	EX LCD	簽名 By

原來號數 TELEGRAM NO.	EP4	等第 CLASS		字數 WORDS	7
發報局 Office from	Z BORSDORFBLZG	日期 Date	3	點 H 5	分 M 45S

LCD STAELHOLSTEIN PEKING CLUB PEKING

REPEAL

BEHRSING

來報紙 RECEIVING

中國電報局

本局號數 JOURNAL NO. 6029

THE CHINESE TELEGRAPH ADMINISTRATION

局 OFFICE

由 From	CPD 22	附註 —REMARKS—	交 To	
時刻 Time	4 點 H 15 分 M	VIA MKDR[redacted]	時刻 Time	點 H 分 M
簽名 By	TLWG		簽名 By	

原來號數 TELEGRAM NO.	Y1 104	等第 CLASS	K	字數 WORDS	7W
發報局 Office from	BLN	日期 Date	21	點 H 17	分 M 10

LCD

STAELHOLSTEIN

PEKING CLUB PEKING

DEPARTED BEHRSING

來報紙
RECEIVING

中國電報局

本局號數
JOURNAL NO.

THE CHINESE TELEGRAPH ADMINISTRATION

局
OFFICE

2647

由 From	CP 10	附註 —REMARKS—	至 To
時刻 Time	18 點H 55 分M	LL	時刻 Time 點H 分M
簽名 By	+MEE		簽名 By
原來號數 TELEGRAM NO.	X46 3303	等級 CLASS	字數 WORDS 10
發報局 Office from	MOUKDENJAP	日期 Date	10 4 40S

STAELHOLSTEIN PEPING CLUB

PEPING

ARRIVING WEDENSDAY EVENING SEVEN FIFTEEN

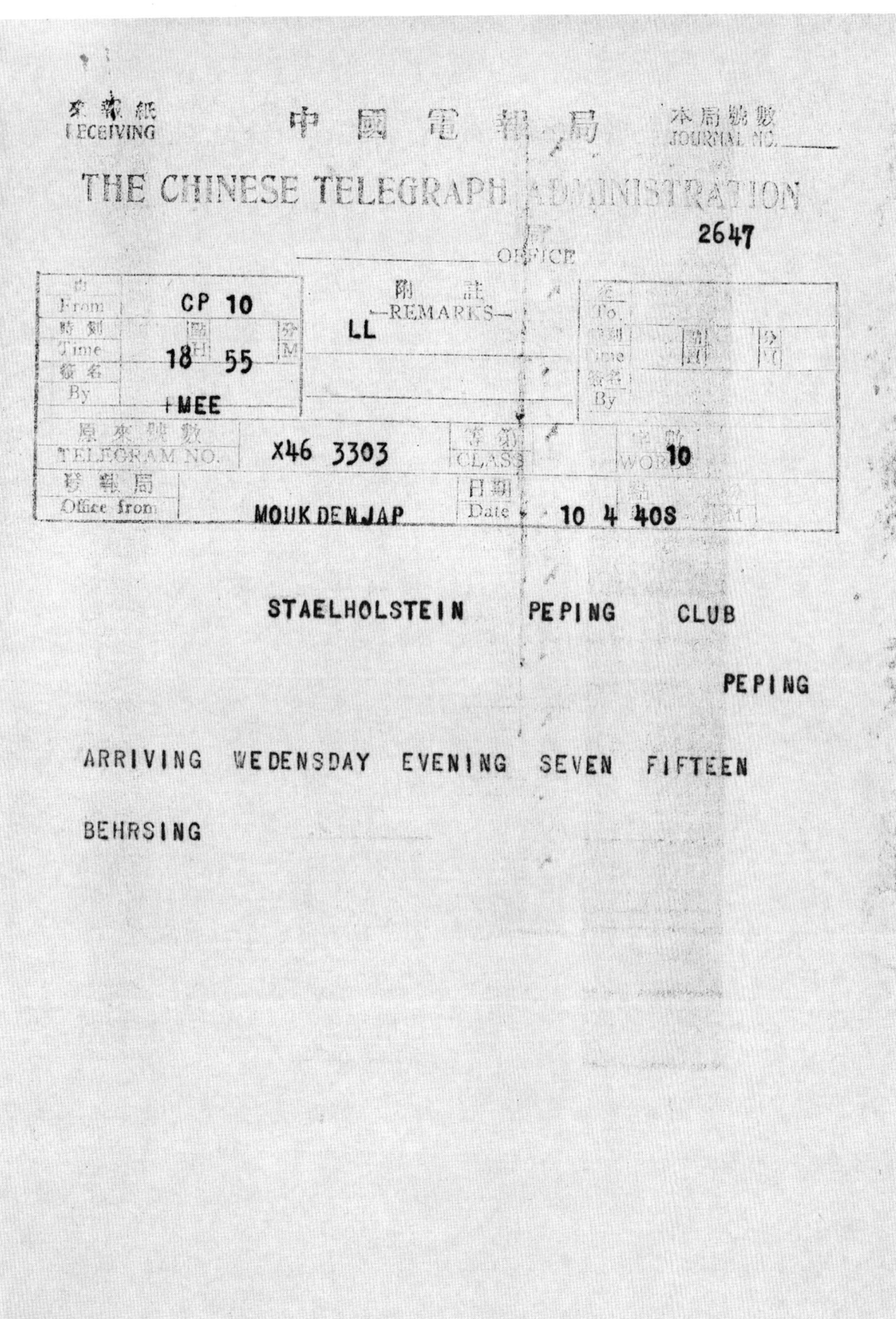

BEHRSING

來報紙 RECEIVING　　中國電報局　　本局號數 JOURNAL NO. ~~34~~54

THE CHINESE TELEGRAPH ADMINISTRATION

PEKING 局 OFFICE　　6

由 From	CFO 13/7	附註 —REMARKS—	交 To	
時刻 Time	8 點 H　0a 分 M	EX LCD	時刻 Time	點 H　分 M
簽名 By	HU		簽名 By	

原來號數 TELEGRAM NO.	EP3	等第 CLASS		字數 WORDS	7
發報局 Office from	LEIPZIG	日期 Date	12	點 H 7	分 M 45P

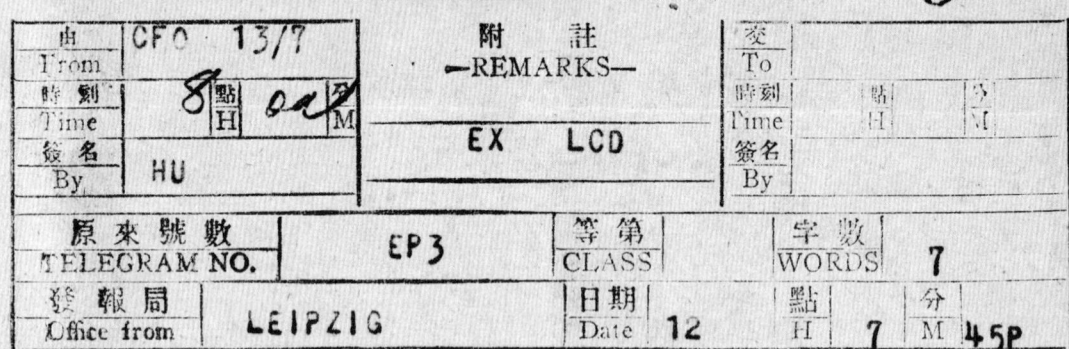

LCD　STAELHOLSTEIN PEKING CLUB

PEKING

ACCEPTED

~~XXXXX~~ BEHRSING

Sehr verehrter Herr Doctor,

Pastor Hahl schreibt mir, dass Sie geneigt wären eine ~~fremde~~ Stellung in China anzunehmen. Leider bin ich nicht in der Lage, Ihnen eine Lebensstellung anzubieten. Ich schlage Ihnen aber hiermit vor, die bevorstehenden deutschen Universitätsferien (Anfang August bis Ende October) zu ~~einem der~~ einer Reise nach ~~China~~ Peking zu benutzen. Ich ~~[illegible]~~ erwarte, dass Sie ~~von~~ vom Tage Ihrer Ankunft (etwa am 15. August) bis zu dem Ihrer Abreise (etwa am 15 October) jeden Wochentag wenigstens sechs ~~Stunden~~ Stunden in meinem sino-indischen Forschungsinstitut arbeiten ~~und~~ ~~mir~~ werden. ~~Ich werde Sie~~ ~~Die Arbeit~~ Ihre Thätigkeit soll darin bestehen, dass Sie mir bei der Übersetzung des Kāçyapaparivarta, ~~[illegible] in's Englische helfen und~~ bei der Zusammenstellung eines catalogue raisonné des gesamten Ratnakūta (fast ausschliesslich chinesisch und tibetisch) ~~und bei anderen~~ ähnlichen Arbeiten helfen. Ich werde im August eine ganze Reihe ~~[illegible] von~~ anderer Assistenten haben ~~von~~ (einen sehr tüchtigen russischen Mongolisten, chinesische Buddhisten, zwei oder drei gelehrte Lamas ~~und wahrscheinlich~~ auch einen japanischen Buddhisten), von denen Sie im Lauf der zwei Monate sicherlich einiges lernen werden. ~~Wenn Sie kommen wollen~~ Ich hoffe sehr, dass Sie meinen Vorschlag annehmen und dass ich wenigstens hier für kurze Zeit, einen Landsmann als Mitarbeiter haben werde.

~~Ich bin in der Lage Ihnen für~~
Ich bin in der Lage, im Ganzen 1600 (ein tausend sechs hundert chinesische Silberdollar) für Sie aufzuwenden und werde Ihnen nach Empfang Ihres Telegramms "accepted" sofort ~~den Gegenwert von~~ 400 chinesischen Silberdollars als Reisegeld telegraphisch überweisen. Am 15. September erhalten Sie weitere 400 chin. Silberdollars und am 15. October 800 chin. Silberdollars (ein Monatsgehalt plus Reisegeld für Ihre Heimreise nach Deutschland).
Im ~~Ok~~ September erwarte ich hier einen meiner amerikanischen Auftraggeber. (~~Profess~~
Wenn Sie ihm gefallen sollten, könnte sich vielleicht aus Ihrer Ferienreise etwas Dauerndes entwickeln; ~~doch~~ ich kann Ihnen aber in dieser Beziehung keinerlei Versprechungen machen.
~~Ein~~ Hundert chinesische Silberdollar ~~sind~~ kann man hier ~~heute~~ für etwas mehr als 8½ englische Pfund Sterling verkaufen. Gewöhnlich bekommt man circa 10 Pfund; der stets schwankende Kurs ist aber augenblicklich ungünstig.
Lessing hat hier vor einigen Jahren mit seiner ganzen Familie von 400 Silberdollar ganz gut gelebt.
Um Ihnen einen Begriff von meinen Beziehungen zur Harvard-Universität zu geben, lege ich eine Photographie meines vorläufigen Ernennungsdocuments bei.
~~Sie müssen für Ihre Wohnung~~ Ich werde Sie bitten für Ihre Wohnung, Ihr Essen etc. selbst zu sorgen.
Meine telegraphische Adresse ist: Staelholstein (ein Wort) Peking Club Peking

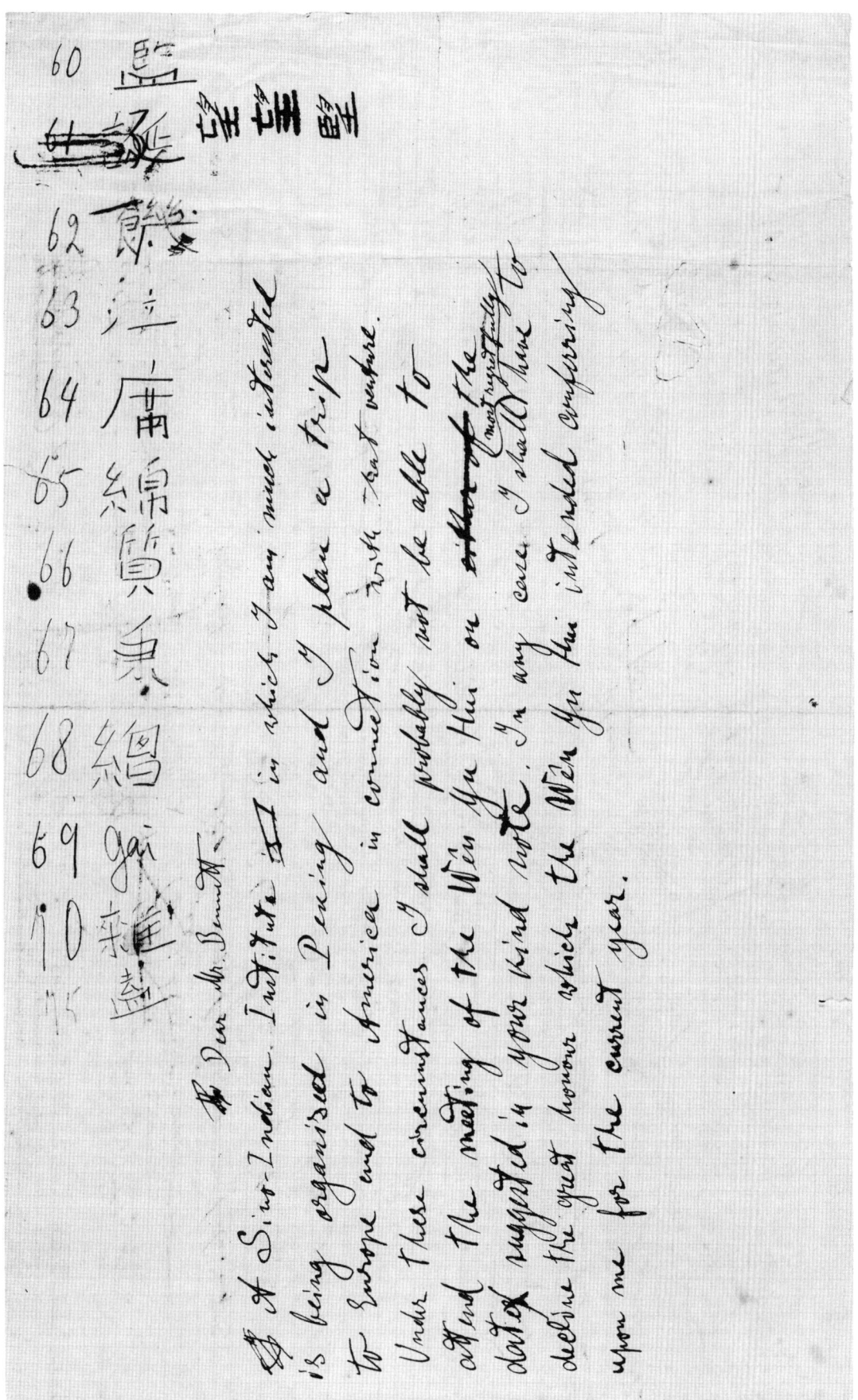

Dear Mr. Bennett

A Sino-Indian Institute in which I am much interested is being organised in Peking and I plan a trip to Europe and to America in connection with that venture. Under these circumstances I shall probably not be able to attend the meeting of the Wên Yu Hui on ~~either of~~ the dates suggested in your kind note. In any case I shall most regretfully have to decline the great honour which the Wên Yu Hui intended conferring upon me for the current year.

VISVA-BHARATI

PRATISTHATA-ACHARYA
(Founder-President)
RABINDRANATH TAGORE

SANTINIKETAN
BENGAL, INDIA

Santiniketan, Sept 30, *192*4.

Dear Baron Holstein,

Gurudeva gave me your letter of June I nearly a month or more ago; I apologise for my inability to reply earlier than what I am doing. I thank you sincerely with all my heart for your kindness in offering me free lodging, simple furniture and coal. I also am eager to work with you and to be of use xxx to you in our common subjects of study and teaching. Gurudeva talked to me about you often, and so also has my friend Prof. Sylvain Levi written to me about you from Paris. I feel very happy and grateful at the thought of living with you.

Gurudeva left for South America on Sept.24. Of course, I am not coming to China this year, as it is now evidently too late. Gurudeva wished me to sail in March, 1925, at which time I shall write to you again. Wkxx When and where will this letter reach you? May I hope to receive a reply? With kind and grateful regards,

Yours sincerely,

V. Bhattacharya

June 4, 1928

GEORGE D. BIRKHOFF
984 MEMORIAL DRIVE
CAMBRIDGE, MASS.

Dear Stäel-Holstein

It was with great pleasure that Mrs. Birkhoff and I learned of your appointment as Professor of Asiatic Philology at Harvard University. We are delighted for personal reasons and also because of the distinction which your appointment brings to Harvard. We hope too that it means that you are to be back in Cambridge next fall.

It was very kind of

you to send us the card from your boat, and Mrs. Birkhoff and I appreciated it very much.

This is my summer for concentrated work since I am hoping to finish a book in the next three months.

With kindest greetings and remembrances from us both,

Sincerely yours,

George D. Birkhoff

SMITHSONIAN INSTITUTION
FREER GALLERY OF ART
WASHINGTON, D. C.
AMERICAN LEGATION, PEKING

19 Ta Yang I-pin Hutung, Peking,
21 Jan., 1926.

My dear Baron:-

Pray accept my very warm thanks for your kindness in giving me the reference to Dr. Wedermeyer's paper in the "Birth Anniversary Volume". I have not as yet had time to do more than glance over it cursorily, but I can see that I shall find it of great interest.

I trust that your double dinner of the other night was not too much for you, and that you are enjoying these splendid winter days to the utmost.

With renewed thanks, and with all good wishes, I am, as always,

Very sincerely yours,

Carl W. Bishop.

Baron A. von Staël-Holstein,
Pi Kuan Hutung, East City,
Peking, China.

60
7
420　　427.

Dear Mr. Bishop

I have much pleasure in accepting your invitation to dinner on ~~the 4th~~ Friday January 7th and I thank you most heartily for your kind wishes.

~~Many thanks for your kind wishes and for the beautiful card!~~

I send you herewith ~~a report~~ two copies of a report on the recently discovered Lama Temple ~~with some photographs.~~ which we discussed the other day. I also enclose two copies of a report ~~concerning~~ which Messrs Priest and March have drawn up and which concerns the Sino-Indian ~~Res~~ Research Institute of Peking. Most of the data have been supplied by myself. The two photographs showing portraits of saints with ~~Tibetan~~ Chinese texts attached are specimina of the unique ~~[illegible]~~ iconographical manuscript mentioned in the report on the ~~book which I want to publish~~ Institute. ~~I want to edit the Buddhist 300 as soon as possible.~~ I have

~~Buddhas~~
~~Ato of the Pao Hsiang Lou as well~~
~~as the 360 pictures of the manuscript as~~
~~I am told I think that soon as~~
~~possible in Peking.~~
~~I am planning an edition~~
~~Both~~ ~~T~~ The 80? Buddhas etc. of the
Pao Hsiang Lou as well as the
360 Buddhas etc. of the manuscript
book ~~are of very great interest should~~
~~be edited as soon as possible and~~
~~It will~~ contain very much hitherto
unknown material and I plan an
edition embodying both groups. Such
an edition (collodium plates) could be ~~done~~
~~as well in~~ made here in Peking as well and
much cheaper than anywhere in the west.
That information I got from several members of the
Geological Survey.

~~by somebody~~
~~members of the Geological Survey~~
~~that plates can be ~~done~~ made here~~
~~as well and much cheaper~~
~~than anywhere in the west.~~

Wishing you a very happy new year and looking forward
to meeting you on the 7th I remain yours sincerely

SMITHSONIAN INSTITUTION
FREER GALLERY OF ART
WASHINGTON, D. C.
AMERICAN LEGATION, PEKING.

19 Ta Yang I-pin Hutung, Peking,
28 Jan., 1927.

My dear Baron:-

A few days ago a friend of Miss Furscott's left in our office a small bronze statue, once upon a time gilded, which has rather puzzled me, as well as one or two Chinese to whom I have shown it. It seems to be a figure of a Lama, but I should be happy to have your authoritative judgment upon it.

Also Professor Tolmatschew, in Harbin, recently sent me a small pamphlet of his, comprising only a few pages, upon the mammoth. Unfortunately Russian is not one of the languages with which I have even a passing familiarity.

Hence I am wondering if I might drop by some time, or if I could prevail upon you to do so, I should be charmed to have you come here; I think I could find a little Black Label Johnny Walker or something of that sort that we could discuss together. Then I could show you both figure and pamphlet and get your opinion of them.

I have been looking up the matter of the Brothers of Dobjin and of the conversion of the Teutonic Order to Protestantism, and I find that my authority was the Introduction written by Jeremiah Curtin to his translation of Sienkiewicz's novel "The Deluge". There he says that the Brothers of Dobjin were founded in 1225 by Christian, first Bishop of Prussia, that they were shattered by

2.

the pagan Prussians almost immediately, and that the remnant of the Order was incorporated with the Teutonic Order a few years later. Dobjin apparently was the name of a castle near Kulm where the new order had its headquarters; hence the name.

In the same introduction Curtin says of the Teutonic order, that it induced Albert, a member of the Franconian branch of the Hohenzollerns to become Grand Master. "He began to reorganize the order, and tried to shake off allegiance to Poland; but finding no aid in the Empire or elsewhere, he acted on Luther's advice to introduce Protestantism and convert Prussia into a secular and hereditary duchy. This he did in 1525. . . . . The military monks married, and were converted into hereditary nobles. Albert became Duke of Prussia, and took the oath of allegiance to Poland. Later the Hohenzollerns of Brandenburg inherited the duchy."

I am happy to be able to tell you that I got off the report on your Lama temple and your Sino-Indian Research Institute in good season. In fact I not merely wrote to Mr. Lodge, my own immediate superior about it, but I also wrote to the head of the Smithsonian himself. I hope earnestly that something may be done about it.

Hoping to have the pleasure of seeing you again soon, I remain, as always,

Very sincerely yours,

Carl W. Bishop.

3 CULTY CHAMBERS
LEGATION QUARTER
PEIPING, CHINA

4 March, 1932.

Baron A. von Staël-Holstein,
The Ex-Austrian Legation,
Peiping, China.

My dear Baron:-

I should be delighted if you would come and have lunch with me next Friday, the eleventh instant, at one o'clock---just a quiet little "stag" affair; I am only asking, beside yourself, Dr. Erkes, for my acquaintanceship with whom I am indebted to you, and one or two others who are interested in Chinese studies. I do hope you can come then.

Pray offer my best compliments and respects to the Baroness, and believe me, with all good wishes,

Very sincerely yours,

C. W. Bishop.

3 CULTY CHAMBERS
LEGATION QUARTER
PEIPING, CHINA

26 September, 1932.

Baron A. von Staël-Holstein,
The Ex-Austrian Legation,
Peiping, China.

My dear Baron:-

While I was in Peitaiho this summer, I received a letter from Dr. J. W. Wigmore, of the Elbert H. Gary Library of Law, at Chicago, Illinois, requesting information in regard to Tibetan works on law. Perhaps I can do no better than quote what he says:

"This Library has the ambition to gather...materials for the legal system of every country in the world. Tibet is now almost the only country thus far not represented. I have interviewed and corresponded with many travelers and writers. They all know a lot about Buddhism, etc., but very few can give any information about Tibetan law, although I know perfectly well from various books on Tibet that there are books and that the Judges refer to them. At last I reveived from Sir Charles Bell a very kind letter in which he wrote out in Tibetan, with transliteration and translation, the title of the book sometimes referred to as The Sixteen Laws, and sometimes (by D. Macdonald) as The Code of Thirteen Judgments......I do not know whether it is block printed or is used in manuscript copies. Our Library would of course expect to pay the cost."

2.

This is a matter quite out of my own field, but I at once thought that possibly you might be able to give me some information; so I replied to Dr. Wigmore that as soon as I could after returning to Peiping, I should ask you about it. Any information that you can give me I should be glad to forward, unless you prefer to write direct to Dr. Wigmore; his address is that which I have given at the beginning of this note. I enclose Sir Charles Bell's which he mentions.

It has been a matter of great regret to both Mrs. Bishop and me that we have not seen more of you and the Baroness; but Mrs. Bishop's almost constant illness for the past year has kept us from attempting anything at all in the way of social activities. Mrs. Bishop has had five attacks of dysentery in a little over a year, and is in fact now at the German Hospital, convalescing from her last attack.

Will you please present my compliments to the Baroness, and believe me, with all good wishes,

Ever sincerely yours,

C. W. Bishop.

P. S. Perhaps if you could just give me the name of a bookshop where they sell Tibetan books such as the one I have mentioned, I could get one of my Chinese helpers to buy it for Dr. Wigmore.

My dear Mr. Bishop,

Mr. Pankratoff, one of my collaborators has seen ~~a copy of~~ the Tibetan law book mentioned in your letter in Mongolia, ~~and he hopes to be able to find a copy a copy for you in Peking. There is however a a Tibetan book store here. A copy and it may a copy may exist in the possession of some private person in Peking. The Tibetan book store~~

You may be able to obtain a copy at the 天清號 (Tibetan) book store (near the 嵩祝寺 monastery) in Peking. If you do not succeed, please write me again, and we shall try to get you a copy from Mongolia. I am very glad to hear that Mrs. Bishop's ~~is getting better~~ health is improving. Please present

mit Empfehlungen

Mirick

my compliments to her and
believe me yours sincerely

SMITHSONIAN INSTITUTION
FREER GALLERY OF ART
C/O AMERICAN LEGATION
PEIPING, CHINA

19 December, 1932.

Baron A. von Staël-Holstein,
Ex-Austrian Legation,
Peiping.

My dear Baron:-

You will perhaps recall my consulting you some weeks ago in regard to a Tibetan law-book which one of the large law libraries in America is anxious to procure for its collection of legal codes from various parts of the world.

Recently my assistant, Mr. Tung, turned up with the accompanying work, which he insists is the book in question. The title (in English transliteration) as given me is as follows: Rgyal-khrims chhen-po zhal-chhe bchu-druk bzhugs so. I had supposed that it was a far larger work than the one Mr. Tung has gotten, and I am wondering whether I might ask you to glance at it and tell me if it is the right book.

zhal che judgment decision SCD
zhal che pa judge magistrate

I trust that you and your family are quite well, and I beg to offer you and the Baroness my warmest good wishes for the approaching Holiday Season. As ever,

Very sincerely yours,

C. W. Bishop.

296
144
16 | 152 9½

My dear Mr. Bishop,

I am sorry to say that the accompanying block print contains nothing but discussions ~~of ms~~ regarding monastic discipline and that it has nothing to do with temporal jurisprudence. ~~The~~ I may add a transliteration of the title of the the book which your assistant bought: ~~is:~~

~~Hdul~~ Hdul ba ~~(monastic discipline)~~

Hdul ba means monastic discipline 19
8
Don gzal bar byed pa means explanation 152
of the meaning

My dear Dr. Brown,

~~I the~~ Many thanks for sending me the Crosses which I ~~have~~ return herewith. I am sorry to say that I have discovered no Indian characters on them. Believe me yours very sincerely

A. Staël Holstein.

Dear Mr. Bishop,

~~[illegible]~~ I have for a long time taken a great interest in the ancient fauna of China, and I find your article on the rhinoceros and wild ox extremely instructive.

~~With man I thank~~ Many thanks for the reprint of your valuable paper!

May I ask to be kindly remembered to Mrs. Bishop?

Believe me yours sincerely

A. Staël Holstein.

LIBRARY OF HARVARD UNIVERSITY
CAMBRIDGE, MASSACHUSETTS

17-го Октября, 1928 г.

Многоуважаемый и дорогой Александръ Августовичъ!

Симъ прилагаю повѣстку (въ черновикѣ) на счетъ свертка, который Вы такъ любезно намъ предоставили. Прошу вписать то, чего не хватаетъ и прибавлять и измѣнять все, что Вамъ кажется цѣлесообразнымъ. Мы тогда передадимъ сущность сообщенія студенческой газетѣ, и выставимъ свертокъ въ Treasure Room

Съ сердечной благодарностью

Остаюсь

Искренно преданный Вамъ

Робертъ П. Блэйкъ

P.S. Прилагаю карту, на которой прошу указать районы, о которыхъ рѣчь идетъ въ сообщеніи.

Р. Б.

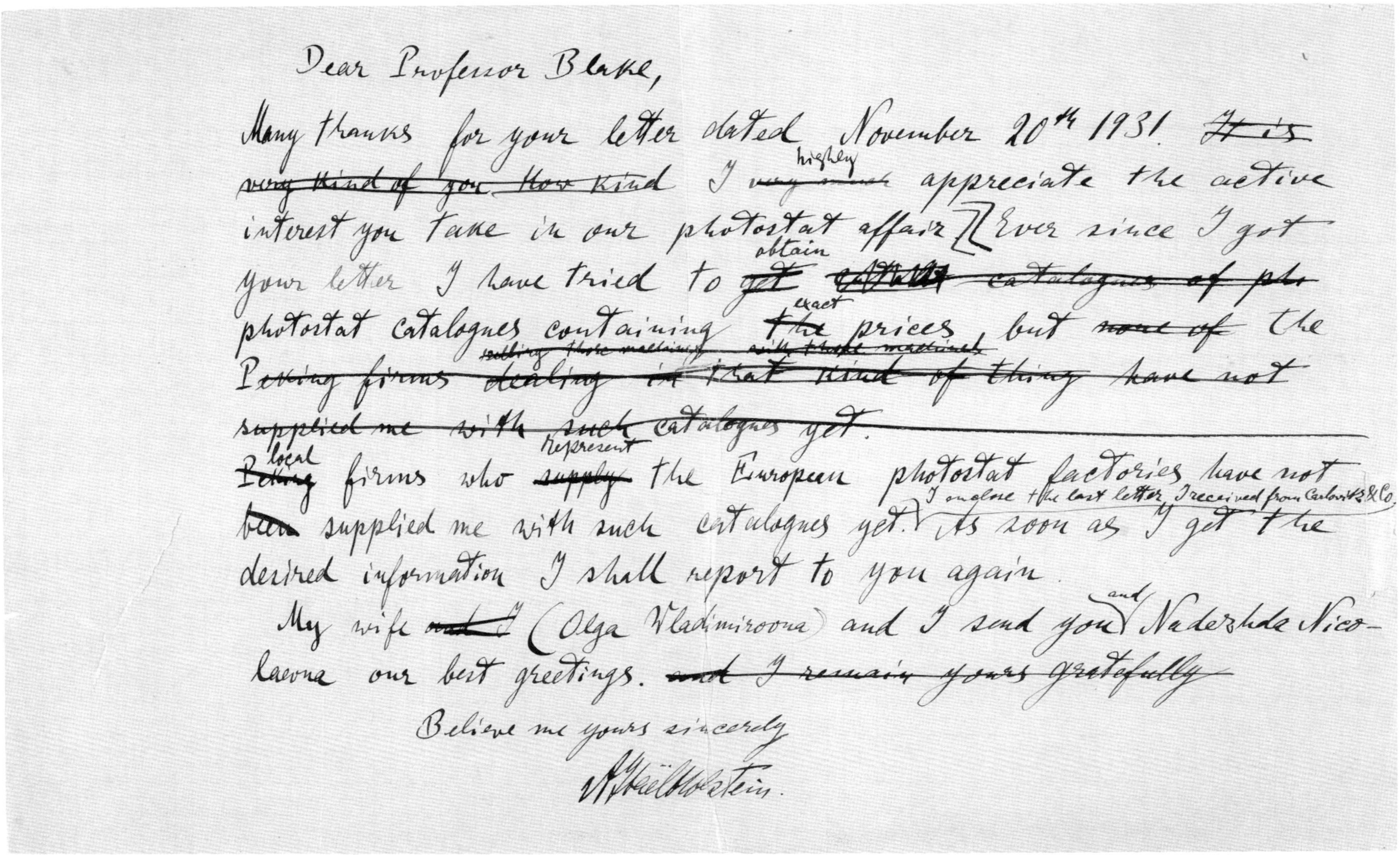

Dear Professor Blake,

Many thanks for your letter dated November 20th 1931. ~~It is very kind of you. How kind~~ I ~~very much~~ highly appreciate the active interest you take in our photostat affair. Ever since I got your letter I have tried to ~~get~~ obtain ~~[illegible] catalogues of pho~~ photostat catalogues containing ~~the~~ exact prices, but ~~none of~~ the ~~Peking firms dealing in that kind of thing have not supplied me with such catalogues yet.~~

~~Peking~~ local firms who ~~supply~~ represent the European photostat factories have not ~~been~~ supplied me with such catalogues yet. I enclose the last letter I received from Carlowitz & Co. As soon as I get the desired information I shall report to you again.

My wife ~~and I~~ (Olga Vladimirovna) and I send you and Nadezhda Nicolaevna our best greetings. ~~and I remain yours gratefully~~

Believe me yours sincerely

A. Staël Holstein.

Former Austrian Legation, Peking July 25th 1933.

Dear Professor Blake,

~~Many thanks for havin~~ I am ~~very much~~ greatly obliged to you for having introduced Dr. Kates to me. I like him very much, and I hope that I shall be able to be of some use to him in the future. At present ~~all my Chine~~ most of my friends ~~(Chi~~ (foreign and Chinese) are absent ~~on account~~ from Peking of the "saison morte", ~~and I have stayed here so long~~ and the fact that I am still here is only due to ~~the difficulties which a strike of the compositors in charge of at the press which printed~~ ~~my edition of the Kaśyapaparivarta commentary. This edition~~ my determination of ~~finishing the edit~~ getting my edition of the Kāśyapaparivarta commentary out before the autumn.

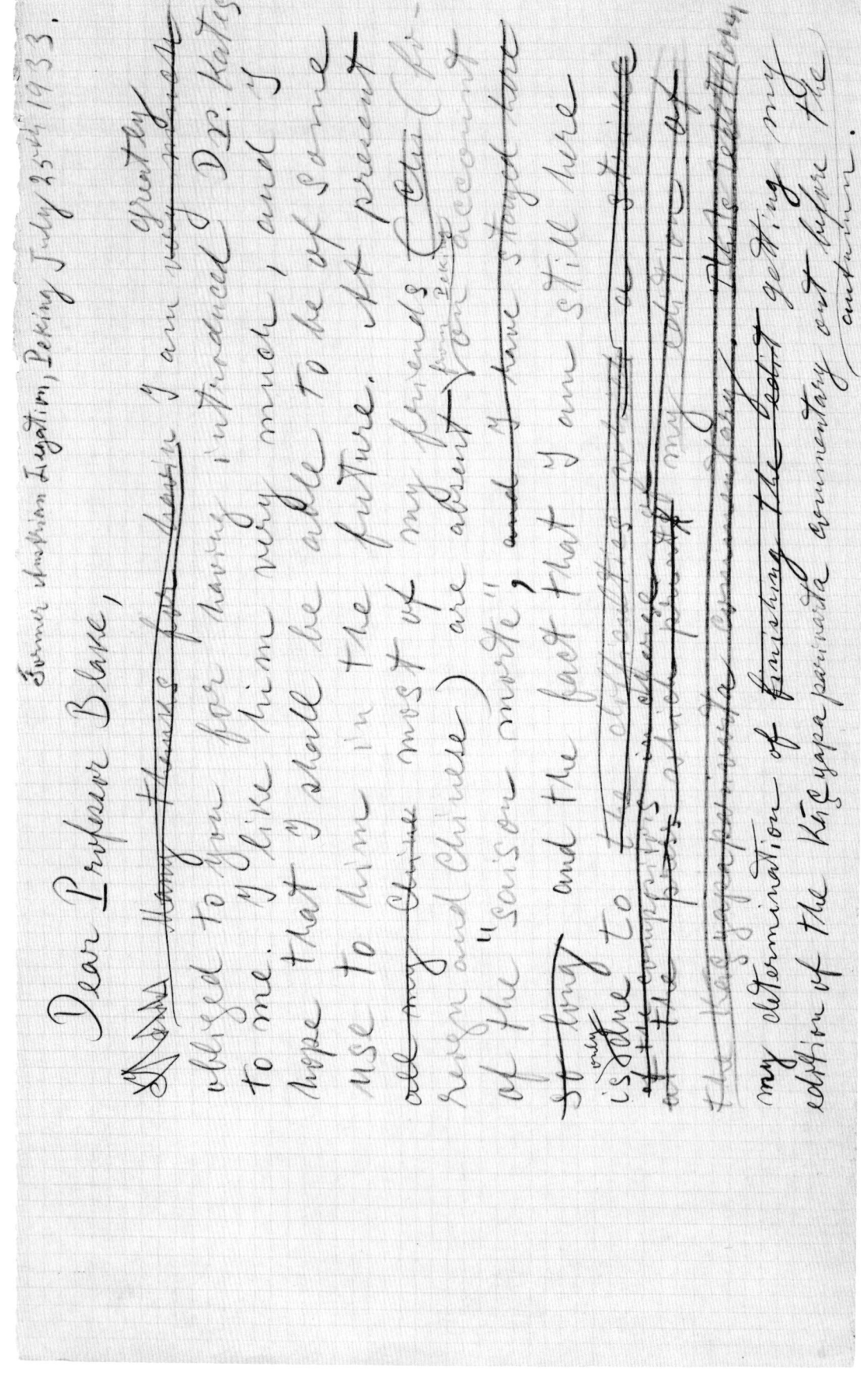

Seeing the books and articles which we have published through the ~~[illegible]~~ presses was not an easy task, because the Chinese compositors

May I ask to be kindly remembered to Mrs. Blake?

Believe me yours very sincerely ~~A. Staël Holstein.~~

Dr. Kertes ~~and Professor Elisséeff~~ has met a few scholars here ~~[illegible] here~~ at a small party which I had arranged for the Elisséeffs. I was very glad to meet my old colleague Elisséeff again, whom I had not seen since 1916. In that year we travelled together from St. Petersburg to Tōkyō.

A. St. H.

were entirely unacquainted with diacritical marks, etc. But now the ice is broken, and the bringing out of our next publications (we have a number of books and papers almost ready for the press) will be less difficult.

LIBRARY OF HARVARD UNIVERSITY
CAMBRIDGE, MASSACHUSETTS

January 23, 1936.

Dear Alexandr Ivanovich:

I have just had the pleasure of inspecting the beautiful red letter xylograph of the Tibetan translation of the larger Suraṃgamasūtra. We are most grateful for this choice and rare gift.

May I thank you also for the reprint of your paper on Tibetan Cycles, which I received not long since and have not yet acknowledged?

With kindest regards from Nadezhda Nikolaevna and myself,

I remain

Very sincerely yours,

Robert P. Blake

Baron A. von Staël-Holstein,
Ex-Austrian Embassy,
Peiping, China.

RPB/P

3 Chen Wu Miao
Nan Chang Chieh
Peiping
January 2, 1934

Dear Baron von Stael-Holstein:

I am sending you a copy of a letter which I have just written to Dean Chase in application for a renewal of my fellowship. With this I am also enclosing a copy of an article which, as I already told you some time ago, has been accepted for publication in the Journal of the American Oriental Society.

I hope that this may be of interest to you, and if you feel that you could support me again in this matter of a fellowship renewal, I should be extremely grateful.

Very sincerely yours,

Derk Bodde

(COPY)

3 Chen Wu Miao
Nan Chang Chieh
Peiping, China
January 1, 1934

Dean George H. Chase
Harvard-Yenching Institute
Boylston Hall
Cambridge, Mass.
U. S. A.

Dear Dean Chase:-

Last August I sent you three articles, two in the middle of the month, the other shortly before September, which I had just written. I have not heard anything from you since that time, but I hope that they reached you safely. I wrote these articles at the suggestion of Dr. Elisséeff, and also at his suggestion sent copies to the Journal of the American Oriental Society, which has accepted for publication the article entitled <u>A Perplexing Passage in the Confucian Analects</u>. This will probably appear in the April number. I am enclosing the letter of comment on these articles written to me by Dr. Shryock of the Journal of the American Oriental Society.

I now wish respectfully to submit my application for a renewal of my fellowship. Of course you realize that this work which I have undertaken requires long study, and I am sure that you understand that I am very anxious to remain here as long as possible so that what I have been doing may have practical results. A brief account of my work during the last half year follows:

Since September I have been taking a course at the Peking National University in which the works of the Taoist philosophers, Lao Tzu and Chuang Tzu, are read and explained in Chinese by Professor Ma Hsu-lun (馬敘倫), whose writings on the subject are well known. Meanwhile with my Chinese teacher at home I have been doing quite a bit of reading in Ssu-ma Ch'ien's <u>Shih Chi</u> (Historical Record), especially those parts of it dealing with the lives of the various philosophers. At present I am reading the works of the Confucian philosopher, Hsun Tzu. At the same time in the National and Language School Libraries I have been reading various western books on Chinese philosophy and culture, and especially the foreign sinological journals. At home I have been reading books by modern Chinese scholars, among them such works as the histories of Chinese philosophy by Hu Shih and by Feng Yu-lan, and the four volumes of the <u>Ku Shih Pien</u>

-2-

(critical discussions by some dozens of contemporary Chinese scholars on ancient Chinese history). I also have been continuing my lessons in the Chinese spoken language, and feel that I have been making good progress.

I hope that this resumé may help you to judge of my work. I myself feel that the past year has been a very profitable one, and that another year would be of tremendous value in putting me on my feet.

With very best wishes for the New Year,

Yours very sincerely,

Derk Bodde

A PERPLEXING PASSAGE IN THE CONFUCIAN *ANALECTS*

By Derk Bodde

One of the most baffling passages in the Confucian *Analects* is *Analects* IX, 1, h which Legge translates as: "The subjects of which the Master seldom sp spoke were--- profitableness, and also the appointments (of Heaven), and perfect virtue." (*Tzu han yen; li, yü ming, yü jen*.)[1] The difficulty here is not primarily a grammatical one, for such a translation may be read from the text without trouble, but rather lies in the fact that the statement made runs counter to everything which the rest of the *Analects* tells us concerning Confucius. It may be granted, to be sure, that *li*[2] (Legge's "profitableness") is not a subject which appears very frequently in the *Analects*. It is almost always disparaged, or attacked directly, in the places where it does occur,[3] and in the one instance in which it is really regarded favorably, it assumes a special meaning having reference to public, rather than individual, welfare.[4]

The same thing, however, can hardly be said about *ming*[5] (Legge's "appointments (of Heaven)"), which appears frequently in the *Analects* bearing the same metaphysical connotation that it possesses in this passage (as distinct from its other meanings, such as "command," "commission," "life," etc.).[6] But it is with the word *jen*[7] (Legge's "perfect virtue"), which forms the keystone of Confucian ethics, that the greatest obstacle to our understanding arises, an obstacle so great as to force Legge to admit in his notes on the passage: "With his not speaking of *jen* there is a difficulty which I know not how to solve. The fourth Book is nearly all occupied with it, and no doubt it was a prominent topic in Confucius's teachings."

Despite such a manifest contradiction between this single passage and the entire remainder of the Analects, western sinologists, such as Zottoli, Couvreur, Chavannes, Soothill, and Wilhelm, all translate in ~~xxx~~ exactly the same manner as does Legge. So, for that matter, does the Chinese translator, Ku Hung-ming.[8] In this they are but following what the majority of Chinese scholars have long accepted as the orthodox interpretation.

Attempts, of course, have not been wanting to find a rational explanation for this puzzling passage. Thus, concerning the strange inclusion of the term jen ("perfect virtue"), Ho Yen of the Wei Dynasty (220-265 A.D.) says: "Few are able to attain to it[jen]. Therefore [Confucius] rarely spoke of it."[9] And Chu Hsi (1130-1200) writes in similar strain: "Ch'eng Tzu says, 'Planning for profit ~~xx~~ is injurious to righteousness; the workings of heavenly decree are abstruse; the way of jen is vast. On all these the Master rarely spoke.'"[10]

But all this is merely explaining the language away. It is absurd to suppose that Confucius hesitated to impart even his most abstruse ideas to such a man as his beloved disciple Yen Hui, at whose death Confucius exclaimed: "Alas! Heaven is destroying me! Heaven is destroying me!"[11] And the essential difficulty persists that jen, when all is said and done, remains one of the commonest topics to be found in the Analects.

The passage has been generally accepted by Chinese scholars as being free from textual corruption, and in Ssu-ma Ch'ien's ~~S~~ Shih Chi it appears word for word the same as in the Analects.[12] The problem lies, then, in finding a reading for the chapter which, without disturbing the existing text, will harmonize itself with what the remainder of the Analects tells us.

In the Hsüeh Chai Chan Pi, a book of the Sung Dynasty, there seems to lie an answer to the problem, despite Wylie's condemnation of it as "only..... a work of second rate standing."[13] This work, which ~~appeared about the middle of the thirteenth century~~ was completed in the year 1250, was written by Shih Sheng-tsu,[14] a follower of Wei Liao-weng (1178-1237),[15] who is noted as being the founder of a school of classical criticism continuing the Confucian teachings of Chu Hsi. Though it deals for the most part with doubtful questions concerning the Yi Ching, ~~thexxxixxxxx~~ it contains one section which specifically discusses the problem involved in Analects IX, 1.[16]

Concerning this passage, Shih Sheng-tsu points out the impossibility of the orthodox interpretation, following much the same reasoning as that given above, and then continues: "In short, what the Master rarely spoke on is only li [profit] and nothing else. Out of this clause [i.e. the first portion of Analects IX,1, containing the opening words, Tzu han yen li] one should make a separate meaning. As regards ming [heavenly decree] and jen [perfect virtue] , these are both what he [Confucius] frequently held deeply forth upon. And this clause [i.e. the remaining portion of Analects IX, 1, containing the words, Yü ming, yü jen] one should make ~~x~~ into a separate single meaning."[17] Shih Sheng-tsu then adds an important grammatical note: "The [two] characters yü are [here] equivalent to the character hsü [a word which may be translated as "to allow," "grant," "give up to," etc.]."[18]

Thus what, according to the orthodox interpretation, was a single sentence, now becomes broken up into two separate sentences through the substitution of a period ~~for~~ instead of a comma after the ~~xxx~~ character li; while the two yü characters, which served as connectives (Legge's "and also..... and.....") become verbs meaning "to give forth," or "share." Interpreted in this way, the passage, newly

-4-

translated, reads: "The Master rarely spoke of profit. (But) he gave forth (his ideas concerning) the appointments (of Heaven), (and also) gave forth (his ideas concerning) perfect virtue." This is not only grammatically correct, but gives a translation thoroughly in accordance with the spirit of the *Analects* as a whole.

To explain how the character *yü* may thus be metamorphosed from a conjunction into a verb, in what may seem to some a rather surprising fashion, Shih Sheng-tsu quotes analogous examples from the Analects which, following Legge's translation, read:

> "There is nothing which I do that is not *shown to* you."
> The Master said: "I *admit* people's approach to me..... If a man purify himself..... I *receive* him so purified."
> The Master..... said, "I *give my approval to* Tien."
> "If I *associate* not with these people..... with whom shall I *associate*?"[19]

In these examples the character *yü* conveys the idea, not easily translated into exact words, but readily grasped in the original, of sharing, or associating, oneself and one's ideas with others, or perhaps of holding forth on (in the sense that an orator holds forth), which last meaning fits well into Shih Sheng-tsu's interpretation of *Analects* IX, 1.

To this exposition of Shih's views, let us add a final proof of our own. The use of the conjunction "and" is to a large extent avoided in Chinese, both in the written and spoken languages. Yet if we accept the traditional interpretation for *Analects* IX, 1, we find that the character *yü* occurs twice in this short sentence with such a meaning--- certainly most unusual. Legge senses this peculiarity when he translates: "The subjects of which the Master rarely spoke were--- profitableness, *and also* the appointments (of Heaven), *and* perfect virtue." The second "and" may be allowable, but the "and also" is certainly most clumsy and unnecessary.

If we look through the *Analects*, we come upon a number of sentences of a type very similar in structure to the one under discussion; that is, sentences in which things or ideas are grouped in the same way into categories. Thus we have:

> The Master's frequent themes of discourse were--- the Odes, the History, and the maintenance of the Rules of Propriety.
> The subjects on which the Master did not talk, were--- extraordinary beings, feats of strength, disorder, and spiritual beings.
> There were four things which the Master taught,--- letters, ethics, devotion of soul, and truthfulness.
> There were four things from which the Master was entirely free. He had no foregone conclusions, no arbitrary predeterminations, no obstinacy, and no egoism.[20]

Comparing these four sentences, we make a most interesting discovery. In not one of them does the character <u>yü</u> occur, either in the meaning of "and," or with any other meaning whatsoever! The "and's" which occur in the translations have been added by Legge solely in order to conform to the demands of English idiom. It seems hardly possible, then, that in <u>Analects</u> IX, 1, which coincides almost exactly with these examples in sentence structure, two <u>yü</u> characters would appear gratuitously, unless they were intended to play a definite part in determining the meaning of the sentence, certainly a part more important than ~~mere~~ superfluous conjunctions such as "and" and "and also." Translation of the character <u>yü</u> according to the formula laid down by Shih Sheng-tsu would seem, then, to be the only possible alternative to falling into a glaring inconsistency.

It is difficult to account for the fact that Chinese scholarship should for the main have disregarded an explanation of a puzzling passage which, when once understood, appears quite logical and natural. Shih Sheng-tsu lived a little too late to have his researches adopted by Chu Hsi and so receive the stamp of orthodox approval. Nevertheless, an extract from his explanation of this passage appears in the <u>Huang Ch'ing Ching Chieh</u>, published by Yüan Yüan in 1829, which Legge praises so highly, but which the eminent translator of the Chinese classics evidently must have overlooked when he studied the passage under consideration.[21]

In any case, Analects IX, 1, affords an interesting example of some of the difficulties besetting the student of Chinese, while Shih Sheng-tsu's explanation exemplifies the use in China of a true scientific method, as applied to textual criticism, at a time when Europe had not yet emerged from the Middle Ages.

Notes

1. 子罕言：利，與命，與仁。

2. 利。　　3. Ana. IV, 12; 16; XIII, 17, etc..

4. Ibid., XX, 2.　　5. 命。

6. Ana. II, 4; VI, 8; XI, 18; XII, 5; XVI, 8; XX, 3.　　7. 仁。

8. Loc. cit., Couvreur, Les Quatres Livres; Ku Hung-ming, Discourses and Sayings of Confucius; Soothill, Analects of Confucius; Wilhelm, Kungfutse Gespräche. Also Zottoli, Cursus Litteraturae Sinicae, Vol. II, p. 279, and Chavannes, Mémoires Historiques, Vol. V, p. 405.

9. 寡能及之，故希言也。

10. 程子曰：計利則害義；命之理微；仁之道大，皆夫子所罕言也。

11. Ana. XI, 8.　　12. Cf. Chavannes, op. cit..

13. Wylie, Notes on Chinese Literature, p. 161 (1902 edition).

14. 學齋佔畢, by 史繩祖. It appears in the 12th 集 of the 學津討原 (edited by 張海鵬), of which I have consulted the 昭曠閣刻本 edition, published in 1805.

15. 魏了翁　　16. Cf. section 子罕言利, in chüan 1, pp. 18b-19b.

-7-

17. 蓋子罕言者，獨利而已、當以此句作一義、曰命，曰仁，皆平日所深與、此句別作一義、

18. 與者，許也、

19. Ana. VII, 23; 28; XI, 25; XVIII, 1. The character 與 occurs twice in the second and fourth examples.

20. Ibid., VII, 17; 20; 24; IX, 4.

21. 皇清經解, published by 阮元. Cf. the section 四書考異, beginning of chuan 459.

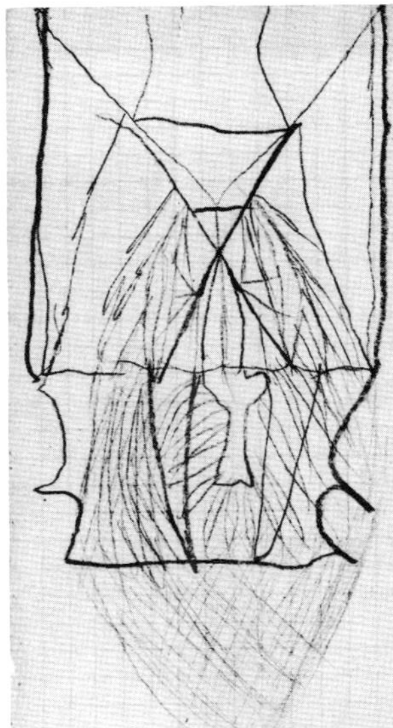

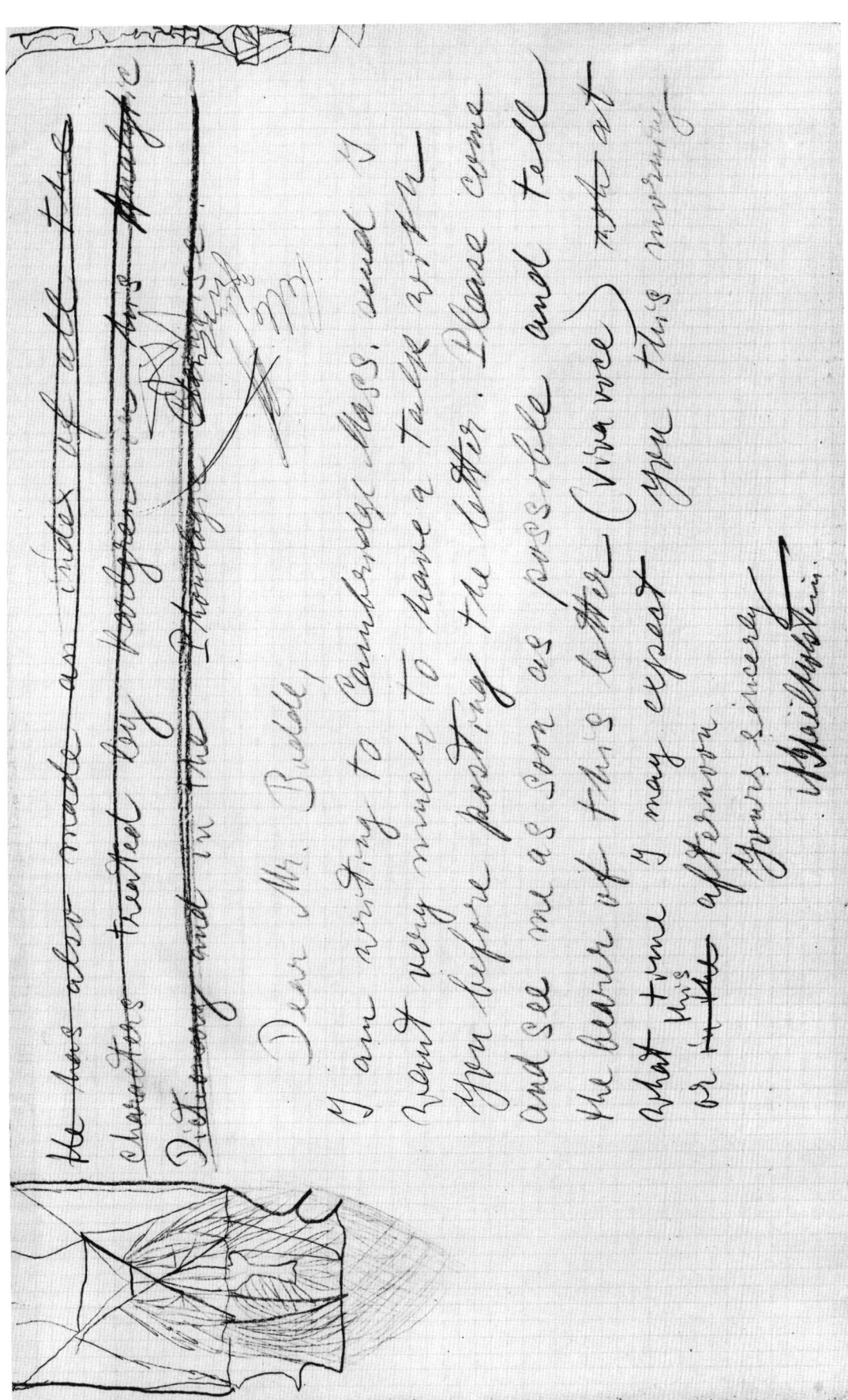

~~He has also made an index of all the characters treated by Karlgren in his Analytic Dictionary and in the Phonologie Chinoise.~~

Dear Mr. Biddle,

I am writing to Cambridge Mass. and I want very much to have a talk with you before posting the letter. Please come and see me as soon as possible and tell the bearer of this letter (viva voce) ~~when~~ at what time I may expect you this morning or ~~in the~~ this afternoon.

Yours sincerely

A. Staël-Holstein.

Peking March 14th 1935

Dear Mr. Bodde,

I think that the books by ~~Mc. Govern~~ McGovern, Suzuki, and de Groot, which you mention, are well worth reading, and I enclose Kimura's charts. ~~(~~ Professor J. K. Tschen thinks that ... is the best history of Buddhism in Chinese.

Cordially yours

A. Staël Holstein

~~Sehr viele Esten haben bekanntlich deutsche Familiennamen. Neulich hörte ich, dass~~ Neulich hörte ich, dass in Estland die deutschen ~~Neulich hörte ich, dass die Esten jetzt ihre deutschen~~ Familiennamen ~~jetzt vielfach abgelegt und von den Esten durch nationale ersetzt werden.~~ ~~Familiennamen ablegen und~~ diese jetzt vielfach abgelegt und nationale Familiennamen angenommen werden. ~~Georg V hat seine würdige Nachahmer~~ Die neugebackene Familie "Windsor" ~~hat würdige~~ hat ihrer würdige Nachahmer gefunden.

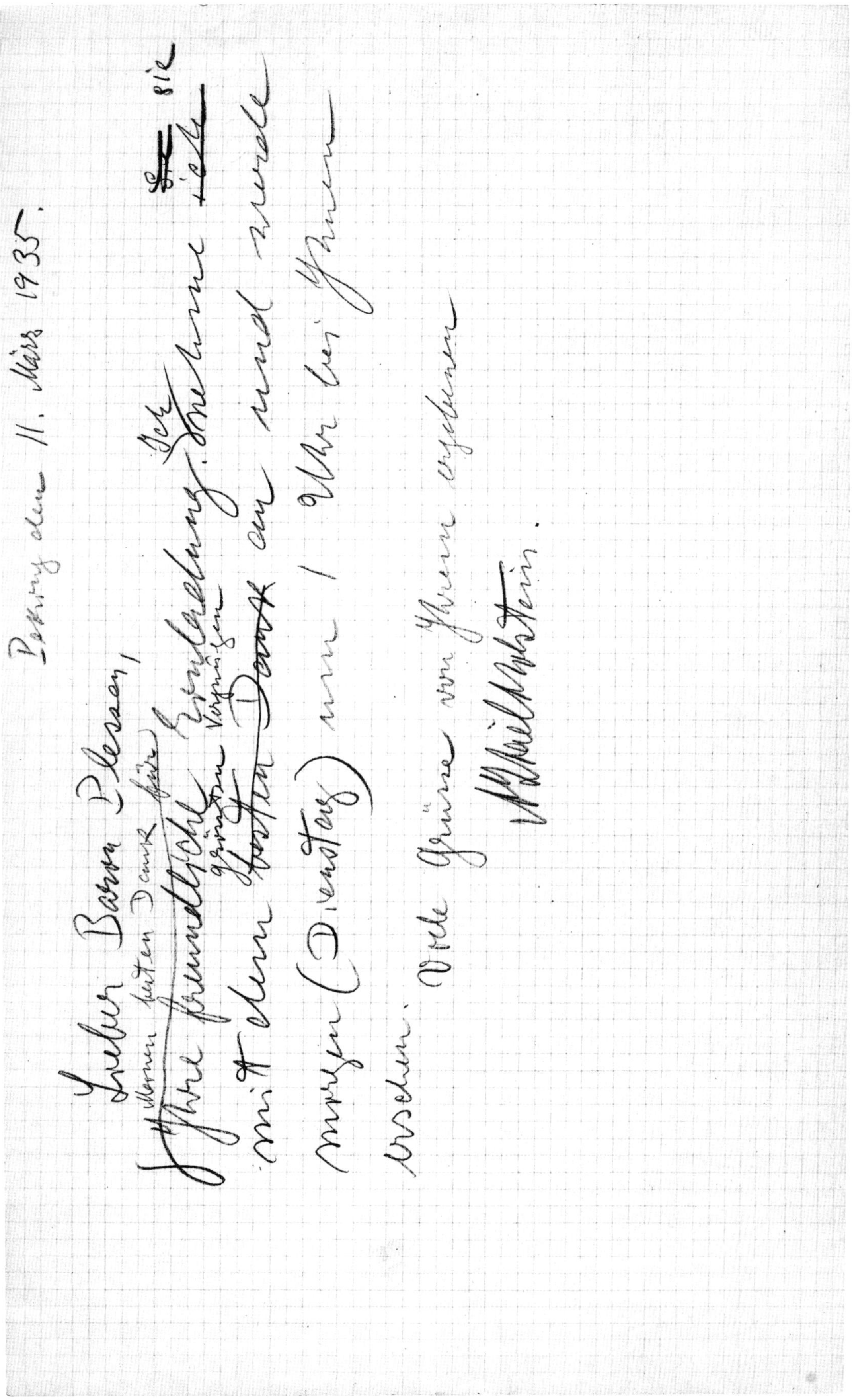

Peking den 11. März 1935.

Lieber Baron Plessen,

Meinen besten Dank für Ihre freundliche Einladung. Ich nehme ~~Sie~~ sie ~~ich~~ mit dem größten Vergnügen ~~besten Dank~~ an und werde morgen (Dienstag) um 1 Uhr bei Ihnen erscheinen.

Viele Grüsse von Ihrem ergebenen

AStaëlHolstein.

Peking, le 4. Juillet 24

Cher Monsieur —

Je suis rentré de mon voyage au P'an Shan où je n'ai pu recueillir beaucoup de renseignements archéologiques mais où je ramène des documents cartographiques et géologiques importants.
Je vais me remettre à mon étude sur le temple des lamas que je vais terminer ce ~~je~~ mois-ci.
Comme je vous l'avais demandé si cela ne vous gêne pas en ce moment, je vous serais reconnaissant de bien vouloir me prêter à nouveau pour une dizaine de jours votre Waddel où je voudrais revoir la question danses et cérémonies. —
Vous voudriez bien me faire savoir le jour où je pourrais le faire chercher.

Pour identifier certains noms chinois du P'an-shan j'avais demandé à notre ami commun Baylin de me prêter son

凝香室鴻雪因緣圖記目錄.

Or le volume qui traite le P'an-shan est entre vos mains. Si vous en avez besoin pour quelque temps je vous prierai de bien vouloir me le confier une journée et je vous le remettrai ensuite.

J'espère que vous êtes toujours en bonne santé et me rappelle à votre bon souvenir.

Cordialement votre

G. Bouillard

Dear Mr. Reid,

Many thanks for your note. I am very glad to hear that you are free tomorrow morning and that you would like to see me. Will you give me the pleasure of your company at lunch tomorrow (Thursday) at 1 o'clock at my house. I shall be delighted to see you. Hoping for ~~th~~ a favourable answer (or on the accompanying slip) I am yours respectfully

A. Staël Holstein.

Lieber Herr Doctor,

~~Erlauben Sie mir, bitte,~~ Nur eine Zeile, um Sie daran zu erinnern, dass ich Sie morgen ~~um~~ um 12 hier zum Lunch ~~[illegible]~~ erwarte. Ich freue mich sehr darauf Sie zu sehen.

Ihr Ihnen ganz ergebener

A. Staël Holstein.

Monsieur
Le ~~D~~ Docteur R. Wilhelm
Attaché Scientifique

Baron A. de Staël-Holstein has much pleasure in accepting Mr. & Mrs. Boyd-Carpenter's kind invitation to dinner on Friday the 29th.

Peking Sept. 27th 1922

Peiping, April 3rd 1932

Dear Dr. Fu,

I am very much obliged to you for your letter and for the rare distinction which the Academia Sinica has conferred upon me. ~~I highly ap I am immensely proud of~~ I highly appreciate the honour and shall try to prove a worthy research fellow.

I also received with many thanks the copy of Kovalevsky's dictionary which you so kindly ~~sent me~~ presented to me. ~~It~~ ~~I am very glad that I possess a complete and which will That valuable work is indeed a~~ I greatly value the volumes of which I never ~~possessed~~ before possessed a complete set.

Believe me yours sincerely and gratefully

Dear Dr. Brown,

One of the Sanscrit formulas which we find on the boards is the following: Namah sattvānām samyaksambuddhānām ("Adoration to the wholly enlightened beings"). The formula Om Manipadme Hum, which we ~~have already~~ discussed before, also occurs. There is, as far as I can see, nothing of special interest on the boards. I am sorry to say that I ~~could~~ have not been able to discover any Indian or Tibetan characters on ~~the~~ your photo which I enclose.

Believe me yours sincerely

No.4 Methodist Mission, Peip'ing,

Dec.15th,1932.

My dear Baron Stael-Holstein:-

Will you be kind enough to examine the ~~eight~~ nine "Crosses" I am sending herewith, together with prints of the same. At your convenience I shall be glad to hear if you find any Sanskrit on them. Thanking you,

I am,

Very sincerely yours,

Mark W. Brown

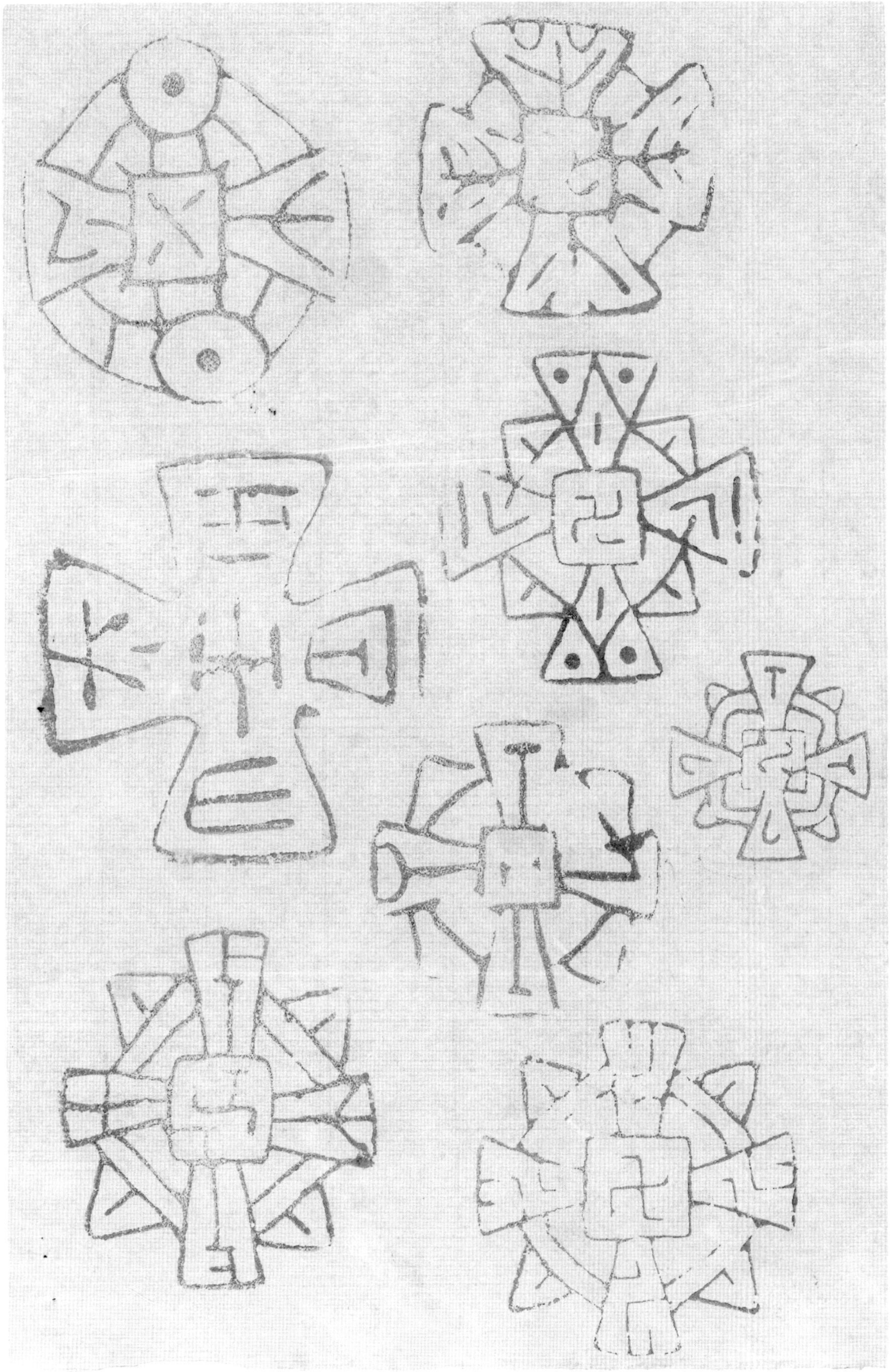

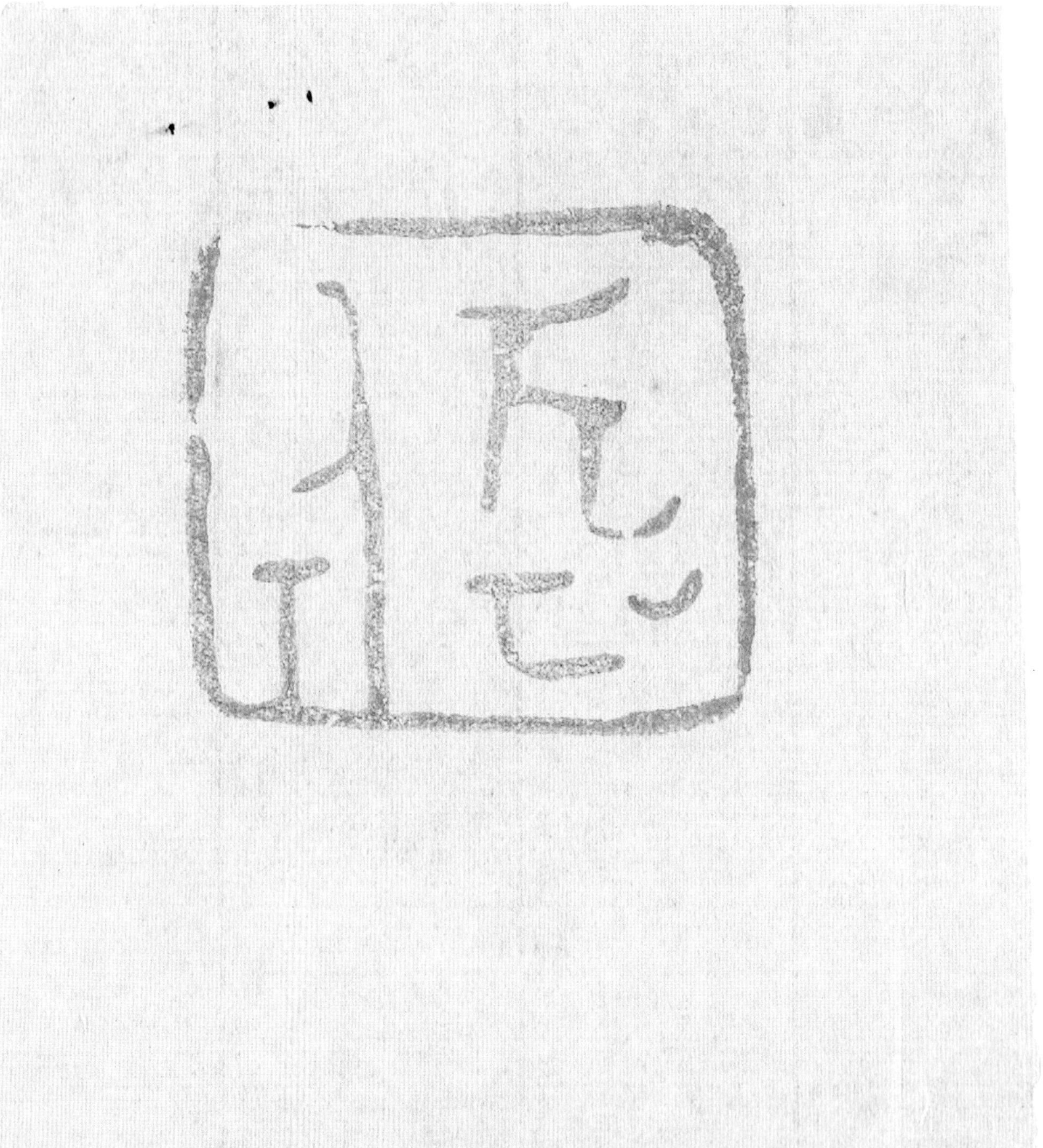

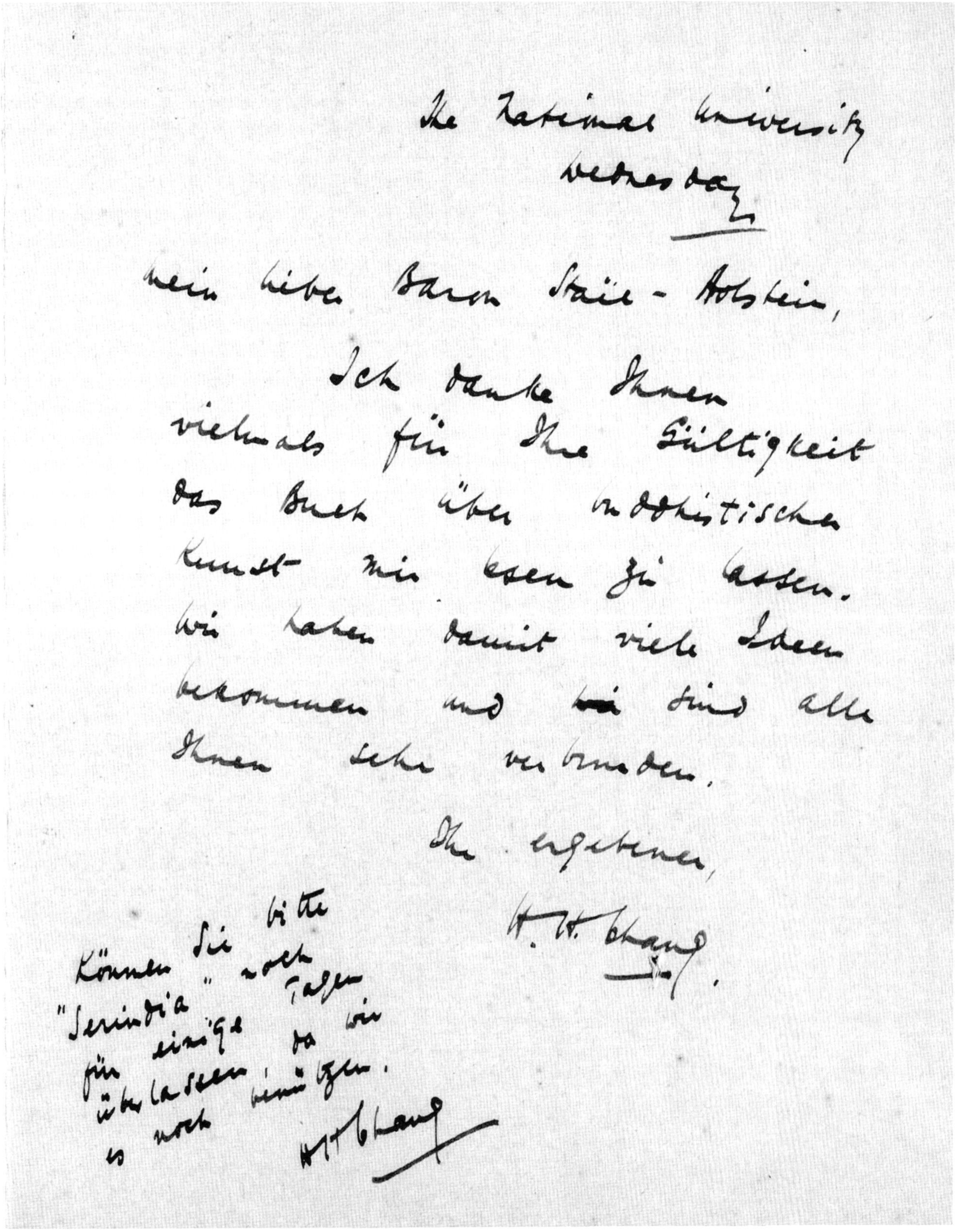

The National University
Wednesday

Mein lieber Baron Staël-Holstein,

Ich danke Ihnen vielmals für Ihre Gültigkeit das Buch über buddhistische Kunst mir lesen zu lassen. Wir haben damit viele Ideen bekommen und ~~wir~~ sind alle Ihnen sehr verbunden.

Ihr ergebener,

H. H. Chang.

Können Sie bitte noch "Serindia" für einige Tagen uns noch überlassen da wir benötigen.

H H Chang

Peking May 14th 1935

Dear Professor Chao,

The Harvard-Yenching Institute of ~~B~~ Cambridge Mass. (not the Peking office of the Institute) will publish a Woods Memorial Volume, and I have been ~~asked~~ requested to ask the Chinese friends of the late Professor J. H. Woods for contributions. ~~Can~~ ~~I think~~ ~~I believe that you collaborate [illegible] collabo~~ I do not think I am wrong in believing that you were one of the closest friends of the late scholar. May I therefore ask you to contribute an article in English (on any oriental subject you love) to the Woods Memorial Volume? If you will send the article to me, I shall forward it to Cambridge Mass. together with other contributions. ~~The article must be in Cambridge Mass. before September~~ ~~Please~~ ~~May I ask you~~ I shall be very much obliged to you if you will send the article to my address before August 15th?

Believe me yours sincerely

A. Staël-Holstein

My dear Baron von Staël Holstein:

I am returning your M.S with thanks, which you kindly lent to me.

I am sorry I did not get to see you that day after receiving your note, as I was going to Tsingtao on business for 10 days. If it will be convenient to you, I should like to call on you Saturday afternoon.

With best regards,

Very sincerely yours,

Yuen Ren Chao

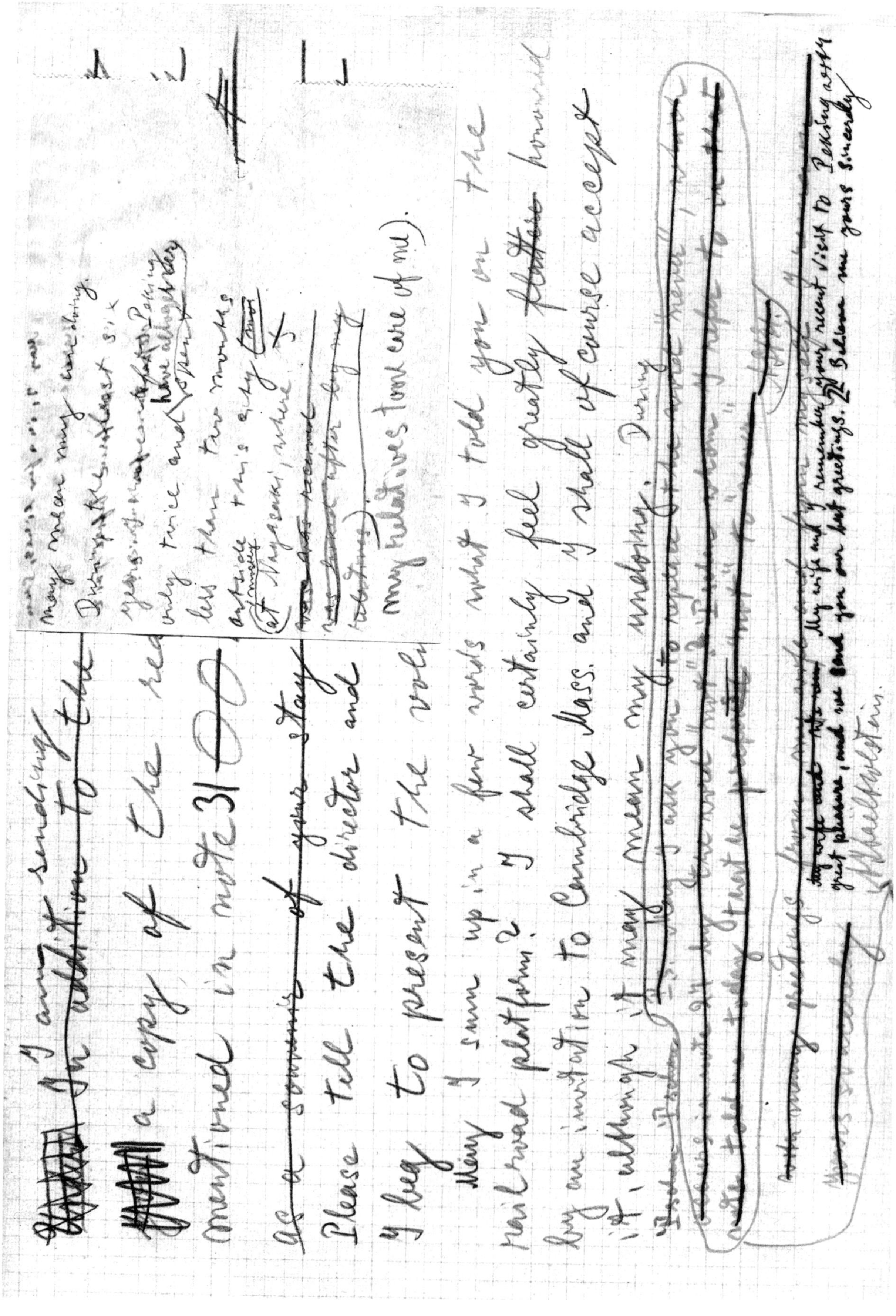

~~In addition to the~~ I am sending a copy of the re[...] mentioned in note 31 ~~as a souvenir of your stay~~

Please tell the director and

I beg to present the vol[...]

may mean my undoing. During the last six years I have been to Peking only twice and have altogether spent less than two months outside this city (not counting my journey at Nagasaki, where ~~I was received~~ ~~was looked after by my relatives~~ my relatives took care of me).

May I sum up in a few words what I told you on the railroad platform? I shall certainly feel greatly ~~flatter~~ honoured by an invitation to Cambridge Mass. and I shall of course accept it, although it may mean my undoing. During

~~May I ask you to replace the word "never", which occurs in note 27 by the word "not"? Peter whom I refer to in that note told me today that he preferred "not" to "never".~~

~~With many greetings from my wife and from myself~~

~~Yours sincerely~~

My wife and I remember your recent visit to Peking with great pleasure, and we send you our best greetings. Believe me yours sincerely

A. Staël-Holstein.

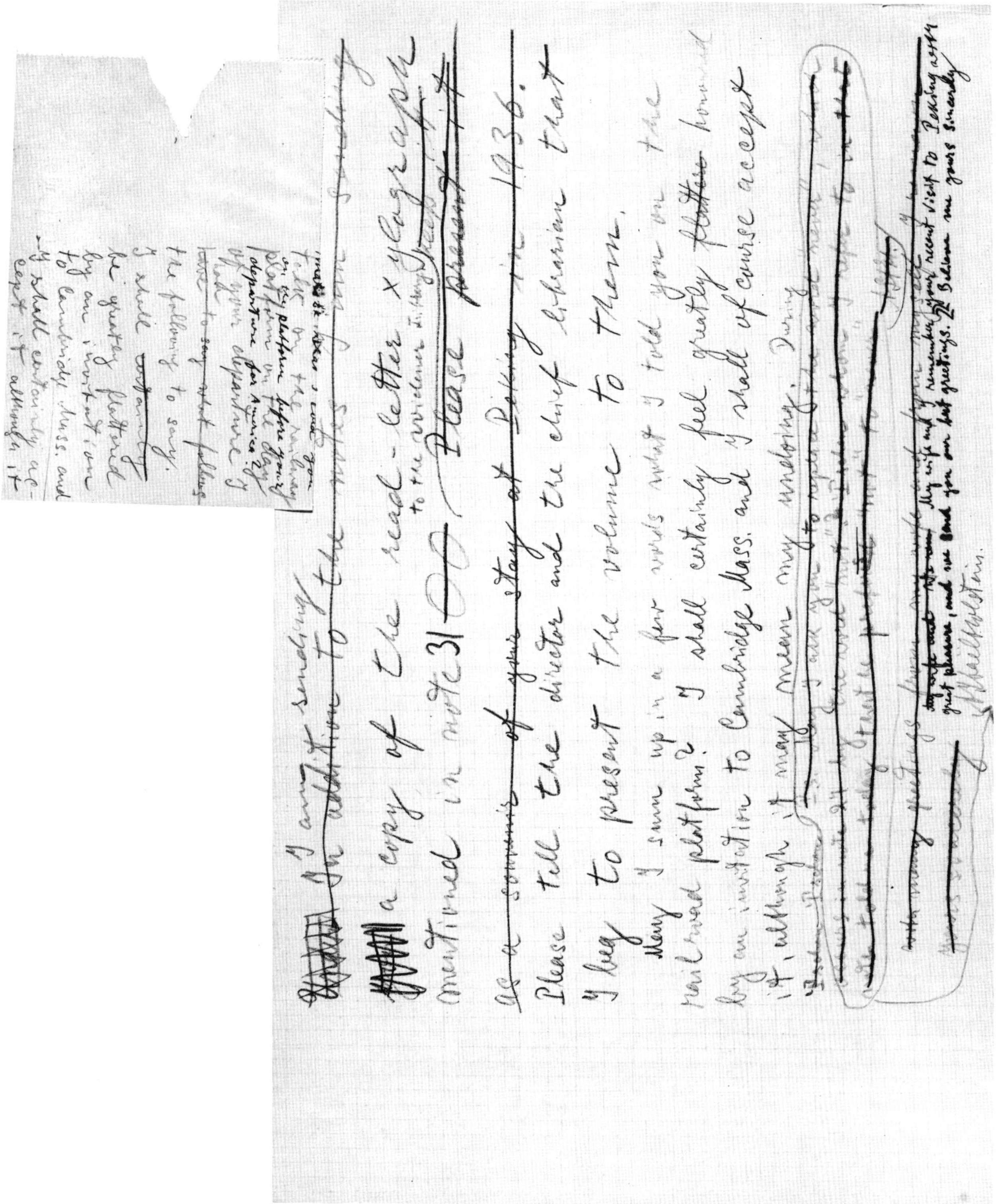

~~In addition to the notes I am sending~~ I am sending a copy of the read-letter xylograph mentioned in note 31 to the Widener Library. ~~Please present it as a souvenir of your stay at Peking in 1936.~~ Please tell the director and the chief librarian that I beg to present the volume to them.

May I sum up in a few words what I told you on the railroad platform? I shall certainly feel greatly ~~flattered~~ honoured by an invitation to Cambridge Mass. and I shall of course accept it, although it may mean my undoing. During

~~with many greetings from my wife and from myself~~

My wife and I remember your recent visit to Peking with great pleasure, and we send you our best greetings. Believe me yours sincerely

A. Staël-Holstein.

~~…~~ on the platform before your departure for America, ~~of your departure I have to say what follows~~ the following to say. I shall ~~certainly~~ be greatly flattered by an invitation to Cambridge Mass. and I shall certainly accept it although it

Charignon

28	14
29	98
30	37
31	70
32	20
33	20
34	12
35	145
	32
	416
30	37
1	70
2	20
3	20
4	12
5	145
	1
	304
	1212
	304
	908

Monsieur et cher collègue,

Le mot kāma signifie ~~l'~~amour, désir, plaisir etc. et le mot rūpa – forme, beauté, qualité couleur etc. Le composé kāmarūpa ce rencontre comme adjectif dans le sens de "capable de prendre diverses formes". ~~Le~~ J'ai souvent trouvé le caractère 楞 comme représentant des ~~l~~ syllabes sanscrite ~~lang~~ lain et ran.

~~Malheureusement c'est tout ce que je puisse vous dire à propos des problèmes~~ ~~intéressants~~ ~~dont vous parlez dans votre~~ ~~intéressante~~ ~~lettre qui m'a beaucoup intéressé.~~

Votre lettre m'a beaucoup intéressé et je regrette profondément de ne vous pouvoir donner que ces maigres renseignements.

Agréez, cher Monsieur, l'expression de mes sentiments distingués.

HARVARD UNIVERSITY

THE GRADUATE SCHOOL OF ARTS AND SCIENCES

24 UNIVERSITY HALL, CAMBRIDGE, MASSACHUSETTS

My dear Sir:

The Harvard-Yenching Institute is now established, and plans are so far made that I write to ask whether you can come to Cambridge next year as a visiting professor to give one whole course or two half courses in Harvard University on such subjects as you may propose. I cannot be absolutely definite yet about financial arrangements, but I am sure they can be made such as to cover fully your expenses of travel and residence in Cambridge for such part of the year 1929 as you are here. (I understand from Dr. North that arrangement has been made through Yenching University to provide for your researches during the whole of the calendar year 1928.)

I am writing by this same mail to Professor Porter, inviting him also to come and giving him somewhat more fully details about our arrangements in regard to courses and some other things that lie in our minds. The essential matter is that we hope to bring together here next year representatives of Yenching University and one or two European sinologists so that we may have a chance to discuss the whole problem of the development of the Harvard-Yenching Institute and its policies.

I need not add, I am sure, that all of us here hope very much that you can answer "Yes" to this invitation. Professor Woods would send personal greetings, I know, if he were here, but he is abroad this year on sabbatical leave. If you could let me know shortly whether you

- 2 -

can come and what subject or subjects you would propose for your lectures, it would help me very greatly in making the necessary arrangements.

I am

Very sincerely yours,

George H. Chase

Baron von Stael Holstein

HARVARD UNIVERSITY

THE GRADUATE SCHOOL OF ARTS AND SCIENCES

24 UNIVERSITY HALL, CAMBRIDGE, MASSACHUSETTS

May 9, 1928

My dear Sir:

At last I am able to write that financial arrangements for the Harvard-Yenching Institute are complete for next year and that your appointment as Visiting Lecturer on Chinese Language and Literature will shortly be made. If official notice does not reach you shortly after this letter, please let me know.

On the basis of your welcome letter of March 16 I have arranged a scheme of courses which, I think, will meet your wishes. I have put the course in Buddhist Mythology down as a half-course in the first half-year with hours to be arranged, and the Introduction to the Kacyapaparivarta as a half-course in the second-half year, with hours to be arranged. Neither of these courses probably will be large, and it is a great convenience to fix the hours after the class meets in such a case. Ordinarily, as you will see from the schedule of courses which I enclose, a course has two or three lectures a week for a period of about twelve weeks. The academic year begins on Monday, September 23, but it would be wise, as Professor Birkhoff suggested, for you to reach Cambridge on or before September 21, since there are always difficulties in settling down, arranging quarters, and so on. If you will let me know your wishes about quarters, I will see what can be done before your arrival. Two of our visiting professors this year have had rooms in the new buildings of the Business School and have found them very satisfactory. It is also possible to get a room at the Colonial Club, which is close by the University and a convenient stopping place, but rooms in the Business School buildings provide a study, bed-room, and bath, and are, I think, rather more convenient.

All of us here certainly look forward to greeting you in the fall, and discussing the problem of the Institute and the way in which it should be worked out.

Cordially yours,

George H. Chase

Professor A. von Stael-Holstein

P.S. The financial arrangement which was finally passed by the Executive Committee of the Harvard-Yenching Institute appropriates $3,000 gold as your salary up to July 1, 1929, and a travelling allowance of $600 gold. These will, of course, be available as soon as you reach Cambridge, but if an advance of the travelling allowance would be helpful, please let me know and I will see that the money is transferred to you at Peking. G.H.C.

HARVARD-YENCHING INSTITUTE

23 University Hall
Cambridge
Massachusetts
October 8, 1928

My dear Professor von Staël-Holstein:

The Educational Committee of the Harvard-Yenching Institute requests the pleasure of your company at a dinner to be held on Monday, October 22, at 7 P.M. at the Faculty Club of the Graduate School of Business Administration to meet the Trustees of the Institute and a few invited guests. The dinner will be formal to the extent of dinner coats, but we hope not otherwise. I hope very much that you can come.

Sincerely yours,

Professor Alexander von Staël-Holstein

HARVARD UNIVERSITY

THE GRADUATE SCHOOL OF ARTS AND SCIENCES

24 UNIVERSITY HALL, CAMBRIDGE, MASSACHUSETTS

October 10, 1928

Dear Professor von Staël-Holstein:

I enclose a statement which I am sure you will be glad to see, as I am. This means, I assume, that the case is in Boston, and can be brought out very quickly when the customs officers are satisfied. I imagine that things will move fastest if you can send me a brief statement of the contents and value of the books in question, and I hope the value does not exceed one hundred dollars so that no consular invoice will be required. Since the shipment is to me, we can probably do best if I make the necessary statement and get the college officials to clear the case and bring it to the Fogg Museum. I hope there will be no further delay.

Sincerely yours,

George H. Chase

Professor Alexander von Staël-Holstein

HARVARD UNIVERSITY

THE GRADUATE SCHOOL OF ARTS AND SCIENCES

24 UNIVERSITY HALL, CAMBRIDGE, MASSACHUSETTS

January 18, 1929

My dear Baron:

Mr. Benedict tells me that there is some unclearness about the examinations which you are to give to the men who have been working with you. This is largely my fault because I undoubtedly have not made clear the distinctions which we observe. The men who are taking Chinese 21, Introduction to the Kacyapaparivarta, should have a written examination on which grades may be returned to the office. If you are in doubt how such an examination should be made out, I am sure Professor Clark will help you with it.

The men who are registered for Chinese 20 -- Messrs. Acker, Sickman, Bingham, and Lee -- should not have a formal examination, but you should report on the blank which will be sent you by the Records Office your impression of the work of each man, giving him an A if the work is very satisfactory, a B if it is of distinctly good quality, but not the highest, and a C if it is ordinary. I should be very glad to talk over the grades that should be given these men with you if that would help; or again, I am sure Professor Clark would give you some advice.

- 2 -

For the second half-year I have arranged that Chinese 21 will go on ~~as another half-course~~, and that the work in Tibetan will be announced as a separate course, Chinese 23. This will make it possible to give the men who take the course a written examination in Tibetan at the end of the year, which, it seems to me, they ought to be able to undertake at that time.

If all this is not entirely clear, please do not hesitate to let me know.

Cordially yours,

George H. Chase

Baron von Staël-Holstein

HARVARD UNIVERSITY

THE GRADUATE SCHOOL OF ARTS AND SCIENCES

24 UNIVERSITY HALL, CAMBRIDGE, MASSACHUSETTS

March 23, 1929

My dear Baron:

I am sure you will be glad to know that the Corporation will act on our recommendation for your appointment on Monday, and that the Secretary of the Corporation has agreed to send you on Tuesday or Wednesday (as soon as he can) a letter stating that this appointment has been made and fixed up with the seal of the University. We all hope that this may prove helpful in straightening out the difficulties of your passport.

One other matter is on my mind. Mr. Acker should have a written examination covering his work in Chinese and related fields on May 15 (what we call a final general examination). I venture to ask you to serve with Professor Clark and Mr. Mei as a committee to set such an examination. I will ask Mr. Clark to be Chairman, and I hope that together you three can arrange a test that will be fair. Shortly after May 15, also, there should be an oral examination, which I hope I may be allowed to attend, but the date and place of this can be arranged later.

Sincerely yours,

Baron A. von Staël-Holstein

HARVARD-YENCHING INSTITUTE

23 University Hall
Cambridge, Mass.
March 30, 1929

My dear Baron:

I write to confirm what I told you a day or two ago that the Trustees of the Harvard-Yenching Institute hope very much that you can come to dine with them at the Faculty Club of the Business School on Friday next, April 5, at six-thirty. I suspect that the Trustees will have to have a formal meeting after dinner, and I hope you will not think them discourteous if they withdraw to hold this meeting in the evening.

Sincerely yours,

George H. Chase

Baron A. von Staël-Holstein

HARVARD-YENCHING INSTITUTE

23 University Hall
Cambridge, Mass.
June 19, 1929

My dear Baron:

There are two things on my mind especially, and I want to write you about one or two other matters.

I submitted the agreement which you signed in regard to things purchased with funds of the Harvard-Yenching Institute to Mr. Coolidge as our legal adviser, and he redrafted the formula in what he thinks is a somewhat better legal form. I enclose this and ask you, if you will, to sign it and return it to me. It does not seem to me that the spirit of the agreement is changed at all, but Mr. Coolidge insists that so long as we make annual appropriations for supporting the Sino-Indian Researches in Peking the agreement ought to read as he has put it, "expects (but has not agreed) to continue such support". I hope you will not think we are unduly legalistic.

The second point is this. After your appointment was made the Secretary of the Corporation pointed out to me that all appointments to professorships nowadays come under an arrangement for a retiring allowance. The scheme is set forth in detail in the printed sheet which I enclose. The Secretary suggested that

- 2 -

the Harvard-Yenching Institute ought to consider whether it wished its professors to share in this scheme, and the Executive Committee, which met last Friday, voted so to do. What it means is that five percent of your salary will be retained by the Treasurer of Harvard University and to this will be added another five percent, contributed by the Harvard-Yenching Institute; this fund, as you see, being available if at any time a professor withdraws, and, if he reaches the retiring age, being used to purchase an annuity. We all think it an excellent plan, partly because it forces saving on professors, and partly because, as Dean Donham says, it is a kind of 100% investment, the Corporation adding each year to the fund what the professor puts in. I wanted to explain this so that you would understand why your salary checks when they reach you have the five percent deduction. If I have not made myself clear, I am sure Professor Woods can explain more in detail when he reaches Peking.

I think you will be glad to know that the Executive Committee voted to invite Dr. Laufer to join the staff of the Institute with the idea that next year, at least, he will be in Cambridge and will take charge especially of our publications, and that later he may from time to time visit Peking. We hope that Dr. Laufer will accept our invitation, though, of course, there is no predicting. Everybody seems to feel that the best chance of the Institute immediately is to publish well the researches of the men connected with it, and certainly Dr. Laufer would be a tower of strength as an editor and no doubt, also, as an adviser.

I hope you had a good trip to Peking and found things

- 3 -

in good shape on your return. We certainly greatly enjoyed your year with us and hope to see you again in the not too distant future.

Cordially yours,

George H. Chase.

Baron Alexander von Staël-Holstein

My dear Dean Chase,

Many thanks for your kind letter dated June 19th 1929. I am very glad to hear ~~that rally~~ about the arrangements for a retiring allowance ~~which~~ and I ~~consider them~~ thank the trustees very much for adding so generously ~~much~~ to the five percent which I, of course, agree to pay.

~~Dr. Laufer will no doubt~~ I have a great respect for Dr. Laufer's scholarship and I beg to congratulate you on the occasion of his appointment.

We expect Professor Woods ~~is expected here~~ in a fortnight, and I shall write to you on the subject of the legal formula ~~immediately~~ after his arrival in Peking.

Peking has certainly changed during the year I spent in America, but it is still a most attractive ~~interesting~~ city. During the last three months I have found a number of very interesting books and some really beautiful pictures. ~~My assistants & I. The~~ During periods ~~Periods~~ of political unrest ~~are always~~ such objects always appear more readily on our ~~the~~ market, than during the rare intervals of peace and tranquillity. ~~The organizo~~ Most of Some ~~The majority of my assistants are already here at work here~~, but ~~others have been~~ the arrival of others has been delayed by floods and war scares. Mr. Schuster has been ~~is~~ studying colloquial Chinese since his arrival here about a week ago. Next Saturday we will start our Sino-Indian and Tibetan

Ex-Austrian Legation, Peking China, September 4th 1929.

To the Bursar of Harvard University.

Dear Sir,

May I ask you to deduct four hundred dollars, the amount of your bill (~~No~~) dated May 9th 1929 and marked "page 215, line 29", ~~1929~~ from the salary (seven thousand dollars a year minus five percent for the retiring allowance fund) which has been promised me by the University?

~~(seven thousand dollars a year minus five per cent for the retiring allowance)~~

Faithfully yours

A. Staël Holstein.

Some of my assistants and I ~~have been busy with our~~ ~~work~~ ~~catalogue~~ ~~since~~ ~~the beginning of June, although the~~ resumed our regular research work, which had ~~been~~ almost stopped during my absence, on July 1st.

Professor Woods

Empress France

Yokohama

~~A~~ many thanks kind letter preparing diamond cutter ~~suitable~~ rooms available ~~kindly~~ please wire ~~exact~~ date arrival Peiping

Stael

Courses. ~~Besides Mr. Schuster there will be two or three students (two of them Chinese and one German)~~ There will be certainly three of us: Mr. Y. K. P... (who was invited ~~to Harvard~~ by the H. Y. Institute, but could not ~~come~~ go to America), Mr. Schuster and myself, but there may be two more. I shall never forget your unvarying kindness during the charming months I spent at Cambridge. Believe me yours most sincerely and gratefully. A. Staël Holstein

HARVARD-YENCHING INSTITUTE

23 University Hall
Cambridge, Mass.
October 8, 1929

My dear Professor von Staël-Holstein:

I have been meaning for a long time to write and congratulate you on your marriage, and at the same time to thank you for sending me the announcement of it. Now your letter of September 9 reminds me that I have been remiss, but I am sure you know how busy we are just at the opening of college and I hope you will forgive me.

Dr. Laufer's appointment is not yet assured, but I think he will come to us in the course of the year.

I am glad to hear that Mr. Schuster has arrived and is starting his study, and that the Sino-Indian and Tibetan courses are already begun.

The opportunities to pick up books and pictures must be remarkable. I don't wonder that you love Peking under present conditions.

The Bursar's office asked me to inquire whether Ex-Austrian Legation, Peking, is the best address to use for you, as you have written it in this letter. They propose to forward

- 2 -

your salary in monthly payments as other professors in the University are paid, and they want to be quite sure of an address. So far, I think, they have sent to you in care of President Stuart. I hope the checks have arrived regularly. If they haven't, of course, you won't hesitate to let me know.

The Chinese Library is now nicely established on the first floor of Boylston Hall, and adjacent to it is a librarian's room, studies for Professor Mei and Professor Hung, and another room for the secretary of the Institute. We expect very soon to provide a stenographer for the Secretary, who will be at the disposal of the professors, and I think altogether the organization will be much better established this year than it was last. Mr. Hollis, as you may have heard, accepted a position as Curator of the Oriental Collection in the Cleveland Museum, beginning October first, but I was lucky enough to engage Mr. Plumer, one of our graduates, who has spent six years in China in the Maritime Custom Service and knows a good deal of Chinese, to take his place. Mr. Plumer will be here only for this year, and I hope before the year is out to find someone who will be more permanent. I think Mr. Hollis rather hated to leave Cambridge, but the position at Cleveland was much better, it seemed to me, than anything that was likely to develop for him in the near future in connection with the Institute.

With kindest remembrances and heartiest good wishes, I am

Sincerely yours,

George H. Chase

Baron A. von Staël-Holstein

~~I take I I~~ The Yenching ~~book keeping~~ business methods represents ~~no doubt~~
The last ~~whisper~~ word of modern book keeping. ~~In spite~~ But still
of ~~its~~ all their ~~up-to-date-ness~~ I am not quite sure that my collaborators
~~would~~ will like the ~~Yenching methods applied to them~~. During the
~~the~~ ~~four~~ three or four most expensive months of my life (getting married,
~~setting up a~~ organizing a new household, inviting scholars from ~~Germany~~
~~and from Jap~~ South China, from Mongolia, from Japan, and from Germany)
~~they left me without a penny~~ they paid me neither
~~salary~~ nor expenses ~~and~~ while making me write reports
and giving out ~~statements~~, ~~which described me~~ as a ~~the~~ grain of
sand ~~in the Yenching ocean~~ the up-to-date ~~the~~ Yenching ~~people~~ book keepers, who ~~describe~~
~~my~~ were supposed to ~~look after~~ take care of me, did ~~control~~ follow closely all my movements
and asked for reports etc., but never paid me a penny. The
fact that I have not been lynched by grocers booksellers etc.
is only due to the kindness of ~~P~~ Professor Woods who obtained
some funds for me. ~~I quite understand~~ the antagonism ~~of the~~ which the

~~It~~ It is ~~quite~~ ~~only~~ not surprising ~~natural~~ that the Yenching people who describe my establishment ~~perhaps because my~~ (a very very young monk, or man, (~~my~~ ... is expected ~~now~~) to join our celibate community next year) as a Buddhist monastery should look upon me and my ~~Buddhist~~ collaborators with the eye of disfavour. ~~The latter has~~ What else could ~~be expected of them? ... Consequently I have to fight for every cent and ... spend my time with financial calculations~~ Could a different attitude be expected from men who may be described as professional enemies of Buddhism, the most important subject of my studies? ~~Mr. ...~~ Professor Porter has always been extremely kind to me and I owe him much gratitude, but he is the only one (in Yenching) who ~~regards my~~ seems to approve of my establishment. ~~As~~ Under these circumstances I think (a return to the scheme outlined at Cambridge in October 1928) ~~a change of regime~~ highly desirable. That would enable me to ~~Could I not correspond with Harvard directly without~~ deal with the Cambridge ~~...~~ trustees directly in all matters, (including finance, and thereby to do away with) ~~avoiding and avoid~~ the Yenching detour which causes irritation to everybody, without any corresponding profit ~~...~~ to the cause. ~~#~~

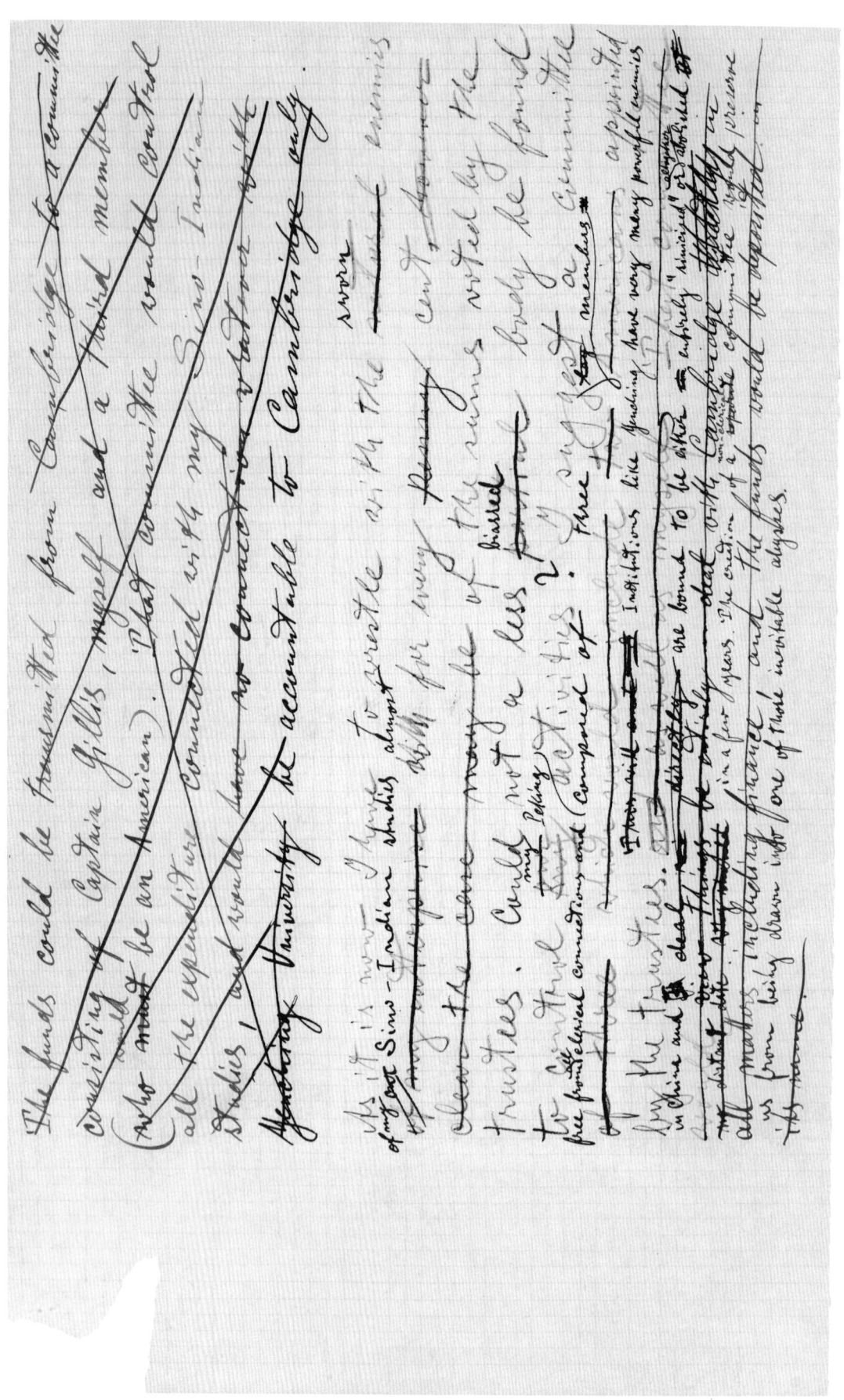

~~The funds could be transmitted from Cambridge to a committee consisting of Captain Gillis, myself and a third member (who must~~ would ~~be an American). That committee would control all the expenditure connected with my Sino-Indian studies, and would have no connection whatever with Yenching University~~ be accountable to Cambridge only.

As it is now I have to wrestle with the ~~natural~~ sworn enemies of ~~my~~ ~~our~~ Sino-Indian studies almost ~~of my enterprise~~ with for every ~~penny~~ cent, ~~however clear the case may be~~ of the sums voted by the trustees. Could not a less ~~partial~~ biassed body be found to control ~~this~~ my Peking activities? I suggest a committee free from all clerical connections and composed of ~~of three which would include two Americans~~ three ~~two~~ members* appointed by the trustees. ~~and as well as myself. That committee would~~ ~~There will~~ Institutions like Yenching have very many powerful enemies in China and ~~I deal~~ ~~directly~~ are bound to be either entirely "sinicised" or altogether abolished ~~at no distant date~~ ~~view things be entirely deal with Cambridge directly in all matters including finance, and the funds would be deposited in its name.~~ in a few years. The creation of a non-clerical ~~separate~~ committee would preserve us from being drawn into one of those inevitable abysses.

The fact that President Stuart practically appoints three trustees makes him what we may call a "super-trustee" and his words ~~appear almost~~ correspondingly important. He told Professor Woods and myself quite distinctly on October 1st 1929 that ~~the details~~ Yenching would never interfere ~~in my relations~~ with my collaborators and that all the details would be left to me. But his subordinates ~~Mr. Greene, who is much more strict, President Stuart's appointee~~, take an entirely different view and, after the President's departure for America, ~~is not content with my wants~~ demanded exactly what President Stuart considered ~~considers~~ as unnecessary ~~(comp. page line 10)~~. ~~The interests of book keeping~~ They ~~He~~ attach a great importance to modern book keeping and are not content with my receipts which prove that all the sums enumerated have actually been paid to the proper persons. They ~~He~~ want still more details and have ~~has~~ forced me to have some of my men paid via Yenching ~~(an hours automobile ride)~~ (comp. page line) which I consider extremely inopportune (comp. page)

My aim is to please American and European Orientalists. If the Yenching people do anything for research they do it with the ulterior aim of protecting their propaganda work from being entirely stopped by the Chinese.

Aus einem Brief von Roger Greene an J. H. Woods (datiert Oct. 25 1929):

..... In the first place, I have approved the account which B. v. S. H. submitted, and have asked Mr. Porter to have it paid immediately, asking him at the At the end of every month (or quarter) Baron de Staël will send Mr. Porter a statement enumerating the payments made by him to his Asiatic assistants and will then receive a single Yenching cheque covering all ~~those pay~~ those payments. This cheque

doomed

linked up with an enterprise

My dear Dean Chase

Many thanks for your kind congratulations. I am also greatly obliged to ~~you~~ ~~much~~ for the 2000 gold which you ~~very~~ so kindly sent me by cable over a month ago. I am very glad to hear that Dr. Laufer will soon join the Institute, and that more spacious quarters have been found for its library.

Mr. Schuster ~~studies~~ reads Sanscrit Tibetan and ~~Ch~~ Buddhist Chinese ~~about 5~~ ~~4–5~~ ~~5 hours for~~ five hours ~~for 4–5~~ with me every week and has not missed a single lecture yet. ~~I hear~~ I also hear that he ~~works well~~ studies Wên Li with Professor Brandt, and that his progress is entirely satisfactory. ~~I enjoy~~ I greatly enjoyed the presence of Professor and Mrs. Woods here, who ~~in Peking.~~ ~~They~~ left about a month ago.

I consulted Professor Woods about the enclosed legal formula bearing my signature ~~signed by myself~~ and he dissipated some doubts which I had concerning it. I feared that I might be unable to write articles in scientific journals without applying for special permission in each case. I was also uncertain about the continuation of my edition of the Ta Pao Chi Ching Lün ~~(San~~ (in Chinese and Tibetan) ~~about~~ half of which was already printed ~~before I left~~ under the auspices of Tsinghua College before my departure for America in 1928. I am now going on with that edition.

P.S. May I ask for the favour of a telegram ~~giving nothing but a fig~~ indicating ~~the~~ ~~sum~~ the amount which ~~##~~ will be paid into my account upon receipt of this letter.

Not long ago I received a letter from the Harvard Bursar, dated October 9th 1929.

I think the following considerations will show that the calculations of ~~that~~ letter) (should be amended.

~~The~~ ~~Bursar's~~ letter ~~dated October 9th 1929~~ (a copy of which I enclose) ~~leaves me without any salary for the period from July 1st until August 31st 1929. I think the following considerations will show that the Bursar's calculations should be amended.~~

I had been fully paid up to December 31st 1928 through Dr. North and Yenching (500 gold a month). I understood that I was to receive the same salary (3000 gold in all) for the six months ending on June 30th 1929, but instead of paying me that sum in the expected six instalments on January 31st, February 28th, March 31st, April 30th, May 30th and June 30th 1929, the Bursar, ~~for reasons unknown to me~~ divided the 3000 gold into ~~twelf~~ twelve parts and paid me 250 gold on Sept. 30th, October 31st, November 30th, December 31st 1928, January 31st, February 28th, March 31st, April 30th, May 31st, June 30th, July 31st, and August 31st 1929. The 250 gold received on July 31st 1929 and the 250 gold received on August 31st 1929 (500 gold in all) therefore really represent~~ed~~ my salary for June 1929. ~~and the~~ ~~implied~~ ~~Bursar's~~ ~~implied~~ ~~statement ignores the fact that as~~ the calculations leave me without any salary for ~~the months~~ the two months ending on August 31st 1929.

~~assumption that I had already been paid for the the two months ending~~

The Bursar's statement ignores this and by counting my new salary ~~(554.16⅔ gold a month)~~ (554.16⅔ gold a month) from Sept. 1st 1929, instead of from July 1st 1929, ~~deprive~~ leaves me without any salary for two months. Was it not definitely stated at Cambridge in April 1929 that ~~the~~ my new financial year was to begin on July 1st 1929?

I suggest that I shall be entitled to claim ~~six months~~ viz. ~~925 gold, six months salary, or 3325 gold, (July, August, September, October, November and December 1929) salary~~, or ~~3325 gold on December 31st minus 2000 gold kindly cabled to me~~ minus 2400 gold ~~(2000 gold kindly cabled to me by you~~ six months' (July August September October November and December 1929) salary, 3325 gold, on December 31st 1929. From that sum of 3325 gold 2400 gold (2000 gold kindly cabled to me by you plus 400 gold, the amount of the bill paid by the Bursar) will have to be deducted, and 925 gold should stand to my credit at the Bursar's office on December 31st 1929. ~~May I ask you to tell the~~ Will you be so kind as to ~~ask~~ tell the Bursar that this amount as well as all other sums which may fall due to me in the future should be paid into ~~my~~ account at Messrs. Kidder Peabody & Co.'s bank (Harvard Square, Cambridge)?

Wishing you a ~~very~~ merry Christmas and a happy New Year I remain yours most sincerely

A. Staël Holstein.

HARVARD-YENCHING INSTITUTE

23 University Hall
Cambridge, Mass.
January 11, 1930

My dear Baron:

First of all, business. I have carefully gone over figures with the Bursar, and find that your failure to receive funds was due to a slip on my part. It is quite true that the fiscal year of the Harvard-Yenching Institute begins on July 1st, but the salary year for Harvard professors begins on September 1st, and the first payment is made on September 30. It was because of my failure to consider this that no salary was assigned you, as it should have been, for July and August. When I discussed things with Mr. Saeger, it appeared to both of us that the reasonable thing was for me somehow to send you as payment for these two months one-sixth of $6,650. Fortunately I found that Dean Donham had some of the funds originally assigned him still in hand, and he agreed to deposit $1108.33 to your account at once. I, therefore, cabled you on Friday, January 10: ELEVEN HUNDRED DOLLARS DEPOSITED TO YOUR ACCOUNT. I hope that the cable reached you without delay.

I found one other slight complication at the Bursar's office. He is holding out a small sum from each monthly payment against the income tax, as he thinks he is bound to do under the income tax law. He said that he would take up the matter with the income tax commissioners and find out whether this must be held for a foreigner holding a Harvard appointment but not resident in this country. If you find, therefore, a slight

- 2 -

discrepancy in the sums deposited hereafter with Messrs. Kidder, Peabody, and Company at Harvard Square, it will be on this account. I hope that the matter will shortly be settled.

I have handed on your message to the Bursar to deposit your salary regularly from now on with Messrs. Kidder, Peabody, and Company.

Thank you for the legal formula, which I will file with the papers of the Institute. I am sure we had no intention of hampering your work in any way, and I don't believe this document will ever rise up and give us trouble.

Professor Woods has not yet reached Cambridge, but we expect him about the 15th. President Stuart is in New York, and will be in this neighborhood until the end of the month. I have, therefore, called a meeting of the Trustees for Monday, January 20, at which I hope we can thrash out some of the new problems that have arisen during the year. Altogether we in Cambridge feel very well pleased with the way things are going. The Publication Committee at the moment is decidedly scattered, since Professor Blake has gone off for some months in Asia Minor and Woods is not back, but I hope in the course of the spring to get things a little more definitely settled about future publication. Professor Hung is most helpful in suggestions and advice.

I am glad to know that Mr. Schuster is making satisfactory progress. Will you give him my kindest remembrances? Dr. Laufer unfortunately after long deliberation decided that he had too many commitments at the Field Museum to justify him in accepting the offer which we made him. This is certainly a matter of great regret, but I don't see that we could do more than we did to attract him.

With best regards, I am

Sincerely yours,

George H. Chase

Baron A. von Staël-Holstein

HARVARD UNIVERSITY

THE GRADUATE SCHOOL OF ARTS AND SCIENCES

24 UNIVERSITY HALL, CAMBRIDGE, MASSACHUSETTS

April 9, 1930

My dear Professor von Staël-Holstein:

Your letter of February 19 ought to have been answered long ago, but it came when I was in the midst of the difficult business of assigning fellowships and scholarships for next year, and I have only now, during this vacation week, found time for the kind of answer I want to write.

Everything you say makes me feel even more that things are going well with your researches and with the students. Certainly I thoroughly approve your spending time to answer inquiries from organizations like the Morgan Library, the Fogg Museum, and individual scholars. It seems to me that this is certainly a very distinct duty of the Harvard-Yenching Institute. I understand, too, why preparation of works for publication is necessarily slow, but I shall look forward to seeing the materials which you send when they are ready, and I am sure the Publication Committee will do everything in its power to advance the publications as they come along. Professor Blake has been away for several months on an expedition to the Sinai Peninsula with Professor Lake, but he is now back, and the Publication Committee will function once more.

At the meeting of the Trustees, held on March 17, the appropriation of LC$26,000 for Sino-Indian Research was renewed automatically. My understanding is just yours, that this appropriation will continue from year to year, and does not require a special request from you unless you wish an increase.

We had a chance also at the meeting to discuss the problem of your accounting and relations to the Institute in general. The only action taken was a vote : To request President Stuart to act on behalf of the Trustees in assisting Professor von Staël-Holstein in his work in every possible way. In the discussion, however, I thought it was quite clear that the Trustees regard you as responsible to the Executive Committee here and not to the Administrative Committee in Peking. The feeling was that President Stuart and Professor Porter can be very helpful if you so desire, especially if any questions arise as to the status of your assistants, but that details should be left to you; and it seemed clear that it was quite satisfactory to the Trustees if you report directly to the Executive Committee after June 30, which closes our fiscal year, how the appropriation of LC$26,000 has been spent. Professor Woods explained the necessity of considerable freedom for you in dealing with your assistants. I shall write Professor Porter also about the deliberations of the Trustees so that there can be no chance of misunderstanding.

I was very glad indeed that we could authorize Captain Gillis to buy the Mongolian Kanjur, and I hope it is proving useful.

Professor Clark tells me that he hopes to have the manuscript for the book on the Buddhas completed before he leaves Cambridge for his vacation in June, and the Publication Committee will then, of course, go ahead with getting the book into type. Professor Clark has, no doubt, written you about details. He is preparing most careful indices, which certainly ought to add a good deal to the value of the book.

- 3 -

The new fellows elected at the meeting of the Trustees were G. T. Bowles, Owen Lattimore, S. Y. Liang, L. C. S. Sickman, G. E. Taylor, and R. K. Reischaur. Mr. Biggerstaff, Mr. Schuster, Mr. Ware, and Mr. Teng Kwei were reappointed for 1930-31. Of these men Bowles and Liang are primarily interested in anthropology, and I suspect will not work with you. Owen Lattimore will, no doubt, continue his studies largely by himself, as he has this year. Mr. Sickman I am sure you know, and he will undoubtedly work with you. Mr. Taylor is a very able Englishman, who has become enormously interested in Chinese history and will devote his year largely to the study of the Chinese language. Mr. Ware, according to his recent letters, expects to reach Peking in the fall of 1930, and will, of course, get in touch with you immediately. He seems to have had a very profitable year in France, and has written very cheerful letters about his progress. Mr. Reischaur and Mr. Teng Kwei were appointed for resident work in Cambridge.

I think there is no other news to give you from the Trustees' meeting. Appropriations for the purchase of books, both in Peking and in Cambridge, were renewed, and a generous appropriation was made for publication.

With every good wish, I am

Sincerely yours,

George H. Chase

Baron A. Von Staël-Holstein

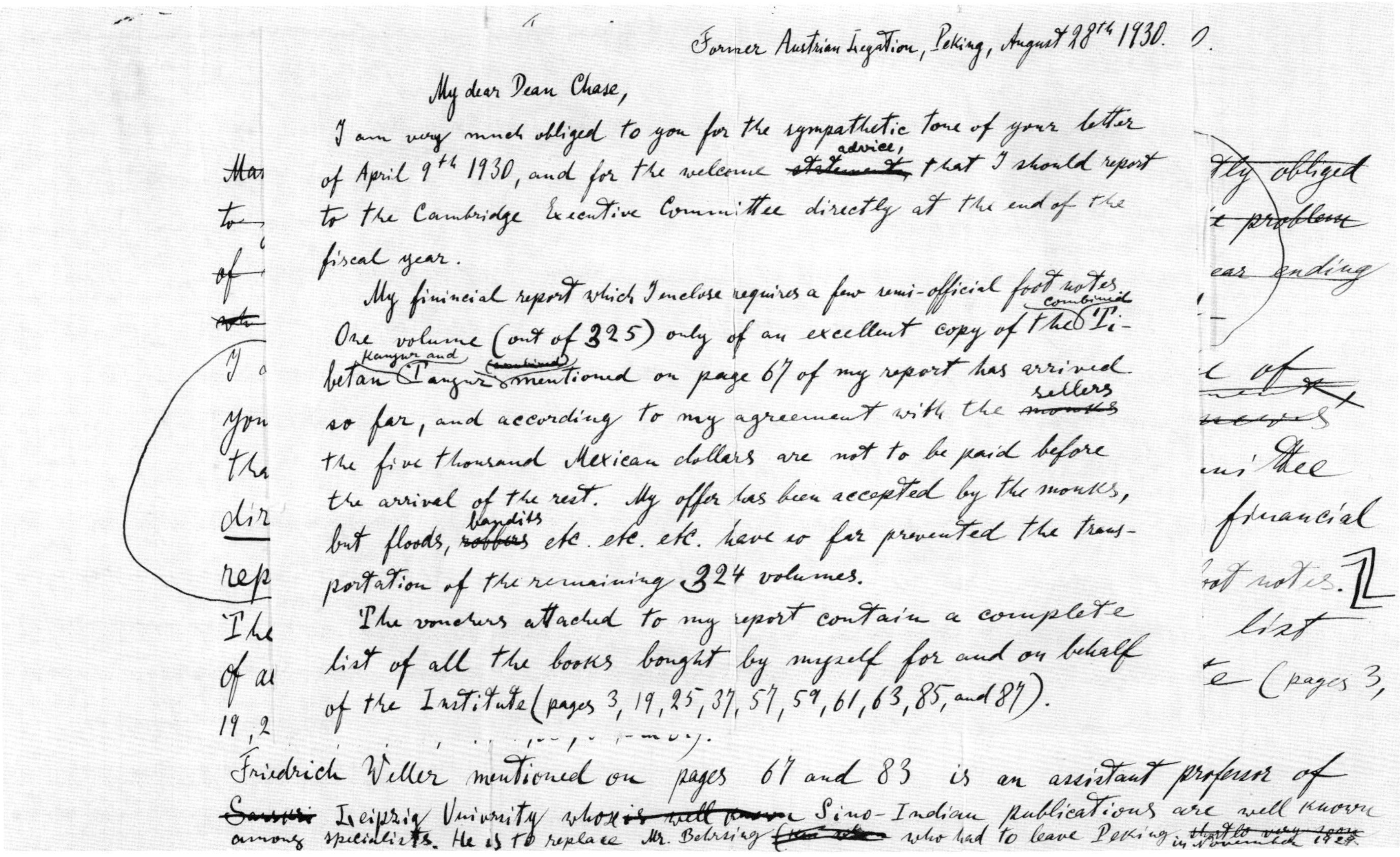

Former Austrian Legation, Peking, August 28th 1930.

My dear Dean Chase,

I am very much obliged to you for the sympathetic tone of your letter of April 9th 1930, and for the welcome ~~statement~~ advice, that I should report to the Cambridge Executive Committee directly at the end of the fiscal year.

My financial report which I inclose requires a few semi-official foot notes.

One volume (out of 325) only of an excellent copy of the combined Tibetan Kanjur and Tanjur ~~combined~~ mentioned on page 67 of my report has arrived so far, and according to my agreement with the ~~monks~~ sellers the five thousand Mexican dollars are not to be paid before the arrival of the rest. My offer has been accepted by the monks, but floods, ~~robbers~~ bandits etc. etc. etc. have so far prevented the transportation of the remaining 324 volumes.

The vouchers attached to my report contain a complete list of all the books bought by myself for and on behalf of the Institute (pages 3, 19, 25, 37, 57, 59, 61, 63, 85, and 87).

Friedrich Weller mentioned on pages 67 and 83 is an assistant professor of ~~Sanskrit~~ Leipzig University whose ~~is well known~~ Sino-Indian publications are well known among specialists. He is to replace Mr. Behrsing [illegible] who had to leave Peking ~~shortly very soon~~ in November 1929.

~~after the departure of Professor Woods for America I have had to do without~~ I have been without a Sanskrit assistant ever since and ~~that~~ had to devote too much time to teaching until I dismissed my pupils on June 26th. ~~We have had I practically~~ neither ~~no~~ Christmas nor ~~and no~~ ~~Easter holidays, and I could not devote~~ spare enough ~~much~~ time to writing ~~before the first of July 1930~~ I have revised our edition of the Vajra-cchedikā text (in three languages) since and rewritten practically all the notes as well as the ~~introduction~~ preface, because some new material turned up at the last moment.) A member of the American Legation has promised me to ~~include~~ send the rather bulky manuscript to America by a diplomatic messenger who will leave Peking about Sept. 20th. In any case I shall despatch the Vajracchedikā manuscript ~~the~~ as well as a detailed account of our various activities and a number of notes, photographs etc. to your address before the end of next month (September).

~~I only learned~~ Owing to a misunderstanding on my part ($ Mex. 25098.47 only ~~of the~~ out of the ~~of the~~ $ Mex. 26000.00 assigned by the trustees for Sino-Indian studies have ~~been left over~~ been spent or definitely promised during the year ending on June ~~1930~~ 30th 1930 which I never suspected. Yenching informs me that the rest ($ Mex. 901.53) must be ~~returned~~ sent back to America, ~~That information reached me the moment~~ I had ~~I intended using~~

~~I possess~~ I (personally) possess the Meiji edition of the Chinese Tripitaka edited in Japan, but we have no copy of the latest ('Taisho) edition of that work, which we ~~must~~ have to consult very frequently. I always intended purchasing that latest edition, and had ear-marked those $Mex. 901.53 for the purpose. A few days ago I was offered an excellent copy of the 'Taisho edition (which is already here in Peking) for $Mex. 1000.00. At the present rate of exchange ~~the~~ the work ~~could not be bought for less than about the $Mex. 1900.00~~ would cost ~~[illegible]~~ much more in Japan (plus transportation charges etc.). Under these circumstances I suggest that the $Mex. 901.53 left over should be returned to me so that I might ~~[illegible]~~ buy the 'Taisho edition of the Chinese 'Tripitaka (the remaining $Mex. ~~[illegible]~~ 98.47 will be inserted into the account for the year ending on June 30th 1931).

~~I can~~ May I ask for the favour of a cable in case you accept my suggestion? ~~I have promised I must~~ I have promised the prospective seller ~~[illegible]~~ a definite answer before October 1st 1930. ~~It would be a great pity if this [illegible] rare chance~~ I would hate missing this rare chance.

I cannot tell you how happy I am to be able to pursue my studies here under so favourable conditions (no ~~[illegible]~~ serious money troubles, all important dictionaries and excellent assistants at hand etc.). My circumstances were very different before the Harvard-Yenching Institute so very kindly took me up.

Believe me yours sincerely and gratefully

A. Staël Holstein.

HARVARD-YENCHING INSTITUTE

Cambridge, Mass.,
October 9, 1930.

Dear Dr. von Stael-Holstein,-

Your letter of August 28th, together with the financial statement, reached me towards the end of September,- luckily in time for me to cable you on September 30th in regard to the purchase of the Taisho edition of the Chinese Tripitaka. I hope that this reached you promptly and that you did not miss what looks like an excellent opportunity.

Everything in the accounts looks to me very decidedly in good order, and I am sure we shall have no financial troubles over that. As soon as Mr. Boyden gets back from Europe, we plan to have a meeting of the Trustees or, at least, of the Executive Committee, and I shall submit your report to them. I am sure it is best to have the report come directly to the Cambridge committee at the end of each fiscal year. The arrangement in regard to balances at the end of the year is one that the Trustees thought wise, and I believe it is the best method of running affairs with a budget. I anticipate that there will be no difficulty in persuading the Trustees to vote Mex. $1,000 which I authorized from unexpended income, thus practically returning to you the Mex. $901.53 which was your surplus. Very few people were about when your letter came and I simply took the responsibility of authorizing the purchase.

A few days ago we had a cable from Mr. Greene, saying that your manuscript had been received,- this I assume to be the manuscript which you spoke of sending through the American Legation. We certainly shall look forward to receiving it, and I shall turn it over to the Publication Committee.

I hope before this letter reaches you you will have got in touch with some of the fellows whom we appointed for work in China this year. I judge that Mr. Ware would reach Peking early in October at the latest and I know that Mr. Sickman planned to work with you. We all feel very much gratified that you have found so much time to work with these students from America and we hope they are not a burden.

#2

Just as soon as I can get a meeting of the Trustees or the Executive Committee, I will arrange for the transmission of the Mex. $1,000. which should come to you.

Everyone here I know would send greetings if he knew that I was writing.

May I finally congratulate you on the birth of your son, though these congratulations must come late? I hope that he is thriving, and I know that he must be a great delight to you.

Cordially yours,

George H. Chase.

Baron von Stael-Holstein,
Ex-Austrian Legation,
Peiping, China.

HARVARD-YENCHING INSTITUTE

Cambridge, Mass.,
December 12, 1930.

Dear Dr. von Stael-Holstein,-

The Trustees of the Harvard-Yenching Institute managed a meeting on Monday last, December 8th, and I presented your financial report, which was accepted and placed on file, as I felt sure it would be. In connection with the meeting, we had a report from Mr. Garside in regard to funds for Sino-Indian research which are transmitted through the Treasurer of Yenching University. He had, as you wrote, listed your balance of $901.53 as one which was not to be carried over. The Trustees changed the report, adding this sum to the balances to be transferred to this year's accounts, which ought to make it perfectly possible for you to use the money for the purchase of the Taisho edition of the Tripitaka, for which you intended to use the funds. I am writing Mr. Garside today and will call his attention to this item, so that I think everything will come out perfectly straight. I didn't even tell the Trustees that I had cabled you to go ahead with the purchase. If there is any complication about the payment of the Mex. $901.53, of course you will let me know.

I hope that all continues to go well with your work. I suppose Mr. Sickman, as well as Mr. Schuster, is working with you, and no doubt some of our other fellows. When you have a good opportunity, I should be very grateful if you would send me some impressions about their work, and especially I should like confidential information as to whether you think Schuster should be appointed to a fellowship for a third year. I personally have the feeling that, having had a fellowship for one year in Cambridge and two years in China, Schuster ought rather to make way for another man, but I don't want to be unjust to him. We all realize that an acquisition of a good knowledge of Chinese is a matter of long time and if, in your opinion, Schuster should have another year, the Educational Committee I know would be very much affected by what you say.

Cordially yours,

George H. Chase

Baron von Stael-Holstein,
ex-Austrian Legation,
Peiping, China.

HARVARD-YENCHING INSTITUTE

17 BOYLSTON HALL
CAMBRIDGE, MASSACHUSETTS

January 5, 1931

Dear Professor von Stael-Holstein,-

On receipt of your recent letter, I immediately consulted Professor Woods and Professor Clark, and both said that they would write you shortly. Mr. Woods tells me that he has written and will soon write again. Mr. Clark I have not seen (your letter arrived just before the Christmas holidays, but I have no doubt that he has written), but his report seemed to be most encouraging. He has been keeping at the manuscript pretty steadily and expects to have the whole thing ready to submit to the Publication Committee soon. Professor Woods's difficulties - as he has no doubt written - were more complicated. I must say that I sympathize with his feeling that some how or other the large amount of work which he has done should be incorporated in any publication. I judged that he had not written you before through his embarrassment and real inability to make up his own mind as to what was a fair procedure.

The question of the publication of your indexes in China I suppose ought to be formally passed upon by the Educational Committee. We are to have a meeting of that committee next week and I will see that the matter is brought up. My own feeling is entirely favorable, and I should be very much surprised if any opposition develops in that committee meeting, but I do think that any proposal of that kind should be passed upon by the full committee and possibly referred to the Trustees at their meeting in April. This was the procedure in the case of Professor Hung's indexes.

I am indeed grateful to you for letting me know your difficulties so frankly and hope I have been of some assistance in the matter. I will write again after the committee meeting next week.

Sincerely yours,

George H. Chase

Professor von Stael-Holstein,
ex-Austrian Legation,
Peiping, China.

Feb. 18th 1931

My dear Dean Chase,

~~Upon rec~~ Many thanks for your letter dated December 12th 1930. I am very much obliged to you for having persuaded the Trustees to return to me the Mex. 901.53 left over from the 29/30 appropriation. I have bought the Taishō Tripiṭaka for the ~~Mex. 1000.00~~ Institute and I shall send you the voucher in question together with the rest of my financial account at the end of this (30/31) ~~financial~~ year. ~~During the~~ In 29/30 and at the beginning of 30/31 Schuster ~~worked with me~~ attended some of my lectures quite regularly, but ~~some~~ about two months ago he ~~asked me wh~~ told me that he intended devoting more ~~then~~ of his time to purely Chinese work and ~~that he~~ asked me whether it would be "all right!" if he ~~stopped attending~~ ~~gave up~~ did not come to (my Sino-Indian classes) (in the future). ~~I regretted the~~ I naturally regretted that question but had to return an affirmative answer, ~~because the Buddhist texts which we interpret I int he has Schuster has already done two years' Sino-Indian work with me (at Harvard and at Peking)~~ because I know that Schuster's motive was ~~and~~ not laziness. ~~but his~~ I hear from all sides that Schuster shows great application and ~~considerable~~ remarkable talent in his ~~Chinese~~ purely Chinese work and I sent you the telegram "strongly recommend Schuster renewal" after ~~considerable~~ having made careful enquiries in different quarters.

Professor J. J. Brandt who teaches classical Chinese at the North China Language School here told me that Schuster was one of the very best pupils he had ever had. ~~and that he had passed an examination held~~ I am now working with Ware (four hours a week), and we are reading the Saddharmapuṇḍarīka. ~~in three languages~~ We compare the Sanskrit, Tibetan, and Chinese versions of that text with one another as well as with a number of ancient commentaries which have, as far as we know, never been studied by westerners before. Besides Ware and myself, Professor Tschen Yin Koh, one of the directors of the National Research Institute (Academia Sinica), and the well-known Berlin sinologue Professor Lessing, who is here on leave, ~~take part in~~ ~~participate~~ attend those Sino-Indian meetings. I conduct them at my house and I hope that Ware will derive as much profit from them as I do. ~~Sickman~~ ~~is still too young an orientalist to~~ ~~is only a beginner and cannot~~ Sickman ~~lacks the philological~~ knows no Tibetan and his ~~Sanskrit and~~ knowledge of Sanskrit and Chinese is too rudimentary ~~not equal~~ ~~advanced enough~~ for that class. ~~and~~ He studies Sanskrit with Professor Weller and Chinese with native teachers. Professor Weller ~~thinks that Sickman~~ speaks very highly of Sickman, who shares Professor Weller's tuition in Sanskrit with my ~~and teaches~~ assistants Lin and Narita.

During the academic year 1929/1930 I conducted the following classes: 1) Sanskrit grammar for beginners (2 hours) 2) comparative study of the Pūrṇāvadāna in Sanskrit, Tibetan and Chinese (4 hours) 3) Indian religious history (2 hours). The classes 1 and 2 were held at my house, but the lectures on Indian religious history were (and are still in 30/31) delivered at the National University of Peking.*)

In ~~II~~ 29/30 I did eight weekly hours' teaching (owing to Professor Villey's presence here) which have been reduced to six in 30/31. I have, however, much more to do in connection with my lectures now than I had last year, because the preparation of the Saddharmapuṇḍarīka in the three languages and the study of the commentaries ~~takes me 2-3~~ is extremely difficult, and takes ~~[illegible]~~ 2-3 ~~[illegible]~~ entire days every week. I think, however, that those

*) Since my return to Peking, ~~eighteen~~ twenty months ago, the National University of Peking has paid me the equivalent of about ~~twelve~~ ~~hundred~~ one thousand U.S. dollars. I consider that sum as a payment on account of the debt which the National University owes me, rather than as a remuneration for those two weekly hours. The National University entirely failed to pay me for three years (July 1925 – July 1928).

laborious days are not wasted. ~~because the fact that~~ The fact that fairly advanced Sino-Indian exercises, in which ~~are carried on at Peking~~ ~~and that~~ the fact well-known scholars like T'schen and Lessing ~~take~~ participate, ~~in them~~ are carried on under the auspices of the Harvard-Yenching Institute ~~H.Y.I.~~ ~~gives us~~ adds a good deal to our prestige. It also encourages Chinese and foreigners alike to pursue those studies which are so important for the proper understanding of things Chinese in general. When I arrived in China 14 years ago there ~~was~~ were practically no Sanskrit and Tibetan books in the Peking libraries, and many ~~most~~ of the leading Chinese scholars here did not even know that ~~there was~~ a difference existed between Sanskrit and Tibetan. ~~It is no Now there~~ Now things look a good deal ~~much~~ better, but much remains to ~~a good deal must~~ still be done in order to ~~procure~~ ~~create the atmosphere which will produce, make it possible~~ encourage Sino-Indian studies in this country. France as well as Germany and Japan are ~~[illegible] producing con-tributing~~ still far ahead of China in their Sino-Indian activities which is certainly not a normal state of things.

Lattimore ~~occasionally~~ asks for my advice ~~and I have recommended~~ occasionally and studies ~~[illegible]~~ the Mongol language with a teacher recommended by myself.

~~I had [illegible]~~ My assistants Lin and Narita study Tibetan under Mr. Pankratoff. ~~[illegible] Last year (29/30) I di. The enclosed photograph from~~ ~~Galitckaya. my very beloved wife is a very good one. She is such a darling little women, with a very strong personality. I call her my busy bee and really she is one. Her energy and vitality can be comparad with that of the great man Mussoliny. She is the incognito ruler of Rus. Ben. Soc. and her diplomacy ~~is of great help for me~~ and her erudition ~~realy [illegible]~~ is of great help to me and my work under her guidance ~~is realy~~ ~~it~~ is renewed and refreched as a tree under fresch rain. I think it will be quite juste if you will elect her as a proffessor ~~of exchange between Europe Asia and America~~~~

~~Owing to Through Pr~~ Professor J. H. Woods recommended me to his brother Colonel Woods and through ~~[illegible]~~ him I obtained a grant for the restauration of certain Peking Temples from Mr. Rockefeller. I attended many committee meetings connected with that restauration ~~during~~ in 29/30, ~~[illegible]~~ and superintended the ~~work~~ actual work with the assistance of an American architect connected with the Rockefeller foundation. ~~[illegible] Mr~~ A document signed by two leading members of the Palace Museum committee ~~(see enclosure A)~~ shows that ~~my initiative is~~ as a consequence of my initiative several other grants were obtained and ~~[illegible]~~ that the preservation of Peking monuments has derived some profit from my stay in China[1]. As soon as the weather permits we ~~shall~~ hope to begin realizing a new plan ~~[illegible]~~ connected with archaeology: we shall collect rubbings of the numerous inscriptions in Tibetan Mongolian and Manchu which are found in Peking with a view of editing them in a large volume[2].

1) ~~[illegible]~~ I was ~~appointed~~ elected a member of the Palace Committee in 1926, and I was the only foreign member at that time. ~~among [illegible] of Chinese~~

~~* Some of those~~ 2 Only a small part of those ~~[illegible]~~ inscriptions has been edited by Dr. Laufer years ago.

~~The Avadana kalpalata of K~~ṣemendra's ~~[illegible]~~ Avadānakalpalatā is a collection of 108 Buddhist legends, and I have discovered a (complete) series of 30 Tibetan ~~[illegible]~~ paintings illustrating them all. No such series seems to exist in any museum, and I think the H. Y. I. should edit them all in colours. I enclose photographic reproductions of ~~those~~ the 30 pictures. Please let me know whether you think that ~~those~~ pictures could be edited ~~in America~~ by the H. Y. I. If not I might send them to Europe where they will surely find a publisher. A number of responsible European* ~~[illegible]~~ ~~[illegible]~~ students of eastern art who have seen ~~them~~ the paintings ~~and pronounced~~ here at Peking, ~~and found~~ find them highly interesting.

*I also possess a large collection of photographs representing oriental pictures which I could not afford to buy.

I have bought those ~~pictures~~ paintings ~~with my own money~~ as well as a great number of other pictures ~~with my own~~ and statuettes with my own money.[1] ~~because the H. Y. I. If you want me to buy things~~ objects of art ~~for~~ ~~the Institute, I shall be very glad to do so.~~ So far ~~as~~ I have bought nothing but books for the Institute, and ~~it is my ambition to create the first Sino-Indian lib.~~ I continue doing so. ~~But it~~ It will take years of patient labour to collect the most important ~~books~~ works on Sino-Indian subjects, a great number of which are out of print, for our library. No library existing in China possesses anything like a complete set of those books.

1) I have not been authorized to buy anything but books for the Institute.

The correspondence with European and Japanese book sellers and the highly complicated negotiations with owners of ~~all~~ rare Chinese Tibetan and Mongolian books occupies much of my time.

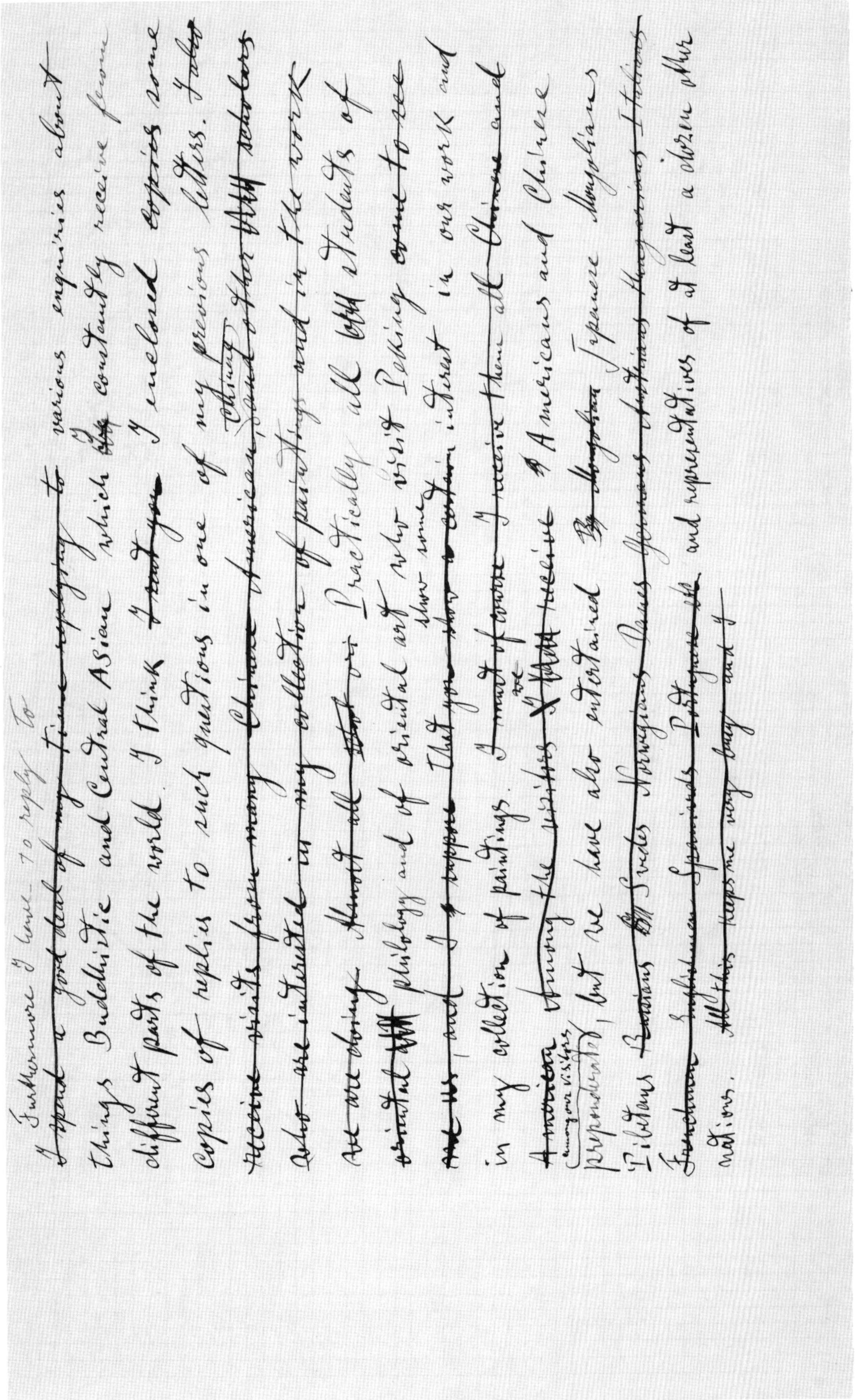

Furthermore I have to reply to ~~I spend a good deal of my time replying~~ ~~to~~ various enquiries about things Buddhistic and Central Asian which I ~~we~~ constantly receive from different parts of the world. I think ~~I sent you~~ I enclosed ~~copies~~ some copies of replies to such questions in one of my previous letters. ~~I also receive visits from many Chinese American, Chinese and other ~~ scholars who are interested in my collection of paintings and in the work we are doing. Almost all ~~~~ or~~ Practically all ~~~~ students of ~~oriental~~ ~~~~ philology and of oriental art who visit Peking ~~come to see me us, and I suppose that you show a certain~~ show some interest in our work and in my collection of paintings. ~~I must of course I receive them all Chinese and American~~ ~~Among the visitors I we ~~ ~~receive~~ ~~A~~ Americans and Chinese among our visitors preponderated, but we have also entertained ~~By Mongolian~~ Japanese Mongolians Tibetans ~~Russians~~ ~~~~ Swedes ~~Norwegians Danes Germans Austrians Hungarians Italians Frenchmen Englishmen Spaniards Portuguese etc.~~ and representatives of at least a dozen other nations. ~~All this keeps me very busy and I~~

~~In January 1931 I wrote to~~ ~~I have~~ ~~Professor Woods~~ ~~I do not know whether Professor Woods has~~ ~~I have written~~
~~Most of my is spent in~~ ~~I consider my~~

In addition to my other ~~duties I~~ ~~correspond~~ activities I keep our accounts and correspond with Yenching as well as with Harvard. ~~I can assure you~~ ~~I am very~~ ~~that~~ All these things keep me rather busy, and I have not been entirely well, ~~Professor~~ ~~grateful to you for your prompt replies. Unfortunately,~~ ~~that~~ for more than a few hours since July 1929. ~~I must say~~ ~~I may~~ ~~correspondence is for the most part an one-sided one. I wish all Harvard authorities were as prompt and kindly correspondents as yourself, my dear Dean Chase.~~

~~Thanking you very much for~~ ~~With many~~ ~~Thanking you very much for all your kindness I remain yours sincerely~~

Believe me yours sincerely and gratefully

A. Staël-Holstein.

~~I must confess that I feel somewhat tired and that I am quite ready for a holiday. I have been lecturing etc. without any considerable interruption ever since 1918 for twelve years.~~

I have written to Professor Woods about the ~~works~~ books which we are preparing for publication

P.S.
President Stuart told me some time ago that you would come out to China this year with dean Donham. I hope very much that you will do so.

Mr. Schuster and the ~~The~~ signatories of this letter ~~and~~ were my most important pupils in 29/30. ~~There~~ ~~The~~ A number of other hearers have not signed the document.

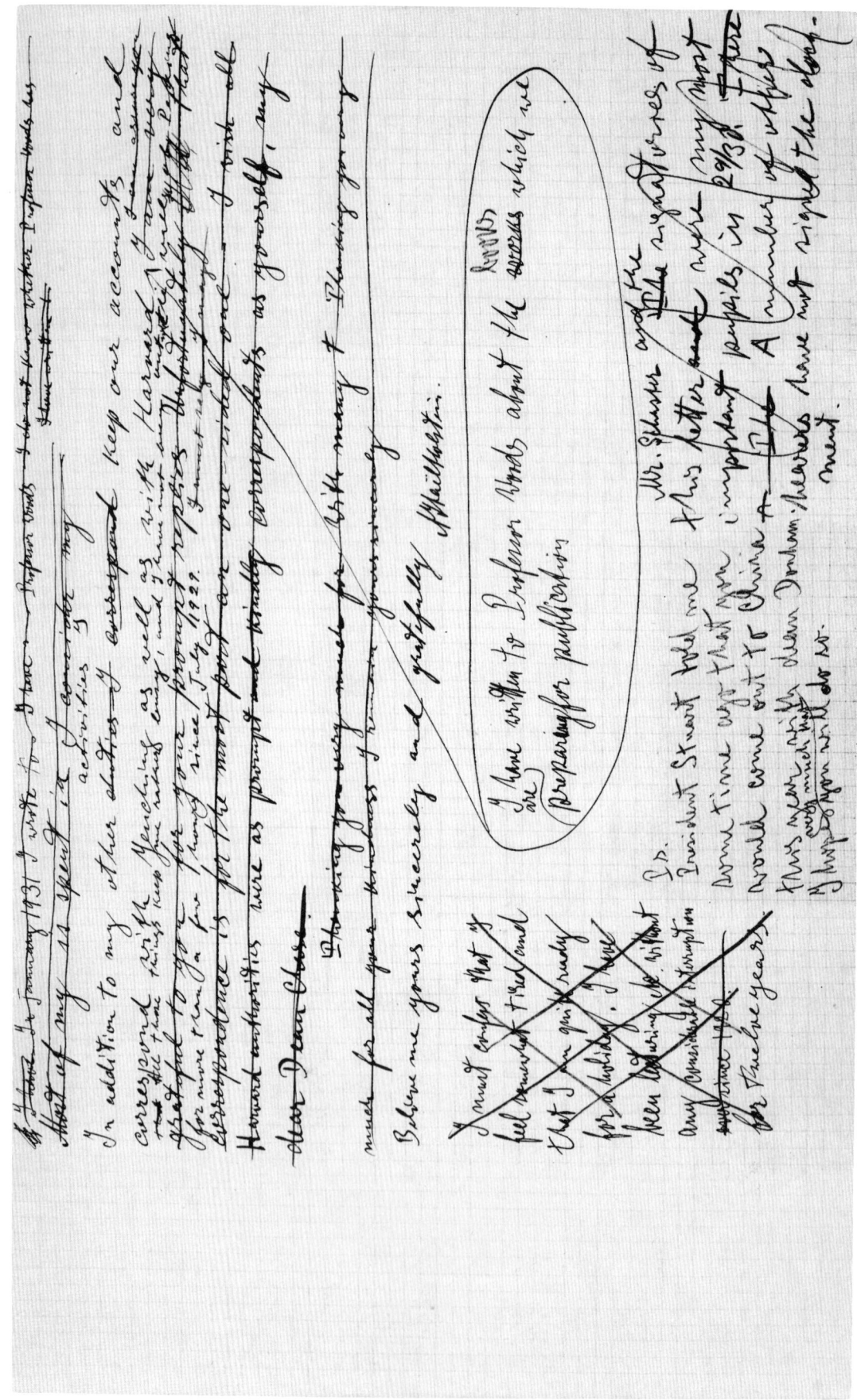

HARVARD-YENCHING INSTITUTE

17 BOYLSTON HALL
CAMBRIDGE, MASSACHUSETTS

March 20, 1931

My dear Professor von Stael-Holstein:-

Your good letter of February 18th reached me some days ago. I am very grateful for the full report which you have given of the work of Messrs. Schuster, Ware and Sickman. The members of the Educational Committee will, I am sure, be very glad to have this information and all the other interesting things that you tell about the Sino-Indian work. Certainly, this must add definitely to the prestige of the Harvard-Yenching Institute.

On your recommendation, Schuster will be nominated for his fellowship for next year, and Sickman also, naturally, we shall support for a further year of work. Mr. Ware has written us that he would like to spend next year in Cambridge, and to this we have agreed. We think it is possible that we may ask him to give the elementary courses in Sanskrit. Professor Clark is offering an introductory course on Indian history and civilization,- this in the Department of History,- and with the new course he may be so busy that he cannot possibly undertake the elementary Sanskrit. We all think that Ware could do this very well and that it would be a good bit of training for him.

When the Educational Committee meets, I will bring up the question of the thirty Tibetan paintings and the possibility of having them published by the H-Y.I. I should think it is the sort of publication that the Institute ought to be glad to undertake.

Cordially yours,

George H. Chase

Professor von Stael-Holstein,
ex-Austrian Legation,
Peiping, China.

HARVARD-YENCHING INSTITUTE

17 BOYLSTON HALL
CAMBRIDGE, MASSACHUSETTS

May 12, 1931

My dear Professor von Stael-Holstein:-

I have no doubt that you have heard by now that Mr. Schuster and Mr. Sickman and Mr. Ware were all reappointed to their fellowships, much to the delight of the Educational Committee. No change was made in the financial arrangements with the Sino-Indian Institute, so that I don't think we shall have any difficulties in the arrangement of funds for next year.

I am writing primarily to let you know that the Trustees referred your proposal for the publication of thirty Buddhist paintings to the Publication Committee, of which Professor Blake is now chairman, and I have asked him to write directly to you. One of our plans for organizing things a little more formally is to have all publication proposals go through the hands of this committee, which consist of Professors Blake, Woods and Porter.

With cordial good wishes, I am

Sincerely yours,

[signature]

Professor A. von Stael-Holstein,
Sino-Indian Institute,
Peiping, China.

Peking Sept. 15th 1931.

My dear Dean Chase,

~~At~~ About eighteen months ago certain Lamas from ~~I~~ Inner Mongolia came to see me and offered to sell me a complete copy (about 325 volumes) of the ~~Coni edit.~~ Tibetan Kanjur-Tanjur (Coni edition). After some bargaining ~~the~~ a very reasonable price (five thousand Mexican dollars) was agreed upon, and the Lamas left one of the 325 volumes (which they had brought to Peking as a sample) at my house promising to send me the remaining 324 volumes in a few weeks. ~~But the 324 volumes never did not come and~~ When the volumes failed to appear I enquired why our contract was not being carried out, and learned that the Lamas of the temple where the books ~~were kept~~ are ~~agreed~~ could not ~~carry on~~ fulfill ~~out~~ their promise because the laymen frequenting that temple would not allow them at the time to part with the volumes. I was told, however, that the Lamas (still) hoped to overcome the laymen's objections. In that position the matter remained until August 1931, when one of the Lamas ~~visi~~ revisited Peking, ~~in order~~ asked for the sample volume, which I ~~returned~~ had to return to him, and declared that ~~the~~ local conditions made the sale agreed upon in 1930 entirely impossible.

Now the question arises ~~shall~~ how the five thousand (Mexican) dollars ~~are~~
~~to be use~~ which ~~were to be paid~~ I agreed to pay for the Kanjur-Tanjur and which
were left with me (not at Yenching) (comp. my expense account for 29/30) are
to be used. ~~Prices have gone up considerably during the last few~~
~~years and We can not now hope to buy a good Tibetan Kanjur-Tanjur~~
(about 325 volumes) or even a good Tibetan Tanjur (about 225 volumes) for that sum,
~~and I suggest that~~ Please do ~~I suggest that you~~ allow me to ~~try and~~
~~buy a good~~ another Coni Tibetan ~~Kanjur-Tanjur for that money whenever~~
~~that should prove possible keep the money until~~ (on behalf of the Institute) use the money
~~for the purchase of Tibetan books~~ or for acquiring a photostat
machine which we badly ~~want~~ need. ~~I again realized how~~
~~A few days ago~~ about a fortnight ago, After many years of fruitless endeavour I succeeded
in finding a copy of ~~the Mongolian translation of~~ a certain Buddhist com-
mentary ~~which now I must use~~ ~~rather which is of considerable size and~~ in one of the ~~local~~ Peking Lamaseries.*
~~The book which could not be bought cannot be bought. The book which is very important~~
~~for my studies~~ The Lamas cannot sell the book which is very important for ~~my~~ our
studies, ~~and~~ but they agreed to lend it to me for a few days. A friend of mine
happens to possess a photostat machine, and he is now making a photographic
reproduction of the book for me. But that friend is frequently absent

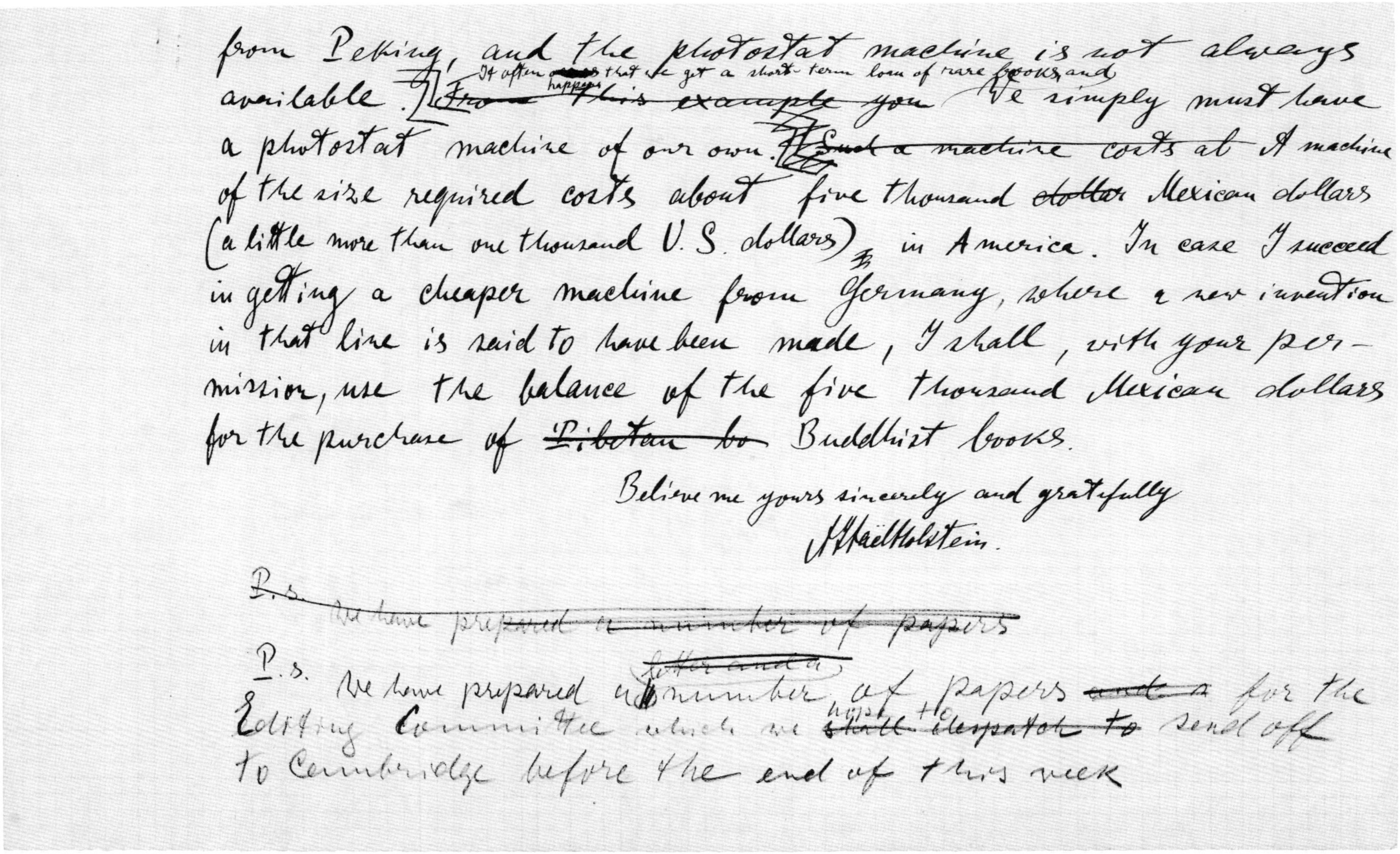
from Peking, and the photostat machine is not always available. ~~From this example you~~ [It often happens that we get a short-term loan of rare books and] We simply must have a photostat machine of our own. ~~Such a machine costs at~~ A machine of the size required costs about five thousand ~~dollar~~ Mexican dollars (a little more than one thousand U.S. dollars) in America. In case I succeed in getting a cheaper machine from Germany, where a new invention in that line is said to have been made, I shall, with your permission, use the balance of the five thousand Mexican dollars for the purchase of ~~Tibetan bo~~ Buddhist books.

Believe me yours sincerely and gratefully

AStaëlHolstein.

~~P.S. We have prepared a number of papers~~

P.S. We have prepared a number [~~letter and a~~] of papers ~~and a~~ for the Editing Committee which we ~~shall despatch to~~ [hope to] send off to Cambridge before the end of this week

*

As far as I know ~~the book does~~ there is no ~~not a~~ (the ~~Tibetan~~ Mongolian translation of the Kāśyapaparivarta commentary) copy of the book in the West and I ~~tried~~ repeatedly tried ~~in vain~~ to obtain one from Mongolia, but in vain.

My dear Dean Chase,

~~About ten days ago I~~ I hope you have received my ~~[illegible]~~ expense account for ~~2~~ 30/31 which I despatched on the 15th of this month, and which was accompanied by a letter ~~dealing with~~ describing ~~[illegible]~~ my endeavours to obtain a ~~[illegible]~~ copy of the Com Kangur (Tangur) ~~attempt to buy certain dealings with certain [illegible]~~. A postscript added to that letter said that ~~I hoped to [illegible]~~ certain papers intended for ~~addressed to~~ Professor Woods and the editing committee would follow "before the end of this week". ~~Unfortunately~~ Since that postscript was written events have occurred ~~[illegible]~~ which make it advisable ~~to wait for~~ to postpone the despatch of those papers. ~~On Friday Since Friday September 18th, the day of the the latest Sino-Japanese incident, the regular postal service has been interrupted, and I. The po~~ The regular postal service via Moukden has been disorganized by the Sino-Japanese incidents of Friday September 18th, and I must wait ~~[illegible]~~ until things quieten down before I ~~send the po~~ entrusting the papers, the loss of which would mean a good deal of wasted labour, to the post office. According to today's papers trains on the Moukden line were fired on yesterday, and ~~it everybody is~~ great excitement reigns everywhere.

~~I~~ Mr. Boddye, a promising young man, has ~~arrived~~ begun his Sanscrit studies under Professor Vallée.

Believe me yours sincerely

A. Staël Holstein.

To

Dean G. H. Chase

University Hall

Cambridge Mass.

U. S. of America

HARVARD-YENCHING INSTITUTE

17 BOYLSTON HALL
CAMBRIDGE, MASSACHUSETTS

October 17, 1931

My dear Baron,-

Your letter of September 15th has reached me, and I am disappointed - as I know you must be - to learn that you cannot get the complete copy of the Tibetan Kanjur Tanjur. I suppose another opportunity is not likely to arise in the near future. It seems to me that your suggestion that the money appropriated for the purchase be used for acquiring a photostat machine is very reasonable. Certainly, there must be a good deal of material for which photostatic copies would be practicallly as good as the original. I know this will appeal to many members of the Educational Committee who have employed the photostat for similar purposes in connection with their work. There will be a meeting of the Educational Committee before the end of the month and a meeting of the Trustees November 9th, and I shall bring up the question of the purchase of the photostat at both those meetings and hope to be able to report favorable action.

With cordial regards and best wishes,

Sincerely yours,

George H. Chase

Baron A. von Stael-Holstein,
Sino-Indian Institute,
Peiping, China.

HARVARD-YENCHING INSTITUTE

17 BOYLSTON HALL
CAMBRIDGE, MASSACHUSETTS

November 18, 1931

My dear Professor von Stael-Holstein,-

At the Trustees' meeting on November 9th, I found everyone in agreement that your request for a photostat is entirely reasonable. At the same time, all the Trustees were opposed to using the funds now in your hands for the purchase of a Tibetan Kanjur Tanjur for the purchase of a photostat. I was therefore instructed to tell you to keep the funds for the Kanjur Tanjur, in the hope of finding another copy. At the same time, the Trustees voted an appropriation of G$250 for the purchase of a photostat,- this on the statement of Professor Blake that there is an excellent instrument which can be purchased for around $200. Professor Blake promised to send you exact details, and I have no doubt that he will do so, if he has not already written.

In this connection, Mr. Ware has urged the great desirability of having a copy of the Kanjur Tanjur in Tibetan here. He further reports that he is not quite sure just what there is in your library in the way of copies of this work. I was asked, therefore, to request from you a statement of just what your library contains in the way of copies of the Kanjur Tanjur. It was thought that, when we had this information, we could decide a little more sensibly about the disposition of the funds for purchase which you hold. I hope you will find this - as we meant it to be - a happy solution of a difficulty about a photostat.

Cordially yours,

George H. Chase

Professor von Stael-Holstein,
ex-Austrian Legation,
Peiping, China.

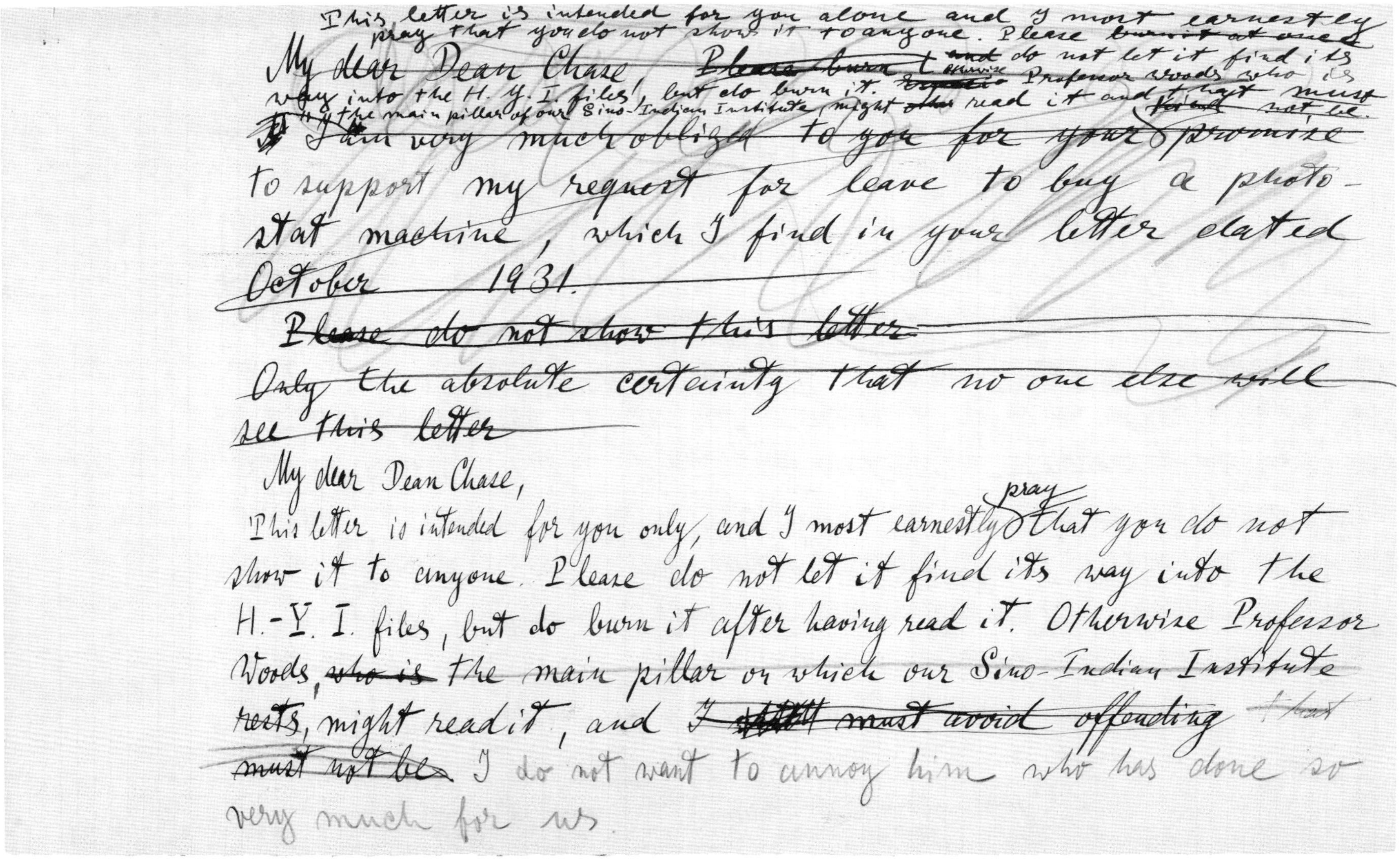

This letter is intended for you alone and I most earnestly pray that you do not show it to anyone. Please ~~burn it at once~~ ~~Please burn~~ I ~~and~~ do not let it find its way into the H. Y. I. files, but do burn it. ~~Otherwise~~ Professor Woods who is the main pillar of our Sino-Indian Institute, might ~~also~~ read it and that must ~~not~~ ~~be~~ not be.

My ~~dear Dean Chase,~~

~~I am very much obliged to you for your promise~~ to support my request for leave to buy a photostat machine, which I find in your letter dated ~~October 1931.~~

~~Please do not show this letter~~

~~Only the absolute certainty that no one else will see this letter~~

My dear Dean Chase,

This letter is intended for you only, and I most earnestly pray that you do not show it to anyone. Please do not let it find its way into the H.-Y. I. files, but do burn it after having read it. Otherwise Professor Woods, ~~who is~~ the main pillar on which our Sino-Indian Institute ~~rests~~, might read it, and ~~I still must avoid offending~~ ~~that must not be~~ I do not want to annoy him who has done so very much for us.

~~We all know that we owe We all (onclud~~

Professor Woods is a great scholar and an excellent friend, but everybody knows that he is not a very prompt correspon- ~~den~~ dent. In reply to a great number of very long and extreme- ly elaborate letters (containing references to Sanskrit, Tibetan, and Chinese codices etc.) in some of which I tried to prove ~~various~~ historico-philological points I received nothing but ~~three~~ ~~few~~ two short notes from him ~~and those which~~ during the last two years. Those notes do not concern themselves with my ~~very~~ carefully worded arguments and leave me in doubt as to whether ~~the letter~~ my letters have ever been ~~properly appreciated at all~~ ~~the~~ read in their entirety or not.* Under these circumstances I fear that the questions which I ~~sent~~ am sending to Professor Woods today will never be answered unless I can count upon your intervention. Please do ~~do try and obtain an answer~~ read the enclosed copy of my letter to Professor Woods ~~and~~ ask him as well

* In my despair I turned to Professor Clark, but ~~found him even worse~~ he treated me even worse. ~~I never received any answer~~ at all to the long letter dealing with the Vajracchedikā which I sent him.

as the other members of the Editing ~~what~~ Committee for an answer ~~and communicate the latt and send the latter~~ and send me the latter as soon as possible. ~~My applying to you is my ultima ratio, because~~ Fourteen month ago we sent ~~finished~~ an important manuscript (which ~~we had compi~~ had cost us many months of very hard work to compile and which we had compiled with the ~~express~~ consent of Professor Woods himself ~~to~~ (comp. page 5 of my letter to Professor Woods) to the Editing Committee ~~Cam~~ at Cambridge, ~~and~~ and but up to this day ~~we~~ no information has reached us as to whether they will print it or not. ~~Such a thing has never happened to me before and I fear that my assistants as well as myself. I have never~~ I fear that ~~all the~~ the other results ~~products~~ of our Sino-Indian efforts will share that sad fate, and that our endeavours ~~enterprise~~ will come to nothing ~~at all~~ unless these disastrous delays are avoided in the future. If ~~they~~ the Editing Committee take over a year for deliberation in each case we risk that ~~all~~ ~~our theories and discovered all rest discoveries~~ ~~our confrères~~ our rivals who ~~[illegible]~~ can publish their works under ~~[illegible]~~ more favorable circumstances will ~~beat us ever~~ always get the better of us. ~~[illegible]~~

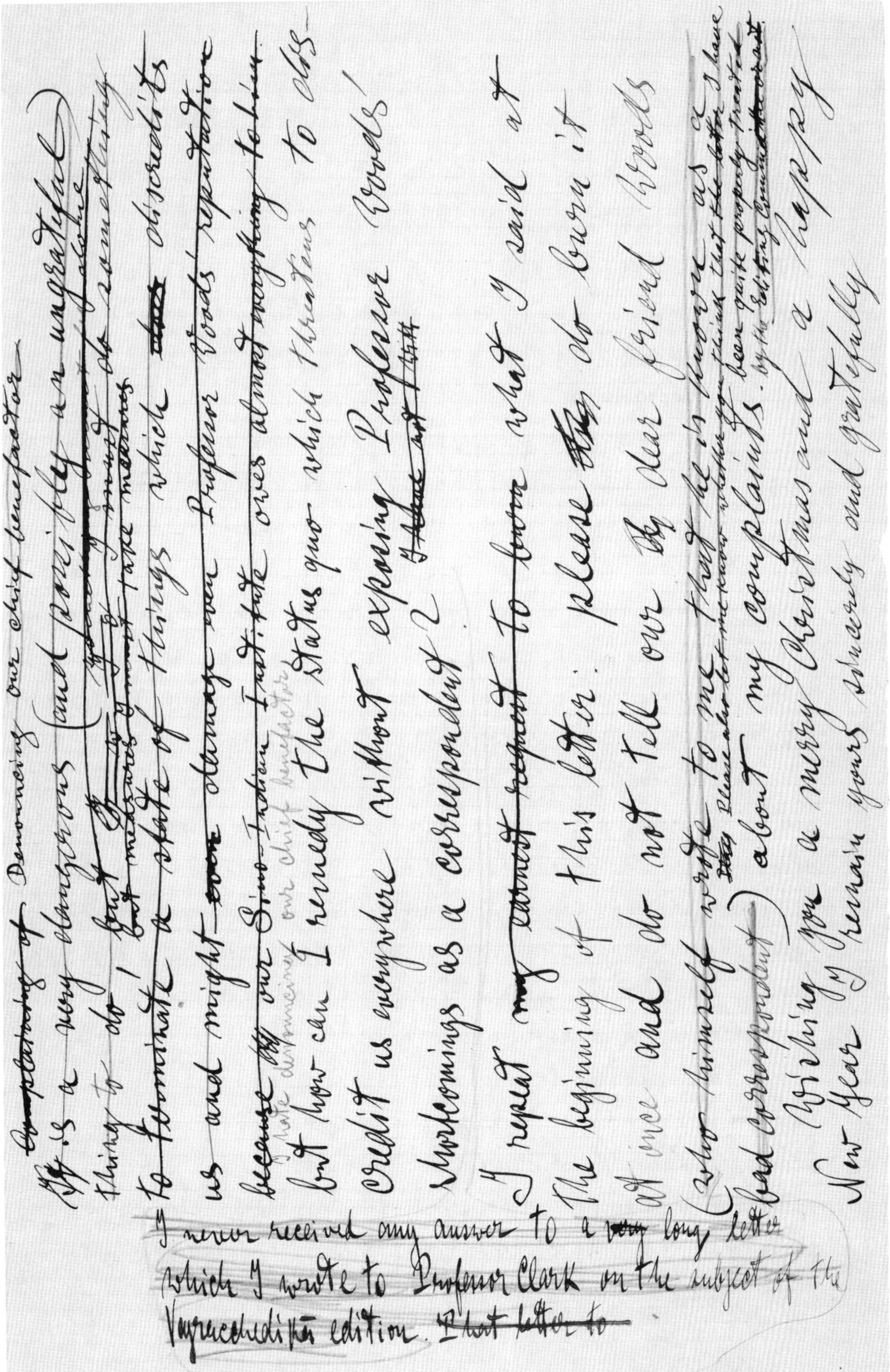

Complaining of Denouncing our chief benefactor
It is a very dangerous (and possibly an ungrateful)
thing to do, but I must do something alone
but measures I must take measures
to terminate a state of things which discredits
us and might even damage even Professor Woods' reputation
because our Sino-Indian Institute owes almost everything to him.
I hate denouncing our chief benefactor
but how can I remedy the status quo which threatens to dis-
credit us everywhere without exposing Professor Woods'
shortcomings as a correspondent? I have not I will
I repeat my earnest request to burn what I said at
the beginning of this letter: please do burn it
at once and do not tell our dear friend Woods
(who himself wrote to me that he is known as a
bad correspondent) about my complaints. Please also let me know whether you think that I have been quite properly treated by the editing Committee.
Wishing you a merry Christmas and a happy
New Year I remain yours sincerely and gratefully

I never received any answer to a very long letter
which I wrote to Professor Clark on the subject of the
Vajracchedikā edition. That letter to

Former Austrian Legation.
Peking, February 25th, 1932.

Dear Dean Chase,

I am very much obliged to you for the very active interest you have shown in our publications, and for supporting my desire to buy a photostat machine. The letters dealing with those subjects which I received from Professor Woods and from Professor Blake have both been replied to.

One of my most cherished personal possessions is a set of the Tibetan Kanjur (Imperial edition). I have bought the volumes during the course of some 1924-1931 years from three different owners and the volumes differ from one another in their make-up. My set is complete now as far as the number of volumes is concerned, but about ten volumes are incomplete; out of some volumes more than two thirds of the leaves are missing. A complete set of the Mongolian Kanjur which belongs to the Harvard-Yenching Institute has been committed to my care by Captain Gillis in 1930. I keep that extremely valuable set in a strong room which I rent for the purpose from the Peking branch of the Deutch-Asiatiche Bank. A few volumes only which my assistants want for their studies are here (Former Austrian Legation) at present. There is no copy of the Tanjur here, and we have to apply to our Chinese or Mongolian friends whenever we want to consult a volume of that collection.

Mr. Schuster is continuing his Chinese studies with his Chinese teachers and is making good progress. He plans to go to Germany in order to continue his studies there, and I have introduced him to Professor Erkes, the Leipzig sinologue, who is here on leave. Professor Erkes has given Mr. Schuster some information

- 2 -

as to the subjects which he will have to study for obtaining a Ph. D. degree in Germany. Mr. Schuster has also on several occasions consulted my friend Professor Lessing of Berlin.

Mr. Sickman has studied Sanscrit with Professor Weller until quite recently (Dec. 1931), and he will read Chinese Buddhist texts with me, or with my assistant Mr. Lin, in the future. Professor Weller tells me that Mr. Sickman has shown much zeal in the Sanscrit class and that he has proved an entirely satisfactory pupil. As far as I can judge, Mr. Sickman's purely Chinese studies too have been carried on with great success.

My general impression is that Mr. Sickman has made very good use of his time since he arrived here in 1930. Mr. Bodde is continuing his Sanscrit studies with Professor Weller and is making equally good progress in the Chinese language which he is studying under Chinese Tuition. Miss Chapin profits from the facilities which the Sino-Indian Institute offers, and has written an excellent article on Buddhist mythology which will shortly appear in Germany. One of the (wissenschaftliche Hilfsarbeiterin) Secretaries of the Berlin Academy of Sciences, Fräulein Dr. von Gabain (recommended by Professors Lüders and Hänisch) who has been sent to China for a year by the Academy in order to continue her Chinese studies, is using our library, and receives instruction here in the Mongolian language from Mr. Pankratoff. She teaches Mr. Pankratoff the Vigur language which is the main subject of her studies.

Lama Śes-rab whom I employed here before going to America returned to Peking after spending some years in India and is now working at the Sino-Indian Institute. He has a fair knowledge of Sanscrit (an accomplishment no other Lama known to me possesses),

- 3 -

and is very well versed in the Buddhist literature of Tibet and Mongolia. He knows no Chinese, but his ability to speak English is of great importance to us. My Chinese assistants can now freely consult a native specialist in Tibetan Buddhism and compare his historical etc. data with those derived from Chinese sources. With the Lamas we had here before discussion was only possible through Mongolian interpreters which was, of course, much less satisfactory.

Mr. Lin is studying Sanscrit as well as Tibetan with remarkable success, and I am sure that his contributions to Sino-Indian studies will be highly appreciated by future workers in that field.

While the team work of the Sino-Indian Institute is thus constantly improving, I must confess that the students of the National University have not shown much interest in our studies during these critical months. They are more interested in politics now, than in Sanscrit. I am still an honorary (entirely unpaid) professor in the National University, but I have not lectured to any Chinese students for several months, and I shall probably not take up those lectures again before the end of the present crisis. I continue, however, my privatissimum on the Lotus Sūtra (four hours a week). I read it (one Sanscrit text, one Tibetan translation, two Chinese translations, and several commentaries) now with Professors Lessing and Tschen Yin Koh. We all regret the absence of Mr. Ware who participated in our work in 30/31. Dr. Rousselle informed me by cable in December 1931 of the "immediate" despatch of his revised Chu T'ien Chuan manuscript to Peking, but it has not

\- 4 -

arrived here yet.

We receive numerous letters like those reproduced below from Chinese and from Foreigners, asking for our advice on Sino-Indian questions, and I am a member of many Committees and Societies dealing with historical, philological, and archaeological subjects. Quite recently I have been elected a corresponding member of the Academia Sinica. That is a very rare distinction (the only foreign philologists who share it with me are Pelliot and Karlgren), and it seems to prove that the efforts of the Sino-Indian Institute are appreciated by the highest authorities in China.

Believe me,

Yours sincerely and gratefully.

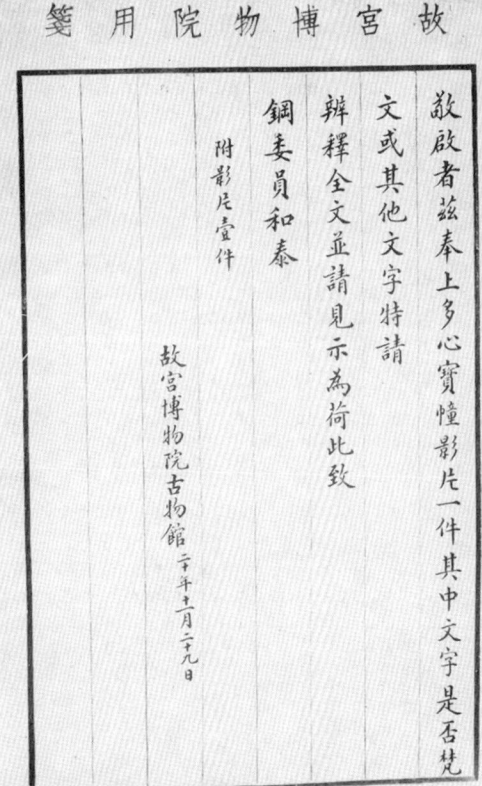

國立北平圖書館
National Library of Peping
Peping (Peking) China

January 13, 1932.

Baron A. von Stael-Holstein,
Ex-Austrian Legation,
Peiping.

Dear Baron:

As we are going to publish our Bulletin specially devoted to the Tangut Studies, I am enclosing copy of the table of contents. There are ~~two~~ three sutras whose Sanskrit original we have not been able to ascertain, and then there may be other inaccuracies which need revision. I shall be very much obliged if you will be kind enough to look it over and insert all corrections.

With many thanks in advance,

Sincerely yours,

T. L. Yuan

故宮博物院用箋

敬啟者茲奉上多心寶幢影片一件其中文字是否梵文或其他文字特請辨釋全文並請見示為荷此致
鋼委員和泰
附影片壹件
故宮博物院古物館 二十年十一月二十九日

HARVARD-YENCHING INSTITUTE

17 BOYLSTON HALL
CAMBRIDGE, MASSACHUSETTS

March 29, 1932

Dear Professor von Stael-Holstein,-

Your letter of the 25th reached me today, and I am delighted to have it so long before the meeting of the Trustees on April 11th. I shall summarize it for the Trustees, and I know they will be glad to have such good reports about Messrs. Schuster, Sickman and Bodde. We are recommending Mr. Sickman and Mr. Bodde for reappointment so that they may have another year in Peiping.

It must be a great comfort to have a lama who speaks English. I should think this would help enormously in the work of the Institute.

It is a pity that students of the National University show no more interest in your studies, but perhaps it is natural, just at the moment, at any rate, that they should be more interested in politics.

Mr. Ware is getting on extremely well here, we all think. He is teaching now the elementary language course in Chinese and hopes to finish his work for the doctor's degree before the end of the year. Next year, Mr. Mei will have leave of absence and Mr. Ware will take over a considerable part of his work.

I am sorry to hear that Dr. Rousselle's manuscript hasn't reached you. I hope it will come along shortly. Certainly, the mails seem very slow these days in all directions.

The copies of inquiries which you sent are certainly most interesting, and I can see that this sort of inquiry must take an enormous amount of your time to answer.

I am greatly pleased at your election to the Academia Sinica, which is clearly a very rare distinction. Surely, the Trustees will be very much pleased by this news.

I shall write again some time after the Trustees' meeting.

Cordially yours,

George H. Chase

Professor von Stael-Holstein,
Sino-Indian Institute,
ex-Austrian Legation,
Peiping, China.

HARVARD-YENCHING INSTITUTE

17 BOYLSTON HALL
CAMBRIDGE, MASSACHUSETTS

April 23, 1932

Dear Professor von Stael-Holstein,-

Since I did not get my letter of March 29th ready much before the time of the Trustees' meeting, I held it until the meeting was over to see if there was anything that I needed to communicate to you.

I am afraid one bit of news is disagreeable. The income of the Institute has been so reduced that all the Trustees here agree that we must cut appropriations for next year just so far as this is possible, and in line with this policy the appropriations for the Sino-Indian Institute was fixed at $3,500 for 1932-33. We realize that this may mean some retrenchment in your activities, but we hope that the favorable exchange will be a certain offset. The reduction is in line with reductions made in many other Institute activities. We granted no new fellowships and cut down appropriations for buying books by Yenching and Harvard to an absolute minimum.

One other matter also came before the Trustees, namely, the question of the use of $5,000 Mex. which you have. The Trustees all felt that this should be kept for the purchase of a Tibetan Kanjur Tanjur and asked me to express the hope that you could find a copy and somehow get it to Cambridge in the near future. We see all the difficulties, but there is such need here of a copy of the Kanjur that I was asked to urge you strongly to do all you can in the matter. President Stuart will probably consult you about it when he returns to Peiping, since he was asked to do so by the Trustees and to let you know exactly their feeling.

With every good wish, I am

Sincerely yours,

George H. Chase

Professor von Stael-Holstein,
Sino-Indian Institute,
ex-Austrian Legation,
Peiping, China.

COPY

HARVARD-YENCHING INSTITUTE

17 Boylston Hall,
Cambridge, Massachusetts.

July 20, 1932.

Dean William Hung,
Acting Executive Secretary,
Harvard-Yenching Institute,
Peiping, China.

My dear Dean Hung:

This will acknowledge receipt of your letter of June 23rd, together with a copy of your letter to Baron von Stael-Holstein in regard to the budget item Y-11, Sino-Indian Institute. My understanding agrees with yours that the Yenching Treasurer's office is authorized to pay the Sino-Indian Institute disbursements in silver not exceeding $14,000. I feel very sure that this was the intent of the Trustees in passing the budget and that the item G$3,500 was inserted simply for the purpose of totaling the whole budget.

Sincerely yours,

(signed) George H. Chase

Peking, September 3rd 1932.

Dear Dean Chase,

~~In~~ on May 6th 1932 I received two hundred and fifty (250.00) U.S. dollars from the Treasurer of Yenching University. ~~[illegible]~~ I sold those U.S. dollars for eleven hundred and fifty two Mex~~ican~~. dollars and fifty cents. ~~Out of that sum I pa~~

| D.A.B. quittung

1146.42
6.08
1152.50

Out of that sum I paid eleven hundred and forty six Mex. dollars and forty two cents (1146.42) for the Leica apparatus, and

| Schmidt quittung

returned ~~the remaining~~ six Mex. dollars and eight cents (6.08) to the Treasurer of Yenching University.

| Yenching quittung

The sample which I enclose seems to prove that the apparatus works quite ~~satisfactory,~~ satisfactorily, and I thank you as well as the (other) Trustees most heartily for having enabled us to buy it.

Believe me yours sincerely and gratefully

| Sample

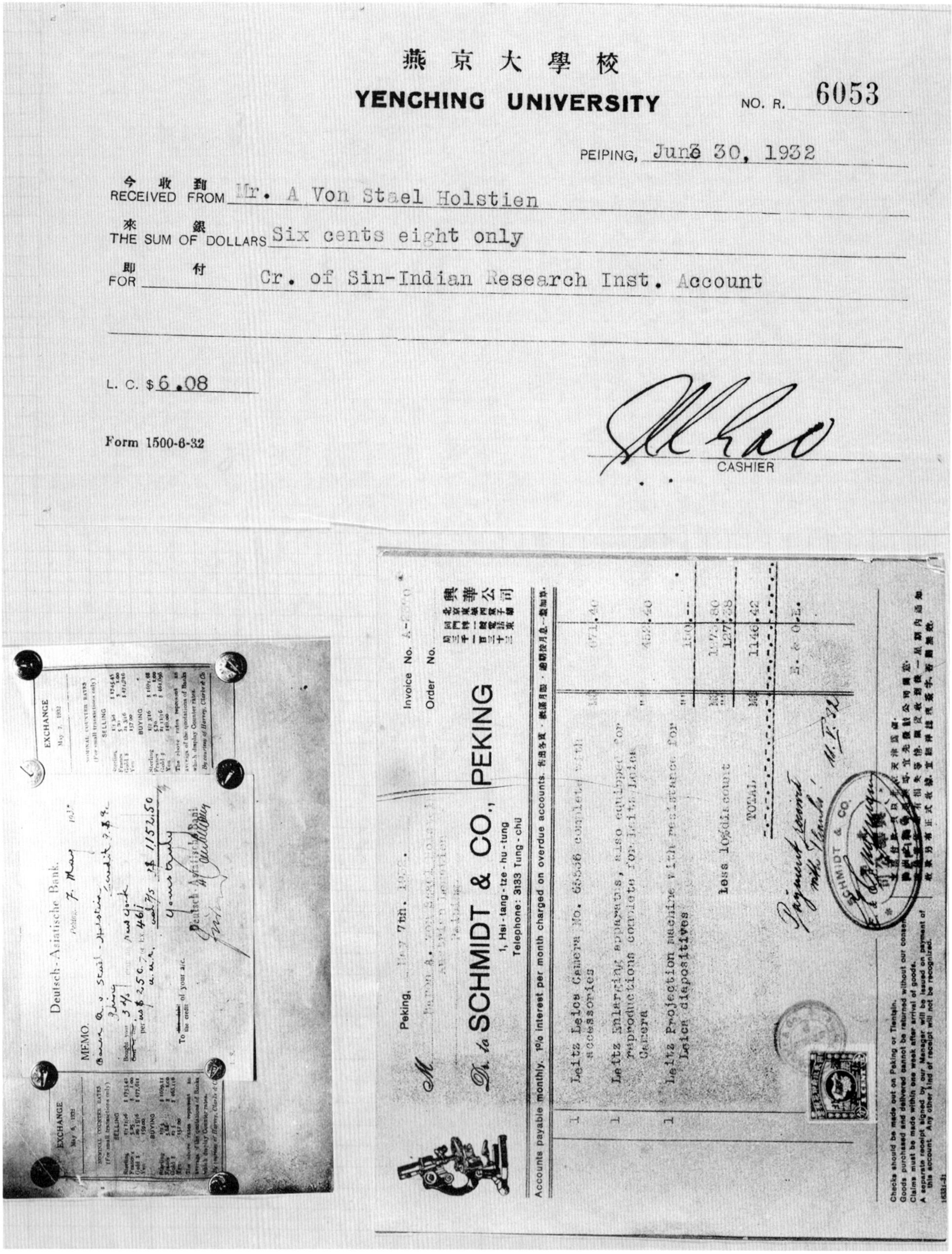

燕京大學校

YENCHING UNIVERSITY　　NO. R. 6053

PEIPING, June 30, 1932

今收到 RECEIVED FROM Mr. A Von Stael Holstien

來銀 THE SUM OF DOLLARS Six cents eight only

即付 FOR Cr. of Sin-Indian Research Inst. Account

L. C. $6.08

Form 1500-6-32

CASHIER

Deutsch-Asiatische Bank.

MEMO.

To the credit of your a/c.

Yours truly

Deutsch-Asiatische Bank

EXCHANGE

SCHMIDT & CO., PEKING

1, Hsi-tang-tze-hu-tung

Telephone: 3133 Tung-chü

Peking, May 7th. 1932.

Invoice No.

Order No.

Accounts payable monthly. 1% interest per month charged on overdue accounts.

1	Leitz Leica Camera No. 65536 complete with accessories	671.40
1	Leitz Enlarging apparatus, also equipped for reproductions complete for Leitz Leica Camera	452.40
1	Leitz Projection machine with resistance for Leica diapositives	150.--
		1273.80
	Less 10% discount	127.38
	TOTAL	1146.42

E. & O.E.

Payment received with thanks 11.V.32

SCHMIDT & CO.

Peking, September 4th 1932.

Dear Dean Chase,

As far as I know, there are only two ~~readab~~ entirely readable Tibetan Tanjur prints in Europe (Leningrad and Paris) and one or two in America (Washington). Ever since I arrived in Peking in 1917 I have tried to buy ~~[illegible]~~ an entirely readable Tibetan Tanjur print for myself, or for certain friends who had asked me to look for one, but I never succeeded ~~in finding one~~ until this spring when a copy was offered to me. I hesitated for ~~a long~~ some time before (paying five thousand Mex. dollars for it on behalf of) ~~acquiring it for~~ The Harvard Yenching Institute, because ~~the price (five thousand Mex dollars) exceeded the sum which I held since 1930~~

~~five thousand Mex. dollars which I held since~~
~~1930 were intended by the Harvard-Yenching~~
~~Institute~~ I had been asked ~~me~~ to buy the Tanjur
and the Kanjur for the five thousand
Mex. dollars which I held since 1930. Please
accept my apologies for paying five thousand
Mex. dollars for the ~~[illegible]~~ Tanjur alone.
My excuse is that an entirely readable Tanjur
print is ~~such~~ so a rare thing that even the
Berlin State Library and a number of other similar institutions have been trying in vain
to obtain one from Tibet for many years. The copies which are obtainable in Tibet, are, ~~[illegible]~~ so I hear, all printed with old worn-out blocks. Comp. my letter dated Sept. 3rd 1932.
~~not to mention~~
~~the Metropolitan Library of Peking which only~~
~~possesses an incomplete and partially unreadable copy.~~
~~copy. If, I had declined the refused~~
~~I think~~

I simply could not refuse the offer, and I am ready to return the five thousand Mex. dollars to you (~~and keep~~ keeping the 'Ganjur for myself), if you so wish.

The copy of the Snar than 'Ganjur which I acquired ~~is quit~~ seems to be quite complete, and I keep it at the ~~D~~ Peking branch of the Deutsch-Asiatische bank.

Believe me yours sincerely and gratefully

'Ganjur [illegible]

Peking September 10th 1932.

Dear Dean Chase,

Apart from the sum accounted for in my letter dated Sept. 3rd 1932, I have received during the special year ending on June 30th 1932 (25.996.51) twenty five thousand nine hundred and ninety six Mex. dollars and fifty one cents from the Treasurer of Yenching University for the year ending on June 30th 1932. Four thousand (4000.00) Mex. dollars have been used for representation and the remaining twenty one thousand nine hundred and ninety six Mex. dollars and fifty one cents (21.996.51) are accounted for on leaves 0—00 below. Of that sum (21.996.51) fifteen thousand two hundred and eighty two Mex. dollars and ninety cents (15.282.90) have been spent in connection with my assistants and six thousand seven hundred and thirteen Mex. dollars and sixty one cents (6713.61) have been paid for books.

~~I possess an almost complete copy of t~~

Some of these books, costing twenty two hundred Mex. dollars, have not been bought for the Sino-Indian Institute ~~at all~~, but for ~~the~~ Cambridge. ~~Mass~~ ~~so that~~ ~~I would have used that money for foreign~~

If it had not been for ~~your~~ the demand expressed in ~~your~~ your ~~(April 1932)~~ letter dated April 23rd 1932, I would ~~not~~ not have bought the Kanjur, ~~for~~ (of which I ~~already~~ personally possess ~~all~~ ~~an a nearly~~ an almost complete copy). ~~and the~~ The money would have been used for foreign books which we ~~stand~~ stand in need of, and for paying my assistants' salaries for June 1932. (I received your letter dated April 23rd ~~April~~ 1932 late in May 1932, at a time when I had already spent or promised practically all the Sino-Indian Institute funds available for 31/32) ~~As it was~~ In order to find the twenty two hundred dollars required for the ~~K~~ Kanjur (comp. my letter dated Sept. ~~4th~~ 1932), I had to cancel ~~some~~ some orders for foreign books and to pay the June salaries on July 1st 1932 ~~Trans~~ (thus transferring them to the year $ 32/33).

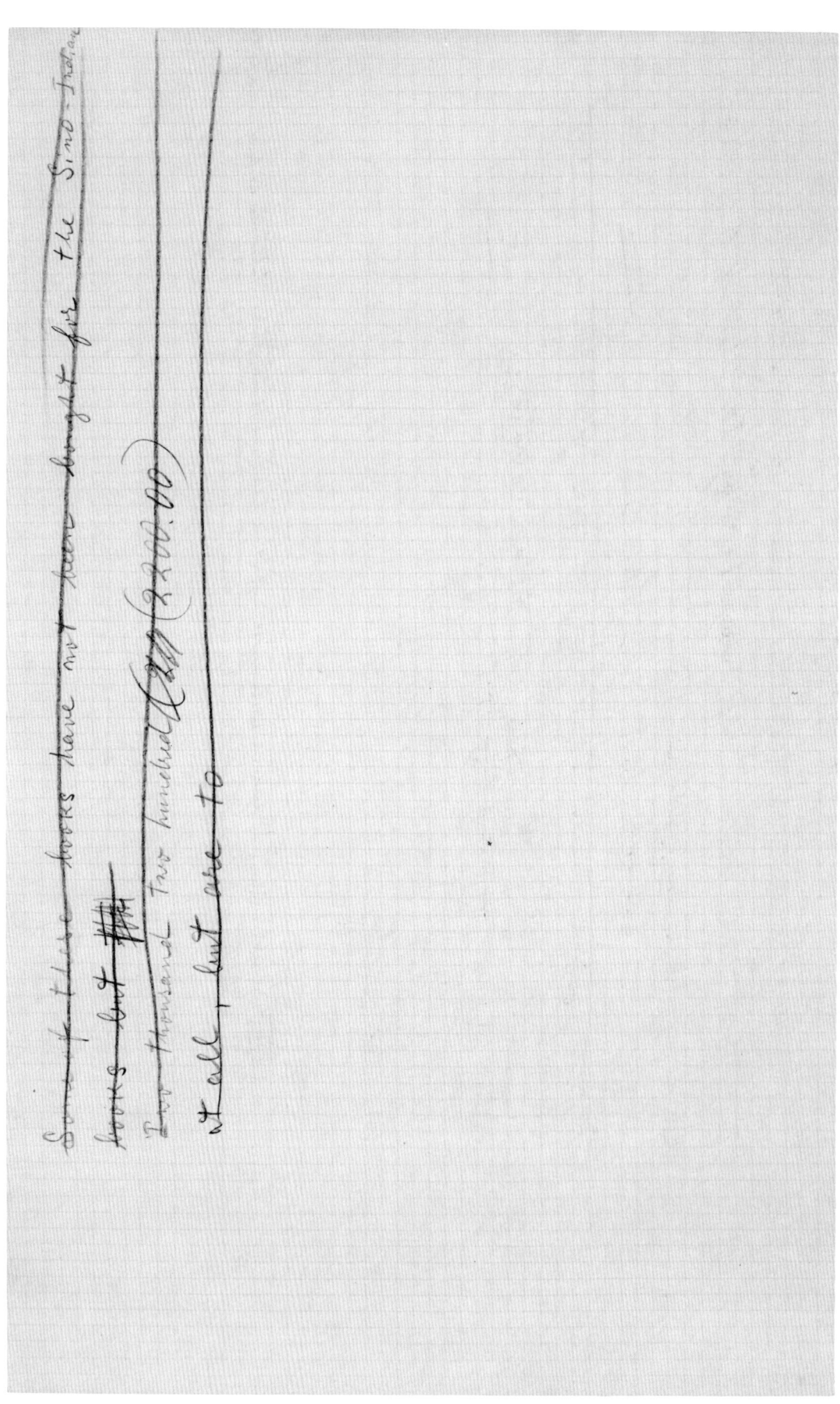

Some of these books have not been bought for the Sino-Indian
books but [illegible]
Two thousand two hundred (2[illegible] (2200.00)
at all, but are to

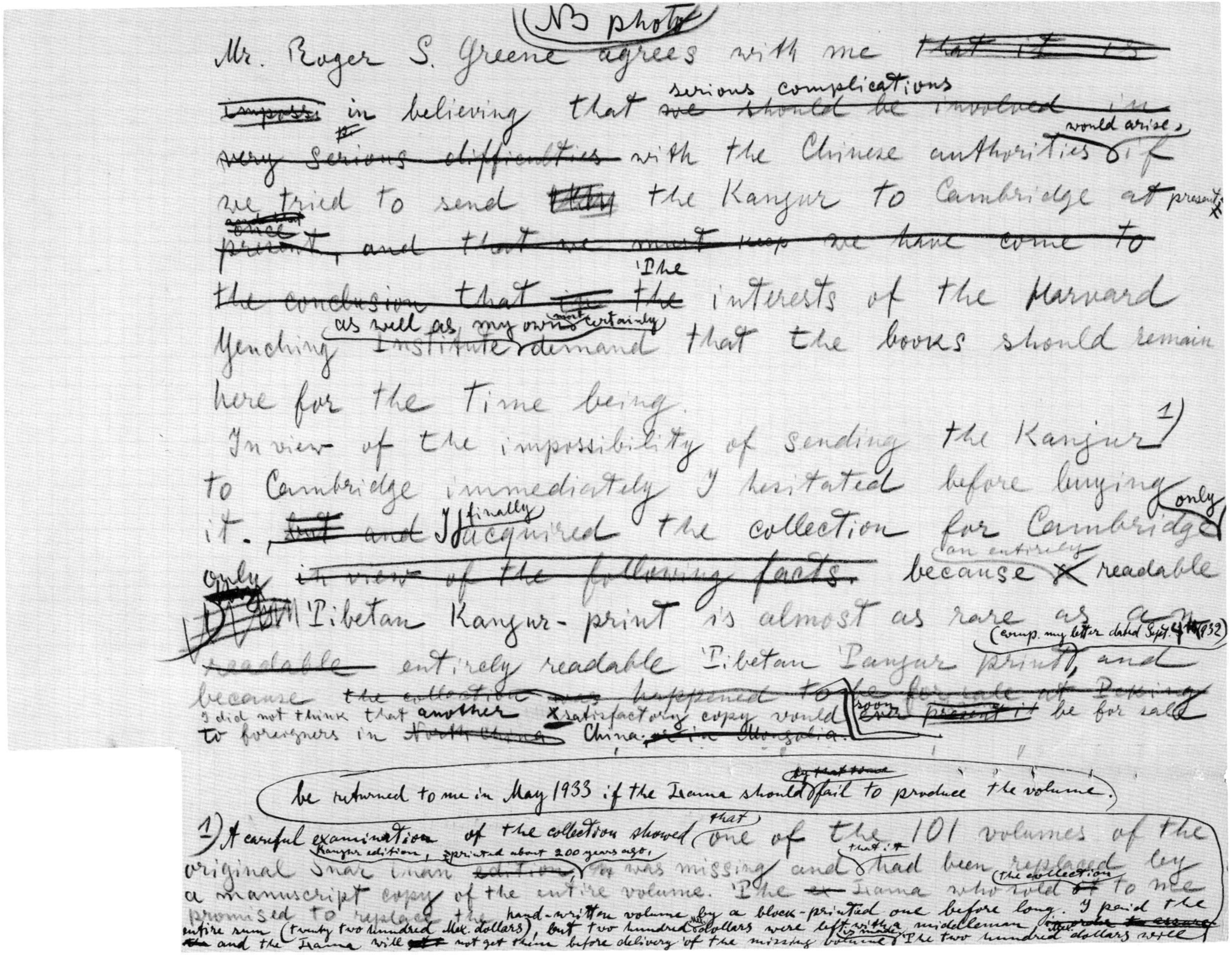

No 3 photo

Mr. Roger S. Greene agrees with me in believing that serious complications would arise with the Chinese authorities if we tried to send the Kanjur to Cambridge at present. The interests of the Harvard Yenching Institute as well as my own most certainly demand that the books should remain here for the time being.

In view of the impossibility of sending the Kanjur to Cambridge immediately I hesitated before buying it. I finally acquired the collection for Cambridge only because an entirely readable Tibetan Kanjur-print is almost as rare as (comp. my letter dated Sept 1932) entirely readable Tibetan Tanjur print, and because I did not think that another satisfactory copy would soon be for sale to foreigners in China. [1]

[1] A careful examination of the collection showed that one of the 101 volumes of the original Snar thang Kanjur edition, printed about 200 years ago, was missing and that it had been replaced by a manuscript copy of the entire volume. The Lama who sold the collection to me promised to replace the hand-written volume by a block-printed one before long. I paid the entire sum (twenty two hundred Mex. dollars), but two hundred dollars were left with a middleman by me and the Lama will not get them before delivery of the missing volume. The two hundred dollars will be returned to me in May 1933 if the Lama should by that time fail to produce the volume.

~~I have not insured~~ The ~~the~~ books

which I have bought for the

Harvard - Yenching Institute

are not insured, but I keep

the ~~most~~ rarest ones, [including the Kangyur] in a

strong room at ~~which I rent from~~

the Deutsch-Asiatische Bank, ~~for~~

Legation street, Peking.

~~that purpose~~

Believe me ~~~~ yours sincerely and

gratefully

A. Staël-Holstein.

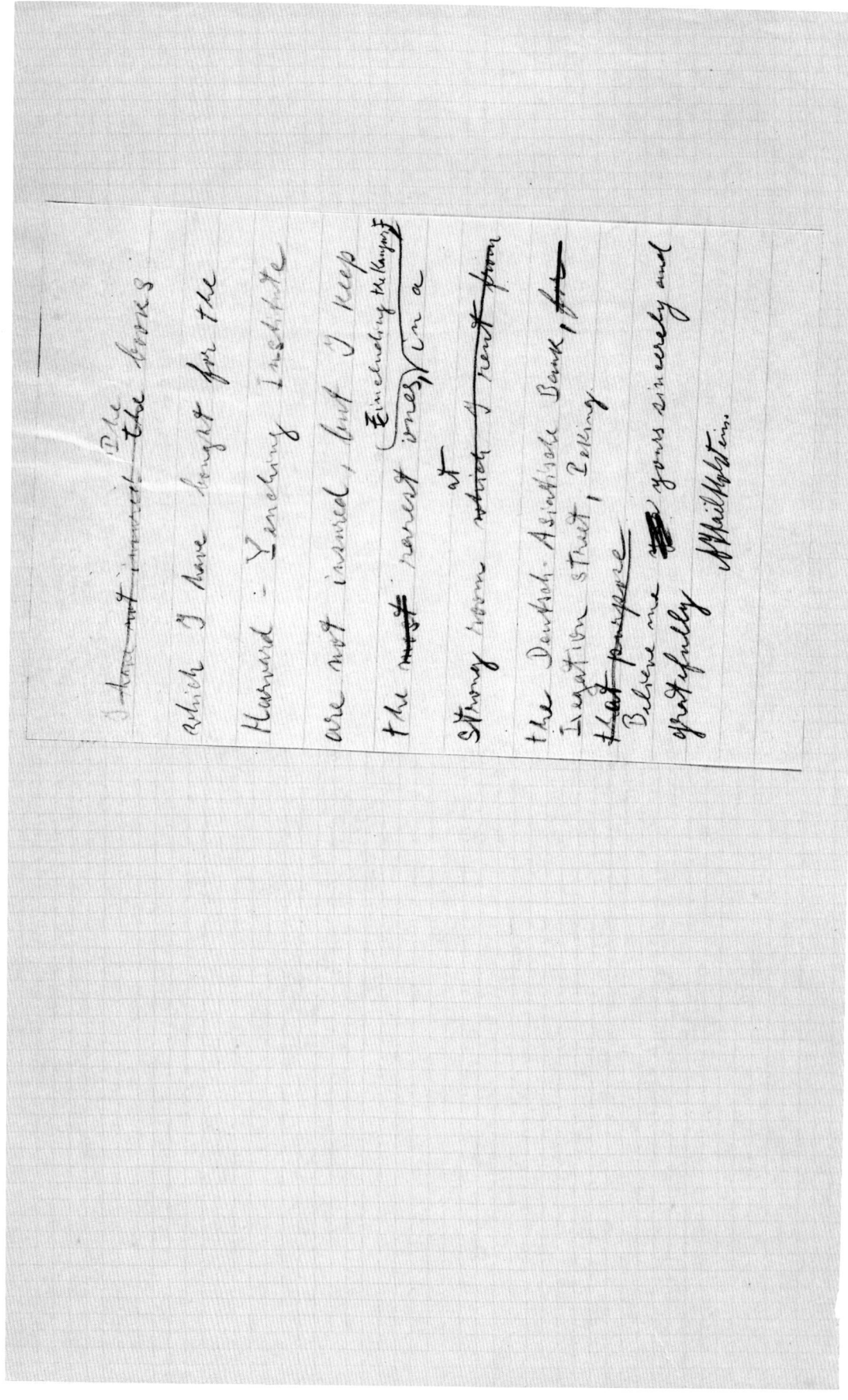

7 ~~Prof.~~ Lessing does not agree with the ~~me or what I say about my~~
9 explanation of the word ẓhin ~~given ab~~ which I give in
3 note 14 above. ~~He suggests the following translation interpre-~~
~~tation of the expression ẓhin spyan ḍran ba: invitation~~
~~of the field He believes that ẓhin "the field" in~~
7 He suggests translating the expression ẓhin spyan
8 ḍran ba as follows: invitation of the field,
8 i.e. invitation of the Three Saints Bcoṅ kha
6 pa, Mkhas grub, and Rgyal chab.

~~I follow A Wang the Shih~~ My translation of dmigs med (Bla maḥi rnal byor, page 12b) by "unfettered" agrees with the Chinese version (無礙) and with what S.C. Das (dict, page 983) has to say about the expression. The Mongolian ~~translator~~ rendering of the term ülü setkikdekü means: ~~"untold"~~, ~~indescribable~~ unimaginable.

9 ~~My explanation The explanation~~ The interpretation of the expression ẓhin spyan ḍran ba
15 which I give in note 14 above is confirmed by the Divyāvadāna ~~(ed. by~~ in which the
5 word kṣetra ~~occurs~~ is, like ~~used in the sense of~~ puṇyakṣetra, ~~(a holy place, or a holy~~
15 ~~person)~~ used in the sense of "a holy person". Comp. the Divyāvadāna, ed. Cowell and Neil,
6 London 1886, pages 388 and 679.

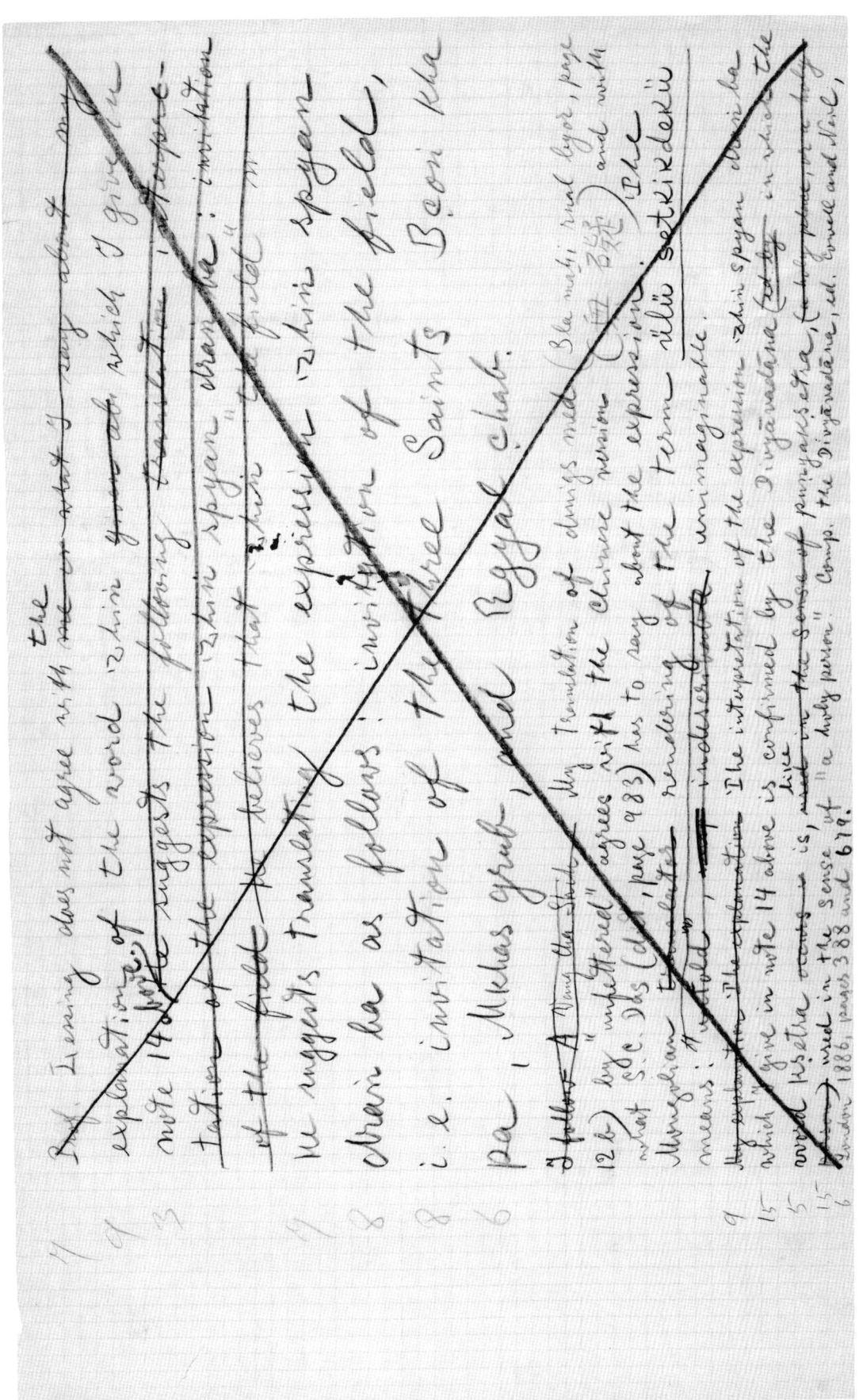

Peking, September ~~18th~~ 1932.

Dear Dean Chase,

Most of the Peking Universities ~~of~~ and Colleges possess some isolated numbers of Oriental journals etc ~~and incomplete series~~ but none of them ~~have~~ has what might be called a fairly complete Sino-Indo-Tibetan library. It has ~~been~~ for many years been my ambition to collect one, and owing to the liberality of the Harvard-Yenching Institute, I have been able to buy all the back numbers of some ~~a number of complete~~ series, like the Pāli ~~Text~~ Text Society's publications, which no other Peking library possesses.

~~I shall be able to. I shall be able ~~ ~~Owing to our reduced finances I shall have to buy all the leave all leave these series~~ (if I do not want to leave the series incomplete) ~~complete, or to buy the newly appearing numbers~~ with ~~for~~ ~~my own money,~~

A reduction of our appropriation by ~~twelve thousand~~ 12.000 Mex. dollars (14.000 Mex. dollars, instead of 26.000 Mex. dollars) would necessitate my ~~force me~~ ~~to~~ ~~force me to~~ buying ~~the~~ newly appearing numbers myself, ~~or leave the series incomplete.~~
~~or result in leaving the various series incomplete.~~
or leave the various series incomplete.

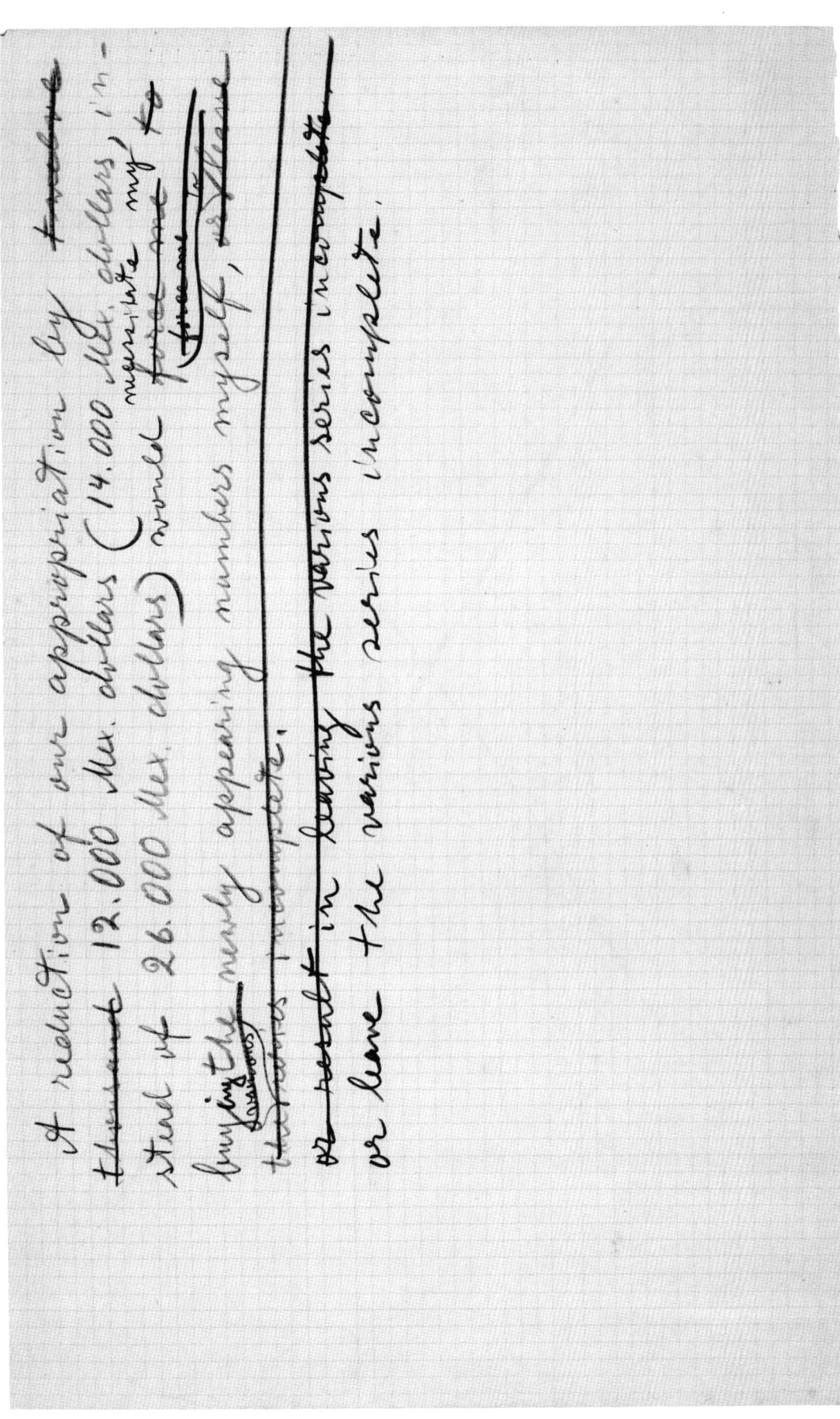

Note 1d 1

The author of the ~~Bla ... rnal~~ Tibetan text of the Bla maḥi rnal ḥbyor is, according to several learned Lamas whom I consulted: the fifth Dalai Lama, Blo bzaṅ ṅag dbaṅ (thub bstan) rgya mcho. The Lamas were unable to produce any proof ~~of~~ for their statement.

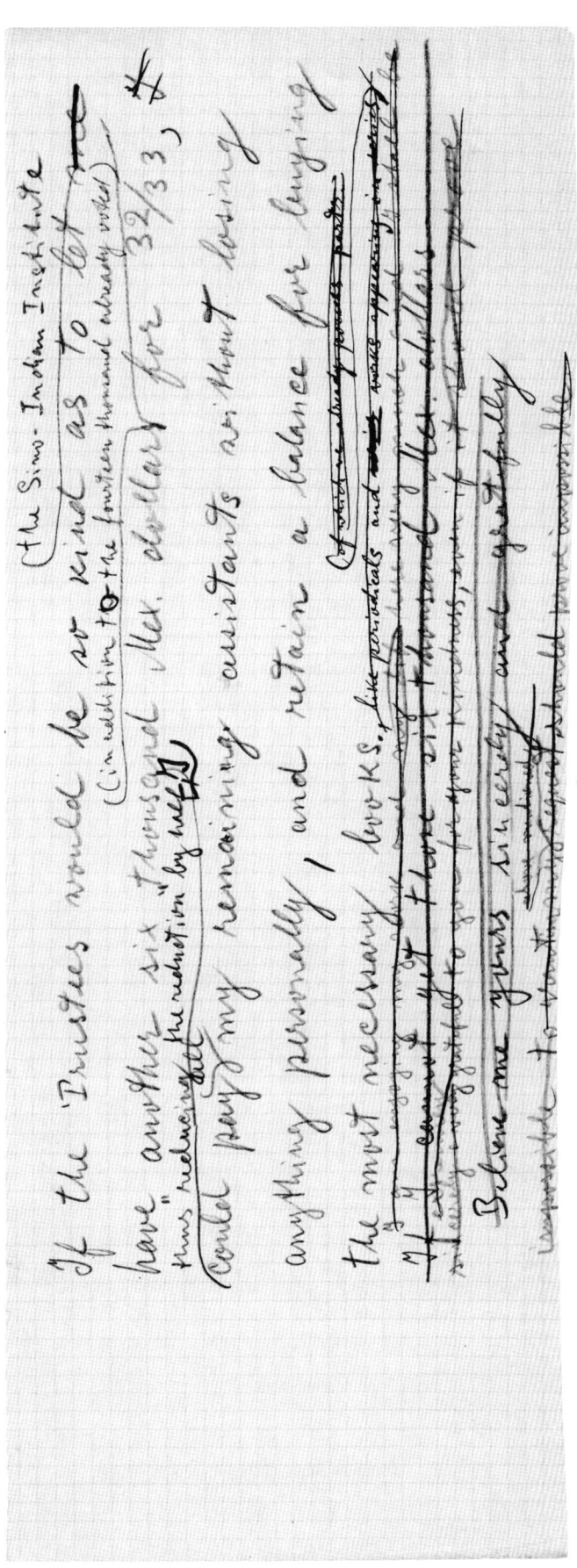

If the Trustees would be so kind as to let ~~me~~ (the Sino-Indian Institute
have another six thousand Mex. dollars (in addition to the fourteen thousand already voted) for 32/33, ~~I~~
could pay (thus "reducing all the reduction" by well [illegible]) my remaining assistants without losing
anything personally, and retain a balance for buying
the most necessary books. ~~(of which we already possess parts)~~ ~~like periodicals and works appearing in series)~~
~~I am enjoying my work and my life here very much and I shall be~~
~~If I cannot get those six thousand Mex. dollars~~
~~sincerely and gratefully to you for your kindness, even if it should prove~~
Believe me ~~yours sincerely and gratefully~~
~~impossible to grant my request should prove impossible~~

But even if I should stop buying books altogether the reduction of the Sino-Indian Institute appropriation by over 46%, (~~as foreshadowed~~ comp. your letter dated April 23rd 1932, ~~14.000 Mex. dollars instead of 26.000 Mex. dollars~~) would result in a ~~quite~~ considerable financial loss (which I am able to bear now, on account of the favourable exchange, but how long will it last?) to me personally; Considering ~~our~~ the various ~~text~~ editions which we have undertaken, as well as ~~our~~ pupils (Messrs. Sickman, Boddeke); ~~I cannot~~ dismiss more than a few assistants at short notice, and I think I must continue employing the great majority of them for the time being, even if my private interests should be seriously affected.

~~My most important collaborator is Professor Veller, who teaches Messrs. Sickman, Bodde, and Lin (in separate classes) now, besides doing his research work and proof reading.~~

I enclose the forty eight pages of ~~this~~ Professor Weller's ~~glossary~~ ~~index~~ index which have been printed so far, as well as two papers ~~written~~ by myself, and the last proof sheet (pages ~~288~~ 296) (of which a few sheets were already printed when I left for America in 1928.) of my Kaśyapa commentary edition. The ~~Pei P'ang~~ Peking printers ~~in charge of our~~ ~~[illegible]~~ ~~editions~~ cannot (or will not) print more than about ten (Commercial Press) or twenty (Pei P'ang) pages of our complicated editions (in a month's time) because only very few workmen here are able to handle the diacritical marks etc. properly.

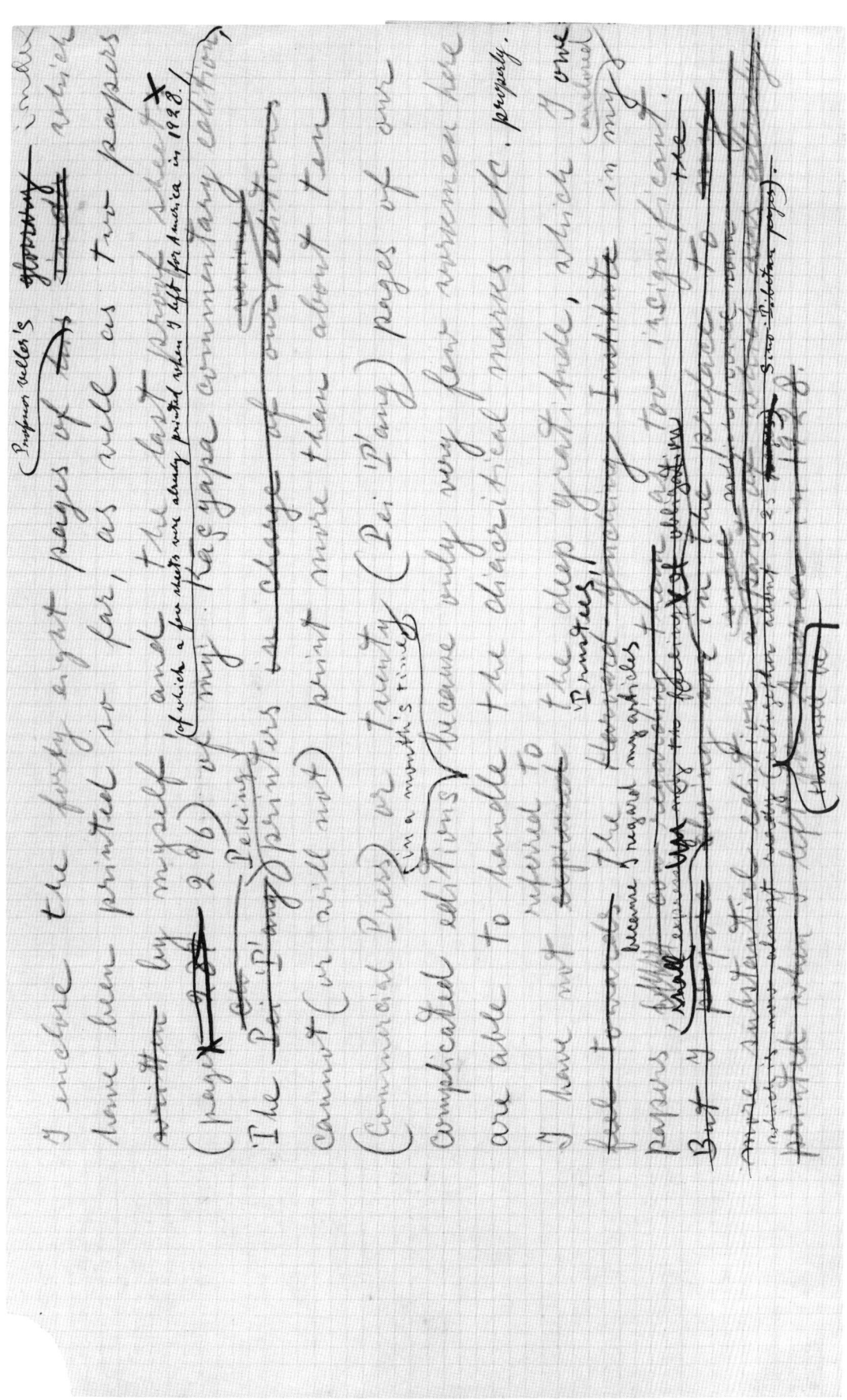

I have not ~~expressed~~ referred to the deep gratitude, which I owe ~~feel towards~~ the Trustees, ~~Harvard Yenching Institute~~ in my enclosed papers, ~~[illegible] regarding them~~ because I regard my articles as too insignificant. ~~I shall express my ~~ my feeling of obligation~~ ~~But I propose doing so in the preface to my the small more substantial edition, a part of which was already which is now almost ready (altogether about 325 Sino-Tibetan pages). printed when I left for America in 1928.~~ there will be

~~But~~ I shall, however, thank the Harvard-Yenching Institute most heartily for
~~for all you have done and are still~~
~~for all you we do for making our~~
~~notwithstanding the depression [illegible]~~
enabling us, to continue our work here, ~~[illegible]~~ in my
preface to the more substantial edition mentioned above.

Believe me yours sincerely and gratefully
A. Staël Holstein.

P.S.
I hope that my report dated Sept. 10th, and my letters dated Sept. 3rd and Sept. 4th have arrived.
ASH.

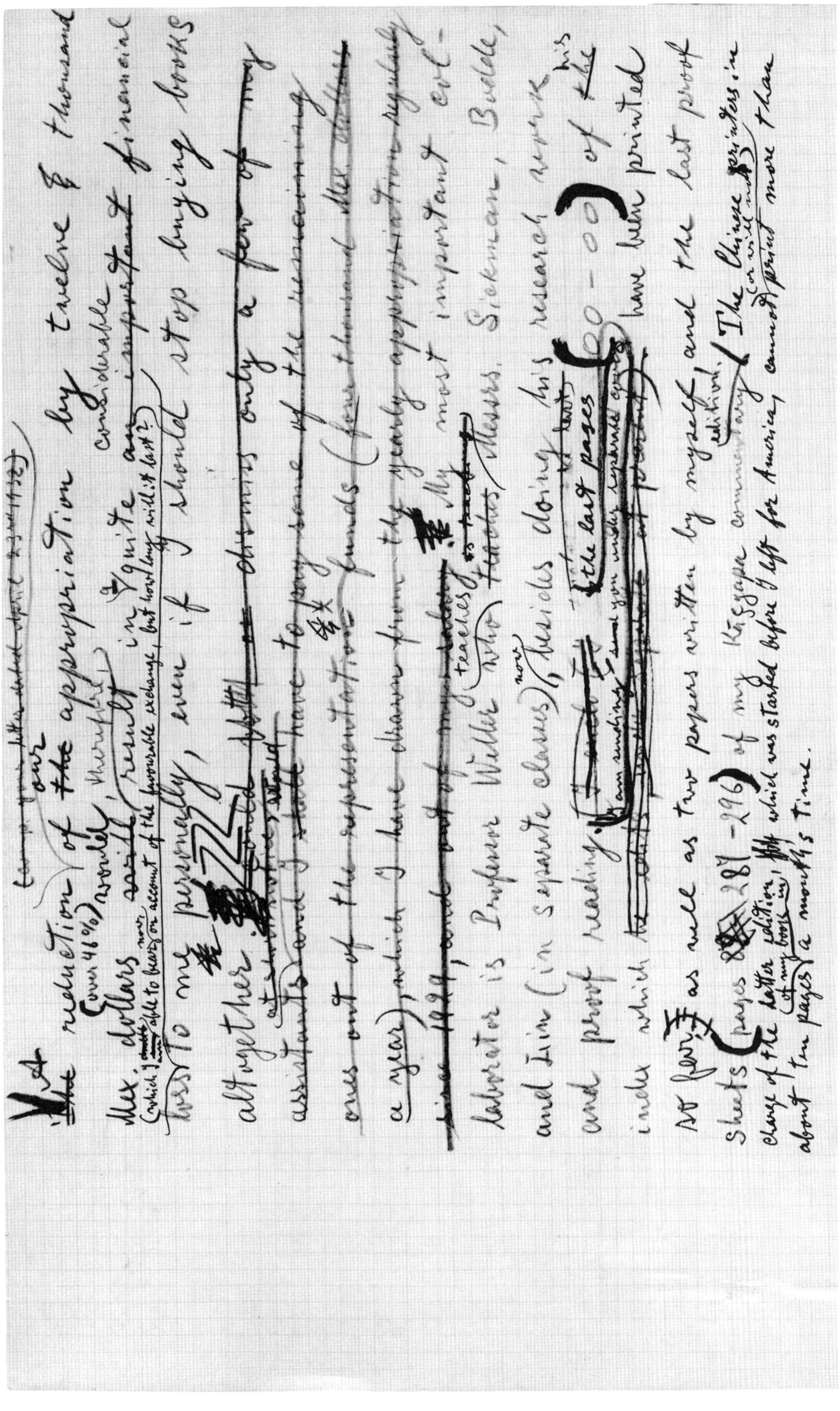

A reduction (over 46%) of our appropriation by twelve thousand Mex. dollars would, therefore, result in a quite considerable financial loss to me personally (which I am now able to bear on account of the favourable exchange, but how long will it last?), even if I should stop buying books altogether. My most important collaborator is Professor Weller who now teaches Messrs. Sickman, Budde, and Lin (in separate classes), besides doing his research work and proof reading. I am sending you under separate cover the last pages (00 – 00) of his index which have been printed so far, as well as two papers written by myself, and the last proof sheets (pages 287 – 296) of my Kāśyapa commentary edition. The Chinese printers in charge of the latter edition (of my books in), which was started before I left for America, cannot (or will not) print more than about ten pages a month's time.

* These four thousand Mex. dollars do **not** cover representation only, but ~~are~~ also ~~used for~~ the following expenses: four furnished rooms (including light heat and service) used daily by the members of the Institute for study lectures etc, ~~for the [illegible] the lectures are held for lectures etc~~ a strong room for keeping the rarest books (including the [illegible] & the [illegible]) (the H.Y. books which I keep at the Austrian Legation (former) are not insured) belonging to the Institute at the ~~[illegible]~~ bank, paper ink ~~etc etc~~ etc. for the Institute. ~~etc etc~~

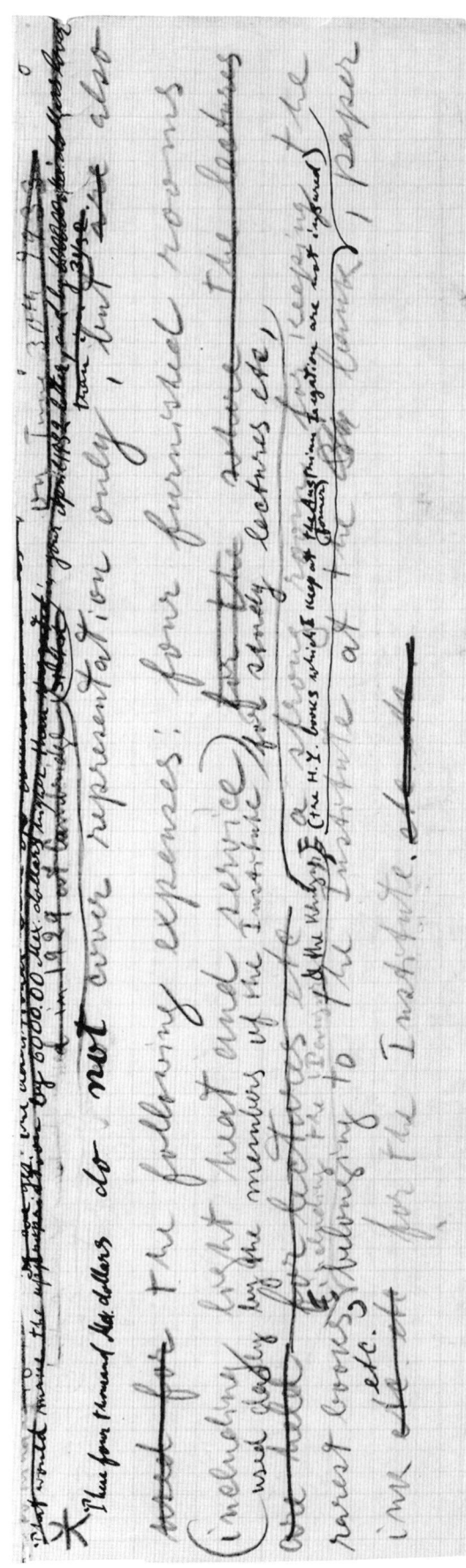

~~I cannot I can only dismiss a~~

~~The inter I~~ ~~Our various~~ ~~enterpr~~ ~~activities~~ some of which ~~began~~ ~~and which~~ take years to mature,
Our
~~The~~ activities, ~~which we have started~~ ~~allow me to dismiss~~
~~but a few of my minor assistants, and if the reduction~~
~~will~~
~~should not be modified, I shall have to pay some~~
~~of the remaining assistants myself.~~
do not allow me to dismiss more than ~~a~~ ~~very~~ a few
assistants at short notice, and I think I must ~~have decided to keep~~
~~the great majority of~~ continue employing the great
majority of them, even if ~~that should~~ ~~result~~ ~~cause me~~
~~serious inconvenience financial embarrassment in diminishing~~
~~my~~ ~~private income.~~ ~~I should suffer serious losses.~~ prejudice.
my private interests should be seriously affected.

~~Note 1d 2.~~

My Lama friends tell me that Bçon kha pa has three tutelary deities: ~~Guhyasamāja~~ Gsaṅ hdus, Bde mchog, and Hjigs byed. Gsaṅ hdus is according to the Tibetan-Sanskrit dictionary published by Bacot (page 1886) = Guhyasamājaḥ. Bde-mchog = Saṃvara, and Hjigs byed = Bhairava. Comp. Grünwedel, Mythologie des Buddhismus, ~~Berlin~~ Leipzig 1900, pages 103 and 67.

HARVARD-YENCHING INSTITUTE

17 BOYLSTON HALL
CAMBRIDGE, MASSACHUSETTS

October 14, 1932

My dear Baron,-

This will acknowledge receipt of your letters of September 3rd and 4th, together with the very clear statement of your account, which I shall submit, of course, to the Educational Committee and the Trustees of the Harvard-Yenching Institute. I think there is no question that all your actions will be approved. I know that Professor Woods will be delighted to know that the Institute possesses a good copy of the Tibetan Tanjur, and I don't think he will feel that the price paid was in any way excessive. If, of course, the Trustees should feel so poor that they prefer to have you keep the Tanjur for yourself and transfer to their account Mex. $5,000. I will let you know, but I think this is a very remote possibility. I anticipate that you will receive a very warm vote of thanks.

I am sure you were right in thinking that it would be impossible at the moment to export this copy and that we must await more favorable conditions, and surely it is wise to keep it at the Peking branch of the Deutsch-Asiatische Bank.

I am very much interested in the note about the one missing volume and your arrangement not to make full payment until the Lama delivers the missing volume.

I shall have more to write, of course, after the meeting of the Trustees in November. All my news about our fellows and their progress seems good and I hope you have a favorable impression of them. About Mr. Sickman, especially, I have heard very good things, and what Mr. Bodde writes makes me think he is turning to studies in philosophy, in which I know that you and the Sino-Indian Institute can help him considerably.

With cordial good wishes and many thanks for sending the reports in so well ahead of the meeting, I am

Sincerely yours,

George H. Chase

Baron A. von Stael-Holstein,
Ex-Austrian Legation,
Peiping, China.

HARVARD-YENCHING INSTITUTE

17 BOYLSTON HALL
CAMBRIDGE, MASSACHUSETTS

November 25, 1932

My dear Professor von Stael-Holstein:-

I have waited to answer your recent letters until the Trustees of the Institute met on November 14th and I was sure just what was to be done.

As I anticipated, the Trustees entirely approved your purchase of the Tibetan Tanjur for Mex. $5,000, which was in your hands, and approved also the storage of these volumes in Peiping until a favorable opportunity occurs for sending them to Cambridge.

The Trustees could not see their way to increase the appropriation for the Sino-Indian Institute by $6,000. They did go very carefully into the budget assignments for the current year and felt that they had, in general, asked the authorities of Yenching University, the Educational Committee here, and the Sino-Indian Institute to accept, roughly, the same reduction in appropriations. We felt that it was only fair to include the sum of G$250 for the photostat in the appropriation for the Sino-Indian Institute and so to reduce the cut from 46% to 41%. At the same time, there was a general feeling that you ought not to be expected to pay L.C.$2200 out of your own funds for the Tibetan Kanjur, and the Trustees voted, therefore, to transfer from another item of the budget this sum and add it to your budget for the current year. We will make arrangements so that this will be transmitted to you through the usual channels.

The suggestion was made by a number of Trustees that, perhaps, it would be possible for you to save something in the amount expended for "representation" and so tide over this difficult year without injuring the growth of the library of the Sino-Indian Institute. We realize, of course, that representation is an entirely necessary expense, but similar expenses here are being drastically cut and we wondered if reduction in this way would not be well understood in Peiping.

For the rest the Trustees who are competent - Professor Clark and Professor Woods - expressed great satisfaction with the photostats of the Tanjur which you sent and with your report in general, which I submitted to them.

Professor von Stael-Holstein, 2

If any difficulty arises about the payment of L.C.$2200, of course you won't hesitate to let me know so that I can straighten out the matter.

With kindest regards and best wishes, I am

Sincerely yours,

George H. Chase

Professor von Stael-Holstein,
Sino-Indian Institute,
ex-Austrian Legation,
Peiping, China.

Former Austrian Legation, Peking, February 28th 1933.

1

My dear Dean Chase,

~~In my last lett Many thanks~~ I am very grateful to you and to the other trustees for the twenty two hundred Mex. dollars which you so kindly added to the 32/33 appropriation of the Sino-Indian Institute. ~~I shall still have to spend most of the representation funds on This will enable me to use a part of the representation funds for their original purpose~~ Professor Weller is teaching Messrs. Sickman and Bodde Chinese. He also reads the Saundaranandakāvya (Sanskrit) with Mr. Lin.

~~Professor Weller's Tibetan index to the Kāçyapaparivarta is now ready ready, and I enclose pages~~

The printing of Professor Weller's Tibetan index to the Kāçyapaparivarta has progressed a little faster during the last months, and I ~~enclose~~ send you (under separate cover) pages 49 – 208 of the index, which will be completed in a few weeks. Professor Weller's Sanskrit index to the

~~we cabled on Dec. 31st 1932, was as follows: Staelholstein~~
~~article already printed Peking journal kindly refuse Oriental Society.~~

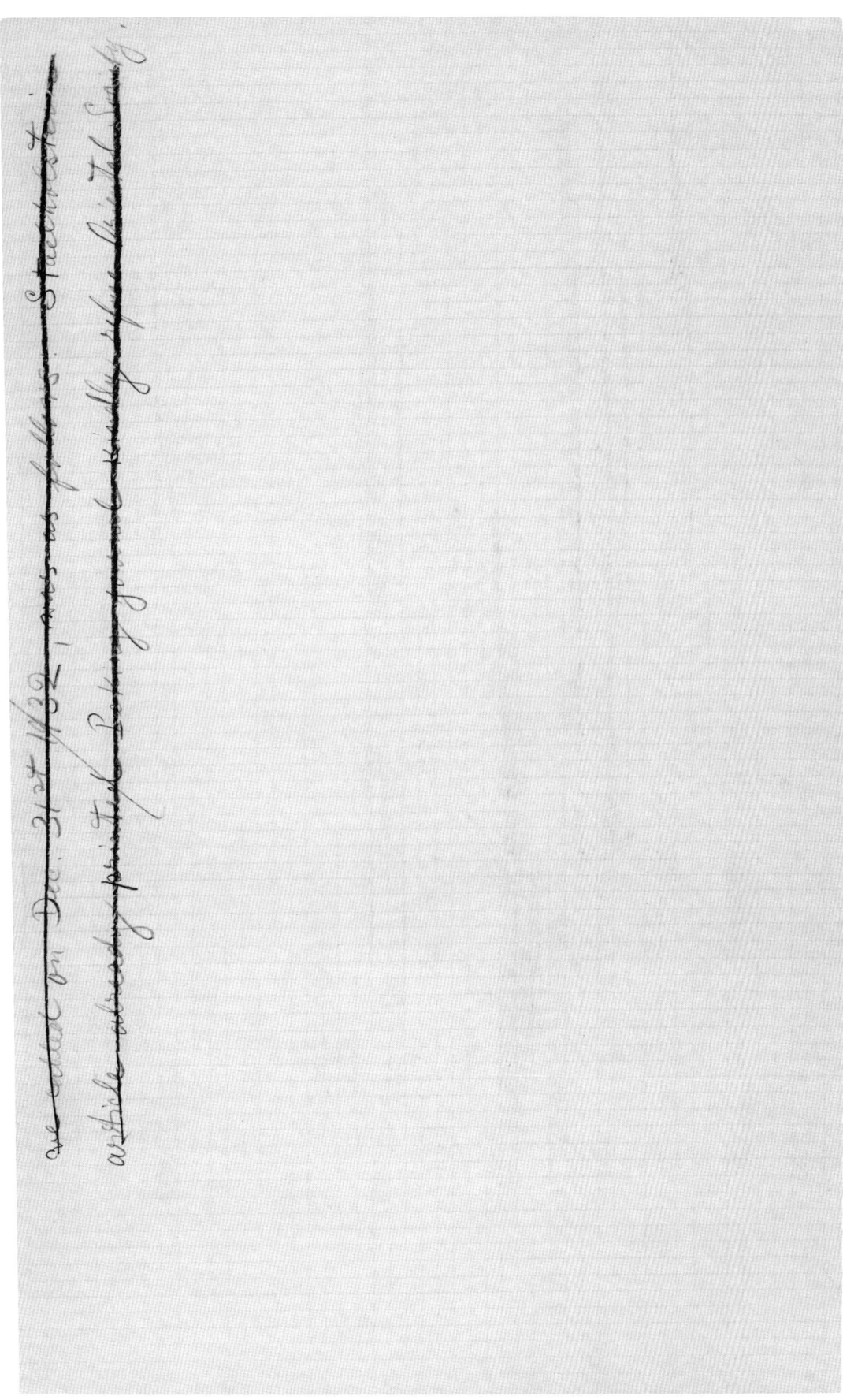

2

Kāçyapaparivarta will ~~All~~ not occupy more than about eighty pages, and we hope that it will be ready (in print) ~~in~~ in July 1933. ~~Professor Weller has been Tea is teaching Messrs. Sickman and Budde Chinese. He also reads the Saundarananda Kavya (Sanskrit) with Mr. Lin.~~

(Not much of) Mr. Pankratoff's Dagurian grammar has been printed ~~so far, I enclose because the spec. mak~~ so far, because a number of special characters had to be made for the purposes of this edition. I enclose pages 1 – 8 of ~~the~~ Mr. Pankratoff's book. ~~#~~ These ~~two~~ pages contain ~~a number of riddles~~ riddles and proverbs. The riddles, proverbs, and a ~~number~~ series of short stories (which will follow) represent the material on which Mr. Pankratoff's grammatical rules are founded. ~~Mr. Pankratoff has lately discovered~~

~~a number of Mongolian vocabularies which~~ 3

Mr. Pankratoff is now working on some newly discovered ~~Mongol~~ Chinese-Mongol vocabularies dating from the ~~XIV~~ XIV - XVII cent. The Mongol words are given in Chinese transliteration, ~~which adds to the interest~~ and Professor Pelliot who ~~is there at present,~~ has already seen the vocabularies, will examine them more carefully in a few days. ~~takes a great interest in the vocabularies~~

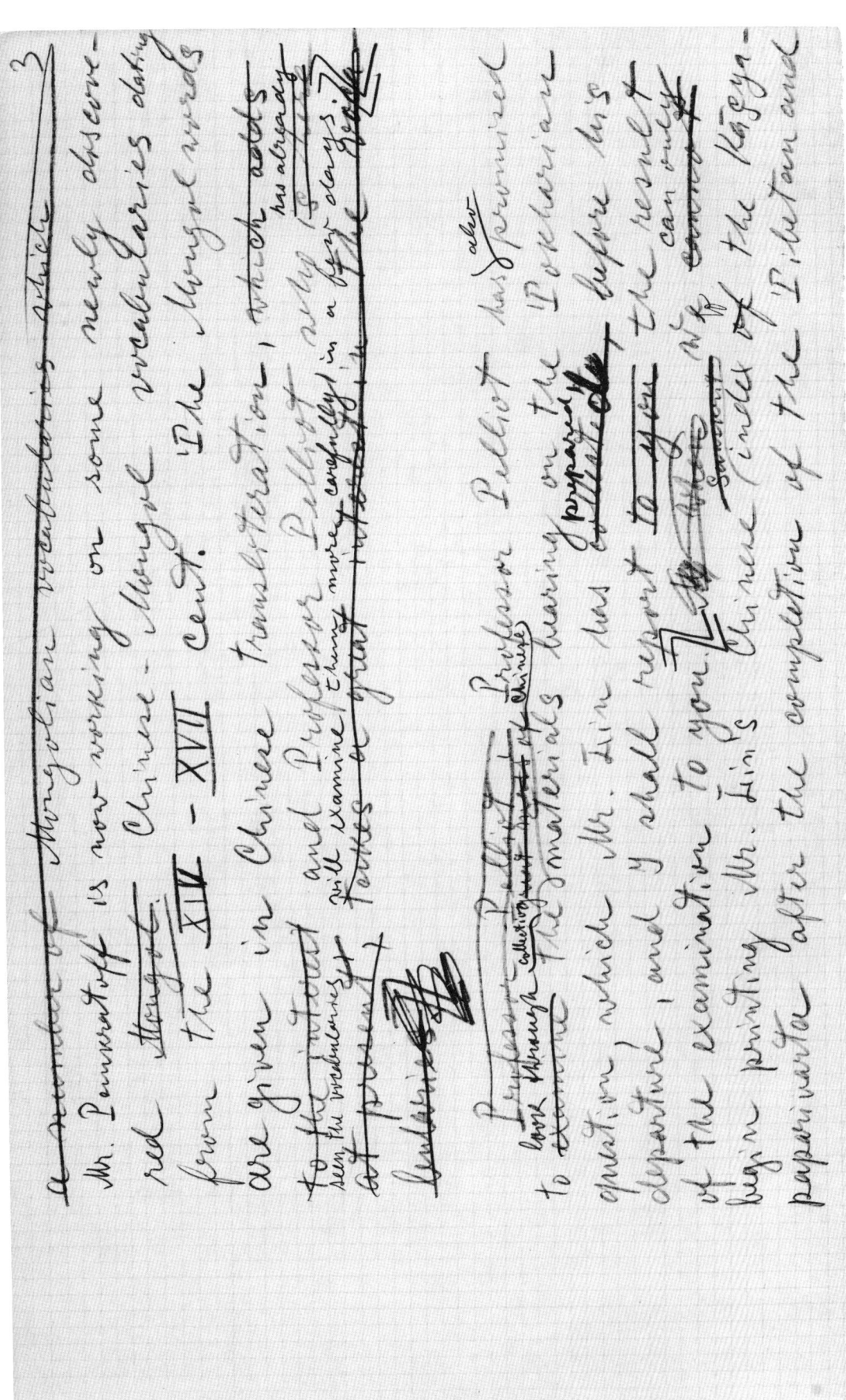

~~Professor Pelliot,~~ Professor Pelliot has also promised to look through ~~examine~~ the collection of Chinese materials bearing on the Tokharian question, which Mr. Lin has prepared ~~collected~~, before his departure, and I shall report ~~to you~~ the result of the examination to you. ~~We When~~ We can only ~~cannot~~ begin printing Mr. Lin's Chinese ~~Sanskrit~~ index of the Kāçyapaparivarta after the completion of the Tibetan and of the Sanskrit indices, because the ~~the~~ (Lazarist press ~~#~~ (Pei T'ang) has only a limited number of men, ~~workmen~~ who are able to ~~do handle the Sanskrit~~ that sort of work.

We have discovered a hitherto unknown supplement to the Kanjur, and Lama ~~Thale-bstan~~ 'Phags ldan ges rab is preparing ~~making~~ a detailed catalogue of the works which the volume contains.

~~M.V.B.~~ Professor Veller agrees with me in believing that Mr. Sickman is a most ~~very~~ serious student, ~~but we think that he is interested in~~ and we ~~think~~ ~~if~~ hope that he will be able to stay here for another year, in order to continue his researches. His field is the history of Chinese art, and he is ~~does~~ not ~~take any great~~ specially interested in philology.

5

Mr. Bodde, on the contrary, is a ~~very promising~~ convinced philologist, and when I examined him the other day I found that he had made considerable ~~prom pr~~ progress in Chinese. This is also the opinion of Professor Weller who, ~~tas,~~ of course, knows Mr. Bodde better than I do. We both ~~hope recommend would not hesitate in recommending Mr. Bodde, if the Trustees asked us, whether his do~~ ~~not hesitate in saying that the intere~~ feel certain that, in the interests of sinology, Mr. Bodde's stay here should be prolonged.

The ~~[illegible]~~ entire Text of the Kāçyapaparivarta commentary (Tibetan and Chinese) which I ~~edit~~ am editing for the National Library ~~[illegible]~~ (about a hundred pages were already printed

6

~~before I left for America)~~ is ~~now ready, and I have~~ ~~page 2 3~~ a proof sheet of ~~page 326.~~ the last page (326). ~~The variae lectiones and the preface are not quite ready yet.~~

The National University of Peking ~~[illegible]~~ (with a K, this is still its official name) possesses a unique edict of Ch'ien Lung addressed to his vassal the ~~King~~ King of Nepal. It is written in Manchu and Tibetan ~~only~~ (no Chinese)! I have translated the edict and added some historical notes to the translation, which are almost ready for print.

I ~~have also written~~ am also working on an article on the Buddhoṣṇīṣaśūraṃgamasūtra of which I have found a hitherto unknown edition in four languages (Chinese, Mongol, ~~[illegible]~~ Manchu and Tibetan). ~~I think I have found some arguments [illegible]~~ I hope to be able to prove that the sūtra never existed in Sanskrit.

I think I can offer a new explanation of the name Avalokiteçvara (Kuan Yin), which will be accepted by some orientalists, and I ~~have~~ am writing a paper on the subject.

I have also found some important documents connected with ~~the history of~~ the Dalai Lamas, and I continue my researches on Tibetan history.

I have, ~~bought~~ not long ago, bought Tibetan illustrations of the Jātakamālā which I want to edit.

I showed my Dalailama documents and the Jātakamālā paintings to Professor Pelliot yesterday, and he agreed with me in considering these materials as ~~[illegible]~~ very much worth publishing.

~~[illegible] I hope that I shall be able to [illegible] [illegible]~~ finish

Another document which I submitted to Professor Pelliot yesterday is the ~~Man Han~~ Yü Chih Man Han Mêng Ku Hsi Fan Ho Pi A Li Ka Li (mentioned in note 28 of my 1932 B. N. L. ~~XI~~ article on a Tibetan text &c.). Professor Pelliot had never heard of it before and ~~thought~~ he thinks that ~~this~~ the publication of my observations on Sanskrit - ~~Chinese~~ syllabary ~~vocabulary~~ almost exhaustive ~~should also be published soon~~ would be of some ~~importance~~ value.

I have a number of other publications in view ~~and I hope that I shall be enabled~~ and I venture to hope that I shall be allowed to finish ~~all~~ my papers in Peking (~~unfortunately not all~~), the only place in the world where most of the necessary documents are available.

~~Owing~~ thanks ~~to Dr. Dipper, my medical adviser, I feel much better~~ quite well ~~now, but I must submit to a very strict diet in order to be able to work. [illegible]~~

If we had not enjoyed the ~~financial~~ support of the Harvard-Yenching Institute, hardly any of the scientific efforts mentioned in this letter would have been possible, and I thank the Trustees most heartily for their liberality.

~~Among I have acquired a number of hitherto unknown~~
~~Iranistic iconographical material whi~~

Professor Pelliot also said that ~~he had never seen~~ the symbolical representations of ~~certain~~ the five senses and of the eight great Buddhist monuments (八大處), ~~were quite~~ which I acquired not long ago, were quite new to him. ~~Lately~~ I have the eight great monuments on a number of pictures, as well as in wood. The eight monuments are described in a poem which exists in several languages, and I intend publishing the poem with notes and with illustrations, as well as ~~the~~ photographs of Lamaism of the seven "personal gems" (including the seven league boots) which have never been properly described yet.

Weller & index
Pommer. Gramm
Stael Comm

Registered A.R.

To

Dean G. H. Chase
University Hall
Cambridge Mass.
U.S. of America

Peking, May 3rd 1933.

My dear Dean Chase,

Messrs. Creel, Sickman, and Bodde as well as myself are very grateful to you for your radiogram "notify Creel Sickman Bodde fellowships renewed" which arrived here on April 27th. I am also ~~very much~~ greatly obliged to you for your radiogram "June JAOS will print an explanatory note" which I received on April 14th. I enclose a photograph of a letter addressed to me by the American Minister which might interest you because it shows that Mr Johnson ~~thinks~~ considers my ~~grievance a well-founded one~~ complaint against the journal a very reasonable one.

In his letter dated January 18th 1932 Professor Woods writes: "With regard to the title of Dr. Weller's index, would it not be more logical to say "Index to the Tibetan Translation of the Kāçyapaparivarta, by Dr. Friedrich Weller, Volume -- of the Harvard Sino-Indian Series, published by the Harvard-Yenching Institute"?

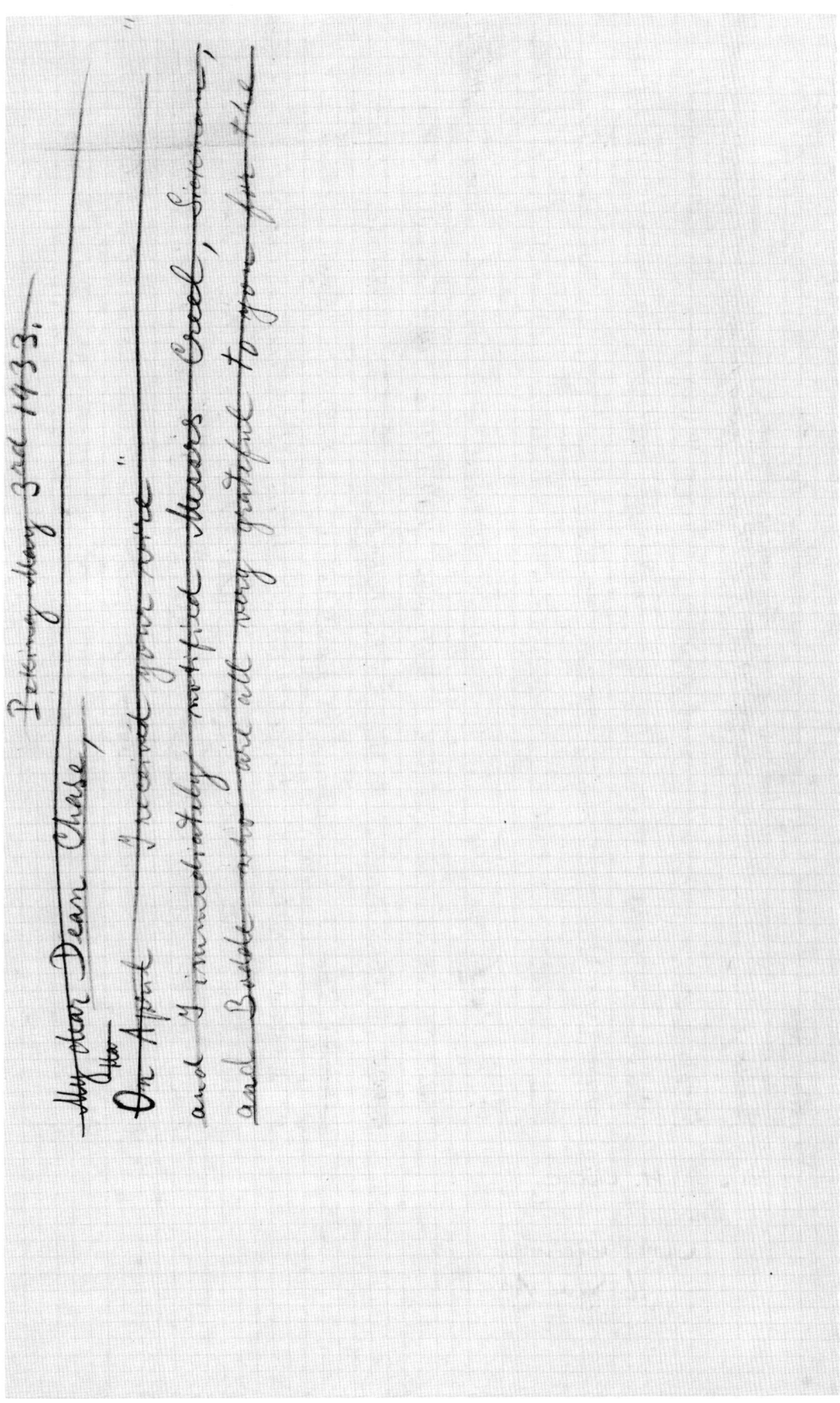

Peking May 3rd 1933.

My dear Dean Chase,

On 4th April "I received your wire"

and I immediately notified Messrs Creel, Siekmann,

and Boddé who are all very grateful to you for the

~~As you~~ I send you (under separate cover) a copy of Professor ~~of~~ Weller's Index to the Tibetan Translation of the Kāçyapaparivarta ~~index~~ and you will ~~see~~ find that we have ~~adopted Professor Woods' suggestion with one modification: we have put "Volume I of the Harvard Sino-Indian Series" first, and "I~~ almost exactly followed Professor Woods' directions. We have, however, had the words "Harvard Sino-Indian Series ~~II~~ Volume I" printed at the head of the title page because we find that ~~[illegible]~~ the volumes of similar ~~series~~ editions ~~[illegible]~~ ~~give~~ generally indicate the name of the series and the number ~~[illegible]~~ of the volume before giving the title ~~[illegible]~~ of the particular work. Pages 1–252 of Professor Weller's Index to the Tibetan Translation of the Kāçyapaparivarta ~~[illegible]~~ are already finally printed, but the title page and the preface are not. We shall finally ~~not~~ print the title page and the preface ~~[illegible]~~ only after having received your permission to do so. ~~[illegible]~~ Will you be so kind as to let me have your permission by a deferred ~~[illegible]~~ telegram?

If you wish us to change the title page or the preface, we shall, of course, have to wait until your directions arrive by letter.

~~I do not write~~ I shall ~~up~~ soon report to you about the progress of the other volumes which we have prepared at the Sino-Indian Institute.

Believe me yours sincerely and gratefully

A. Staël Holstein.

P. s.

~~[illegible]~~ I venture to write to you about the index because I hear that Professor Woods has gone to Europe.

~~[illegible]~~ Idem.

HARVARD-YENCHING INSTITUTE

17 BOYLSTON HALL
CAMBRIDGE, MASSACHUSETTS

May 9, 1933

My dear Professor von Stael-Holstein:-

I have waited to answer your letter of February 28th until everything was clear about the note for the JAOS. Just lately, I have heard from Prof. Norman W. Brown that he intends to place in the June number a note as follows:-

> In consequence of a misunderstanding of the editors of this Journal, the editors of Eastern Art, and Baron A. von Staël-Holstein, the Journal published in Volume 52, part 4 (December, 1932) an article by Baron von Staël-Holstein entitled "Notes on Two Lama Paintings" at the same time when a revised version of the same article entitled "On Two Tibetan Pictures representing Some of the Spiritual Ancestors of the Dalai Lama and of the Panchen Lama" appeared in the Bulletin of the National Library of Peiping, December, 1932."

He wrote me that he felt that this brief note covers the case, and it seemed to me that this was so. I don't wonder that you were disturbed at the double publication, but everyone, of course, would understand that it must have come about through some misunderstanding. Certainly, you ought not to feel that your friends here would ever suspect you of trying to arrange any double publication of this sort.

The members of the Educational Committee were greatly interested in all the details of your report and thoroughly agreed that you ought not to be disturbed in your schemes for publication. Next year, when Mr. Mei will return to us, we shall get along with Mr. Ware and Mr. Mei for the teaching of Chinese, adding to them Mr. Sidney Gardner, who is to give an introductory course on the history of China; and Mr. Kishimoto will continue to teach Japanese language and will offer a course having to do with the cultural background of Japanese history. With these courses we can, I think, take care of the men who will be studying here. We all feel very much pleased that you have been able to get rid of work with beginners and are very glad that you have had more time for advanced instruction. From out point of view, certainly, everything seems to be going very satisfactorily with the Sino-Indian Institute, and I gather that your feeling is similar.

Professor von Stael-Holstein, 2

We have been more and more convinced of the desirability of giving our fellowship holders - provided they are worthy - fairly long terms of tenure, and for the coming year no new fellows were appointed to go to China. This was partly due, of course, to the falling off in income of the Institute, but partly to the feeling that the older men should be carried forward.

The meeting of the Trustees was rather later this year owing to Dean Donham's absence from Cambridge, and so only lately have the details of the budget for 1933-34 been arranged. I am happy to say that we were able to make the same appropriation (LC$14,000) for the Sino-Indian Institute for 1933-34 that we made for 1932-33, and we hope this will prove adequate. Some other items were cut considerably from the amounts for the present year, and it is clear enough that we shall not get through 1933-34 without cutting deeply into reserve funds, but there was no proposal, either in the Educational Committee or in the meeting of the Trustees, to cut the Sino-Indian budget. We all hope, of course, that things will improve somewhat during the coming year, but I suspect that the Trustees will still be in a very saving mood in the spring of 1934 and will feel that the reserves should be built up somewhat before any expansion is undertaken.

Sincerely yours,

George H. Chase

Professor von Stael-Holstein,
Sino-Indian Institute,
ex-Austrian Legation,
Peiping, China.

HARVARD-YENCHING INSTITUTE

17 BOYLSTON HALL
CAMBRIDGE, MASSACHUSETTS

May 9, 1933

Dear Professor von Stael-Holstein:-

I am writing a separate letter about a separate matter. The Trustees, at their meeting, decided that it would be very helpful for the Institute if Prof. Elisséeff, who has greatly impressed us all during the year, returned to Paris by way of China, and it worked out that his plans allowed this. He is therefore, planning to sail May 26th on the PRESIDENT HARRISON from San Francisco, which will bring him to Shanghai on June 19th and to Peking some time later. We have told him to get in touch with you as soon as he reaches Peiping, and I have specially written to the holders of fellowships, asking them to find out through you or Professor Porter when Professor Elisséeff will arrive and to be sure to have a conference with him. He has made a number of very helpful suggestions - as it seemed to me - about the programs of study which the fellows are pursuing, and I am sure that personal conferences with him will help them; and we are anxious for him to see the type of men that we have been appointing.

You know Professor Elisséeff, I understand, and of his reputation as an excellent scholar. We regard him as a thoroughly good fellow whom we have all come to admire greatly during his year with us.

Very sincerely yours,

George H. Chase

Professor von Stael-Holstein,
Sino-Indian Institute,
ex-Austrian Legation,
Peiping, China.

HARVARD-YENCHING INSTITUTE

17 BOYLSTON HALL
CAMBRIDGE, MASSACHUSETTS

June 27, 1933

My dear Baron:-

I am late in acknowledging your letter of May 3rd because of the difficulty with the end of the year, but I did get Professor Clark to look at the title page of Dr. Weller's index and his opinion agreed with mine that the arrangement which you made was an improvement on that suggested before, so I know Miss Bayley cabled you:

"Title page, preface entirely satisfactory,"

and I hope this arrived in good time.

I shall certainly look forward to hearing about the progress of the other volumes which you have prepared at the Sino-Indian Institute. Certainly, it is good news that things are going forward with the publications and, of course, the Institute is proud to have a share in them.

I am off to the country at the end of the week, but I shall be back in Cambridge now and then during the summer.

With every good wish, I am

Sincerely yours,

George H. Chase
per B.

Baron von Stael-Holstein,
Sino-Indian Institute,
Ex-Austrian Legation,
Peiping, China.

Peking, August 29th 1933.

My dear Dean Chase

Many thanks for your telegram (dated May 16th 1933) and for your letters (dated May 9th and June 21th 1933). ~~They have greatly encouraged me~~ I highly appreciate the encouraging statements which they contain, and I enjoy my work at the Sino-Indian Institute more than ever since I received them.

~~Our photographer has been abs~~ ~~I send~~ I am sending you ~~to-day~~ (under separate cover) Professor Weller's index and my edition of the Kāçyapaparivarta-commentary. ~~The Artist~~ ~~I could~~ ~~I had asked Tsinghua University and the National Library to publish my edition before I went~~

√I was very glad to meet my old colleague Elisséeff again, whom I had not seen since 1916. In that year we travelled together from St. Petersburg to Tōkyō. ~~[illegible]~~ At the time of Elisséeff's ~~[illegible]~~ [recent] visit ~~some~~ [here] ~~most~~ [most] of my friends (foreign and Chinese) were absent from Peking on account of the summer vacation, ~~but I managed to introduce him to some s~~ and I could [not] introduce him to ~~the leaders of Ch all the~~ as many intellectual leaders as I should have wished. I arranged, however, a number of small parties for him, at which he made the acquaintance of some local scholars.

~~to America in 1928., and could That is the reason why I could my edition could not be printed in the Harvard Sino-Indian Series~~

The latter could not appear in the Harvard Sino-Indian series, because a part of it had already been (printed under the auspices of ~~published by~~ (The National Library and Tsinghua University before I left for America in 1928. I shall send you a much longer letter ~~detailed report~~ before the end of next month.

Believe me yours sincerely and gratefully A. Staël-Holstein.

~~I have spent the whole summer in Peking, and I intend I am leaving Peking for a holiday of about three weeks after having spent the whole summer here, and I shall send you a detailed report after my return. [illegible]~~

Peking, October 5th 1933.

My dear Dean Chase,

In September 1932 I reported to you that ~~the~~ ~~the~~ one of the volumes of the printed Kanjur which I bought for Cambridge [illegible] was missing and that it had been replaced by a manuscript copy of the entire volume. The Lama who sold the collection to me promised to supply the missing printed volume before long. I paid the entire sum ~~[illegible]~~ (twenty two ~~thousand~~ Mexican dollars), but two hundred Mexican dollars were left with a middleman, and the Lama was not to get them before delivery of the missing printed volume. The two hundred Mexican dollars were to be returned to me in May 1933, if the Lama should fail to produce the printed volume. The volume never came, and ~~I received~~ the money (was returned to me in May 1933). ~~What shall I do with the [illegible] two hundred Mexican dollars?~~ There is practically no hope of finding the ~~printed~~ missing printed volume. What ~~shall I do with~~ is to be done with the two hundred Mexican dollars? Shall I use them for the purposes of the Sino-Indian Institute or shall I return ~~[illegible]~~ the sum to you?

Peking, ~~September~~ October 7th 1933.

My dear Dean Chase,

During the year ending on June 30th 1933 I received twelve thousand one hundred and eighty four Mexican dollars and eighty three cents (12184.83) ~~[illegible]~~ on account of assistants from the Treasurer of Yenching University, ~~and I paid~~ and I had to pay ~~I could not dismiss~~ ~~I had to pay~~ (fourteen thousand ~~four~~ two hundred and ~~eighty~~ forty four Mexican dollars and eighty three cents (14244.83) to my assistants during the same period. (and the deficit ~~was~~ ~~[illegible]~~ of two thousand ~~three hundred~~ and sixty Mexican dollars (2060.00) was made up as follows: I ~~paid~~ used two thousand ~~one hundred~~ and sixty ~~(more than~~ Mexican dollars (2060.00) out of the four thousand Mexican dollars (4000.00) which I received ~~on account~~ of representation ~~and I used the~~.

~~On account~~ In order to cover the resulting deficit I ~~had to~~ used two thousand and sixty Mexican dollars (2060.00) out of the four thousand Mexican dollars (4000.00), which I received on account of representation from the Treasurer*, for ~~my~~ the assistants.

~~The total sum paid to the assistants~~ Professor Weller (comp. page below) received six thousand one hundred and eighty four Mexican dollars and eighty three cents (6184.83), Mr. Pankratoff (comp. page below) four thousand eight hundred Mexican dollars (4800.00), Mr Lin (comp. page below) one thousand nine hundred and twenty Mexican dollars (1920.00), Lama Thabs ~~[illegible]~~ ges rab (comp. page below) six hundred and twenty Mexican dollars (620.00), ~~and Mr. Teng seven hundred and twenty Mexican dollars (720.00)~~.

* During the year ending on June 30th 1933 I received altogether

8090.71
8094.12
16184.83

~~sixteen thousand one hundred~~ ~~from the Treasurer~~ of ~~Yenching University.~~ sixteen thousand one hundred and eighty four Mexican dollars and eighty three cents (16184.83) from the Treasurer of Yenching University.

Mr. Tʻêng [(comp. page below)] four hundred and eighty Mexican dollars (480.00), and Mr. Ku [(comp. page below)] two hundred and forty Mexican dollars (240.00).

~~I understand that last year the autumn meeting of the Trustees was held on November 14th, and I hope that this ~~belated~~ report~~

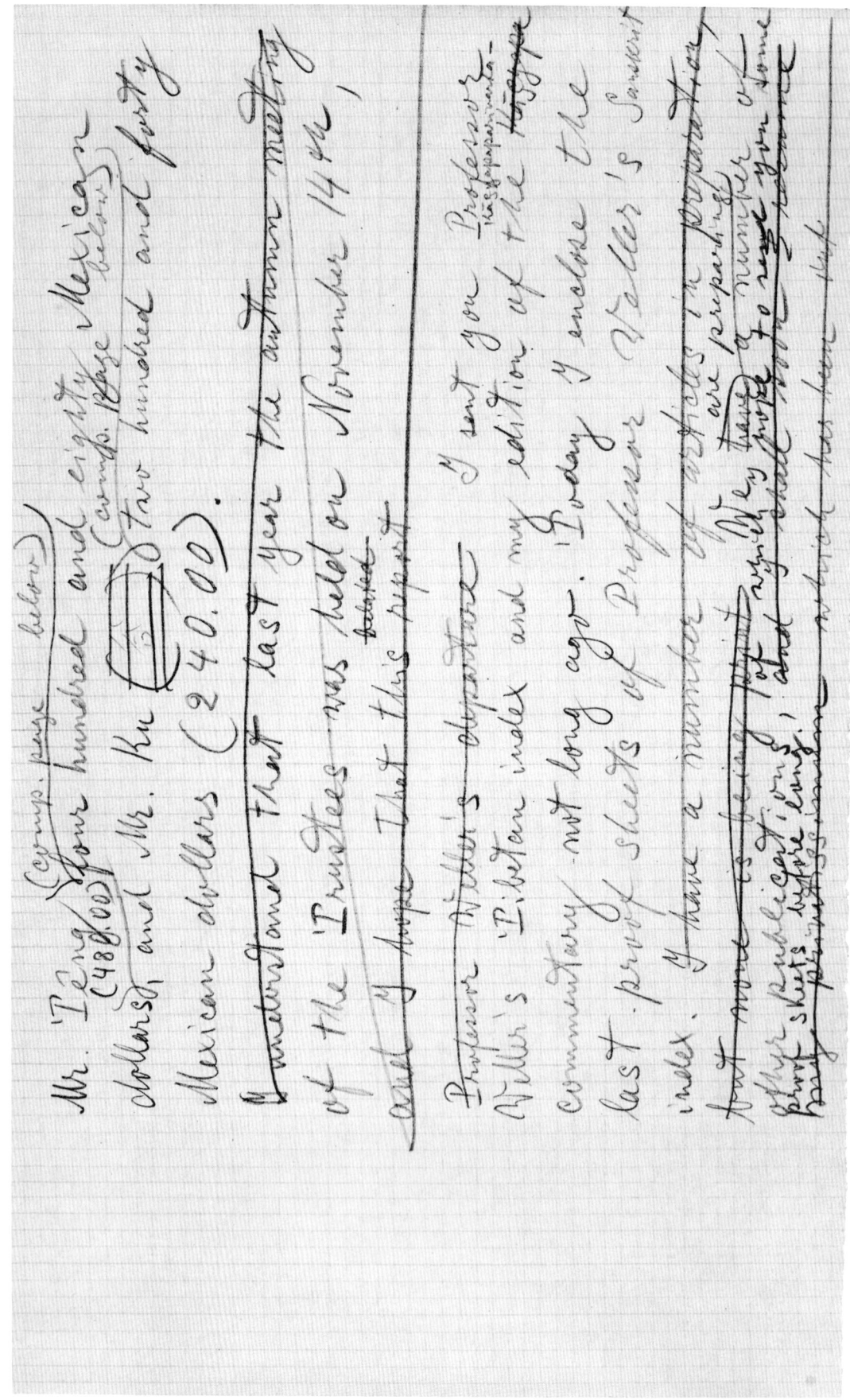

~~Professor Weller's departure~~ I sent you Professor Weller's Tibetan index and my edition of the Kāśyapaparivarta-~~Kāśyapa~~ commentary not long ago. Today I enclose the last proof sheets of Professor Weller's Sanskrit index. ~~I have a number of articles in preparation, but none is being print~~ We ~~I~~ ~~have~~ are preparing a number of other publications, of which ~~I~~ hope to ~~send~~ you some proof sheets before long. ~~and I shall soon resume my printing of the ... which has been ...~~

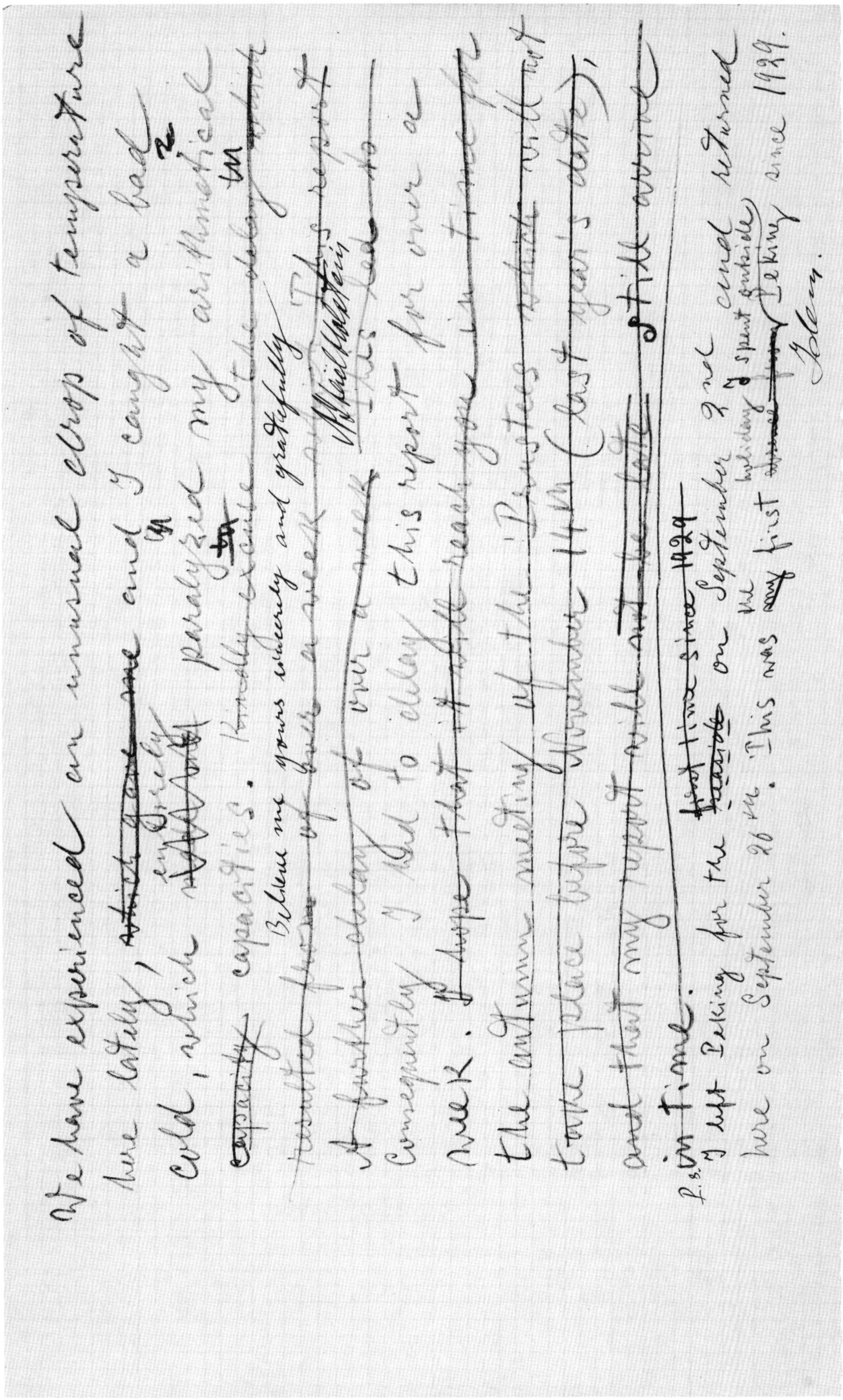

We have experienced an unusual drop of temperature here lately, ~~which gave me~~ and I caught a bad cold, which [entirely] ~~[illegible]~~ paralyzed my arithmetical ~~capacity~~ capacities. ~~Kindly excuse the delay which resulted from of over a week~~ ~~This report~~ ~~A further delay of over a week~~ ~~This led to~~ Consequently I had to delay this report for over a week. ~~I hope that it will reach you in time for the autumn meeting of the Trustees which will not take place before November 14th (last year's date), and that my report will not be late still arrive in time.~~

[Believe me yours sincerely and gratefully]

[A. Staël Holstein]

P.S. I left Peking for the ~~seaside~~ [~~first time since 1929~~] on September 2nd and returned here on September 26th. This was ~~my~~ [the] first ~~absence from~~ [holiday I spent outside] Peking since 1929.

Yolan.

HARVARD-YENCHING INSTITUTE

17 BOYLSTON HALL
CAMBRIDGE, MASSACHUSETTS

November 27, 1933

Dear Professor Stael-Holstein,-

I have been waiting to acknowledge your recent letters and the report of the Sino-Indian Institute until after the Trustees' meeting, which was held on November 13th.

The Trustees, as always, were greatly pleased with the report, which gives such a clear picture of the activities of the Sino-Indian Institute. The members of the Educational Committee asked me to inquire whether the report could be sent earlier in future years so that it might be considered by that committee before the Trustees' meeting on the second Monday in November.

In regard to the LC$200, which you received when the printed volume of the Kanjur was not delivered, the Trustees

<u>VOTED</u>: That Professor A. von Stael-Holstein be permitted to use, toward the deficit in expenses of the Sino-Indian Institute for 1932-33, the sum of LC$200, retained from the price of the Kanjur, purchased by him for the Institute, until a missing printed volume of the set was delivered to him.

It seemed to all of us that this was much the most reasonable disposition of the balance.

Everything here goes ahead normally. Mr. Gardner is this year offering, for the first time, a course in the history of China, which is taken by a small number of students, but we hope to be able to continue the course in future years, when it ought to grow. Professor Mei is back after a year in China, and we are happy this year in having Laurence Binyon as visiting professor on the Norton lectureship. He is lecturing on Chinese art very charmingly and making a very distinct impression. Our graduate students are continuing to hold informal meetings about once a month, which serve an excellent purpose in bringing them together and giving them a feeling of solidarity.

Our principal worry is, of course, about finances. No one seems to be at all sure of what course the dollar will take, but we have hopes that before the spring meeting something will be settled, so that we may know a little bit better where we stand.

Cordially yours,

George H. Chase

Professor A. von Stael-Holstein,
Sino-Indian Institute,
Peiping, China.

Peking, February 25th 1934.

My dear Dean Chase,

Some of my ~~wisest and most~~ oldest and ~~wisest~~ most experienced neighbours have, with ~~some~~ a great deal of concern, observed the extreme modesty which I display whenever ~~they meet me~~ I ~~see~~ meet them. In order to prevent this ~~exaggerated~~ excessive modesty from degenerating into what is now generally called "an inferiority complex" they suggested not long ago, that I should start a collection of Compliments.

Our sadly reduced circumstances (the Sino-Indian appropriation, which used to be 26 thousand Mex. dollars, has lately been cut down to 14 thousand Mex. dollars) ~~seriously~~ considerably interfere with my collecting activities, because ~~we~~ I cannot subscribe to very many journals. In spite of this handicap my collection ~~that~~ is progressing fairly well.

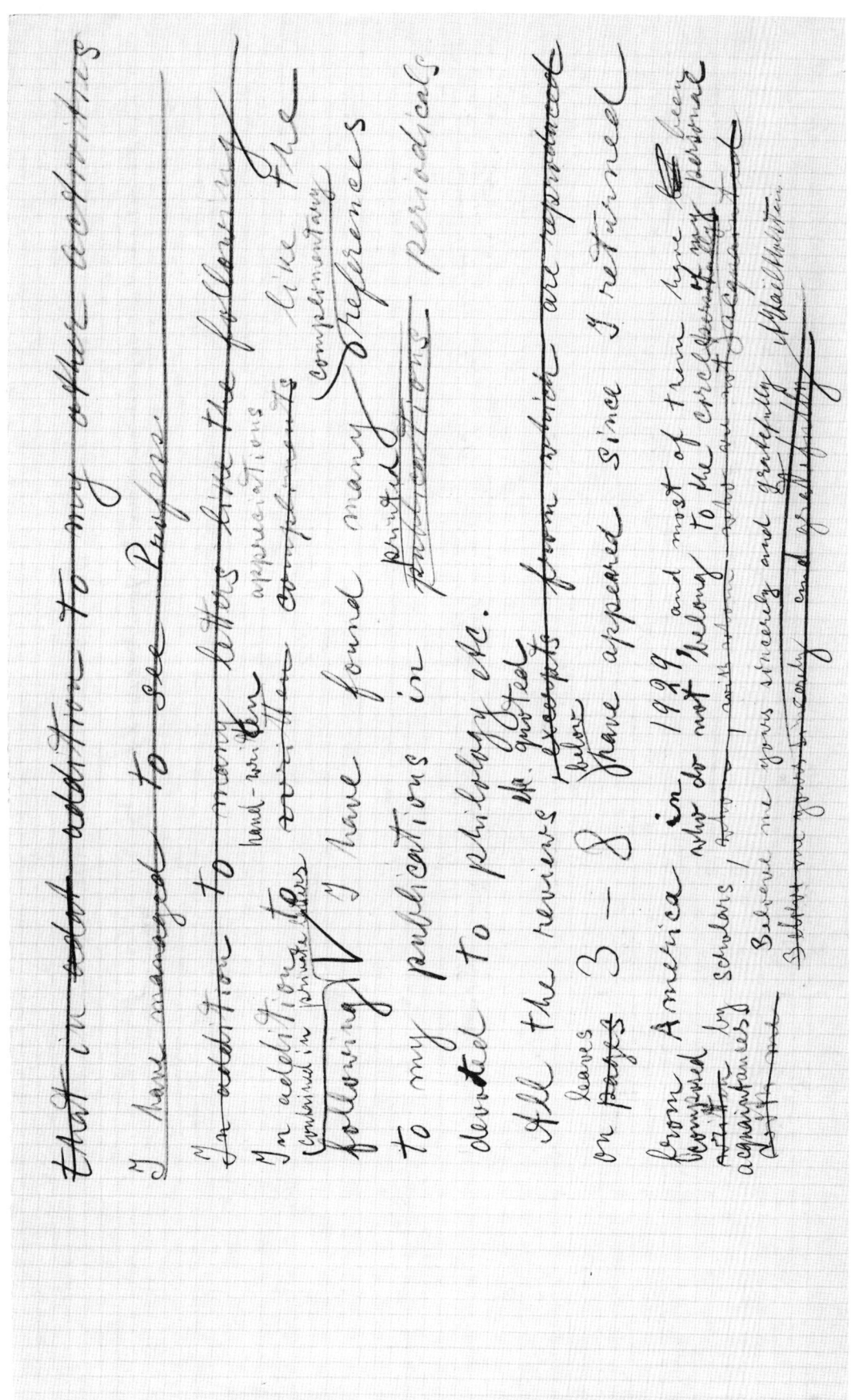

~~that in adat addition to my other activities~~

~~I have managed to see Profess.~~

~~In addition to many letters like the following~~

In addition to ~~written~~ hand-written ~~compliments~~ appreciations like the following (contained in private letters) I have found many ~~references~~ complementary references to my publications in ~~publications~~ printed periodicals devoted to philology etc.

All the reviews etc. ~~excerpts from which are reproduced~~ quoted below on ~~pages~~ leaves 3 – 8 have appeared since I returned from America in 1929, and most of them have ~~been~~ been ~~written~~ composed by scholars, who do not belong to the circle ~~of~~ of my personal acquaintances ~~who, with whom who are not acquainted with me~~

Believe me yours sincerely and gratefully A. Staël Holstein.

~~Believe me yours sincerely and gratefully~~

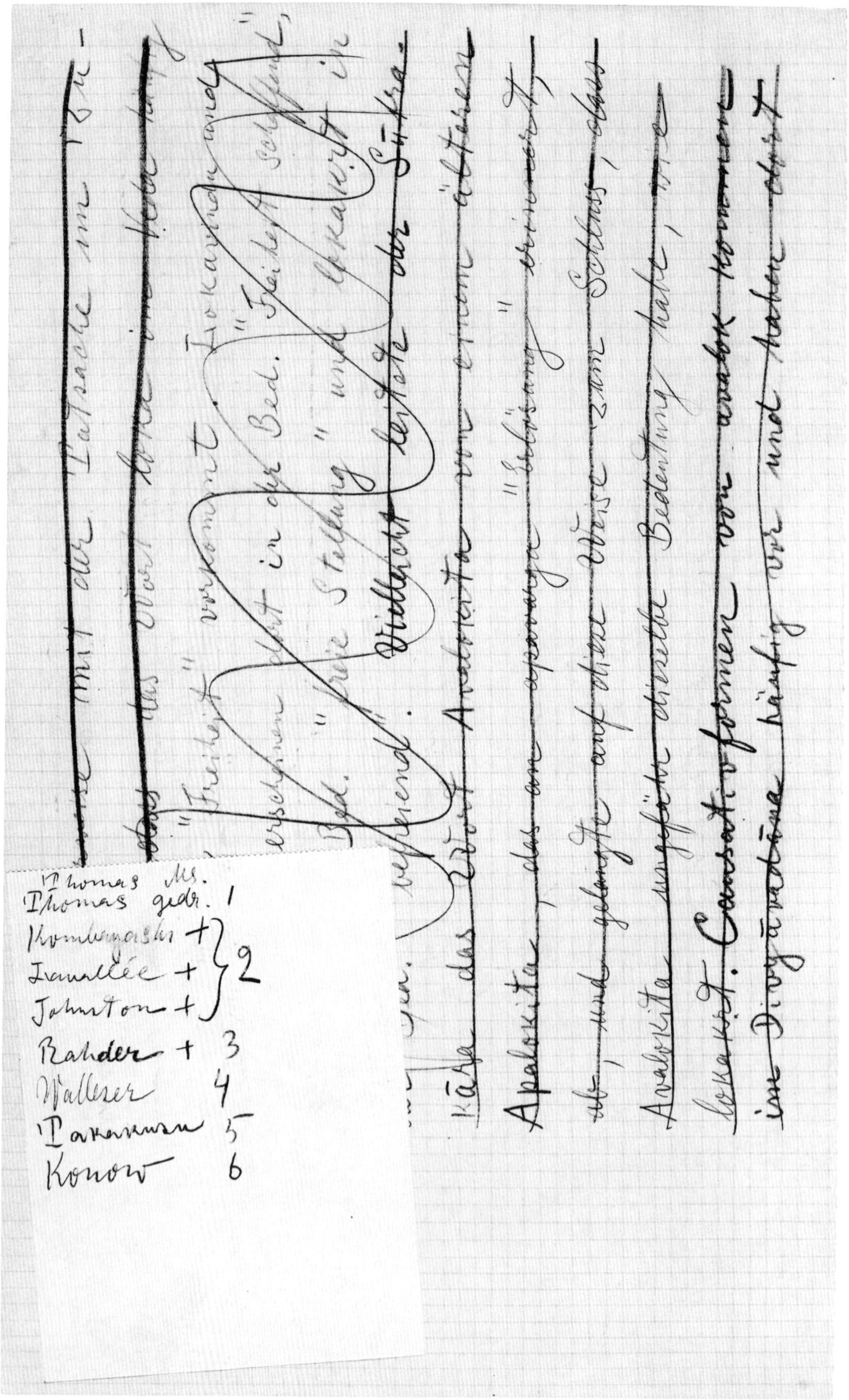
Thomas Ms.
Thomas gedr. 1
Kombumashi + }
Lavallée + } 2
Johnston + }
Rahder + 3
Walleser 4
Takakusu 5
Konow 6

~~…weise mit der Tatsache im Zu-~~
~~… dass das Wort loka im Veda häufig~~
~~… "Freiheit" vorkommt. Lokavinda und~~
~~… erscheinen dort in der Bed. "Freiheit schaffend",~~
~~… Bed. "freie Stellung" und lokakṛt in~~
~~… Bed. "befreiend". Vielleicht leitete der Sūtra-~~
~~kāra das Wort Avalokita von einem älteren~~
~~Apalokita, das an apavarga "Erlösung" erinnert,~~
~~ab, und gelangte auf diese Weise zum Schluss, dass~~
~~Avalokita ungefähr dieselbe Bedeutung habe, wie~~
~~lokakṛt. Causativformen von avalok kommen~~
~~im Divyāvadāna häufig vor und haben dort~~

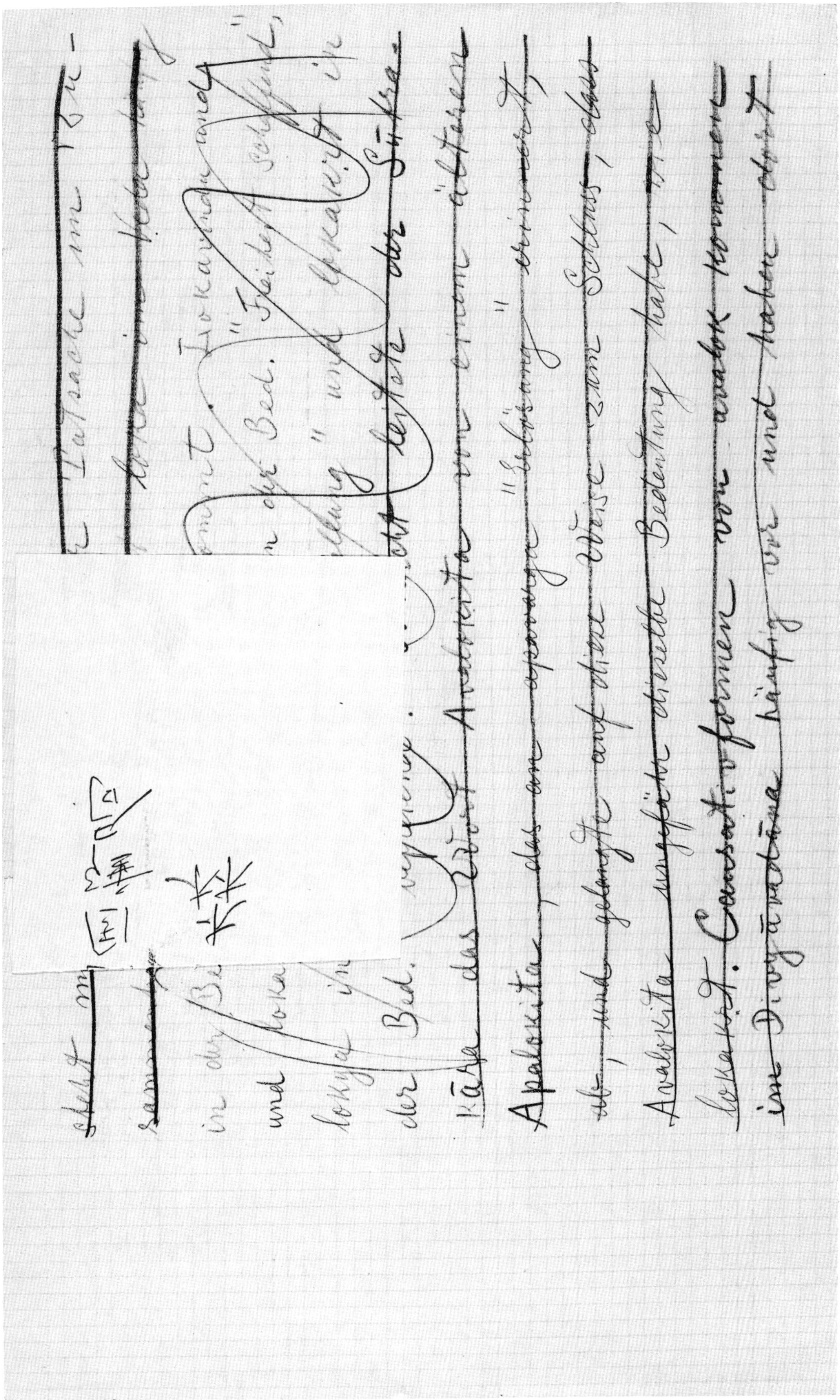

stellt m... Tatsache im Zu-
sammen... loka im Veda häufig
in der Be... kommt. Lokavanda und
und loka... n der Bed. "Freiheit schaffend",
lokya in... llung" und lokakṛt in
der Bed. "verschaffend". ... leitete der Sūtra-
kāra das Wort Avalokita von einem älteren
Apalokita, das an apavarga "Erlösung" erinnert,
ab, und gelangte auf diese Weise zum Schluss, dass
Avalokita ungefähr dieselbe Bedeutung habe, wie
lokakṛt. Causativformen von avalok kommen
im Divyāvadāna häufig vor und haben dort

Anm.:

I send you ~~a few~~ only some ~~samples~~ of the foreign compliments I received. ~~I do not think it necessary to refer to the Chinese compliments, because~~ ~~fact that the highest Chinese authorities~~

~~I think I need not refer prove the in detail to the ~~Ch~~ fact that the highest Chinese authorities value my publications, because this has~~ No Chinese compliments are attached to this letter, because a number of ~~I think that you have already received~~ documents, ~~proving showing~~ which seem to prove that the highest ~~Chinese~~ authorities of this country appreciate ~~value~~ my work ~~publications~~ ~~have already been forwarded~~ were sent to your address long ago.

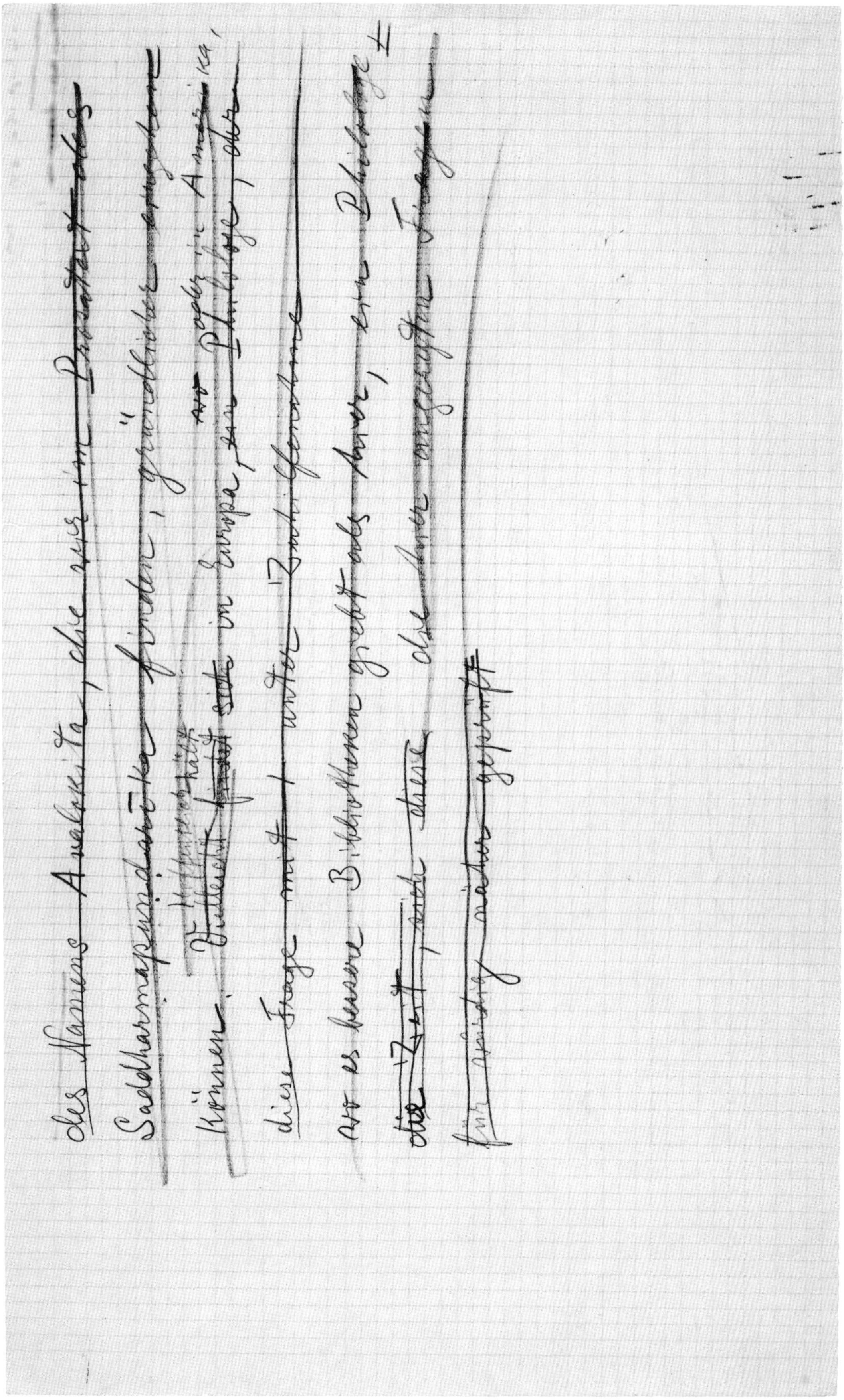

des Namens Avalokita, die wir im Prosatext des
Saddharmapuṇḍarīka finden, gründlicher angehen
können. Vielleicht Hoffentlich hält sich in Europa, wo oder in Amerika, ein Philologe, der
diese Frage mit / unter Zuhilfenahme
wo es bessere Bibliotheken giebt als hier, ein Philologe
die Zeit, sich diese die hier angeregten Fragen
für würdig näher geprüft

Peking, February 27th 1934

My dear Dean Chase,

~~Kindly excuse the delay~~ I am very sorry to hear that my last report ~~was late for the~~ did not reach Cambridge in time for the meeting of the Educational Committee, and I ~~hope that this letter shall try~~ hope that I shall never be late again. Z I am very much obliged to you and to the other Trustees for the vote concerning the two hundred Mex~~ican~~ dollars.

(My knowledge of purely Chinese things)
is extremely limited. ~~I have never read any purely Chinese text,~~
The only Chinese texts, which I have [seriously] studied, are translations of Indian originals, and I have hardly ever touched any Confucian or Taoist books. ~~[illegible]~~ This being so, I am not ~~in a position~~ [able] to appreciate the progress made by Messrs. Sickman and ~~[illegible]~~ Bodde properly. ~~I see them, [however] from time to time, and I am~~ As long as Professor Weller, who ~~was~~ [is] ~~of~~ a qualified teacher of Chinese (he has held a "Lehrauftrag" for Chinese at Leipzig for a number of years),

was ~~here~~ in Peking) I could ~~report~~ consult him ~~and~~ before sending you reports concerning Messrs. Sickman and Bodde. ~~But our sadly reduced circumstances~~ ~~(the~~ But I ~~could not~~ was not in a position to keep Professor Weller here on account of our sadly reduced circumstances (~~a~~ the Sino-Indian appropriation, which used to be 26 ~~th~~ thousand Mex. dollars has recently been cut down to 14 thousand Mex. dollars), and he has returned to Leipzig. ~~about ten months ago.~~

I see Messrs. Sickman and Bodde ~~at~~ from time to time, and I am under the impression

that they are ~~doing very well~~ working ~~very satisfactorily~~ hard in
their respective fields. I examined
Mr. Bodde the other day as well as
I could, and ~~that~~ found that his knowledge
of Chinese characters ~~had considerably~~ was very satisfactory.
~~increased since last February 3. 1932.~~
~~I am now teaching Mr. , an extremely~~
~~gifted young Chinese scholar, who already~~
~~knows~~ Sanskrit. Mr. an extremely
gifted young Chinese scholar, who already ~~knows~~
a great deal of ~~Sanskrit~~ (Tibetan, is making ~~goo~~ excellent progress ~~in Sanskrit~~

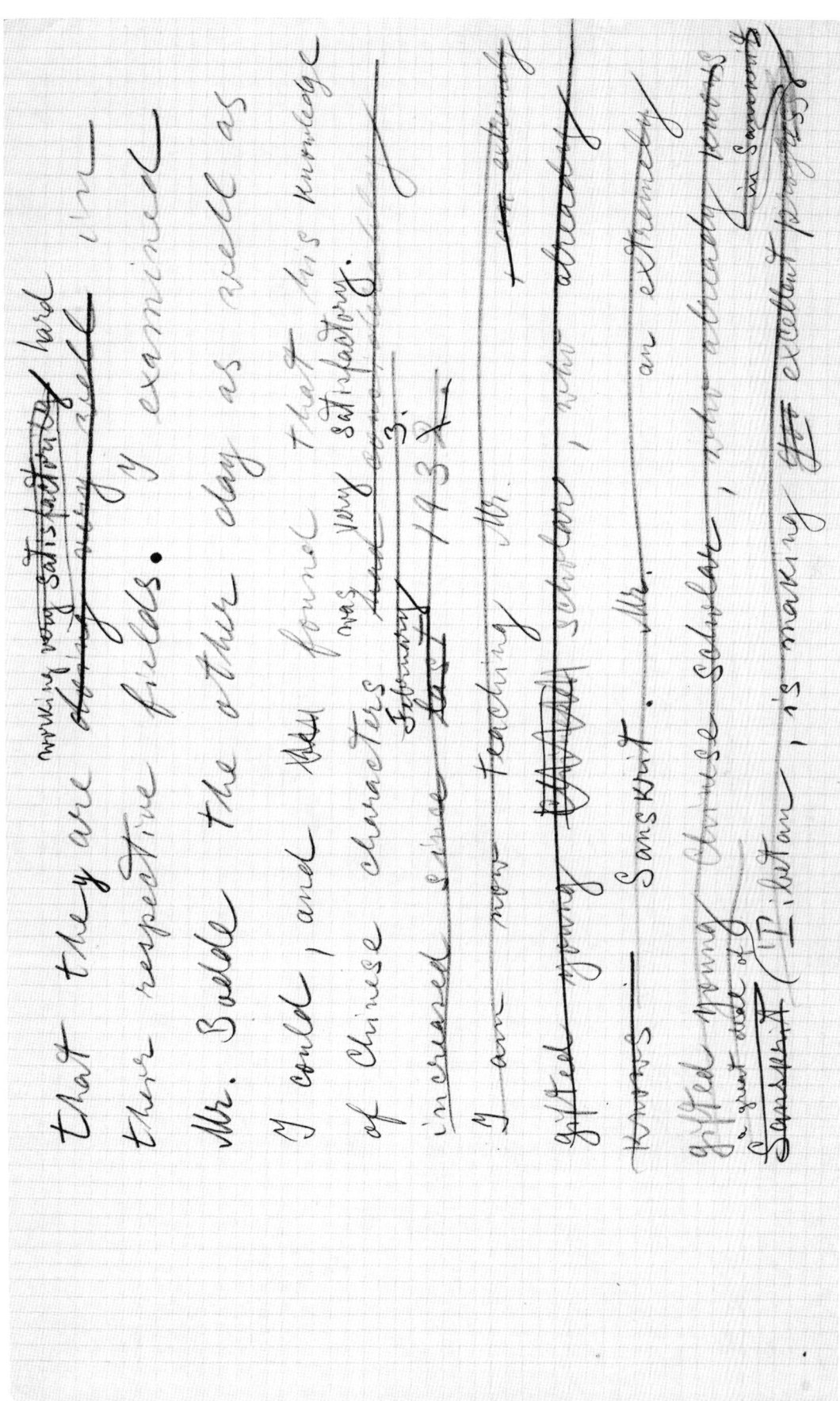

I am now ~~teaching~~ giving Sanskrit lessons to a young Chinese ~~scholar~~ linguist, ~~who is a~~ (Mr. Y. N. Li), who is connected with the Academia Sinica. He already knows a great deal of Tibetan, Mongolian etc. and promises to become a fine Sino-Indian scholar.

I ~~am~~ also continue my "privatissimum" on the Sino-Tibetan commentary of the Kāçyapaparivarta. In addition to Professor Y. K. Tschen Dr. Walter Liebenthal attends the "privatissimum". He is a pupil of Professor Lüders (Berlin) × ~~who~~ and has travelled to China at the expense of the "Notgemeinschaft der deutschen Wissenschaft". Dr. Liebenthal, ~~whose doctor's dissertation I am sending you under separate cover,~~ has promised to complete ~~the Chinese~~

He is a pupil of Professor Lüders (Berlin)
and has come to China at my ~~invitation~~ suggestion.
Our extremely reduced circumstances
did not allow me to pay ~~for~~ ~~this Jewish refugee's~~ his ~~the~~ ~~passage~~ journey
from Berlin to Peking, and we have to thank ~~the~~ the Notgemein-
schaft der deutschen Wissenschaft ~~has helped~~
~~us by for making~~ for enabling him to ~~accept~~ join
~~my invitation~~ our group of Sino-Indian students.
~~Dr. Liebenthal, whose doctor's dissertation I am~~
~~sending you under separate cover, has~~
~~promised to compleete the~~

I greatly admire the ~~leaders~~ authorities of the Notgemein-
schaft (Prof. Lüders etc.) for ~~having~~ found (one thousand marks) the money Dr. Liebenthal needed in spite of the fact that he
is a Jew, who ~~considers~~ regards himself as a refugee.
I venture to hope that circumstances will not necessitate a further reduction of the Sino-Indian
appropriation, and that I shall be able to keep
Dr. Liebenthal here for some time. He has promised to complete the

index ~~of~~ to the Chinese translations
of the Kāśyapaparivarta, which Mr. I. K.
Iin had almost ~~begun~~ finished. Mr. Iin left us, ~~in~~
~~Augus~~ to our great regret, in August 1933,
and has gone to Paris, where he now
holds the position of Chinese instructor
at the École des Langues Orientales
Vivantes. He wants to return to the
Sino-Indian Institute in ~~thd~~ 1935, but
I could promise him nothing definite ≠
in view of the unsettled condition of world finances~~, which has~~

~~I had (very foolishly, I admit) already made~~
~~certain financial engagemen arrangements~~
~~for FY 32/33, and the result was~~ I still
deplore the (whenever I inspect my banking account.) ~~results of my rashness.~~ ~~The~~
~~fact that my assistants cann~~ ~~I cannot~~
~~make any definite contracts precise which my with my as-~~
~~sistants, who have to live from hand to~~
~~mouth, is a great serious handicap. Serious studies~~
Mr. ~~Lin~~ I. K. Lin is regarded as ~~a great~~
~~asset~~ something like a national asset by
the ~~Am~~ Chinese Academy of Sciences, who greatly

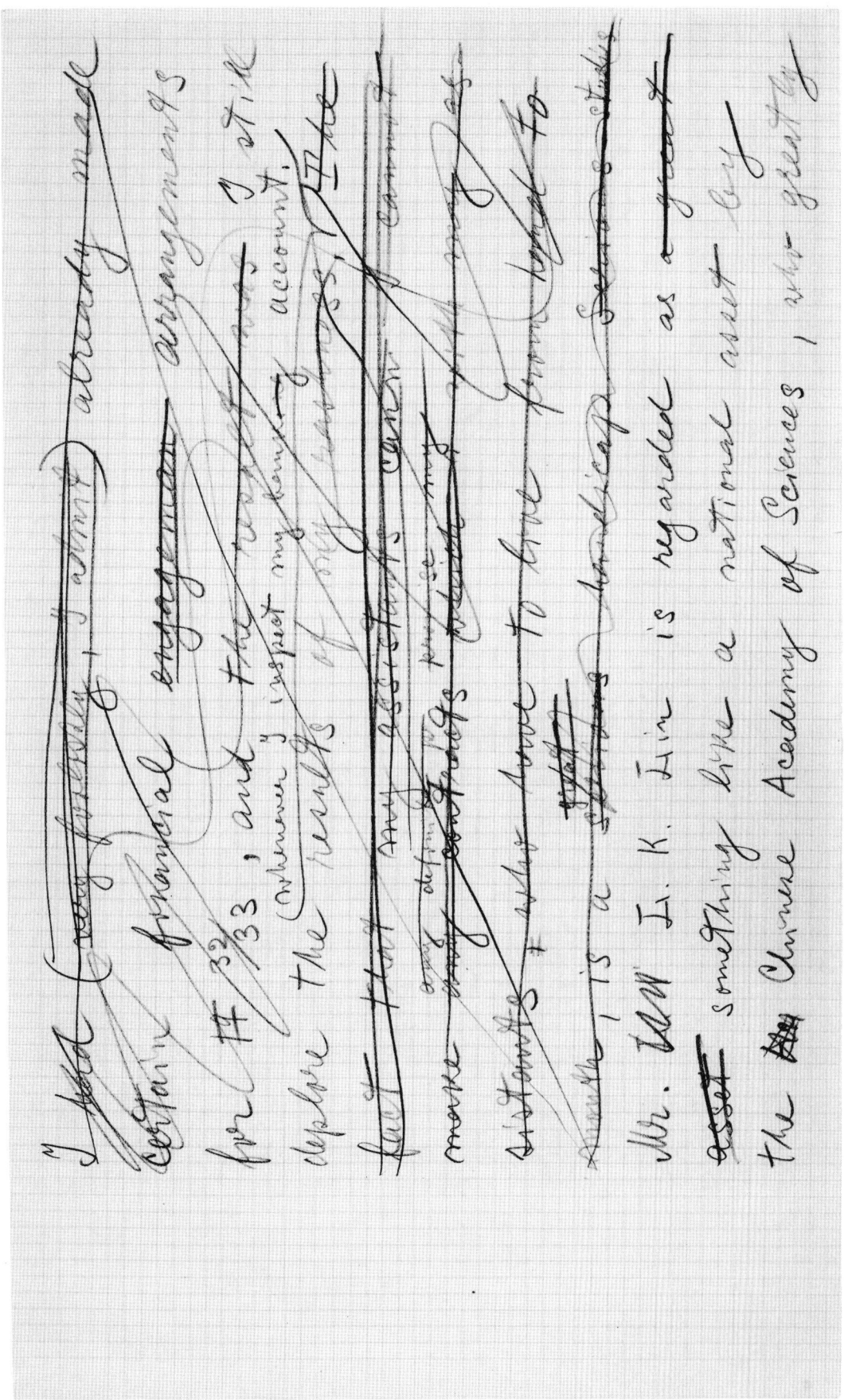

value his knowledge of Sanskrit and Tibetan ×
(acquired during his four years' study at the
Sino-Indian ~~Ir~~ Institute). The authorities of the Chinese Academy
proved ~~their (interest)~~ the interest they take
in Mr. Lin by paying ~~his~~ for his passage
to ~~Fran~~ France. ~~Another former pupil~~
~~of mine, Mr Mr T. C. Yü, is being sent~~
~~to Europe by the Chinese Government,~~

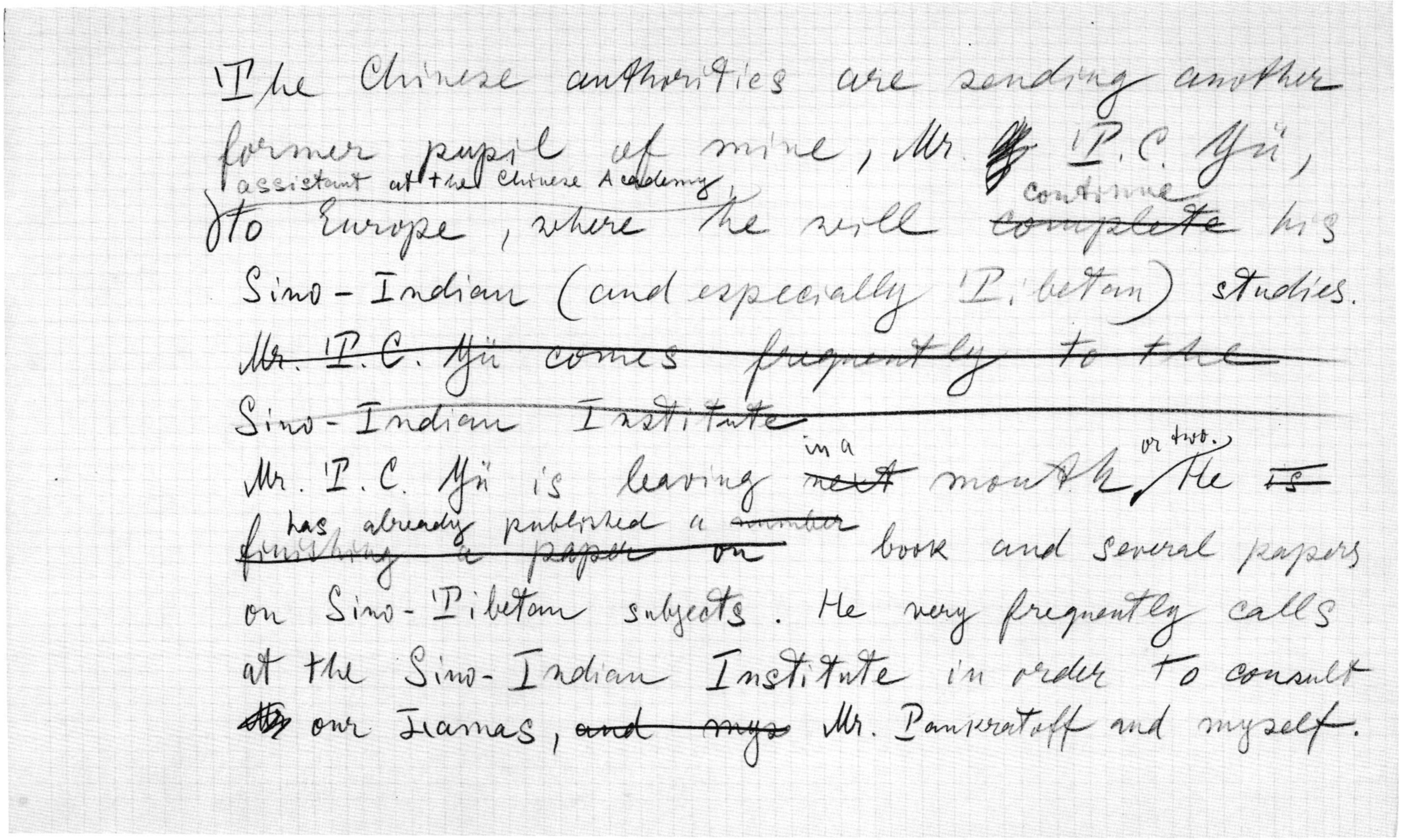

The Chinese authorities are sending another former pupil of mine, Mr. ~~[illegible]~~ T. C. Yü, assistant at the Chinese Academy, to Europe, where he will ~~complete~~ continue his Sino-Indian (and especially Tibetan) studies. ~~Mr. T. C. Yü comes frequently to the Sino-Indian Institute~~

Mr. T. C. Yü is leaving ~~next~~ in a month or two. He ~~is finishing a paper on~~ has already published a ~~number~~ book and several papers on Sino-Tibetan subjects. He very frequently calls at the Sino-Indian Institute in order to consult ~~[illegible]~~ our Lamas, ~~and mys~~ Mr. Pankratoff and myself.

Mr. Pankratoff's Dagurian grammar, which is being printed ~~ters~~ at the Pei 'P'ang, has not made much progress lately, because the few competent type-setters available have been busy with my ~~pref~~ articles and Professor Weller's Sanskrit index, the last ~~pages~~ 28 pages (proof sheets) of which I am sending you under separate cover. ~~index of which I enclose the last pages~~

~~An article by Mr. Pankratoff (on the Kao Seng Chuan) has been accepted by the Bulletin of the National Library of Peking and will soon appear.~~

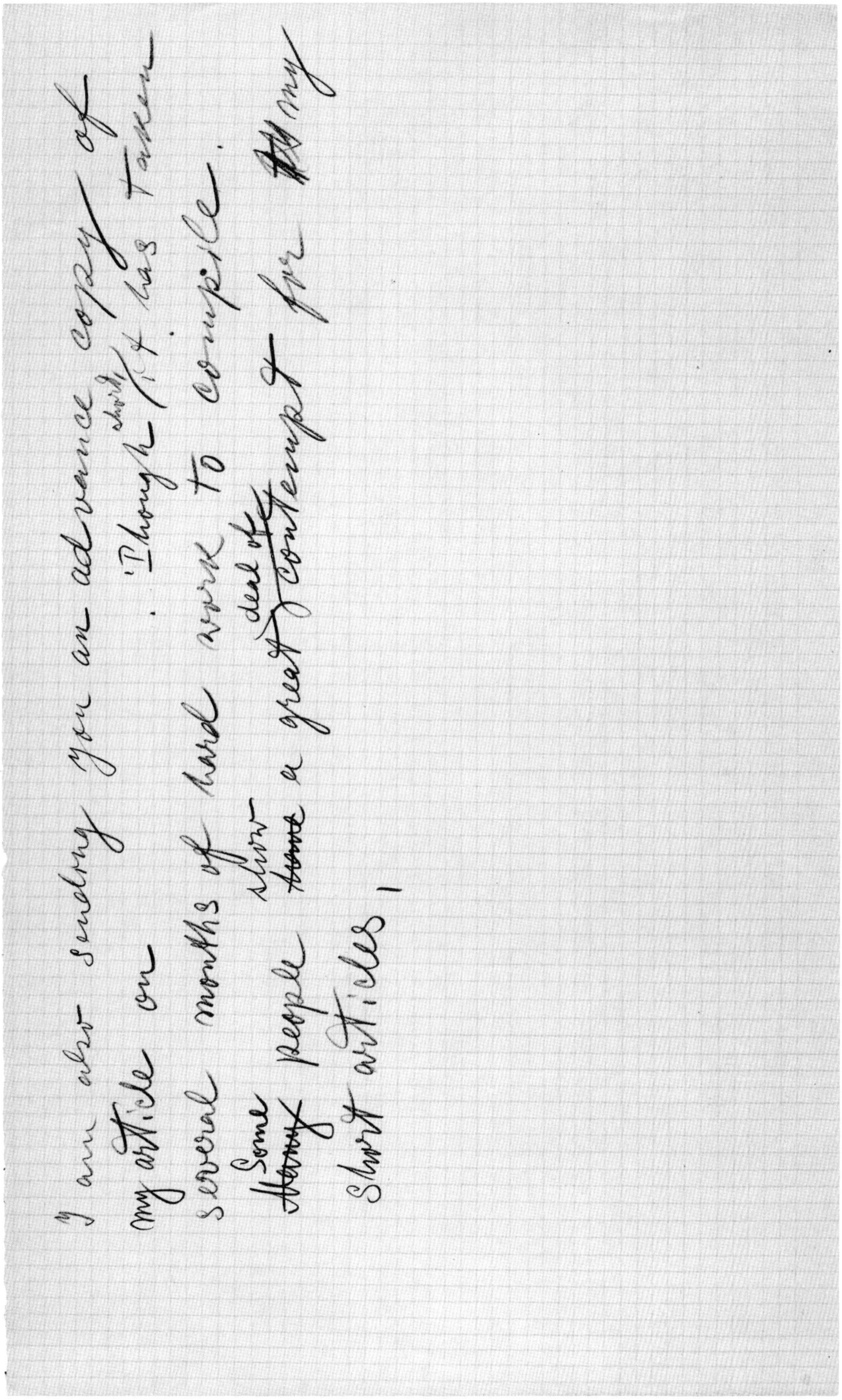

I am also sending you an advance copy of
my article on . Though short, it has taken
several months of hard work to compile.
~~Heavy~~ Some people ~~have~~ show a great deal of ~~contempt~~ contempt for ~~the~~ my
short articles.

~~but I find some encouragement~~

but I am encouraged to produce more of ~~s~~ such apparently insignificant papers by the ~~fact~~ that certain miniature treatises of mine ~~which of mine (of mine)~~ the St. Petersburg Academy, the Berlin Academy and the Royal As. Soc. published ~~published~~ ~~miniature treatises, which I wrote~~ ~~in the~~ over twenty years ago, are still being discussed ~~quoted~~ by well-known scholars. ~~See~~ ~~Arch. Survey of India~~ See the Memoirs of the Archaeological Survey of India, No. 38, Calcutta 1930, pages 5-6, the Journal of the Royal As. Soc. 1933, page 221, and the Asia Major vol. IX, pages 456 and 466. and Asia Major.

You will find that the ~~latest article~~ ~~the~~ format ~~size~~ of my latest article is the same as the format ~~size~~ of the first volume of the Harvard Sino-Indian Series. I have chosen this format ~~size~~ because I want to publish a volume of "Parerga Pekingensia" (about 200 pages) ~~c~~ consisting of short articles in the Harvard ~~Oriental~~ Sino-Indian Series. I shall be very much obliged to you, if you will kindly allow me to have such a volume of the Harvard ~~Oriental~~ Sino-Indian Series printed at Peking. ~~do so~~. The articles will deal with a number of little discoveries, which we have made during the last few years.~~, and they must be published here in China, because~~ Various Chinese institutions, such as the Academia Sinica and the Peking Historical Museum, keep asking ~~me~~ us to contribute to their periodicals, and I shall have to apply for your permission to do so, if ~~any~~ our articles cannot be published in the Harvard Sino-Indian Series.

Believe me yours sincerely and gratefully

A. Staël-Holstein.

P. S.

I have written an article on the name Avalokita, which has been accepted by the authorities ~~of~~ Yenching University and will soon appear in the Yenching Journal, ~~I of however pr~~ but I ~~hope~~ venture to that ~~my~~ the majority of future articles will ~~appear~~ be published in the Harvard ~~Oriental~~ Sino-Indian Series.

Note 1

~~After~~ Long after his arrival in Germany, Professor Weller has published an account of what he calls "das Sino-Indian Institute der Harvard University" ~~der Harvard-Universität~~ (des Harvard-Yenching Instituts would perhaps be more correct?) in the "Asia Major" (vol. IX pages 658–663). He calls me "Herr Institutsdirektor" in his account, although, I think, I have never ~~assumed~~ used that title since I returned from America in 1929.

Ann. 2

I enclose page 1 of the Sino-Indian index to the Kāçyapaparivarta, and I hope that ~~the Educa~~ you will allow us to print the whole of it in the same style.

~~Anfang~~ Am 3. März 1934 geschrieben & abgeschickt.

My dear Dean Chase,

The notes to my article on the Kanjur (of which I sent you two copies) are printed with ordinary ~~type~~ (not small) type, and the fear that the Educational Committee may object to this unusual procedure causes me ~~sleepless nights.~~ great anxiety. ~~About~~ ~~[illegible]~~

I have ~~not~~ good reasons for choosing the ordinary (large) type for my notes: my notes contain many quotations from Chinese and if ~~the Roman~~ I used small type for the English text I would have to use small Chinese characters as well, and this is extremely inconvenient.

About two years ago the Educational Committee insisted

Two years ago the Educational
Committee insisted upon
upon our Professor Weller's index
being printed with small type.*
and thereby delayed the
publication of the work for
a whole year. The Educational
Committee do, probably, not
realize that we have to deal

~~My dear Dean Chase,~~

About two years ago the Cambridge Mass. Educational Committee objected to the type ~~I was~~ you were using for one of our books and thereby delayed the publication of the first volume of the Harvard Sino-Indian Series for a whole year.

upon ~~Professor Weller's index being~~
~~printed with small type, and there-~~
~~by delayed the publication of the~~
~~work for a whole year~~ ~~They~~ ~~This~~
~~That was very discouraging, and~~ I venture
to hope that the Committee will ~~not~~
not protest ~~about~~ against the way, in which
I print my notes. I do ~~quite~~ admit that
it is an unusual way, but I humbly
beg that they accept my explanation and

do not refuse to sanction my plan for external reasons.

Believe

~~The~~ Small type characters with diacritical marks did not exist in our printing office and they had to be specially made. At first we were told that this could be done in ~~a~~ two months, but as a matter of fact it took ~~much longer~~ about 1 year.

HARVARD-YENCHING INSTITUTE

17 BOYLSTON HALL
CAMBRIDGE, MASSACHUSETTS

May 5, 1934

Dear Professor von Stael-Holstein,-

I hope you aren't thinking me a very bad correspondent. As a matter of fact, I thought I had better wait to answer your recent letters until the Trustees had finally settled budgetary matters and other things for the year 1934-35. The question of funds was so complicated that we had to postpone action until a special meeting, which was not held until Monday last. I am happy to tell you that the budget for the Sino-Indian Institute was finally established as LC$14,000., the same as last year. We all hope that general business will improve, so that there will be no need of further cuts in the appropriation for the Sino-Indian Institute, but every business man in this neighborhood feels so uncertain about the future that we are, naturally, a good deal upset.

The Educational Committee felt that your request to be allowed to use ordinary large type for notes in articles was entirely reasonable, and we so reported to the Trustees, although I think the Trustees have really little to do with such matters. At any rate, you can go ahead without any worry about criticism from sources here.

The Educational Committee also voted, formally, that you be allowed to publish a volume of "Parerga Pekingensia" in the Harvard-Sino-Indian Series. Everyone felt that this would be an excellent plan and heartily approved the proposal.

We were interested, too, in the appreciations which you sent from letters and reviews, though I think I ought to assure you that no one here, at any rate, felt any doubt about the quality and value of the publications issued by the Sino-Indian Institute.

The Trustees were more generous than I had hoped for in regard to fellowships, agreeing to reappoint all the men at present on fellowships (except Mr. Sickman, who had been notified that the present was his last year), and to take on one new man, Mr. Kates. We were a good deal cheered by the fact that Fairbank was granted a fellowship by the General Education Board, and Dr. von Erdberg, a woman who has been working for several years with Langdon Warner, obtained a fellowship grant from the Council of Learned Societies. Mr. Biggerstaff also, who has finished all his work here, obtained a grant for two years of research in China from the

Professor von Stael-Holstein, 2

Social Science Research Council and I suppose will be in Peiping before this letter. All this seems to show that other bodies with financial backing are becoming interested in training men in knowledge of Far Eastern affairs and is, I think, distinctly encouraging. We all rather thought that next year, when a good many of our fellows finish their terms, we might go slowly for a year or two in appointing new fellows until we found out how far places are open for the men already trained. I shall be very glad if you think this is a good policy.

I need not add, I am sure, that everyone was greatly interested in your reports and grateful to you for giving us such a complete picture, and I know that all your friends here would send best greetings if they knew that I was writing.

Sincerely yours,

George H. Chase

Professor A. von Stael-Holstein,
Sino-Indian Institute,
ex-Austrian Legation,
Peiping, China.

P.S. One of the instructors awhile ago called my attention to the fact that he had two works of yours which are not in the Harvard Library:

"On a Peking, a St. Petersburg, and a Kyoto reconstruction of a Sanskrit stanza transcribed with Chinese characters under the Northern Sung Dynasty;"

"On a Tibetan text translated into Sanskrit under Ch'ien Lung (XVIII cent.) and into Chinese under Tao Kwang (XIX cent.).

I venture, therefore, to ask whether copies of these are available and whether you would be willing to send a copy of each for the library. If there are othersof your publications, also, that are not here, of course we should be delighted to have them. I realize, of course, that it is quite likely that a number of such publications are out of print.

July 14th 1934 (abgesch. July 17th 1934)

~~I enclose a photographic reproduction of the bill for printing~~

Dear Dean Chase,

Many thanks for your letter, which says that ~~in which you write that~~ the budget for the Sino-Indian Institute was established as 14000.00 Mex. dollars and that I ~~am allowed can go~~ am allowed to publish a volume of "Parerga Pekingensia" in the Harvard Sino-Indian Series. The first part of volume II (Index to the Sanscrit text of the Kāçyapaparivarta by Friedrich Weller) ~~of this series~~ is now almost ready (the last proofs of the last pages are being examined), ~~and~~ the second part ~~is in pro~~ of volume II (Index to the Chinese translations of the Kāçyapaparivarta by W. Išibašal and A. K. Tojin) ~~are is in~~ is in preparation and the first twenty pages of volume III (Parerga Pekingensia by myself) have been printed. The only volume, however, which has been entirely finished is volume I ~~, of which~~

(Index to the Tibetan translation of the Kāśyapaparivarta by Friedrich Weller). ~~I sent you several copies of it and you are probably~~ On the title page of ~~the~~ the I volume, which was approved by ~~the~~ ~~Ed. Committee~~ your telegram dated May 16th 1933, we find the words "Published by the Harvard-Yenching Institute Cambridge Massachusetts", ~~$~~ 450* copies of the I volume are stored here, at the Sino-Indian Institute, and ~~I wonder what should be how th~~ I await your instructions as to how they shall be disposed of. and I suppose that the ~~bulk of the~~ copies should be sent to Cambridge Mass. ~~If you will allow me to keep fifty copies here I shall try and~~

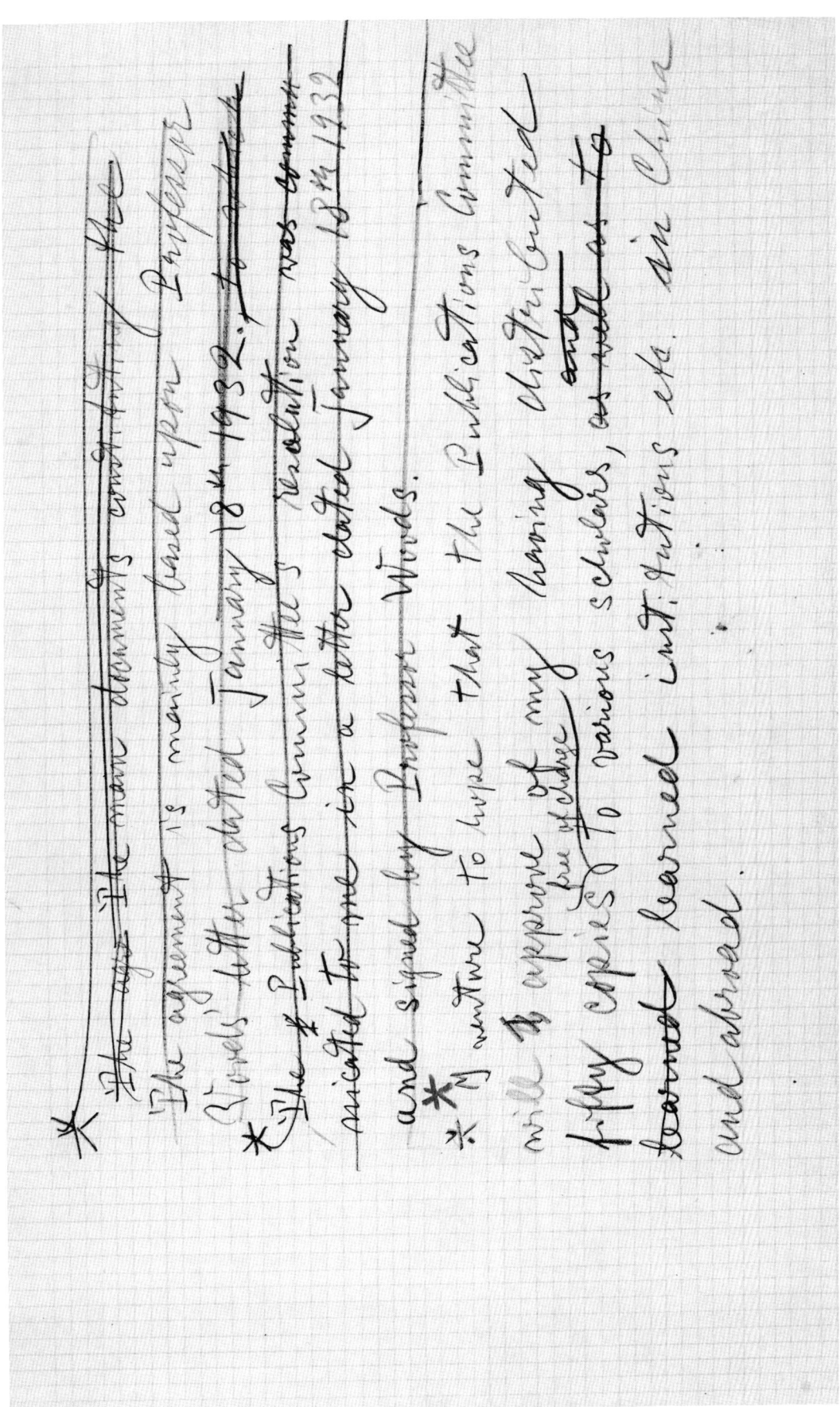

* ~~The agr The main documents constituting the~~
~~The agreement is mainly based upon Professor~~
~~Woods' letter dated January 18th 1932. to which~~
* ~~The Publications Committee's resolution was commu-~~
~~nicated to me in a letter dated January 18th 1932~~
~~and signed by Professor Woods.~~
* * I venture to hope that the Publications Committee
will ~~t~~ approve of my having distributed
fifty copies [free of charge] to various scholars, ~~as well as to~~ ~~and~~
~~learned~~ learned institutions etc. ~~in~~ China
and abroad.

sell them here and in Europe. Please do
let me know what the price of volume
I of the Harvard Sino-Indian Series (in
a photographic reproduction of
U.S. dollars?) will be. I enclose the bill of
(1070.00 Mex. $) (one thousand and seventy Mex. dollars) ± for
printers' bill which I have paid
the I volume of the Harvard Sino-Indian Series,
which I have paid out of my own resources. Who will
finally bear the cost of printing this and
the future volumes of the Harvard Sino-Indian
a resolution of the Publication Committee
Series? According to the letter of the
one-half of the cost of printing should be
borne by the Publication Committee of Cambridge Mass., and the other
myself in 31/32 one half of the cost of printing
the Harvard Sino-Indian Series should be born by
the Bd. Committee of Cambridge Mass., and the other

* I learnt of the Publication~~s~~ Committee's resolution from Professor Woods' letter dated January 18th 1932, which says:

"'The committee felt that, because of the financial depression throughout the world and here also, it ought to ask you to find one-half of the sums necessary for these publications out of this year's appropriation for the Sino-Indian Institute or out of the appropriation for some following year."

half should be paid out of the regular appropriation of the Sino-Indian Institute. I wonder whether the Publication Committee will still be guided by this arrangement in spite of the fact that the regular appropriation of the Sino-Indian Institute has been reduced from twenty six thousand (26000.00) Mex. dollars to fourteen thousand (14000.00) Mex. dollars since the resolution was passed.

~~Will you be so kind as to let m~~
~~I am very anxious to know whether~~ [Will] the ~~Aid~~ [Publication] Committee, ~~will~~, considering our [sadly] reduced circumstances,
let me have ~~the~~ one thousand and seventy
~~(1)~~ Mex. dollars (the entire ~~pri~~ cost of printing
volume I) or merely five hundred and
thirty five Mex. dollars (half the cost of
printing volume I)? ~~V~~ I may be allowed to a add
that we will hardly ever publish more than
one or two volumes of the Harvard ~~&~~ Sino-Indian
Series a year, and that consequently we shall
never have to apply to ~~you for~~ the ~~Aid~~ [Publication] Committee
for more than ~~an~~ about one or two thousand
Mex~~ican~~ dollars in addition to our regular appropriation.

V I shall be very grateful to you for an early answer to this question, because I ~~must~~ am making my financial plans for 34/35, and ~~[illegible]~~ 535 Mex. dollars make a considerable difference. If we shall have to do without them, either some assistants will have to be dismissed or fewer books will have to be ordered.

If you so wish the cost of printing the future volumes of the Harvard Sino-Indian Series could be reduced by about one third by having merely three hundred copies (not five hundred copies) of each volume printed.

Believe me yours sincerely and gratefully

A Staël Holstein.

P.s. ~~enclose~~ ~~send you under separate cover~~
I ~~enclose~~ copies of the following publications:
~~1) On two Tibetan pictures~~
1) On a ~~Sanskrit~~ Tibetan text
2) On a ~~Tibetan~~ Peking a St. Petersburg and a Kyoto reconstruction
~~4) A Commentary to the Kāçyapaparivarta edited in ... Tibetan and in Chinese~~
~~5) On a Peking edition~~
~~All these~~ Comp. the post script ~~of~~ to your letter dated May 5th 1934.
Idem

I went to see Alan Priest today in the Chinese house which he has taken for a few months. It is wonderfully situated and has an observation platform overlooking the Forbidden City and the palace moat. In addition to the ancient Imperial buildings ~~of the pala~~ one can, sitting on the platform, study the life of rare aquatic birds (the ~~white~~ beautiful water pheasant etc.) who live among the lotus leaves of the moat.

HARVARD UNIVERSITY

THE GRADUATE SCHOOL OF ARTS AND SCIENCES

24 UNIVERSITY HALL, CAMBRIDGE, MASSACHUSETTS

August 23, 1934

Dear Baron von Staël-Holstein:

Your letter of July 14 has arrived together with the two reprints (On a Tibetan text translated into Sanskrit under Ch'ien Lung (XVIII cent.) and into Chinese under Tao Kuang (XIX cent.) and--On a Peking, a St. Petersburg, and a Kyōto reconstruction of a Sanskrit stanza transcribed with Chinese characters under the Northern Sung dynasty). Fortunately, Professor Blake was in town at the same time with me, so I have answers to your questions about the Sino-Indian Series.

Both of us think that we should, of course, keep to the agreement about sharing the cost of publication of the three volumes of the Sino-Indian Series already authorized, but we also think in view of the ~~publication~~ financial difficulties of the Institute that we ought to say that the agreement for sharing expenses applies to the three volumes only, and probably the question of payments ought to be brought up newly in connection with later volumes. We both heartily approve the distribution of fifty copies free of charge to scholars, institutions, etc. Would it be a great deal of trouble, if you sent me a list of scholars and institutions outside of China to whom the copies were sent? What is on my mind is that probably Professor Elisséeff and Professor Clark may think of some others to whom we ought to send complimentary copies, and certainly we do not want to send two to any one person. As for distributing the remaining copies, we suggest that you ship one hundred copies

Baron A. von Staël-Holstein 2 August 23, 1934

to the Harvard University Press, Cambridge, Massachusetts. I have asked at the Press and find that they think there will be no difficulty about duty. They point out, however, that if the value of the shipment is over one hundred dollars (which, of course, it will be), a consular invoice must accompany the shipment. No doubt the shippers in Peiping would know about this, but I thought it worth while to hand on the information.

The people at the Press also want to know what price should be charged for the volume in dollars. We ought to arrange things so that the price in China and the price in Cambridge, Massachusetts, is not very different, and, of course, this is difficult with fluctuating exchange. If you let me know your idea, I will see what the people at the Press think and write again about this matter.

We also thought that probably the simplest way of arranging the finances would be for you to keep such receipts as came from sales in Peiping and for us to keep any result of sales in this country and in Europe. Does this accord with your ideas?

Miss Bayley is having a long vacation this year and has gone to Europe. She will be back in September and as soon as she comes I will take up the question of how we shall transmit 535 Mex. dollars to you; but this letter will enable you to make plans. Certainly I hope you won't have to dismiss any assistants or cut down severely on the books that you wish to order.

I didn't take up with Mr. Blake the question of the number of copies to be printed for future volumes. I suppose it is true that three hundred copies would probably cover the demand for a good many years. Anyway,

Baron A. von Staël-Holstein 3 August 23, 1934

this is not a pressing question at the moment, and I will write again about it after people are back and I can get a little more advice.

Good luck to the progress of Volumes II and III of the Series.

Cordially yours,

George H. Chase

Baron A. von Staël-Holstein

13
4
5200.00
181.62
Pavseratoff 5381.62
Lie 1050.00
'Pêng 1020.00
Lama 600.00
Ku 315.00
8366.62
Iiin 320.00
8686.62

~~Sino-Indian expense account for 19.. the year ending~~

Dear Dean Chase,

During the year 33/34 I received fourteen thousand (14000.00) Mexican dollars from ~~Yenc~~ the Treasurer of Yenching University. ~~Four thousand (4000.00) Mex. dollars (were) I spent for representation (which includes~~ (including office ~~expenses~~: ~~writing material, heating, coolie hire, photographing receipts and other documents etc.), and the remaining ten thousand Mex. dollars~~ (eight thousand six hundred and eighty six Mex. dollars and sixty two cents (8686.62) ~~...... Mex. dollars~~ I paid ~~Mex. dollars~~ to my assistants: Mr. Pavseratoff (5381.62 Mex. dollars, comp. pages ... - .... below) Mr. Iiin (320.00 Mex. dollars, comp. pages below) Dr. Liebenthal (105.00 Mex. dollars, comp. pages .... - .... below) Mr. 'Pêng (1020.00 Mex. dollars, comp. pages .... - ..... below) Lama 'Thabs-bkan ye çes (600.00 Mex. dollars, comp. pages ..... - .... below), and Mr. Ku (315.00 Mex. dollars, comp. pages ..... - .... below). Four thousand Mex. dollars were

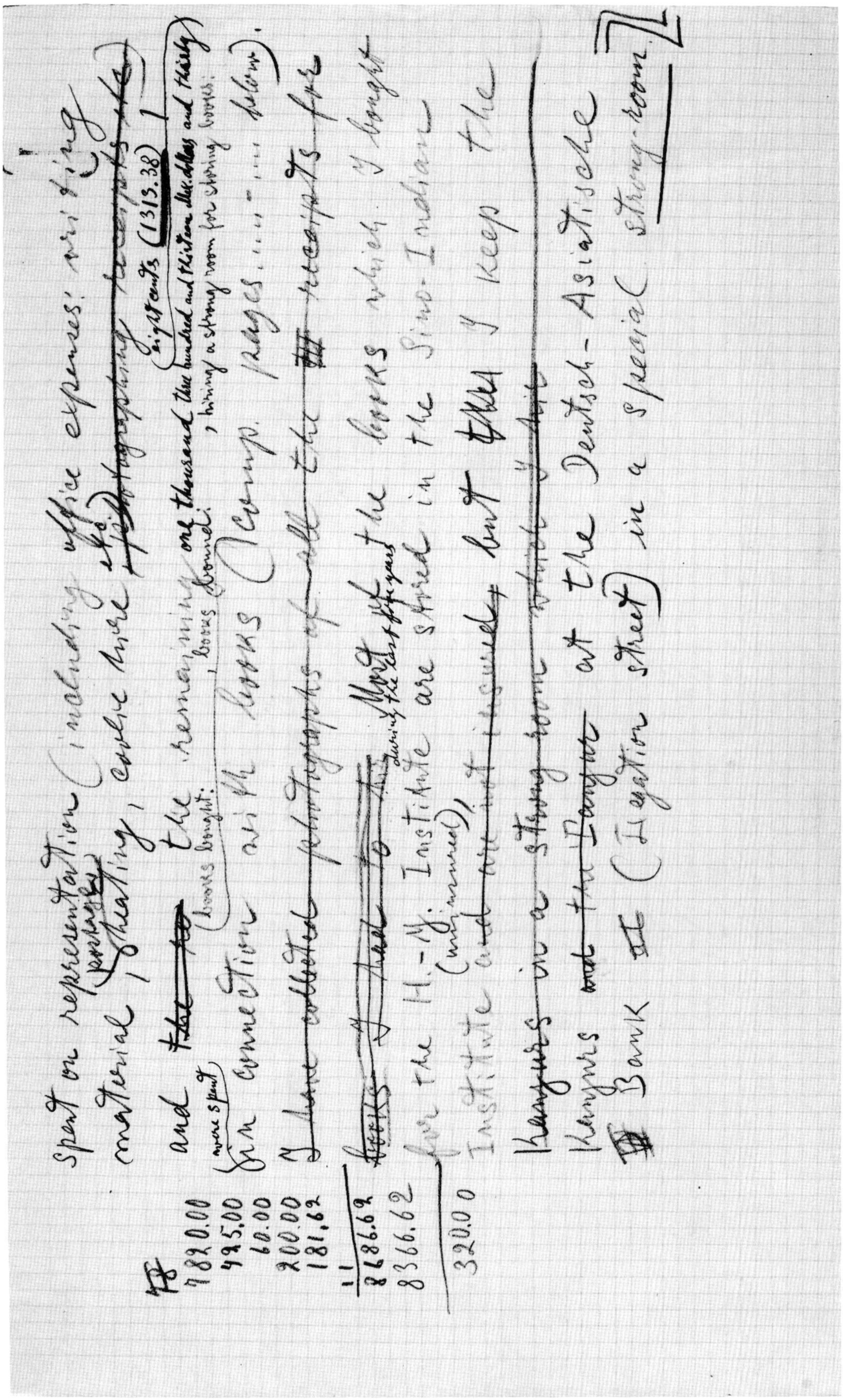
spent on representation (including office expenses: writing material, postage, heating, coolie wire etc ~~photographing receipts etc~~)

and ~~the to~~ the remaining one thousand three hundred and thirteen Mex. dollars and thirty eight cents (1313.38) [

were spent (books bought: , books bound: , hiring a strong room for storing books:

in connection with books (comp. pages ..... – ..... below).

~~I have collected photographs of all the receipts for books I had to~~ Most of the books which I bought during the last five years for the H.-Y. Institute are stored in the Sino-Indian Institute ~~and are not insured,~~ (uninsured), but I keep the ~~Kanjurs in a strong room which I hir~~ Kanjurs ~~and the Tanjur~~ at the Deutsch-Asiatische Bank ~~at~~ (Legation street) in a special strong-room.]

7820.00
425.00
60.00
200.00
181.62
8686.62
8366.62
320.00

Peking: October 23rd 1934.

Dear Dean Chase,

~~About ten days ago I sent~~ Many thanks for your letter dated August 23rd 1934. The (Shanghai Commercial Press (a Chinese concern) sell the) Kāśyapaparivarta Text edition ~~costs~~ for six Mexican dollars per copy, and I ~~venture to suggest that the price of the edition of the commentary to the Kāśyapaparivarta. I we should be two U.S.A. dollars.~~ think that the price of Professor Weller's index, ~~which is of should be the same i.e. two U.S.A. do a~~ should be two U.S.A. dollars. The size of the two books is about the same.

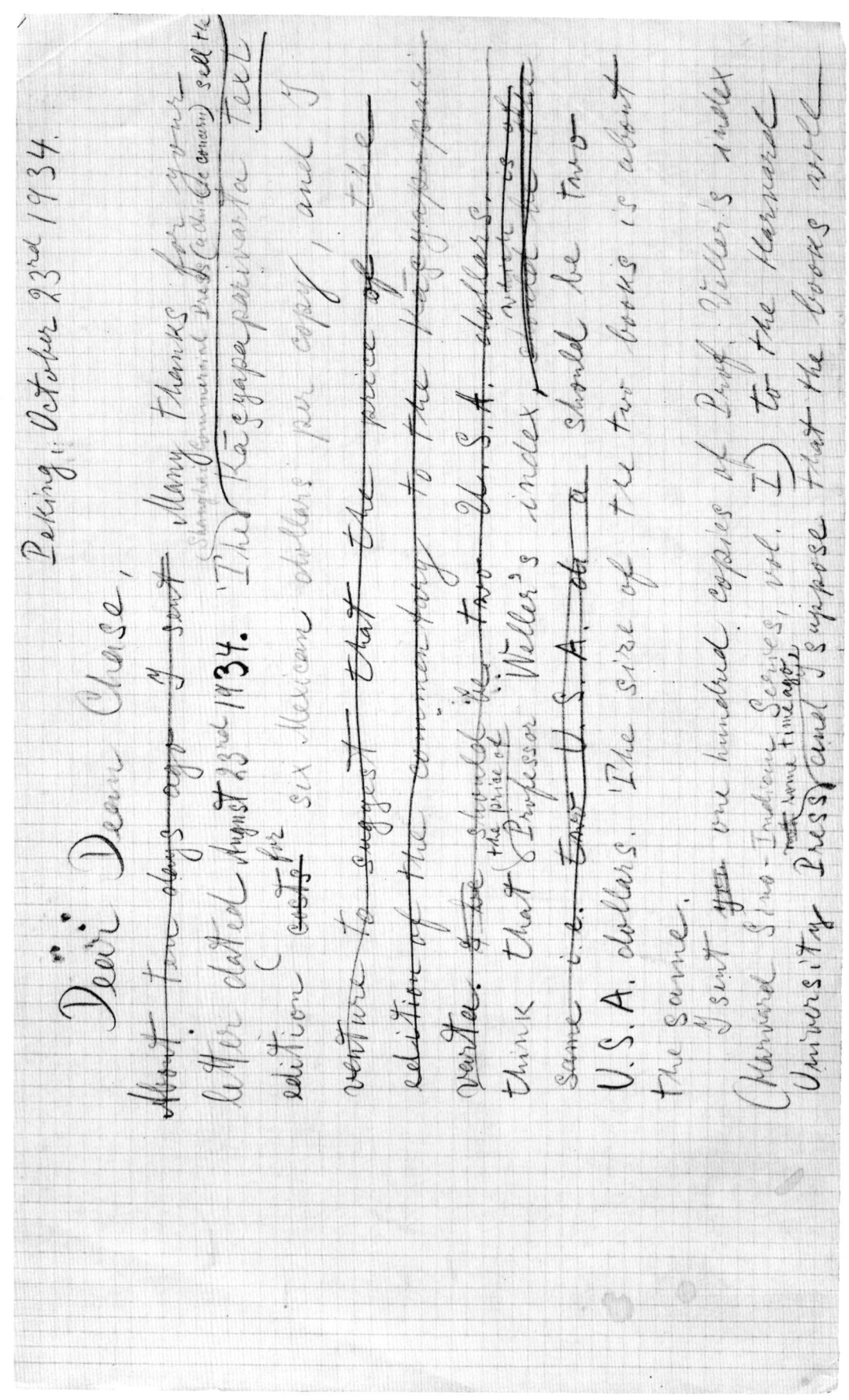

I sent ~~you~~ one hundred copies of Prof. Weller's index (Harvard Sino-Indian Series, vol. I) to the Harvard University Press ~~not~~ some time ago, and I suppose that the books will

On the other hand ~~I regard it as quite natural, that, accor~~ the Harvard University Press ~~wants to~~ will keep ~~the sums obtained~~ whatever it can get for the copies of Professor Weller's index, ~~(which it will receive)~~ which I sent to Cambridge. ~~Shall I think~~ I regard this as an excellent arrangement.

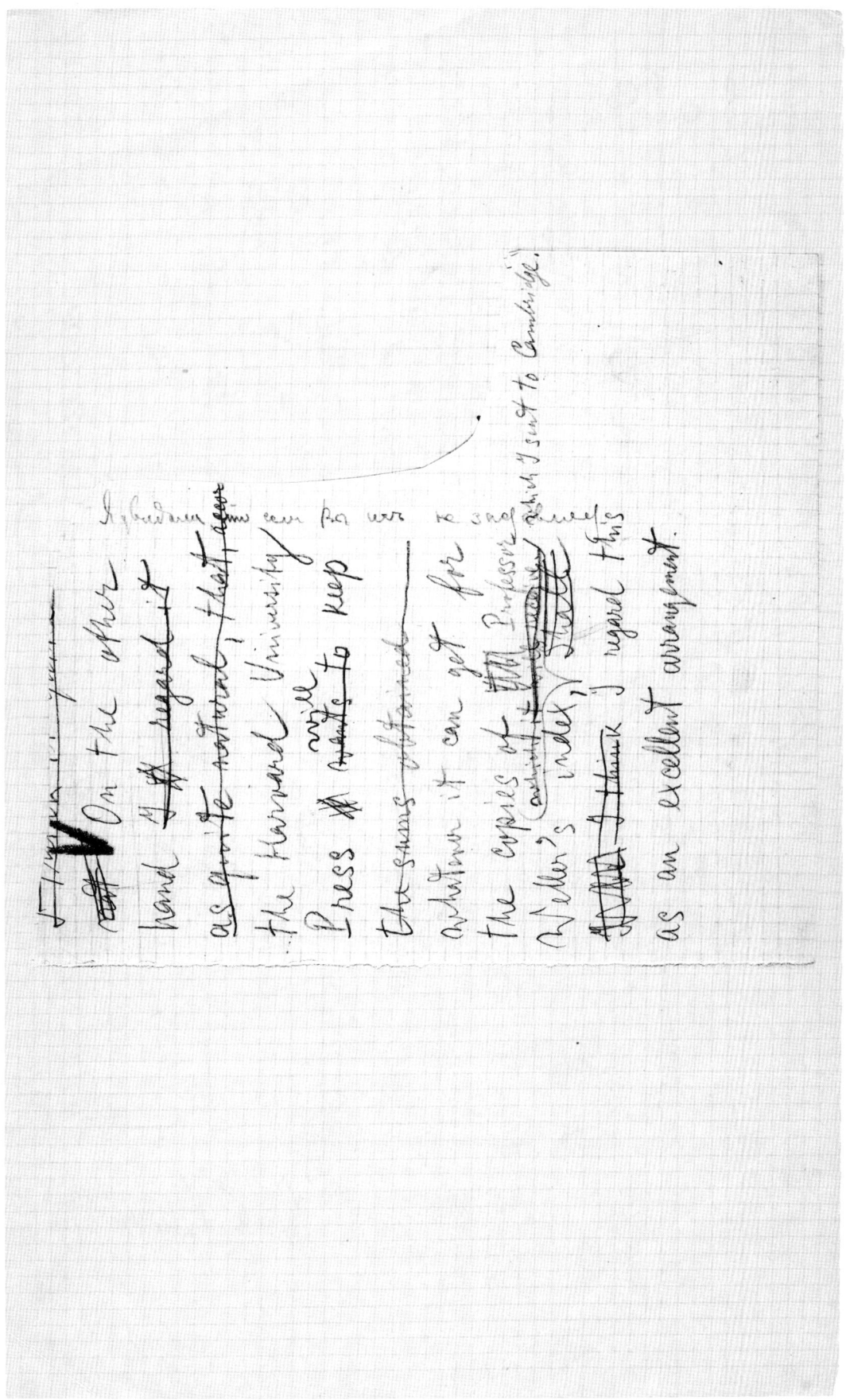

arrive in Cambridge before this letter reaches you.
~~I quite agree with your suggestion as to the disposal of~~ ~~In accordance with your instructions about~~ ~~+ As soon as I hear from you~~

As soon as I learn [from you] ~~what~~ the price of ~~the~~ ~~9 Ro~~ the I volume of the Harvard Sino-Indian Series will be, I shall try and sell some copies. ~~here as well keeping the money~~ The proceeds [of the copies sold by me] ~~of I~~ will, in accordance ~~with~~ [with] your wish~~es~~, be devoted to the needs of the Sino-Indian Institute. ✓

~~You as~~ In your letter you ask me to send you "a list of scholars and institutions outside of China" to whom copies of vol. I have been sent by me.

As far as I can ascertain I sent ~~copies~~ [seventeen] copies ~~to~~ of vol. I to: ✓
The remaining copies were distributed in China.

Believe me yours sincerely and gratefully
A. Staël Holstein.

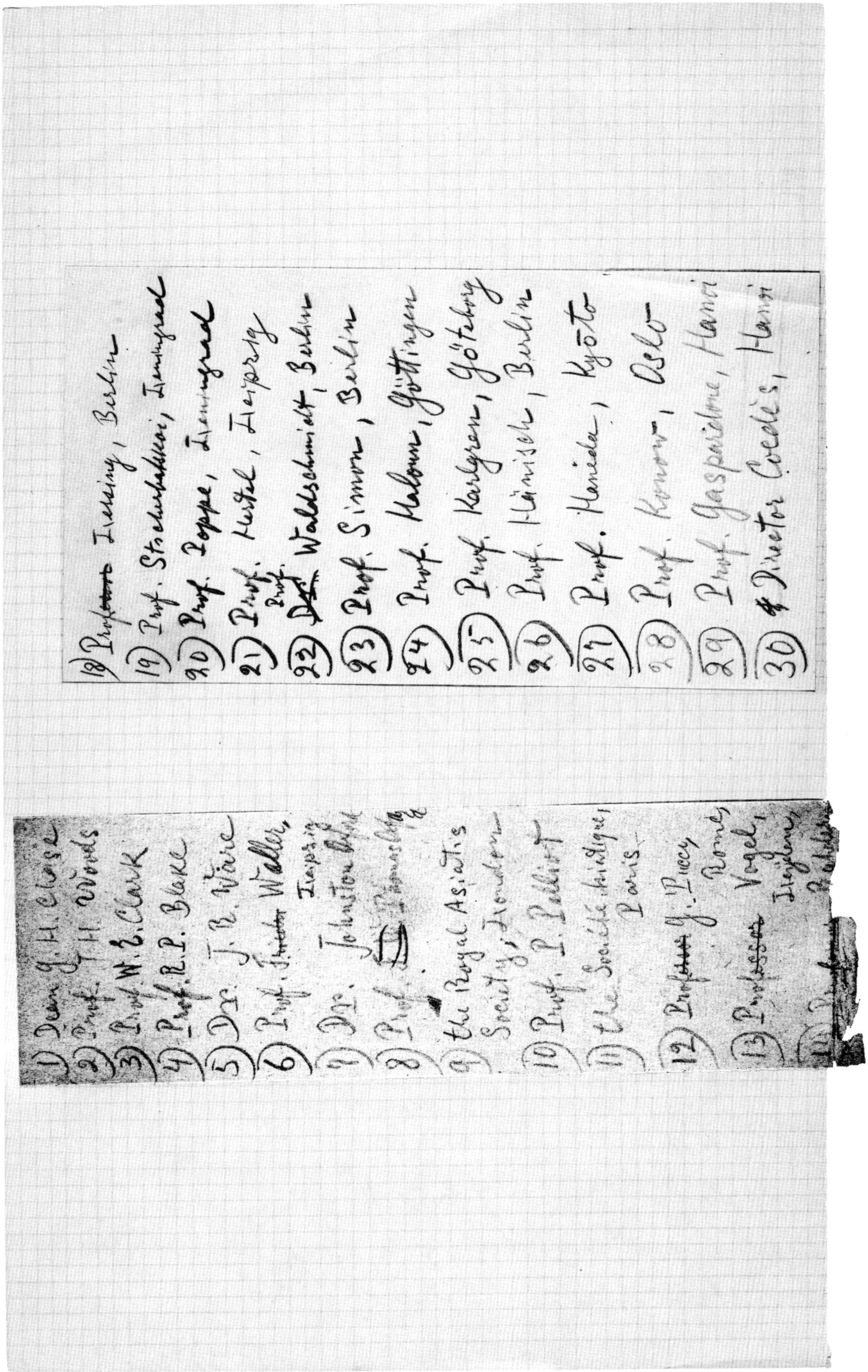
1) Dean G. H. Chase
2) Prof. J. H. Woods
3) Prof. W. E. Clark
4) Prof. R. P. Blake
5) Dr. J. R. Ware
6) Prof. ~~[illegible]~~ Waller, Leipzig
7) Dr. Johnston, Oxford
8) Prof. ~~[illegible]~~ Thomas, Oxford
9) the Royal Asiatic Society, London
10) Prof. P. Pelliot
11) the Société Asiatique, Paris
12) ~~Professor~~ G. Tucci, Rome,
13) ~~Professor~~ Vogel, Leyden,
14) ~~Professor~~ Rahder

18) ~~Professor~~ Lessing, Berlin
19) Prof. Stcherbatskoi, Leningrad
20) Prof. Poppe, Leningrad
21) Prof. Hertel, Leipzig
22) ~~Dr.~~ Prof. Waldschmidt, Berlin
23) Prof. Simon, Berlin
24) Prof. Haloun, Göttingen
25) Prof. Karlgren, Göteborg
26) Prof. Hänisch, Berlin
27) Prof. Haneda, Kyōto
28) Prof. Konow, Oslo
29) Prof. Gaspardone, Hanoi
30) Director Coedès, Hanoi

In your letter you ask me to send you "a list of scholars and institutions outside of China" to whom copies of vol. I have been sent by me.

As far as I can ascertain, I have sent copies of vol. I to:

1) Dean G. H. Chase,
2) Prof. J. H. Woods,
3) Prof. W. E. Clark,
4) Prof. R. P. Blake,
5) Dr. J. R. Ware,
6) the Yale University Library,
7) Prof. Weller, Leipzig,
8) Dr. Johnston, Oxford,
9) Prof. Thomas, Oxford,
10) the Royal Asiatic Society, London,
11) Prof. Pelliot, Paris,
12) the Société Asiatique, Paris,
13) Prof. Tucci, Rome,
14) Prof. Vogel, Leyden,
15) Prof. Rahder, Leyden,
16) Prof. de la Vallée Poussin, Brussels,
17) Prof. Walleser, Heidelberg,
18) Prof. Lüders, Berlin,
19) Prof. Lessing, Berlin,
20) Prof. Stscherbatskoy, Leningrad,
21) Prof. Poppe, Leningrad,

22) Prof. Hertel, Leipzig,
23) Prof. Waldschmidt, Berlin,
24) Prof. Simon, Berlin,
25) Prof. Haloun, Göttingen,
26) Prof. Karlgren, Göteborg,
27) Prof. Hänisch, Berlin,
28) Prof. Konow, Oslo,
29) Prof Gaspardone, Hanoi,
30) Director Coedès, Hanoi,
31) M. Bacot, Paris,
32) Prof. Hackin, Paris,
33) Mr. J. van Manen, Asiatic Society of Bengal, Calcutta,
34) Prof. Lévi, Paris.

The remaining ~~seventeen~~ sixteen copies have been distributed in China.

Believe me yours sincerely and gratefully
A Staël Holstein.

P.S.
~~Less than~~ Many thanks for the ~~five hun~~ seven five hundred and thirty five Mexican dollars (half the cost of printing volume I of the Harvard Sino-Indian Series)!
The Harvard University Bursar's che~~que~~ck arrived less than ten minutes after I had signed this letter.

Idem.

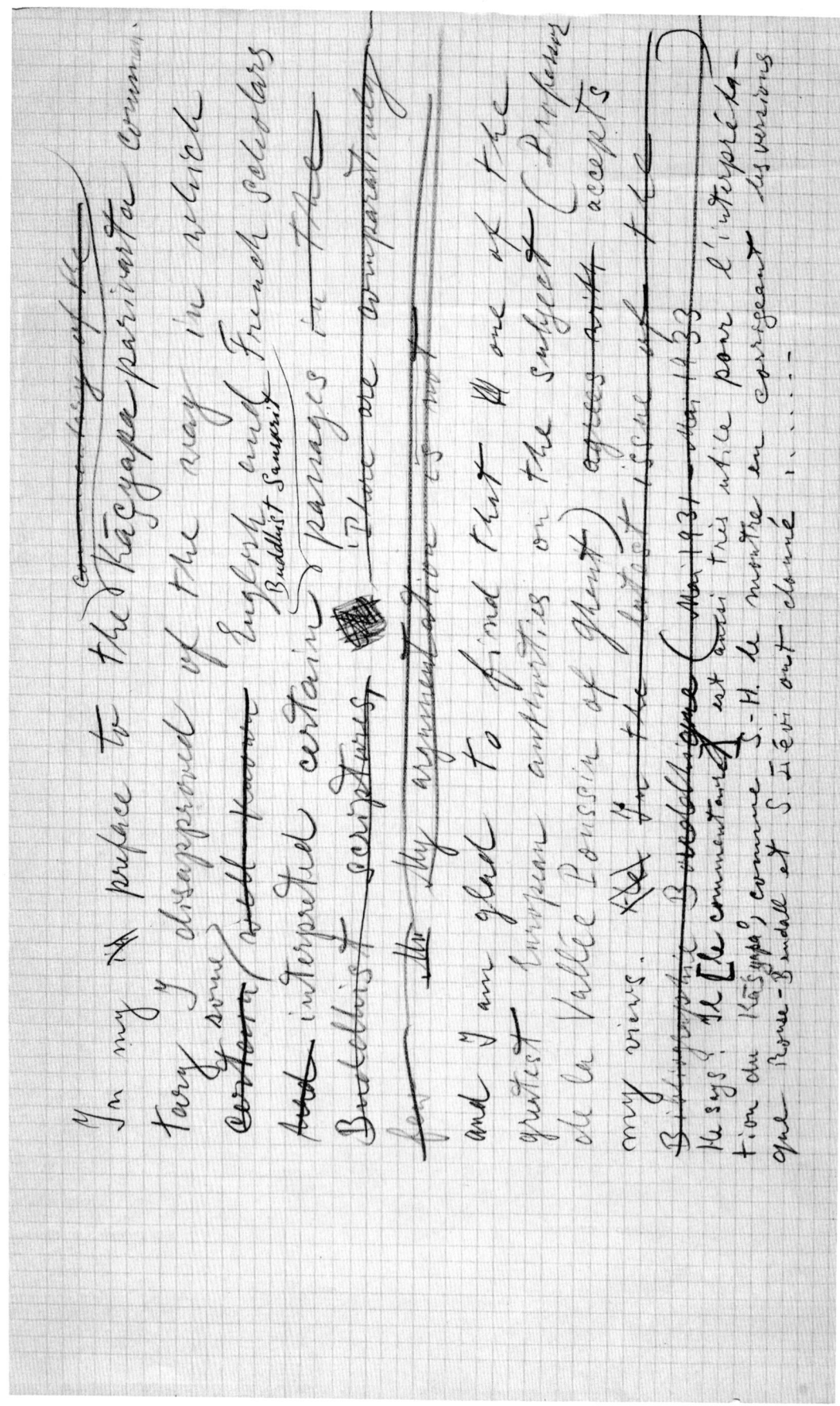

In my ~~H~~ preface to the ~~commentary of the~~ Kāçyapaparivarta commentary I disapproved of the way in which ~~certain~~ (by some) ~~well known~~ English ~~and~~ and French scholars ~~had~~ interpreted certain (Buddhist Sanskrit) passages ~~in the Buddhist scriptures,~~ ~~There are comparatively few~~ ~~The~~ ~~My argumentation is not~~

and I am glad to find that ~~H~~ one of the greatest European authorities on the subject (Professor de la Vallée Poussin of Ghent) ~~agrees with~~ accepts my views. ~~He~~ ~~In the latest issue of the Bibliographie Bouddhique (Mai 1931 – Mai 1933)~~

He says: Il [le commentaire] est aussi très utile pour l'interprétation du Kāçyapa, comme S.-H. le montre en corrigeant les versions que Rouse-Bendall et S. Lévi ont donné ......

I note with ~~great~~ satisfaction ~~that~~ Professor de la Vallée Poussin ~~writes~~ publishes what follows in the latest issue of the "Bibliographie Bouddhique" (Paris 1934, pages):

'These words prove that Professor de la Vallée Poussin (Ghent) agrees with me in regarding certain interpretations published by Professors Lévi (Paris) and Bendall (Cambridge, England) as erroneous. ~~He evidently~~

'The Belgian scholar, who accepts my corrections, is regarded as a great ~~authority~~ international authority.'

~~Professor de la Vallée Poussin's note on my edition of the commentary is~~ Comp. (Bibliographie Bouddhique IV-V, Paris 1934, pages 47-48.) is ~~quite~~ shorter than ~~most~~ some reviews, photographic reproductions of which I sent you in March 1934, but the reviews ~~of~~ by Professor Lüders and Professor Tucci, photographic reproductions of which I ~~not~~ enclose with this letter, are ~~quite~~ of a quite considerable size.

I venture to send you these reproductions, because they show that the work which ~~is being done~~ we do here under the auspices of the Harvard-Yenching Institute, finds an echo in Europe.

~~As~~ I do not ~~know a~~ read Japanese and being ~~unable~~ no longer able to keep a Japanese assistant, ~~(the ap~~ because the appropriation of the Sino-Indian Institute has been reduced (from 26 thousand Mex. dollars to 14 thousand Mex. dollars) ~~I am almost entirely ignorant of the~~

I cannot report to you on the reception which
our publications have met with in Japan.

HARVARD-YENCHING INSTITUTE

17 BOYLSTON HALL
CAMBRIDGE, MASSACHUSETTS

December 10, 1934

Dear Professor von Stael-Holstein:-

Your letter of October 24th ought to have been answered long ago, but I wanted to make sure that the price of $2. for the Kacyapaparivarta text edition agrees with the ideas of the Publication Committee here. It took me some time to get the attention of Blake. Now he has told me that this is all right, and I shall inform The Press of the decision.

Some days ago, I had notice from the American Express Company office in Peiping of the shipment of the one hundred copies of Professor Weller's index with a statement that they had ordered all invoices and other papers sent to me on arrival of the shipment in the U.S.A. As soon as the documents reach me, I will turn them over to The Press, and I have no doubt that the books will arrive in Cambridge shortly after that. Evidently, there has been considerable delay somewhere. I don't suppose this is really harmful.

I am glad you like the arrangement for the division of receipts. I am sure that will make everything simpler for all people concerned. The list which you sent of persons to whom complimentary copies have been sent will surely be very helpful to the Publication Committee when they consider the question of sending further complimentary copies from here.

I haven't yet been able to get Mr. Blake to rule on the number of copies that might well be printed of future volumes of the Sino-Indian series. He wants to take that up with the Publication Committee and thinks the whole matter should be pretty carefully canvassed. I shall try to look after him and to let you know soon, and I judge, anyway, that the matter isn't particularly pressing.

Now that Professor Elisséeff is established in Cambridge as Director of the Institute, I think it would probably be better if you wrote to him rather than to me. I shall miss hearing from you, but I am sure, as a matter of routine, time will be saved by direct correspondence, and, although I have no intimation to that effect, I think Dr. Elisséeff might well think it queer that correspondence came to him through the Chairman of the Educational

Professor von Stael-Holstein -2- December 10, 1934

Committee rather than directly. He will, of course, report on your activities to the Educational Committee and so I shall get your news reasonably promptly.

I am delighted to hear that the 535 Mexican dollars arrived safely.

Cordially yours,

George H. Chase

Professor von Stael-Holstein,
Sino-Indian Institute,
ex-Austrian Legation,
Peiping, China.

During the last two years I have published
a book and some articles, copies of all of which
I have from~~f~~ time to time forwarded to
a number of Harvard orientalist professors. Not
one of them has acknowledged any of my writings
or Professor Weller's very elaborate index, which ~~a~~ was lately published
in the Harvard ~~Oriental~~ Sino-Indian Series. ~~On account
of this silence I have developed the symptoms
of a serious inferiority complex, and my
medical advisers recommend a collection of
compliments as the ~~only~~ best remedy for ~~my~~ the ailment.~~

~~From this silence and from the fact that they practically~~
~~On account of th~~ Considering this silence as well as ~~and~~
the fact that they practically never answer
my letters I venture to write to you about
what I am doing.

My latest hobby is: collecting compliments.

~~No~~

The only reaction to the copies of my ~~my~~ publications (three ~~short~~ articles and one book) which I sent to the Harvard ~~orientalists~~ professors ~~(in~~ 1932 and 1933 (and evidently studied) has been an icy silence. ~~This means my sad~~ Is this due to the fact that most of my ~~[illegible]~~ efforts have resulted in short articles? (Some of ~~my~~ the short articles which I wrote in 1908 - 1914 are still discussed in ~~scientific~~ philological ~~periodicals~~ serials of good standing, see Corp. Inscr. Ind., Arch. Survey of India and the ~~[illegible]~~ number of ~~the~~ "Asia Major" which appeared in 1933) ~~Or are they~~ Or do they ~~disapprove~~ altogether disapprove of my ~~work~~ writings which ~~have been~~ seem to

~~Saddharmapuṇḍarīka-Stelle~~

~~flows out of the mouth of~~ (the mouth of a)

~~a an a fine Vaidūrya horse's~~

~~head (made of Vaidūrya) fixed to the western~~

~~part of the Anavatapta~~

~~lake~~

Peking February 27th 1935.

Dear Dean Chase,

Many thanks for your letter dated December 10th 1934. I had a letter from the late Professor Woods ~~of at~~ dated three days earlier, in which he ~~[illegible]~~ described ~~spoke of his future plans and of~~ the philosophical ~~questions~~ problems, ~~at the solution of~~ which he had lately been examining and ~~working and he spoke. He speaks of~~ ~~He also~~ mentioned ~~[illegible]~~ his "plan of work for these last years". How very sad for all ~~of us that no years but only a few weeks were~~

of us that he had ~~two~~ years but merely ~~only~~ a few
weeks before him! I have already told ~~written~~
~~to Mrs. Woods that I mourn with him~~
~~with her and that~~
Mrs. Woods how deeply grieved ~~affected~~ I am by the loss of this
old ~~and faithful~~ friend ~~affects me~~ and
how grateful ~~grateful~~ I feel ~~am~~ towards ~~to~~ her late husband
~~for the numerous important~~ services I
for all that he did for me.
In your letter dated December 10th 1934 you
say: "I haven't yet been able to get Mr. Blake
to rule on the number of copies that might well
be printed of future volumes of the Sino-Indian Series.

He wants to take that up with the Publication Committee." May I ~~so~~ now enquire, ~~whether the Committee has arrive~~ what decision the Committee has arrived at? I am rather anxious to know the Committee's decision because without it I cannot go on printing volumes ~~two and~~ II and III of the Series. ~~Both these volumes cannot~~. The printing work has been at a standstill for months and must evidently remain so until I learn how many copies shall be printed. I think 300 copies are quite sufficient.

Did you ever receive my letter dated September 1934?

I have just written a long report and addressed

it to Professor Elisséeff. I hope that the ~~of~~ 100 copies of Professor Weller's index have in the mean time safely arrived at Cambridge.

Believe me yours sincerely and gratefully

A Staël Holstein.

Geschrieben, datiert & abgeschickt am 3 März 1935

Dear Dean Chase,

~~Ever since I came to China I have collected~~ — Before the war I had a large collection of various ~~documents~~ oriental manuscripts, pictures and photographs, which have nearly all perished during the revolution without leaving any trace. This experience has taught me a lesson, and I am trying to get as much ~~of my~~ new collection (started after my arrival ~~in China~~ in the Far East in 1916) published as possible. Professors ~~Clark has~~ Konow (Oslo) and Thomas (Oxford) have already published certain documents (the originals of which are in the [illegible] Library) discovered by myself in Peking, and Professor Clark's book on ~~the~~ my pantheons ~~collected by myself~~ ~~is~~ will soon appear. A unique series of ~~photographs~~ 30 Tibetan pictures* is now being prepared for the press in Paris (under the direction of Professor Hackin of the Musée Guimet). ~~and some other pictures may soon appear in Germany~~ In 1932 I ~~I enclose The Jātakamālā is a~~ published two ~~F~~ of my pictures and sent you a copy of the publication.

The Jātakamālā or Garland of Birth-Stories has been translated ~~into~~ from Sanscrit into English by Professor J. S. Speijer (Sacred Books of the Buddhists vol. I, London 1895), but no illustrations of of ~~I two~~ this famous work have, as far

as I know, ever been published. ~~I enclose~~ I possess
photographs of 15 Tibetan pictures illustrating
the entire Jātakamālā and I enclose three
of them. ~~Do you think Do you think~~
~~that ###~~ If you think that someone in America
would care to publish the Jātakamālā-illustrations,
I shall send you the remaining 12 photographs.
~~No knowledge of oriental languages is required~~
~~for the publication of the illustrations~~
No knowledge of any oriental language is required for writing
the necessary explanations, but I believe that some acquaintance
with the history of oriental painting would be desirable.
The pictures show a good deal of Persian influence.

In ~~February~~ 1931 I sent you ~~some~~ photographs of some of the 30 pictures, and you very kindly acknowledged the receipt of them (on March 20 1931) with the following words:

I never learnt, however, what the Educational Committee thought of the photographs. ~~I have paid for all the pictures as well as~~ All the original pictures as well as all the photographs, which I possess, have been paid for out of my own personal funds.

HARVARD-YENCHING INSTITUTE

17 BOYLSTON HALL
CAMBRIDGE, MASSACHUSETTS

April 17, 1935

My dear Professor von Stael-Holstein:

On receipt of your letter of February 27th, I got in touch with Mr. Blake and sent you, on March 27th, a cable reading "Three hundred copies approved". I hope it was perfectly clear that this meant the approval of 300 copies of volumes 2 and 3 of the Harvard-Sino-Indian Series and that you were able to go ahead. I don't quite understand why Mr. Blake had not written you before, but I suppose the excuse must be the usual one that he is a very busy man with all sorts of things to do, and this is simply one that he didn't get done.

I find, on inquiry at the Press, that they received the 100 copies of Professor Weller's index on December 29th.

I did receive your letter, dated September, 1934, which was your report for 1933-34 and which was presented to the Trustees at their meeting on November 12, 1934.

Professor Woods's death certainly was a serious loss to all of us. It does seem an awful pity that he should die just when he had been freed from academic duties and really would have had time for his own work. Mrs. Woods is now back in Cambridge and some time ago informed Mr. Blake that she proposed to give all Woods's books which are desired to the Harvard Library. Under this bequest, the Chinese-Japanese Library will receive some very welcome duplicates of periodicals and the Sanskrit collection will be very considerably augmented.

At the last meeting of the Trustees, Professor Clark was elected to fill the vacancy caused by Professor Woods's death. I am sure this is an excellent choice. We all rely very much on Clark's judgment, and he will feel a little more intimately associated, I am sure, with the work of the Institute.

I hope you will be pleased to know that, in spite of the uncertain financial conditions, the appropriation for the Sino-Indian Institute was kept the same for 1935-36 as for 1934-35. The Treasurer seems to feel that the Institute's income has reached its lowest point, unless everything goes to pieces in this country, and we all hope his prediction is correct; but the Trustees have a feeling that they have cut into their surplus as much as they safely can and that economy must be the watchword for the next few years.

-2-

I was very sorry to hear that you have to be on such a strict diet and have to watch your health so carefully. I hope that this heroic treatment will, in the end, effect a permanent cure. I am one of those lucky people who still can eat and drink anything, but I know that the time will come some day when I shall have to "watch my step".

Sincerely yours,

George H. Chase

Professor A. von Stael-Holstein,
Sino-Indian Institute,
17 Boylston Hall,
Cambridge, Mass.

of short articles in the Harvard Oriental
Series. Do you think that the Harvard-
~~Orient~~ Yenching Institute will be able
and willing to bear the entire expense
of this and of ~~the all other~~ the future volumes
of the Harvard ~~Oriental~~ Sino-Indian
Series? The ~~present~~ financial arrangement, under which the first volume of the Series was published, ~~which~~
is based upon a letter, ~~which I~~ re-
ceived here in 1932, and involves ~~means~~ ~~that~~ a penalty
on production. The more ~~we~~ y produce

the less money I ~~get~~ retain for assistants and for buying other people's books. It should also be pointed out that a few months after the above-mentioned letter was written the ~~appropri~~ Sino-Indian appropriation was reduced from 26 thousand Mex. dollars to 14 thousand Mex. dollars.

~~the less money we get for assistants and books.~~

I shall be extremely grateful to you if you will allow me to ~~print the~~ publish the "Parerga Pekingensia" (about 200 pages, 1,500 copies, ~~price~~ cost about 8 or 9 hundred Mex. dollars) as a volume of the Harvard Sino-Indian Series and if you will take the entire expense of ~~all~~ the future Harvard S. I. S. volumes (vol. II, III etc.) ~~upon yourself~~ ves. ~~III~~ ~~I have already paid the bill for vo enclosed bill~~

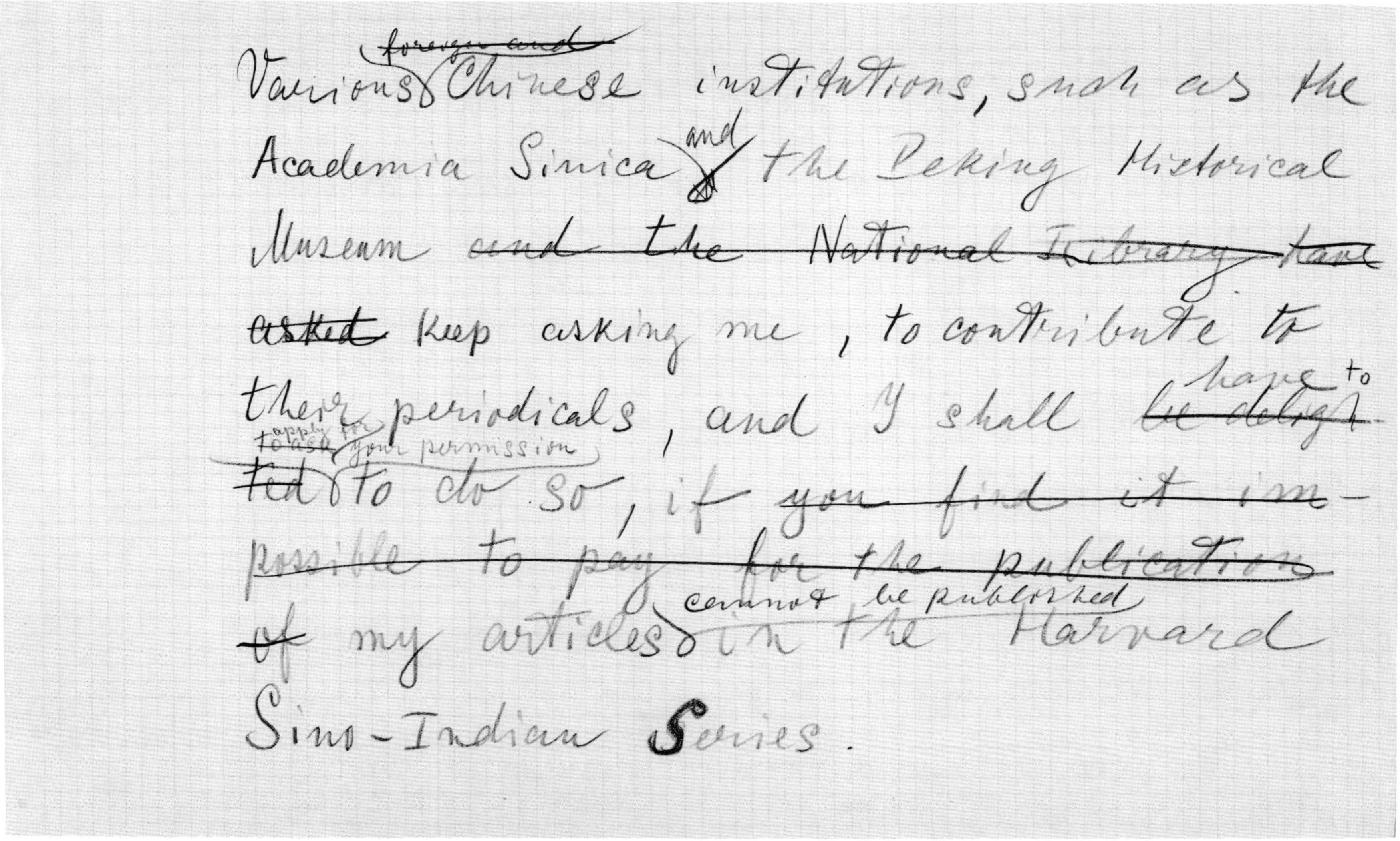

Various ~~foreign and~~ Chinese institutions, such as the
Academia Sinica and ~~&~~ the Peking Historical
Museum ~~and the National Library have~~
~~asked~~ keep asking me, to contribute to
their periodicals, and I shall ~~be delig~~ have to
~~ted~~ ~~to ask~~ apply for your permission to do so, if ~~you find it im-~~
~~possible to pay for the publication~~
~~of~~ my articles cannot be published in the Harvard
Sino-Indian Series.

I hope I shall ~~never~~ not be forced to
send any more manuscripts abroad, ~~(except~~
~~two articles which I have already promised to~~
~~European institutions), because many quotations~~
~~from Pali Sanskrit, Tibetan and~~
~~Chinese [books] occur in my papers, which~~
~~necessitates~~ which makes
because I must read the proof-sheets myself.
~~self. I cannot leave this task to others~~
~~anyone else. No one I know will~~
self. ~~No one else will be willing to spend the~~
~~time~~ spare the time, ~~which is necessary to correct all~~
~~the quotations in Sanskrit Tibetan and Chinese, which~~
~~my papers contain.~~

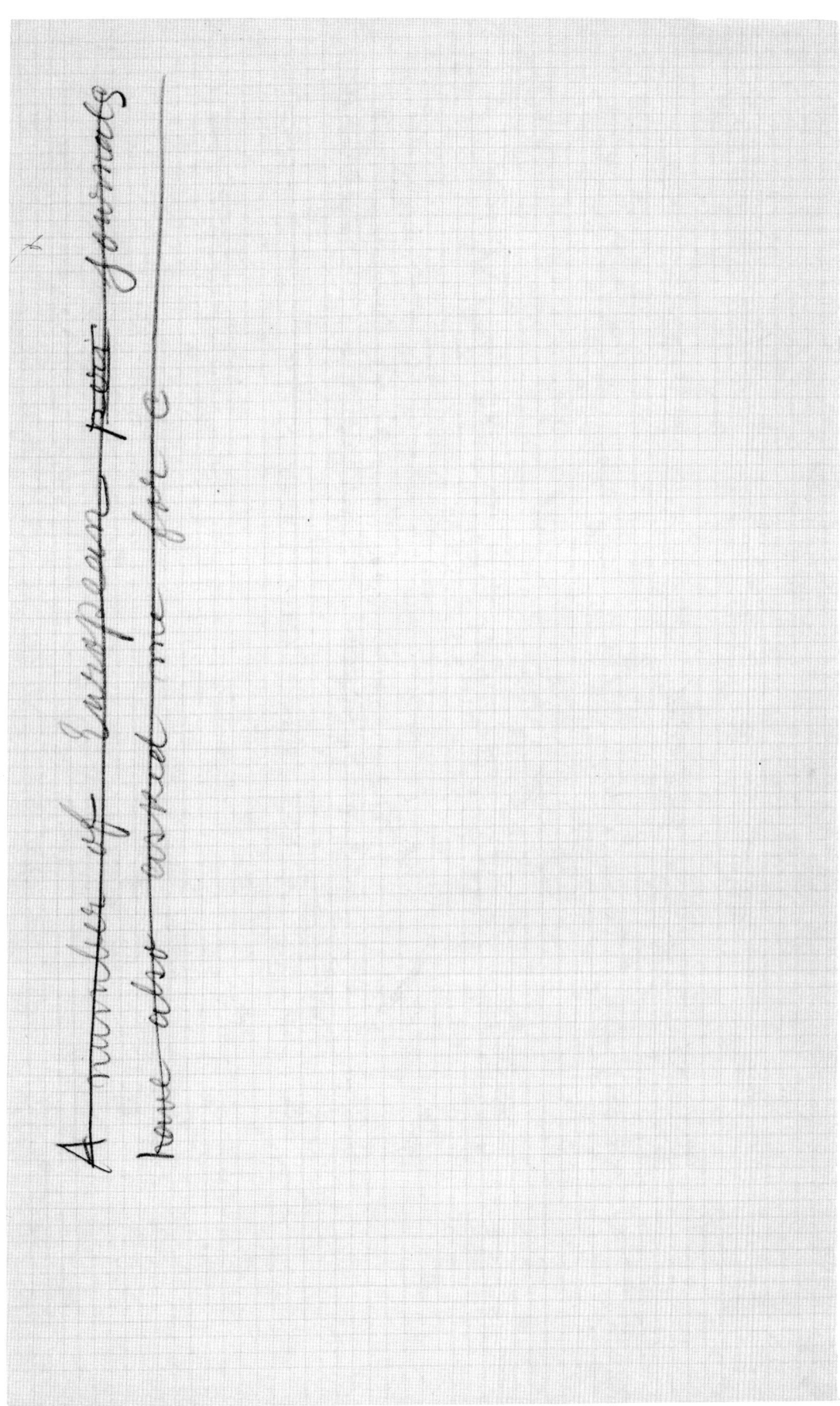

~~A number of European ~~per~~ journals~~
~~have also asked me for~~

No one else can be expected to devote ~~a sufficient amount enough time to them~~ the time to my proof-sheets, which is necessary to correct the numerous quotations from Sanskrit, Tibetan and Chinese properly, and sending the manuscripts as well as the proof-sheets ~~across~~ across the seas may again lead to serious complications. ~~is evidently impossible may lead to serious to new complications. with the editors, which I must I want to avoid like those connected with~~

~~After After sen~~ For sending a certain manuscript to ~~you~~ I was severely reprimanded in a letter (dated) which contains the following phrase: I am surprised

I have already paid the enclosed bill for volume I, and I think I am entitled to receive a draft for Mex. dollars ~~under~~ (half the cost) under the (rather unsatisfactory) arrangement mentioned above. ~~I shall~~ The other half ~~will~~ I shall ~~be~~ defray~~ed~~ out of the ~~app~~ Sino-Indian appropriation for 33/34, and it will appear in my financial report ~~which~~ for this year.

P.S. I have ~~also~~ written an article ~~which~~ on the name Avalokita, which has been accepted by the authorities of Yenching University and will soon appear in the Yenching Journal.

I am — Sir,

V This is the first academic ~~day~~ year since ~~19~~ 1918/1919 during which ~~that~~ I have practically ~~not~~ nothing to do with beginners, and I must say that I greatly enjoy the freedom from elementary work. I now read the ~~very difficult~~ Kāśyapa-parivarta commentary (Tibetan and Chinese only) with ~~Professor~~ Messrs. Tschen Yin Ko and ~~Dr~~ Creel (four hours a week). We compare the commentary (Sanskrit, Tibetan, and Chinese) with the various versions of the text of the sūtra, and the preparation for this privatissimum occupies a ~~good~~ great deal of my time.

before I left for America) is now ready, and I enclose a proof sheet of the last page (326). The variae lectiones and the preface are not quite ready yet. Z

~~In Wednesday's An~~ From an American gentleman who is in a position to know all the facts of the case we receive the folling communication:

Yesterday's (October 2nd 1929) issue of your valuable newspaper contains (on page 4) a list of the scholars attached to the "Chinese research institute in connection with Yenching." That list ~~contains~~ includes the name of Baron Alex. von Staël-Holstein. ~~who appears there as a subordinate of Mr. Ch'ên Yüan the director of the said~~ institute. ~~With all respect to Mr. Ch'ên Yüan~~ It should be quite clearly ~~must be~~ stated that Baron Alex. von Staël-Holstein, is professor of Central Asian philology in Harvard University, [redacted]

is not a member of the Yenching School of Chinese studies ~~and~~ but is, only by courtesy, a visiting professor at Yenching

國 立 北 京 大 學

THE NATIONAL UNIVERSITY OF PEKING

PEKING, CHINA.

July 12, 1927.

Baron A. von Stael-Holstein,
7 Pi Kwan Hutung,
Peking.

Dear Baron Stael-Holstein:

Owing to the financial difficulties prevailing in all government institutions, we regret that the University has not been able to pay your salaries regularly. The arrears for the last twenty-two months (September 12, 1925 - July 12, 1927) have amounted to Eight Thousand and Eight Hundred Dollars ($8,800.00). Deducting One Hundred Forty -Eight Dollars ($148.00) which were paid to you as a part of your salary for September, 1925, the amount still due to you is Eight Thousand Six Hundred and Fifty-Two Dollars ($8,652.00).

The University will not fail to bring the matter to the attention of the Government which, I am confident, will take steps to refund you the arrears by some instalment plan.

Yours very sincerely,

Ta-tsi Chen

Dean

鋼和泰先生大鑒：前日奉訪，未克晤談，良用悵惘。曾託林藜光先生代達鄙忱，懇邀

清誌

先生學識淵博，誨人不倦，久深欽仰。擬懇

增加授課時數，並兼任研究所國學門

導師，以嘉惠學子。如承

國立北京大學用箋

概允月薪當照從前數目致送，俟候

教言，無任翹企。專此，敬頌

台綏

弟陳大齊啓

十七年十月十二日

國立北京大學用箋

國立北京大學
THE NATIONAL UNIVERSITY OF PEKING
PEKING, CHINA.

The Office of
The Chancellor.

July 9, 1926.

Baron A. von Stäe-Holstein,
7 Pi Kwan Hutung,
East City, Peking.

Dear Baron,

I am exceedingly sorry that, on account of the general financial difficulty which prevails in all government institutions, the University is not able to pay you at the present moment your salaries for the last sixteen months (March 15, 1925 — July 15, 1926) amounting to six thousand four hundred dollars (local currency) $6,400.00.

(2)

國立北京大學

THE NATIONAL UNIVERSITY OF PEKING

PEKING, CHINA.

I fully understand your present difficulties, and can assure you that, if some means could be found to advance to you this amount in the form of a loan, this University will be willing to undertake the repayment of that loan according to some instalment plan to be arranged.

Sincerely yours

Monlin Chiang

Acting Chancellor

39 Kirkland St
Cambridge
Mass.
October 13, 1929

Dear Staël:-

The news of your marriage was a surprise, but a very pleasant surprise. Our congratulations and best wishes.

Received your letter with the photographs. They will add greatly to the appearance of the book. I was going to write you asking if you could get Çākyamuni and better photographs of Akṣobhya and Çamvara.

I spent two months before I went away this summer in making a card index of the Tibetan names, ransacking the literature on the subject, and making a card index of as many of the Sanskrit names as I could reconstruct. This Autumn I have spent over a month reconstructing as many Sanskrit names as possible from the Chinese. About 500 of the Palace collection can be made out satisfactorily. I have not yet made out a considerable number of the Buddhas (Fo), the "mountain mothers", "mountain princes", "western mothers", and many of the "vajrasana" "tien-mus". Weller's Tausend Buddhanamen des Bhadrakalpa may help some. Also I have not yet been able to secure access to d'Oldenbourg's edition of the Mahāmāyūrī in Zapiski Vostočnago otdyeleniya Imp. Russk. Arkheol. Obstchestva, vol. 11, 1897-8 published Petersburg 1899. I feel sure that it would be of assistance.

The Sādhanamālā is of great help, as is Rosenberg.

I have recently made out the names of nine of the Daçabhūmis among the Fo-mus, but the tenth is elusive.

I have not yet worked systematically at the fifty or so names which seem to be merely transcriptions of the Sanskrit names. They ought to be easy but I have not made out many of them — and Lévi's index in connection with his paper on the yakṣas in the Mahāmāyūrī (Journal asiatique 1915) has not helped much.

I shall not postpone the book indefinitely in order to try to make the identifications complete. It will be better to publish soon even if a quarter of the names have to be left in Chinese and Tibetan.

Sincerely
Walter E. Clark

My dear Clark,

Many thanks for your interesting paper on the sources for early Buddhist history. I am very proud to see that you mention my name in connection with the Kanjur analysis. I hope that we shall soon be able to let you have ~~some spec~~ at least a small part of our catalogue raisonné of the Tibetan and Mongolian Kanjurs, ~~[illegible]~~ as well as of the corresponding Chinese texts.
~~I also~~ I am very glad to hear that my Vajracchedikā manuscript has arrived at Cambridge Mass.
~~I hope that the Editorial Committee have received~~ I shall be very much obliged to you if you will
~~my Vajracchedikā manuscript. Please~~ look it through and ~~correct~~ change whatever you like ~~I shall~~ Please do not consult me about those emendations,
I accept all your emendations in advance. ~~But please do not send us have I~~ and persuade the Committee that the book should be printed in America, or in ~~England~~ Europe as soon as possible. ~~I have worked very hard at the manuscript and Do not It~~ In China it would take years and could ~~[illegible]~~ never be done really well under present

conditions. My Kāçyapaparivarta ~~has been~~ was ~~well~~ well received by a number of authorities (comp. Sir Charles Eliot in the China Journal, and La Vallée Poussin in ~~the~~ Le Muséon), and the Vajracchedikā ~~has been~~ is arranged on a similar plan. ~~The only difference~~ The various readings of the Vajracchedikā, however, should be printed on the same pages as the corresponding chapters of the texts, because the ~~Vaj~~ various readings of the Vajracchedikā are important while the various readings of the Kāçyapaparivarta ~~(which we will shall print in the translation volume~~ are not. ~~the~~ The various readings of the Kāçyapaparivarta will appear in the ~~translation~~ second volume (notes indices etc.) of the K. p. which we are preparing now. But I think that the Vajracchedikā notes should ~~be~~ not appear in another volume and not even at the end of the first volume, because the reader should be able to compare ~~the~~ ~~[illegible]~~ the amplified versions with the primitive ones ~~[illegible] without~~ with the greatest ease possible. I have spent ~~very~~ much time and energy on that edition and I am very anxious to see the book published.

~~I have mentioned the fact that Woods is preparing a translation of the Vajracch.~~

~~I am afraid that it will be~~

~~In case the proof reading. We are, of course, ready to read the proofs of the Vajracch. edition here, but I fear that sending the proof~~ Please ~~tell~~ ask Woods to accept my best New Year's greetings. I see from Dean Chase's letters that Woods ~~[illegible]~~ has been acting as a true friend ~~[illegible]~~ towards us, and I ~~[illegible]~~ thank him very much for the interest he takes in our welfare. But ~~I cannot he is~~ ~~I cannot say that he is the best of my corre~~ I regret that he never ~~writes to~~ answers my letters.

~~My dear Clark,~~

A few days ago ~~Mr~~ our pupil Carl Schuster ~~[illegible]~~ ~~came to me~~ told me that ~~no~~
~~and said that he had not received a no funds~~
~~he had~~ he was almost starving because no fundes
had been forwarded to him by the Harvard Bursar
for a long time. ~~[illegible] He has been granted a fel~~
I lent him U.S. $200 and promised ~~that I~~ to write
to you about ~~it. He [illegible]~~ his money troubles. He has
received nothing on account of the Harvard-Yenching
year beginning on July 1st 1930, ~~[illegible]~~ and he ~~he~~ must
have some funds before the New Year. ~~[illegible] May~~
~~I ask you~~ Will you be so kind as to ask the Harvard-
Yenching authorities at Cambridge to cable ~~the~~
~~sums~~ (a letter would be too slow) ~~the funds~~ the sum
due to Schuster care of myself? My cable address is:
Staelholstein (one word) Augofoo ~~Peking~~ Peiping.

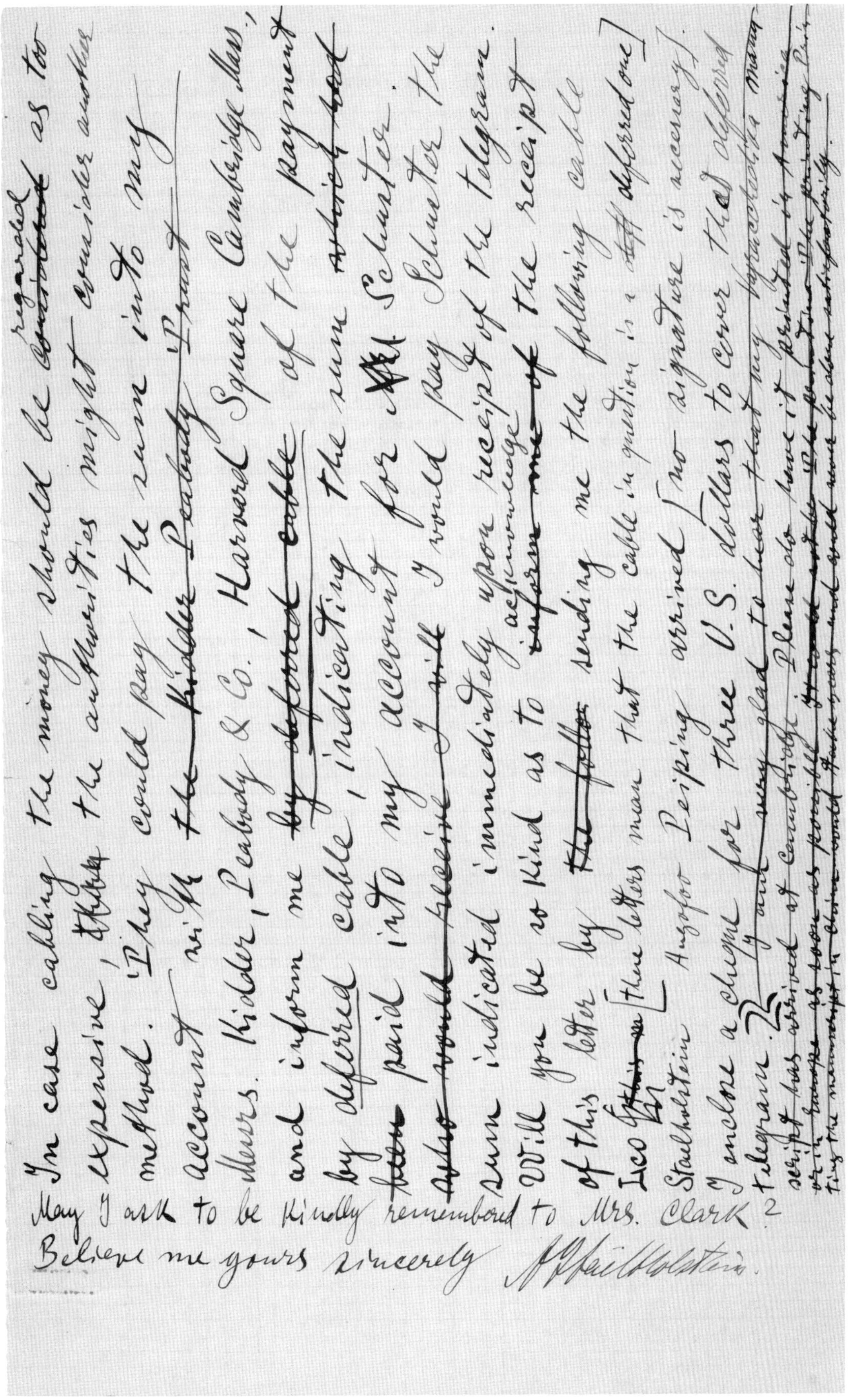

In case cabling the money should be ~~considered~~ regarded as too expensive, ~~then~~ the authorities might consider another method. They could pay the sum into my account with ~~the Kidder Peabody Trust~~ Messrs. Kidder, Peabody & Co., Harvard Square Cambridge Mass., and inform me ~~by deferred cable~~ of the payment by deferred cable, indicating the sum ~~which had been~~ paid into my account for ~~Mr~~ Schuster. ~~who would receive I will~~ I would pay Schuster the sum indicated immediately upon receipt of the telegram. Will you be so kind as to ~~inform me of~~ acknowledge the receipt of this letter by ~~the follow~~ sending me the following cable LCO ~~this m~~ [these letters mean that the cable in question is a ~~stff~~ deferred one] Staelholstein Angofoo Peiping arrived [no signature is necessary]. I enclose a cheque for three U.S. dollars to cover that deferred telegram. ~~I am very glad to hear that my Vajracchedika manuscript has arrived at Cambridge. Please do have it printed in America or in Europe as soon as possible. It could not be The printing The printing Printing the manuscript in China would take years and could never be done satisfactorily.~~

May I ask to be kindly remembered to Mrs. Clark? 2

Believe me yours sincerely A. Staël Holstein.

HARVARD UNIVERSITY

INDIC PHILOLOGY
WALTER E. CLARK
39 KIRKLAND STREET

CAMBRIDGE, MASSACHUSETTS

Oct. 4, 1933

Dear Staël:

You must have been wondering what has happened to our Tibetan Pantheon. It cost me two years hard work. Over a year ago the plates had been printed, the Tibetan and Sanskrit indexes were in galley-proof, and I was trying to make arrangements for the publication of the Chinese index by some process of engraving. Then, after a long procrastination, the Harvard-Yenching Institute decided to purchase a font of Chinese type. Negotiations with a Japanese firm have been under way this past year and seem, finally, to have been completed. We are hoping to receive the type shortly. Then we shall proceed immediately to the printing of the Chinese index and the publication of the whole.

The "Mountain Mothers" and the "Western Mothers" still baffle me, but I have succeeded in identifying a considerable number of queer groups, mainly on the basis of the Sādhanamālā and some other Śanskrit texts of the later Tantric type.

Have you any definite suggestions concerning the title page? Should we call it the Staël-Holstein Collection of Tibetan Pantheons, or something of the sort, and place my name as author on the title page under this?

Shall I re-write the material which you gave me concerning the Palace collection and the Three Hundred Sixty collection into a short preface and sign your name to it, or shall I incorporate this material into my own introduction, giving to you full credit for the information?

Sincerely yours,

Walter E. Clark

Peiping November 28th 1933 (abgeschickt)

Dear Clark,

I am ~~very~~ glad to hear that ~~the book~~ your book will soon appear, and ~~The notes few notes which I~~ I highly appreciate your intention of calling it the Staël-Holstein collection of Tibetan Pantheons. ~~and I do not consider~~ ~~I think I think I think I shall be very grateful if you will say I am also very I shall be very grateful to you if you will say in your introduction that I gave you some information in addition to the photographs I gave you some bits of~~ ~~information~~, ~~but I believe that~~ the latter are ~~not important or rather~~ too insignificant ~~and that a preface or my name should not~~ ~~they should~~ for a special preface. Please incorporate them into your introduction. ~~This is a short~~ ~~I published a very short article~~ some remarks concerning the 360 collection in 1928 ~~volume I of the No I of volume I of the Bulletin of the [Peking] Metropolitan Library in 1928~~ and I enclose a copy of them. I have

I certainly agree with you in thinking that your name should be placed on the title page under this.

~~It is~~ ~~You~~ In your letter you very kindly mention the fact that, ~~I gav~~ in addition to the photographs, I gave you some ~~informa-tion~~ material concerning the palace collection and the 360 collection. I believe that the bits of information I ~~a~~ gave you are too insignificant for a ~~pref~~ special preface. Please incorporate them into your introduction.

I published some remarks concerning the 360 collection in the first volume ~~(May 1928) of~~ of the Bulletin of the [Peking] Metropolitan Library. ~~for 1928 (No 1).~~ ~~The official designation of this periodical is now~~ My article was printed in 1928. Now (1933) the official English designation of the periodical is: Bulletin of the National Library of Peiping.

Peking is no longer a metropolis and its name has been changed to Peiping.

Ever since I published my Halle-Wittenberg thesis in A. D. 1900, I have called myself ~~baron A. von S~~ baron (or Freiherr) A. von Staël-Holstein on (the title-pages of my publications) ~~you will possibly~~ I hope that you will excuse ~~me~~ (my keeping) that comparatively ancient, though insignificant, philological "firm" intact in spite of ~~all the my reduced~~ [the greatly changed] circumstances. ~~In~~ [The laws of republican] Germany, where most of my friends and relatives live, regard (and have always regarded) all the titles of nobility as parts of the respective names. The other Teutonic barons, practically all of whom rigorously preserve their traditions,

I enclose a copy of the first pages of my article on the Kanjur, and I feel that I owe you an apology in connection with ~~the title~~ page I ~~title~~ page

~~most of whom now live in Germany~~ ~~(and rigourously observe their traditions)~~ Bavaria, would be greatly surprised* if I voluntarily renounced this heritage, however ridiculous it might appear to ~~the~~ some outsiders.*

~~Even excellent republican~~ I am encouraged in my persistence by the fact that even ~~the~~ excellent Americans ~~republicans~~, such as ~~like~~ President Lowell and ~~Mr. Johnston~~ his ~~Nelson~~ Secretary, the U.S. ~~American~~ ~~Minister in Peking~~, have repeatedly addressed me as a baron in their communications.

* ~~I know of~~ According to the "Neue Freie Presse", a German official ~~who was~~ has ~~been~~ lately been dismissed the Service because, ~~he had~~ ~~voluntaril~~ in order to please the authorities when the Marxists were in power, he had given up a title of nobility.

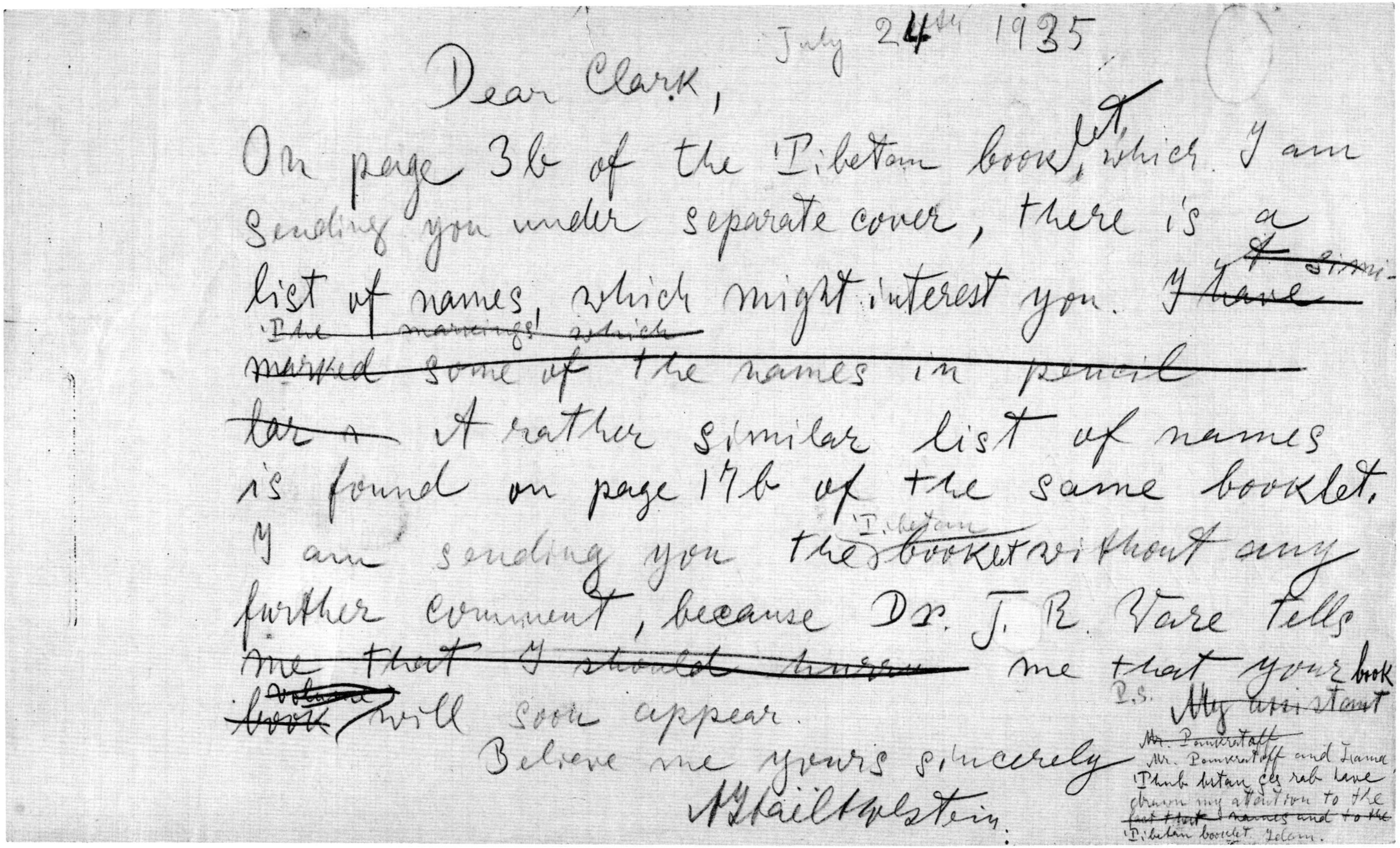

July 24th 1935

Dear Clark,

On page 3b of the Tibetan booklet, which I am sending you under separate cover, there is a list of names, which might interest you. ~~I have~~ ~~[illegible] simi-~~ ~~'The [illegible]' which~~ ~~marked some of the names in pencil~~ ~~lar [illegible]~~ A rather similar list of names is found on page 17b of the same booklet. I am sending you the ~~booklet~~ Tibetan ~~without any~~ further comment, because Dr. J. R. Ware tells ~~me that I should [illegible]~~ me that your ~~volume~~ ~~book~~ book will soon appear.

Believe me yours sincerely

A. Staël Holstein.

P.S. ~~My assistant~~ ~~Mr. Pomeranzoff~~ Mr. Pomeranzoff and Lama Thub bstan ges rab have drawn my attention to the ~~fact that~~ names and ~~to the~~ Tibetan booklet. Idem.

P. S.

It is due to the efforts of Mr. Pankratoff and Lama Dhabs ~~bstan~~ [Golen] ges rab, [two of my assistants,] that I am able to send you the booklet and the pencil notes, which you will find on page 3.6.

Y. Golem

KIRKLAND HOUSE
HARVARD UNIVERSITY

Cambridge, Massachusetts
26 October, 1936

Dear Staël-Holstein:

A manuscript of a book on Lamaistic iconography was offered to the Harvard-Yenching Institute for publication by a Mrs. Gordon of New York. It was an amateurish re-hash from secondary sources with an effort at tables which might make it easier for art museums and collectors to identify images. Her Tibetan was in a state of confusion, a jumble of different transliterations from various books. We rejected it as a semi-popular compilation which contained nothing new. Since then it has been presented to other committees. Professor Pope has heard that you had in view a book on Lamaistic iconography and has asked me to write you to ask if this is so, or if you know anything about Mrs. Gordon.

The indices of the Pantheon are now in final form, so far as I can do them with my limited knowledge. The introduction is in final proof, and all that remains is the printing of the captions on the plates.

Sincerely yours,

Walter E. Clark

Professor A. von Staël-Holstein

Dear Clark

I am very glad to hear that your book is nearly ~~ready~~ finished.
I ~~[illegible]~~ have a number of articles almost ready for print,
~~Some~~ some of ~~them~~ which deal with ~~iconography,~~ Tibetan images, but I never contemplated any ~~[illegible]~~ work on iconography which could serve as a general work of reference. I am not acquainted with ~~the~~ any ~~Mrs~~ Mrs. Gordon, who is interested in Tibetan ~~[illegible]~~ mythology.

Wishing you and Mrs. Clark a very ~~[illegible]~~ happy New Year

I remain yours sincerely

Peking Club
June 16th 1921

Dear Mr. Crane,

I enclose the letter to the living Buddha of the Tsoogool monastery (between Manchuli and Tchita) in Transbaikalia. I hope you do not mind my saying in the letter ~~that~~ you want to „worship ~~the~~ his lotus feet." ~~If~~ ~~It~~ Considering ~~his divine position~~ the Buddha's super-divine position I could do no less.

Wishing you a pleasant journey
I remain yours sincerely
AStaelHolstein.

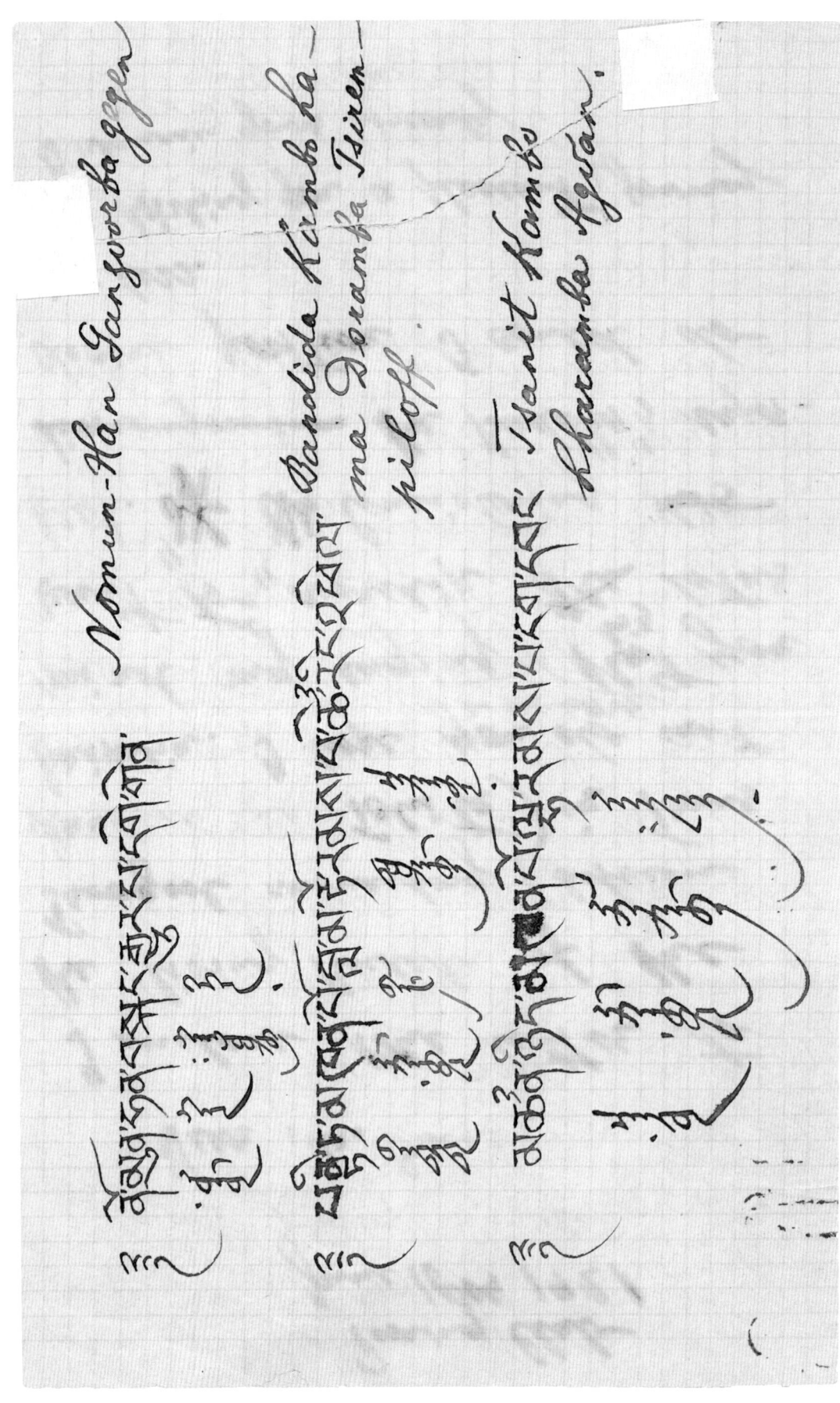

ནོ་མྱུན་ཧན་བསྐར་རྒྱུར་པ་དགེ་གེན Nomun-Han Gangoorba gegen

པཎྜི་ཏ་མཁན་པོ་བླ་མ་རྡོ་རམས་པ་ཚེ་རིང་ཕི་ལོབ Bandida Kambo lama Doramba Tsirempiloff.

མཚན་ཉིད་མཁན་པོ་ལྷ་རམས་པ་ངག་དབང Tsanit Kambo Lharamba Agvan.

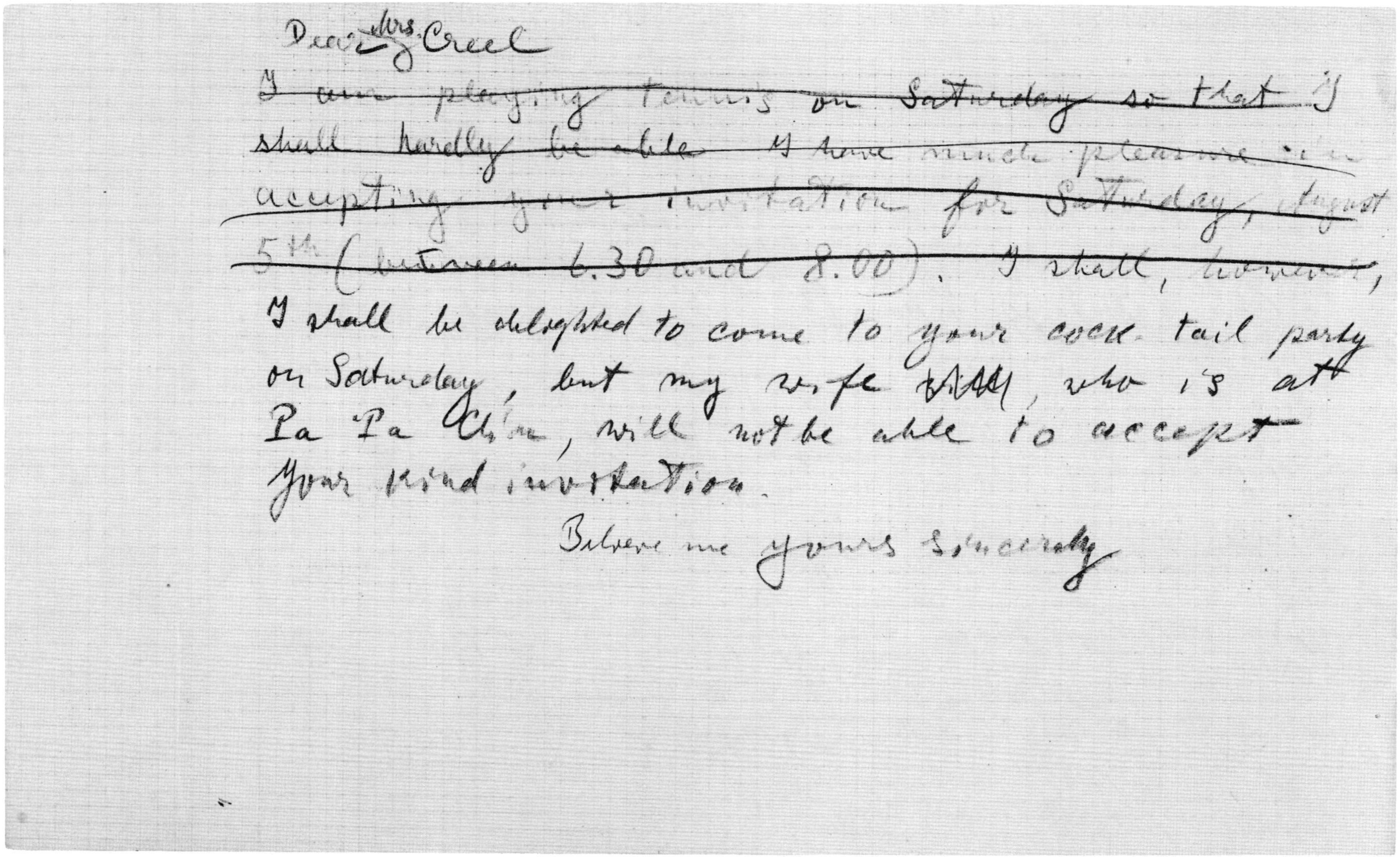

Dear Mrs. Creel

~~I am playing tennis on Saturday so that I shall hardly be able I have much pleasure in accepting your invitation for Saturday, August 5th (between 6.30 and 8.00). I shall, however,~~

I shall be delighted to come to your cock-tail party on Saturday, but my wife ~~[illegible]~~, who is at Pa Pa Ch'u, will not be able to accept your kind invitation.

Believe me yours sincerely

Pekin Thursday December 28th 1933.

Dear ~~Mr~~ Dr. Creel,

My wife and I shall be very pleased if you and Mrs. Creel will ~~come to our house on Saturday~~ ~~join our party.~~ come to a small cock tail party which we are planning for Saturday January 6th (6 p. m.).

Wishing you a very happy New Year

~~Yours sincerely~~ I remain yours sincerely

A. Staël Holstein.

THE EAST CHINA CHRISTIAN EDUCATIONAL ASSOCIATION
ANHWEI CHEKIANG KIANGSU

J. A. ELY, C. E.
TREASURER

REV. EARL H. CRESSY.
GENERAL SECRETARY.

20 MUSEUM ROAD, SHANGHAI

15th February, 1924.

Baron De Stael Holstein,
Peking Club,
Peking.

Dear Sir:

I had hoped to be able to get to Peking and see you again before going on furlough, but that has been impossible and I am leaving for the States in a few days.

I was much interested in your article in the journal of the Royal Asiatic Society. The other day in Nanking I was discussing Buddhism with the Commissioner of Education of this province, and on mentioning you he told me that he had been to see you in Peking. He is lecturing on Buddhist Philosophy at the Southeastern University and I had a most interesting time with him. I am hoping during my time at home, to do a bit of study along this line, and look forward to seeing you when ~~you~~ I return to China.

The occasion of this letter is the situation in the departments of philosophy in a number of Christian Colleges and Universities in this part of China. Last week a conference was held in Nanking of the sixteen Christian Colleges and Universities in China. In the

- 2 -

sectional conference on Philisophy, the question came up as to the place which Hindu Philosophy should have in the curriculum, along with questions as to source material and whether the work could be better done in English or Chinese. Many of us feel that the subject is of no little importance and that it would be desirable to work out a policy and suitable courses of study and plans for research.

I suggested to the sectional conference that they could not do better than to seek your advice and counsel in this whole matter, and as a result of this suggestion, Dr. H.F. MacNair, of St. John's University, who is dean of a Summer School to be carried on this year cooperatively by six Christian Colleges and Universities at St. John's University, has asked me to write on his behalf, to invite you to give a course of lectures and conduct a seminar at the Summer School. The lectures should be adapted to men of college grade, and the subject that would perhaps be of greatest value in our present situation would be the coming and influence of Hindu Philosophy and the Chinese form which it has assumed. You will know better than I as to what phase of it will be of most value.

As to the seminar, what we have in mind is to bring together professors of philosophy from the several institutions and one or two others who are specially qualified and have you advise as to the scope of the courses which should

- 3 -

be offered in our Christian Colleges and Universities, source materials and related topics in Chinese History and Religion.

I wish that the Summer School were in a position to supplement this invitation with some fitting financial arrangement. Its budget is a very small one and the best that it is able to do is to provide railway transportation for the round trip, board and lodging at the home of one of the professors, and a small amount of about $100.00 additional to cover further expenses.

I hope that it may be possible for you to come to Shanghai and render us this great service. The six Christian Colleges and Universities concerned have together about 1800 students and 220 faculty members. We are not putting sufficient emphasis upon courses dealing with Chinese thought and research along these lines. Your coming would give impetus to this. Will you please reply to Prof. H.F. MacNair, St. John's University, Shanghai.

With best personal regards, I am,

Very sincerely yours,

Earl H. Cressy

EHC/S

The Royal Palace
Stockholm
Feb. 12th.

To
Baron A. v. Staël-Holstein.

Dear Sir,

On behalf of H.R.H. the Crown Princess of Sweden I write to thank you so very much for the kind wishes and the very interesting book you kindly sent her. Her Royal Highness very much appreciated your kind attention, and she wants me to tell you that she well remembers when she met you in China.

Yours truly
Stina Reuterswärd
Lady in waiting to H.R.H.
the Crown Princess of Sweden.

The
Sino-Indian Research Institute
of Peking

Dear Professor ~~Vogel,~~ de la Vallée Poussin,

Many thanks for your articles which I have read with the greatest interest. ~~[illegible] May I suggest the following emendation of the lines discussed [illegible]~~

I entirely agree with your emendation of pāda 66 of the (Atyam) ~~H~~aṃgrīnāmāṣṭaçataka (ṛsibhir munipuṃgavaiḥ), and I think that pāda 67 should be reconstructed as follows: yauvarājy[y]ābhiṣiktas] tvaṃ. ~~It seems [illegible]~~ After having read your notes [(Mél. chin. et bouddh., p. 420)] [I] regard it as improbable that ~~[illegible]~~ 法天 should have used the character 曜 (yao) which occurs only once in ~~[illegible]~~ the three hymns, instead of 喻 ~~[illegible]~~ (yü) or 愈 (yü), in order to represent the Indian syllable yu. If we read [ṛsibhir munipuṃgavaiḥ] yauvarājyābhiṣiktas tvaṃ] and consider pādas 66-67 as one

The
Sino-Indian Research Institute
of Peking

The
Sino-Indian Research Institute
of Peking

sentence (which ~~as~~ you suggest) we get a very satisfactory sense:

'Thou art anointed to ~~of~~ yuvarājaship ~~dom~~ (yauvarājya) by the Buddhas, who are the Kings of the Munis.

~~Your index to the Abhidharmakośa is~~
~~I am sending you (under separate cover)~~
~~In a few days I shall send you~~ my edition of the commentary ~~to the Kāśyapaparivarta, I am quite aware of~~ ~~I am afraid that this is not~~ ~~I sh~~ and I shall be very much obliged to you if you will kindly publish a few encouraging words about my latest efforts.

* Since 1929 I ~~am a professor of Central Asian philology~~ ~~professor~~ in Harvard University, the authorities of which have so far ~~very kindly~~ ~~have~~ allowed me ~~so far~~ to live in Peking.* ~~I must, however,~~ ~~I pr~~ I like this city ~~Peking~~

*I am in charge of ~~preside here over~~ the Sino-Indian Institute of Peking, which depends entirely upon American liberality. Professor Weller ......

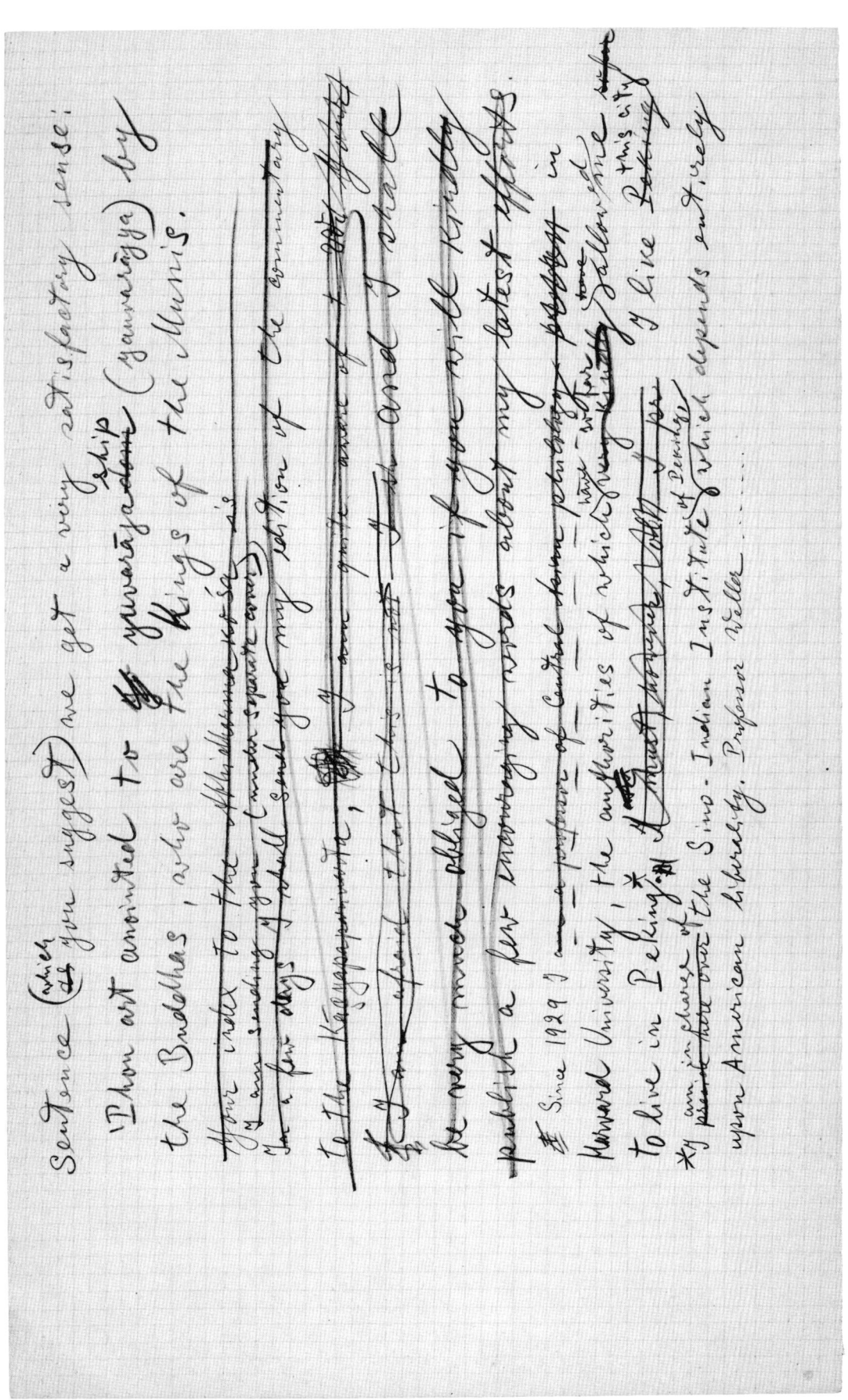

very much, and I hope that ~~I shall be allowed~~ the authorities will let me remain ~~here to stay there~~ for ~~another~~ a few more years. ~~This~~ In order to obtain an extension of my leave, which ~~by~~ has to be renewed every year, I must, however, be able to prove that my work is appreciated in Europe. May I ask you to publish a few encouraging words about my edition of the Kāçyapaparivarta commentary, which I ~~send you~~ am sending you under separate cover, ~~as well as~~ or about ~~the~~ my three articles, which appeared in 1932? A few printed words from you would, ~~as~~ I am sure, considerably impress the American authorities, upon whose decision my fate depends. [illegible] The decisive meeting of the authorities is to take place in the early spring of 1934.

Believe me yours sincerely

A. Staël Holstein.

Mon cher collègue et ami,

J'ai bien reçu il y a quelques jours votre lettre du 29 juillet, et je reçois aujourd'hui, 18 septembre, les volumes de F. Weller et le vôtre. – Ne doutez pas que je n'aie le vif désir de vous être agréable. Je ne publierai rien ces temps-ci (ayant sous presse le 2e vol. de mes Mélanges Chinois-Bouddhiques), mais je vous enverrai sous peu (en dactylo) le texte du cpte-rendu des 2 voll. qui paraîtra dans Mélanges 3 (1933-34) s'il plaît à Dieu!

Le loisir me manque pour étudier Sthiramati; je me borne à lire la préface. La remarque sur .. śrutam / ekasmin samaye est fort curieuse. Pour le svārtha ("utilité personnelle". Le "jeu de soi" de S. Lévi est incompréhensible en français). était-il besoin de Sthiramati pour être fixé sur l'avayava- et samāsārtha ?

Je ne vous cacherai pas que nous attendons avec impatience accrue 1. le texte sanscrit amendé (quelques soient les précisions), 2. la traduction, 3. l'index chinois, 4. l'introduction.

La lecture yauvarājyābhiṣiktas est en effet très bonne.

Peut-être pourriez vous me faire ou donner ou envoyer contre dollars les publications de la 支那內學院 de Nanking et aussi

ling tomb k'o engrave

de 金陵刻經處 de la même ville.

Voici longtemps que je n'ai pas de nouvelles d'Oldenburg et de ཤེར་ཨད་སྐི. Restez vous en contact avec eux? Devaient m'envoyer (de Russie) de petites choses.

Croyez, cher Monsieur, à mes sentiments très distingués et amicaux

Lavallée Poussin

66 Avenue Molière
Uccle-Bruxelles
Belgique.

Dear Professor de la Vallée Poussin,

~~Many thanks~~ I am very much obliged to you for your kind letter ~~and~~ as well as for your readiness to review ~~[illegible]~~ my edition (and to send me a type-written copy of the compte-rendu). ~~[illegible]~~ The 支那內學院 has ~~so far only~~ as far as I know published only ~~four~~ small volumes which I am sending you under separate cover. ~~The fifth volume which you will also find in the book parcel is supposed is a catalogue to contain all the~~ I am also forwarding to your address a catalogue of Buddhist books which is supposed to include practically all the publications of the 金陵刻經處. ~~[illegible] Nearly all the~~ The great majority of the books edited by the latter ~~[illegible]~~ seem to be sūtras or śāstras found in the Japanese editions of the Chinese Tripiṭaka. I shall be only too glad to send you the Chinese publications which you need. ~~Please let me know about your wishes~~ ~~May I ask you, however, to~~ Please let me know about your wishes. ~~The type-written~~ Believe me yours sincerely and gratefully

A. Staël Holstein

Dear Woods,

Would not it be a good thing to talk ~~our~~ matters ~~with Mr Boyden~~ (tomorrow, I think) over à trois with Mr. Boyden before his departure for Japan?
I sent him a second (verbal) invitation ~~message~~ through Mr. Roger Greene's brother, ~~yesterday, who is in constant commun[illegible] but he has not come to my house yet. He did not~~ but he has not yet fulfilled his promise to call here. Could you not bring him to my house this evening between 6.30 and 8 o'clock for a cocktail?
~~My~~ The "hall of the Arhat's" an important feature of my establishment is not quite ready yet, and I think I shall postpone my Chinese party until the completion of the necessary alterations.

My dear Professor Yuan,

~~[illegible]~~ I have much pleasure in accepting your kind invitation for Wednesday October 9th, 1 o'clock. My wife ~~regrets very [illegible]~~ thanks you very much for having included her, but regrets that she will be unable to come on account of a bad cold. Believe me yours most sincerely AStaelHolstein.

Le baron et la baronne de Staël-Holstein remercient Monsieur et Madame Ed. H. de Tscharner pour leur aimable invitation (dimanche, 13 octobre, 1 heure), à laquelle ils auront l'honneur de se rendre.

Peking le 8 octobre 1929.

Hanoï, 17 juillet 1922.

ÉCOLE FRANÇAISE
D'EXTRÊME-ORIENT

Cher Monsieur,

Je vous prie d'excuser le retard que j'ai mis à vous envoyer les fascicules du *Bulletin* de l'École dont vous aviez besoin. Ils sont partis il y a cinq jours. Pour le *Sūtrālaṃkāra* de Sylvain Lévi, M. Finot reste intraitable...

Nous préparons un volume consacré à l'œuvre de l'École depuis 1900. Je me permettrai de vous l'envoyer, et, si vous y voyez mentionnés des articles qui vous intéressent, vous n'aurez qu'à me les demander.

Nous avons eu le malheur de perdre M. Péri, mort des suites d'un accident d'automo-

lui. C'était un esprit rare, remarquable à la fois par son érudition profonde et sagace et par son intelligence artistique. Ses travaux sur la littérature dramatique japonaise sont bien connus; ceux qui ont trait à l'histoire du bouddhisme le sont à peine, parce qu'il a utilisé exclusivement les textes chinois; il a été sans doute le premier à étudier sérieusement le bouddhisme purement chinois, en particulier dans les ouvrages incorporés au Supplément du Tripiṭaka de Kyōto.

Nous attendons impatiemment votre 迦葉品; M. Toussaint nous a apporté l'heureuse nouvelle que vous vous êtes décidé à enrichir votre ouvrage d'une traduction. En passant à Nankin, j'ai rendu visite à 歐陽漸, le maître de votre élève. C'est un homme à l'esprit ouvert et fort éveillé, mais je crains que son institut, comme c'est trop souvent le cas en Chine, n'existe que sous forme de programmes éloquents et grandioses. Il m'a dit qu'il souhaitait vivement que son disciple se rendît en Europe.

J'ai visité un certain nombre de monastères au 浙江 et au 福建 ; je n'ai pas réussi à y rencontrer un moine érudit. Dans le principal monastère de 普陀, notamment, une des armoires contenant le Tripitaka a failli s'écrouler quand je l'ai fait ouvrir. Décidément, je ne crois pas que la Chine offre rien de bien intéressant dans ce domaine. Chez le clergé annamite, c'est l'ignorance crasse.

Veuillez agréer, cher Monsieur, l'expression de mes sentiments respectueux.

P. Demiéville

P. S. Je vous prie de conserver le Winternitz, dont je n'ai nul besoin. Si vous avez besoin d'autres livres, veuillez me les signaler : je pourrai peut-être vous les procurer.

J'ai envoyé à 胡適 un certain nombre de fascicules du Bulletin de l'École ; je vous serais fort reconnaissant de le lui faire savoir, car la poste chinoise m'inspire quelque inquiétude. Je viens également d'écrire à 黃建.

P. Demiéville

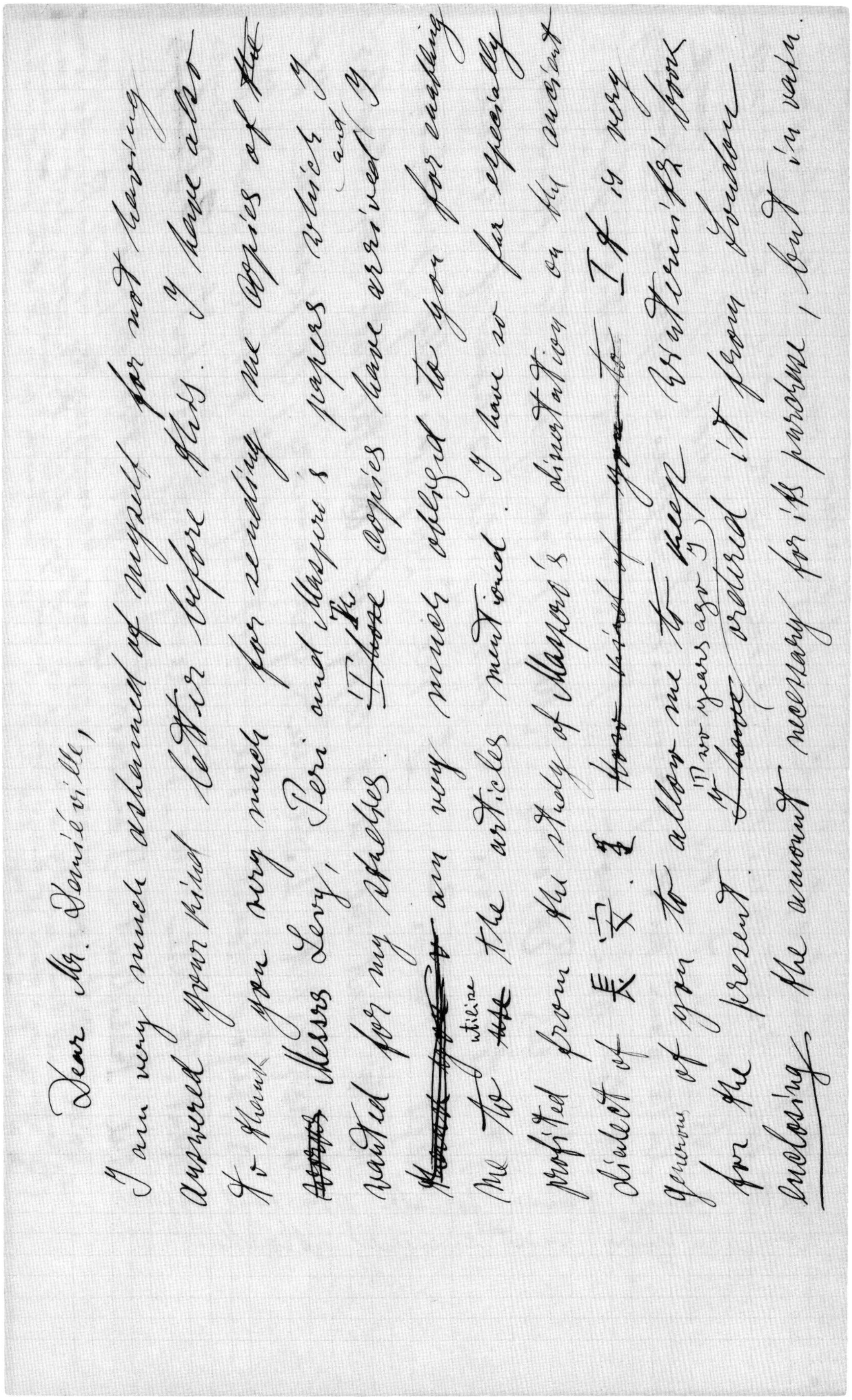

Dear Mr. Demiéville,

I am very much ashamed of myself for not having answered your kind letter before this. I have also to thank you very much for sending me copies of ~~the~~ Messrs Levy, Péri and Maspero's papers which I wanted for my studies. ~~Those~~ The copies have arrived and I ~~thank you~~ am very much obliged to you for enabling me to ~~use~~ utilize the articles mentioned. I have so far especially profited from the study of Maspero's dissertation on the ancient dialect of 長安. ~~How kind of you to~~ It is very generous of you to allow me to keep Winternitz' book for the present. ~~I have~~ Two years ago I ordered it from London enclosing the amount necessary for its purchase, but in vain.

A friend of mine has ~~written~~ a year ago written to Leipzic for Winternitz' book with the same sad result. As I want the book very much I shall ~~keep~~ with your kind permission refrain from returning it to you now. I enclose a letter for Mr. des Rotours. May I ask you to forward it to him in case he should have left Hanoi? ~~I~~ He very kindly promised me to send me a ~~I~~ copy of ~~the~~ the late Mr. Cordier's lithographed Tibetan grammar, if possible. It is beyond doubt the best of its kind and I want to use it in teaching my students. ~~B~~ ~~Perhaps~~ Maybe the President Toussaint has got two copies of the work. Will you please present my compliments to the President Toussaint?

I have several times spoken to Mr. Hu who is now Dean of all the faculties about the possibility of offering you a chair at this University. He seemed to be very much in favour of asking you to come to Peking and I hope that he will do it soon. Unfortunately he is ill at the present moment.

With many thanks for all your kind offices I remain yours most sincerely A. Staël-Holstein.

ÉCOLE FRANÇAISE
D'EXTRÊME-ORIENT

Hanoi, 22 janvier 1923

Cher Monsieur,

Je vous remercie vivement de votre aimable lettre du 10 décembre. Elle m'est parvenue trop tard pour que j'aie pu remettre à mon ami des Rotours celle que vous y aviez jointe; je l'ai fait suivre à son adresse à Paris. Des Rotours n'est resté que cinq jours à Hanoi, étant pressé de continuer son voyage. J'ai reçu depuis lors de ses bonnes nouvelles de Bangkok et de Penang.

Nous avons communiqué au directeur et au secrétaire de l'École votre désir d'acquérir un exemplaire du second tibétain du Dr Cordier. La malchance veut qu'il n'en reste aucun exemplaire disponible. M. Toussaint, auquel j'ai transmis vos messages, n'en possède de son côté qu'un seul. Je crains donc, à mon sincère regret, de ne pouvoir vous procurer cet ouvrage actuellement. Il est d'ailleurs question, depuis quelque temps déjà, d'en publier à Paris une édition imprimée. J'ai songé à faire copier pour vous ~~ch~~ l'exemplaire de l'Ecole française ; mais nous n'avons aucun copiste capable de reproduire l'écriture tibétaine ; et il me semble qu'une copie du texte français, sans les citations de tibétaines (données presque exclusivement en écriture indigène), serait fort dispendieuse. Si toutefois je me trompe sur ce dernier point, et qu'une pareille copie vous paraisse utilisable, je suis tout prêt à la faire exécuter et à vous l'envoyer.

En attendant, je me permets de vous expédier le dernier fascicule de notre Bulletin. Comme je vous l'ai dit dans ma dernière lettre, si vous trouvez mentionnés dans ce fascicule des travaux, publiés par l'École, qui vous intéressent, je serai heureux de vous les faire tenir.

Nous avons eu la visite de M. Sylvain Lévi, revenant de l'Inde et du Népal,

où il a fait un voyage fructueux. Il
passe maintenant quelques mois au Japon;
il y fera des cours sur les origines du
tantrisme et les rapports du bouddhisme
avec le jaïnisme. Il avait l'intention
de rentrer en France, si possible, par le
Transsibérien. Si ce projet est réalisable,
il s'arrêtera sans doute à Pékin, et
sera enchanté de faire la connaissance
de vos élèves chinois, notamment de
黃建, dont je lui ai parlé. Il
emmène lui-même à Paris un
jeune Bengali qui étudie le
bouddhisme chinois et prépare une
traduction du 釋迦方志. Si

ÉCOLE FRANÇAISE
D'EXTRÊME-ORIENT

la voie du Transsibérien est impraticable, il rentrera directement par ~~Sibérie~~ l'Indochine.

Je vous suis extrêmement obligé d'avoir bien voulu songer à moi pour une chaire à l'Université de Pékin, et d'en avoir entretenu M. Hou. Sur le conseil de M. Lévi, je me suis décidé à demander une prolongation d'un an de mon terme de séjour à l'École française. Il est donc fort probable que je resterai ici jusqu'au début de l'année prochaine. Pour plus tard, M. Lévi m'a proposé de me rendre au Japon afin de m'occuper de la préparation de l'encyclopédie bouddhique projetée par l'association internationale des sociétés asiatiques. Mais cette proposition était assez vague. Vous savez qu'on parle de cette encyclopédie depuis 1902 .... Je ne sais si M. Lévi obtiendra cette fois des précisions, sinon des garanties, sur la contribution japonaise. Si le travail dont il m'a parlé ne peut être entrepris, je serai certainement fort heureux de trouver une situation à Pékin, où je disposerais de ressources de toutes sortes pour poursuivre mes études sinologiques.

J'espère avoir, d'ici là, publié un ou deux travaux qui me donneraient quelque assurance pour oser risquer un enseignement. La publication du Bulletin est considérablement retardée par l'impression de l'index des vingt premiers tomes, qui dure depuis plusieurs mois et n'est pas près encore d'être terminée. M. de Rotours m'a dit que la Commercial Press, elle aussi, me faisait languir. Nous avons appris avec joie votre intention de joindre à l'édition des textes une traduction.

Veuillez, je vous prie, me rappeler au souvenir de M. Hou et de 黄建, en présentant au premier mes voeux de guérison.

Agréez, cher Monsieur, mes sentiments

nous pour vos offres bienveillantes et l'assurance
de mes sentiments les plus dévoués

P. Demiéville

Dear Mr. Demiéville,

Many thanks for your kind letter dated January 22nd 1923 and all my apologies for ~~this~~ this late reply. I am also very much obliged to you for trying to get me a copy of Cordier's Tibetan grammar and for actually sending me a copy of the history of the École Française d'Extrême-Orient.

Monsieur Sylvain Lévi spent about ten days in Peking ~~about~~ a little more than three months ago. I saw him several times nearly every day during his visit and he also made the acquaintance of my late pupil Huang-chien. I say "late" because Mr. Huang died about two months ago from scarlet fever. This is a very great loss for oriental learning and for me personally. I do not know who is going to take his place as my Chinese assistant; I shall hardly ever find anyone so devoted to my particular line of studies in this country.

Monsieur Sylvain Lévi left here, I think, on the first of May for France via Siberia. ~~I have~~ None of his Peking friends have received any ~~as~~ direct news from him since he crossed the frontier of Manchuria, but we have learnt from the Soviet newspapers that he has been much fêted at Moscow and at Petrograd.

T'sai-yuan-p'ei who used to be Chancellor of the National University (and who took ~~an~~ a great interest in Buddhist studies) has left Peking many months ago on account of differences with the politicians; a few weeks ago he ~~flott~~ married a Miss Chow and ~~left for~~ sailed for Belgium where he intends staying one or two years. They say that upon his return to China he will once more assume the office of Chancellor which is at present vacant.

Our friend Hu-shih who used to be, ~~the sec~~ as dean of the facultties, the second in command, has fallen ill; he has also left Peking and nobody knows whether and when he will return. Hu-shih was, as you know, the chief promoter of "western" orientalism in China and during ~~his~~ the absence of both Ts'ai-yuan-p'ei and Hu-shih nothing much can be done for extending the personnel of the oriental department.

~~I am very sorry for~~ I regret that very much, because I hoped that we might invite you and some other European scholars to collaborate in a field which ~~off~~ surely offers many great possibilities. As things are ~~at~~ all these plans will have to remain in abeyance for the time being.

~~With~~ Monsieur Sylvain Lévi promised to send me ~~the~~ Winternitz' book from Europe. May I keep your Copy of it until I get Monsieur Sylvain Lévi's parcel?

With many thanks for your kindness I remain

Yours sincerely A Staël Holstein

ÉCOLE FRANÇAISE
D'EXTRÊME-ORIENT

Hanoi, 10 février 1924

Monsieur

Je suis très honteux de n'avoir pas encore répondu à vos bienveillantes lignes du 7 août 1923, d'autant plus que je crains maintenant que celles-ci ne vous atteignent plus à Pékin. J'ai appris avec un vif regret la mort de votre brillant et sympathique élève; c'est là, comme vous le dites, une perte réelle pour les études orientales, et aussi pour la Chine; parmi les « Jeunes Chinois » que j'ai rencontrés au cours de mon voyage en Chine, il était le seul, avec Hou Che, qui m'eût donné l'impression d'être sérieux. J'ai envoyé une lettre de condoléances à son maître M. 歐陽漸 de Nankin, auquel j'ai rendu visite en revenant de Pékin. Je me permets de vous en présenter également, car outre la peine qu'a dû vous causer ce regrettable événement, j'imagine la difficulté que vous aurez eue à trouver un successeur capable de vous assister utilement.

Je vous dois des remerciements, tardifs eux aussi à ma sincère confusion, pour l'intéressant article sur les Hutuktu de Pékin, que vous avez bien voulu m'envoyer avec le volume de Winternitz. En en préparant un compte rendu qui paraîtra dans le prochain numéro du Bulletin de l'École, j'ai trouvé, soit dans des ouvrages européens dont vous ne disposiez pas, soit dans les sources chinoises, quelques renseignements complémentaires confirmant les dires de votre lama, sauf sur quelques points de détail ; j'espère que vous ne m'en voudrez pas de les publier.

Le même numéro contiendra des comptes rendus de tous les ouvrages de Hou Che. Je les ai lus et médités attentivement, et en définitive mon impression est nettement favorable. Le dernier numéro du T'oung pao contient un compte rendu de Pelliot d'un ouvrage de Hou che composé en anglais en 1915 et réédité récemment à Chang-hai : c'est la "thèse" par laquelle il a débuté. Pelliot ne connaît aucun des ouvrages qu'il a publiés depuis lors ; il se prononce favorablement, mais avec une réserve montrant qu'il ... se méfie un peu.

Mon ami des Rotours m'a envoyé de ses bonnes nouvelles ; il se remémore ses voyages au coin du feu. Il m'a écrit que M. et Mme Sylvain Lévi sont rentrés de Varsovie à Paris ... en avion !

Je vous suis mille fois obligé d'avoir pris la peine de me tenir au courant des possibilités de mon engagement comme professeur à l'Université de Pékin. Depuis cinq jours je n'appartiens plus à l'École française, mais je compte prolonger mon séjour à Hanoi jusqu'à la fin de mars ou au début d'avril. Je me rendrai ensuite en Chine ou au Japon, car je suis décidé à ne pas rentrer en Europe, où je n'ai rien à faire, avant de m'être assuré une situation quelconque en Extrême-Orient. Si donc il se présentait une occasion à l'Université de Pékin, je serais toujours disposé à la prendre en considération. La "Jeune Chine" est extrêmement mal vue ici : c'est presque une crise de sinophobie. Sylvain Lévi lui-même, qui est pourtant d'une indulgence excessive à l'égard des Orientaux, a jugé, paraît-il, l'Université de Pékin d'une façon tout à fait pessimiste. J'ai passablement réfléchi sur ces questions depuis mon retour de Chine, et je crois, en définitive, que le public français a une tendance à exagérer et que la situation intellectuelle de la Chine est loin d'être désespérée.

En dépaquetant votre colis, j'espérais presque y trouver votre édition et votre traduction du Ratnakūṭa; M. Toussaint se joint à moi pour souhaiter que la Commercial Press ne tarde pas davantage à nous livrer votre œuvre. Mon travail sur Nāgasena est enfin à l'impression.

Veuillez agréer, Monsieur, l'expression de mes sentiments les plus dévoués et reconnaissants

P. Demiéville

MAISON FRANCO-JAPONAISE

~~20 NITCHÔMÉ NAGATACHÔ, KÔJIMATCHI-KOU,~~

~~TOKIO~~

~~TÉLÉPHONE: GINZA [illegible]~~

19 mars 1928

n° 1 Mita-Kōunchō,
Shiba, Tokyo.

Cher Monsieur,

Mille mercis de vos aimables voeux. Les charmantes photographies m'ont fait plaisir, mais plus encore votre souvenir.

Voulez-vous me permettre de vous parler d'un de mes anciens étudiants d'Amoy, qui voudrait aller étudier le sanscrit auprès de vous? C'est un garçon d'une trentaine d'années, qui était maître d'école et a fait des économies pour entrer à l'université. Je lui ai appris quelques éléments de sanscrit, et depuis mon départ il a continué à étudier tous seul à Amoy où il habite avec sa vieille mère. Mais naturellement il lui faudrait un maître; je l'ai encouragé à aller auprès de vous, et il paraît décidé à se rendre à Pékin après avoir terminé ses études à l'université d'Amoy — c'est-à-dire en septembre prochain. Toutefois, avant de quitter Amoy où il a de graves charges de famille, il désirerait être assuré que vous serez encore à Pékin l'automne prochain, et aussi renseigné sur les conditions dans lesquelles il pourrait "recevoir vos instructions". Il m'a demandé de le renseigner sur vos projets, sur l'organisation de votre Institut Sino-indien, sur l'institution où vous enseignez actuellement, etc. et aussi de le recommander à vous.

auriez-vous peut-être la bonté de lui écrire un mot directement, pour éviter un retard ? Je vois d'après ses lettres qu'il voudrait être fixé bientôt, pour prendre des mesures nécessaires à son départ. Vous trouverez ci-dessous son nom et son adresse. S'il vous déplaît de lui écrire directement, peut-être voudrez-vous bien m'envoyer les renseignements qu'il désire, et que je lui transmettrais.

C'était de beaucoup mon meilleur étudiant à Amoy, et un des Chinois les plus distingués que je connaisse. Il est intelligent, très travailleur, d'esprit sérieux et déjà mûr, parfaitement désintéressé et courtois, et ne s'attache qu'à l'étude. Il sait fort bien l'anglais, connaît et écrit bien le chinois classique, et il est décidé à se consacrer tout entier à l'étude du bouddhisme... si la vie le lui permet.. Depuis mon départ d'Amoy il a étudié seul les volumes du "Sanskrit Tutor" publiés à Trivandrum par Sambasiva Sastrizal, et a bien pioché la grammaire ; mais évidemment, sans la direction d'un maître il n'aboutirait à rien. Il serait malheureux qu'un garçon si bien doué et riche de promesses soit abandonné à lui-même dans ce trou d'Amoy. Il n'a aucun préjugé à l'égard des étrangers, et je suis sûr que s'il devient votre étudiant vous n'aurez qu'à vous louer de son commerce. A mon égard il a toujours été charmant.

Ici notre Dictionnaire avance lentement mais régulièrement. L'impression

MAISON FRANCO-JAPONAISE
28 NITCHÔMÉ NAGATACHÔ, KÔJIMATCHI-KOU,
TOKIO
TÉLÉPHONE: GINZA 4906 & 7209

du premier fascicule est commencé. La lettre B qui contient tant d'articles importants est à peu près terminée. Le travail est long car nous sommes obligés de vérifier et de compléter à chaque pas les encyclopédies japonaises, et aussi de remanier entièrement le plan des articles et la disposition des matériaux, car la science japonaise se signale par un manque d'esprit de synthèse et une incapacité d'ordonner les idées, qui rendraient impossible une traduction directe des encyclopédies japonaises.

M. et Mme Lévi quitteront le Japon à la fin de mai, pour rentrer en France par étapes, en passant en Indochine, aux Indes néerlandaises, au Népal, en Abyssinie, en Syrie ... Le successeur de M. Lévi comme directeur de la Maison Franco-Japonaise sera un botaniste, M. Blaringhem. Il arrivera au début de l'an prochain, et jusque là c'est moi qui assurerai l'intérim. M. Henri Maspero, professeur de chinois au Collège de France, viendra également au Japon pour s'occuper des travaux d'orientalisme entrepris à la Maison Franco-Japonaise.

Veuillez agréer, cher Monsieur, l'assurance de mes sentiments d'ami fidèle

P. Demiéville

Voici le nom et l'adresse de l'indianiste en question :

福建省厦門城霞溪仔頂井仔巷

門牌第四号

林藜光

A few days ago Mr. Elis informed me by telegram that he would arrive at Peking "in time." That is certainly good news, but the Japanese assistant is of still greater importance

Cher Monsieur,

~~Je vous suis infiniment reconnaissant pour votre lettre et pour le ll~~

Je suis tout à fait confus ~~de~~ de ne pas vous avoir ~~pas~~ remercié plus tôt pour votre ~~aimable~~ lettre, pour la dépêche et pour la soie, que vos amis français de Yokohama m'ont ~~fait parvenir~~ envoyée. ~~Mais j'ai une excuse. Les photographies ci-jointes prouvent~~ J'ai aussi reçu le premier fascicule du Hōbōgirin, qui m'a beaucoup impressionné. ~~Je n'ose à peine~~ Je n'ose même pas espérer que ~~nous~~ se produira jamais quelque chose d'aussi parfait ~~à Pékin~~ avec mes assistants pékinois.

I am very glad to learn from your letter that there is some hope of my getting ~~an English speaking Japanese~~ a Japanese assistant, but ~~But could not~~ Takakusu seems to be ~~hopeless~~ far too slow. Could ~~you~~ not you get me one without the aid of Takakusu? The conditions are: six hours' attendance at the Institute on ~~every~~ week days and Two hundred Chinese dollars a month. In case we like one another I hope that the assistant will stay much much longer. I enjoyed the hours I spent with you at Yokohama and at Kamakura ~~very~~ enormousely and I ~~th~~ thank you very much for all your kindness. May I ask to be remembered to Madame Demiéville? Hoping to receive your telegram in the near future I remain yours most sincerely A. Staël-Holstein.

The Institute is situated in the ~~Legation Quarter~~ Ex-Austrian Legation [compound] (Legation Quarter) and ~~is~~ ~~under the special prot~~ Japanese [and the Institute's] troops are [especially] ~~in~~ charged with its protection. My ~~next~~ door neighbour is a Japanese infantry officer who lives here with his family. He may possibly ~~then~~ let a room to my Japanese assistant (who will of course [have to] pay for it out of his salary), but I have not consulted him ~~yet~~ on the matter ~~yet~~. There are many other Japanese families in the Legation Quarter and I am ~~almost~~ [quite] certain that a suitable lodging can be found here for my Japanese assistant. ~~I pre~~ But I do not like talking to any ~~future landlord~~ Japanese landlord before the arrival of the assistant at Peking. ~~In case of need I could appeal to Mr. Yoshizawa, the Japanese minister, with whom I am personally acquainted.~~ ~~It will~~ I will ~~send~~ [wire] you two hundred Chinese dollars as the assistant's travelling expenses as soon as I get your telegram "heureka". Please do not bind me for ~~longer~~ any longer period than ~~six~~ four months. I promise to pay the assistant's travelling expenses ~~(in~~ (200 Chinese dollars) [back to Japan] at the end of that period [if required].

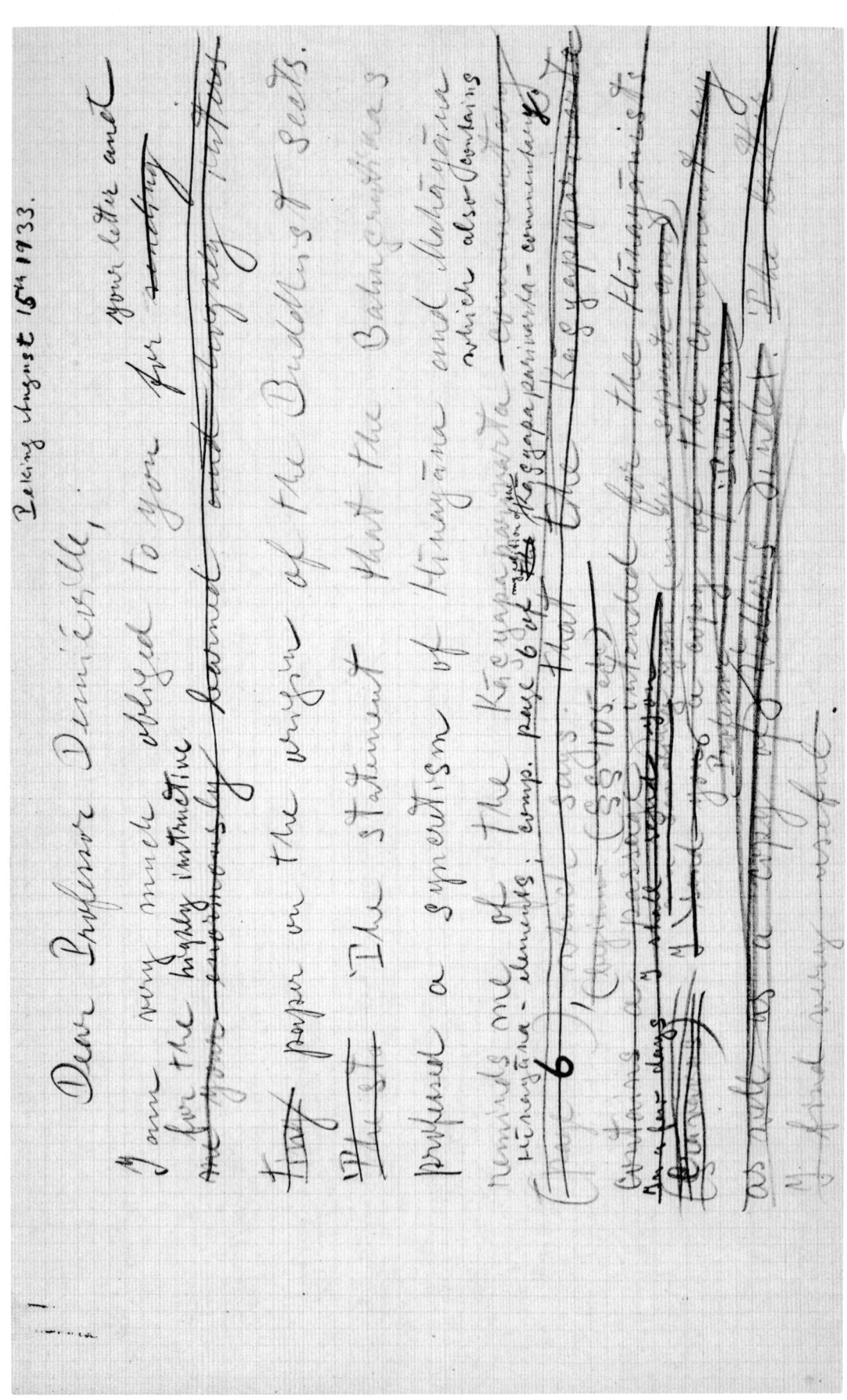

Peking August 15th 1933.

Dear Professor Demiéville,

I am very much obliged to you for your letter and ~~sending~~ for the highly instructive ~~me your enormously learned and highly interesting~~ ~~thy~~ paper on the origin of the Buddhist sects.

~~The sta~~ The statement that the Bahuçrutīkas professed a syncretism of Hīnayāna and Mahāyāna reminds me of the Kāçyapaparivarta ~~commentary~~ which also contains Hīnayāna-elements; comp. page 6 of my edition of ~~the~~ Kāçyapaparivarta-commentary.

~~(page 6), which says that the Kāçyapaparivarta (beginning (§§ 105 etc.) contains a passage intended for the Hīnayānists~~

~~In a few days I shall send you (under separate cover) I send you a copy of the commentary as well as a copy of Professor Stael's Tibetan Index. The latter I find very useful.~~

~~On 9th~~ ~~I am sor~~

~~Mr. Liu has ~~been~~ helped me very much in reading the proof sheets of the edition, and I regret his departure for Europe leaves a gap which will be difficult to fill.~~

I send you under separate cover a copy of this edition as well as a copy of Professor Weller's index. The former was printed at the Commercial Press (Chinese management) and the latter at the Imprimerie des Lazaristes which is much more efficient.

I regret very much I part from Mr. Lin (which has occupied him [illegible] which he has worked for a long time, with great Mr. Lin's Chinese index, as for is not ready yet, and I tried in vain to make him stay here until that work the completion of that work. On the other hand I must admit that he should not miss the opportunities which Paris offers Paris off he will enjoy in Paris. His stay there will certainly be of the greatest importance for his scientific career, and if If the budget of the Sino-Indian Institute had not been reduced as so drastically cut, I should certainly have paid for Mr. Lin's voyage travelling expenses. to France. In view of the financial depression, which has struck us, all I can do is to wish him a happy voyage to France.

May I ask to be kindly remembered to Madame Demiéville.

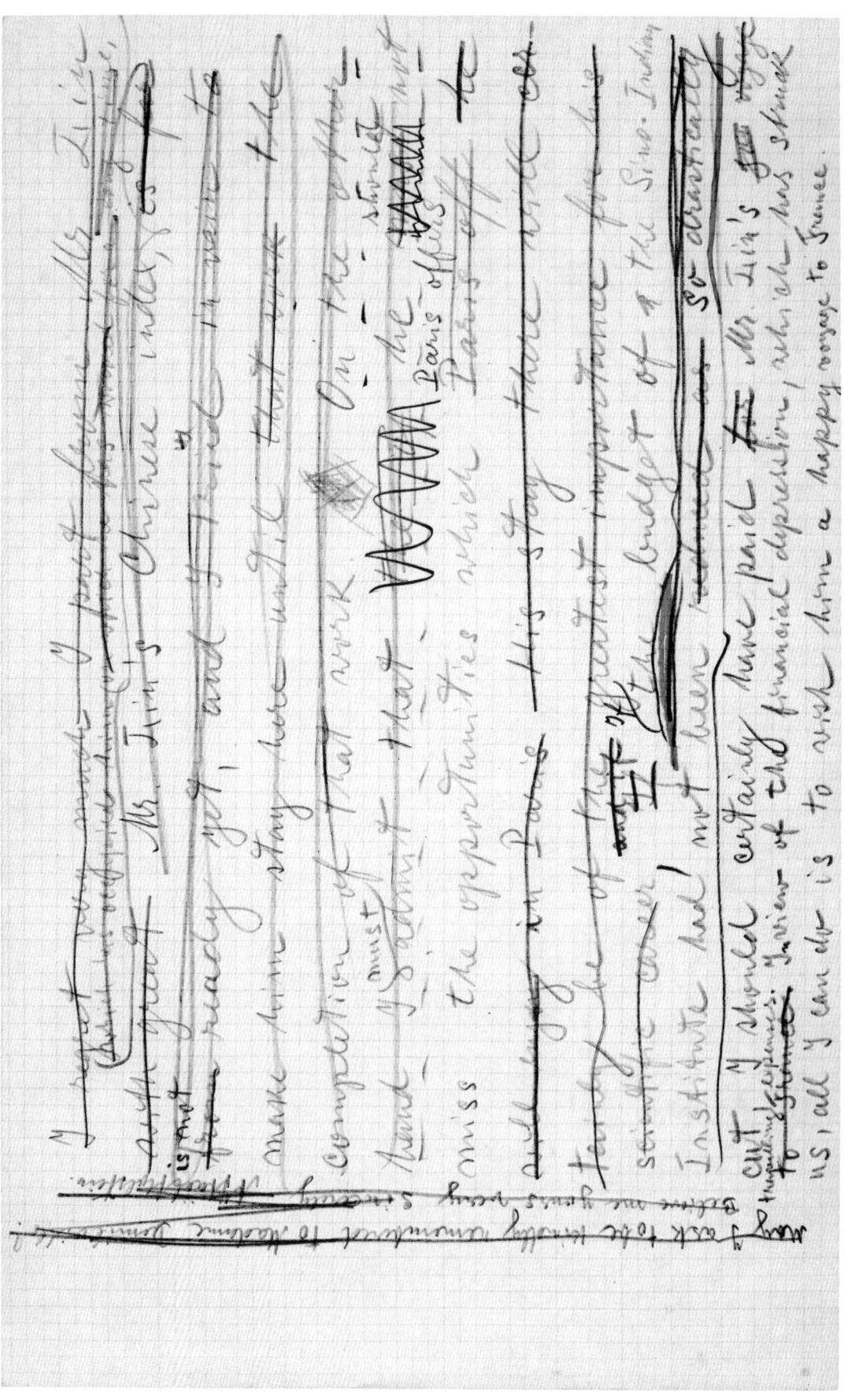

Believe me yours very sincerely

~~Seeing the commentary edition through the press was not an easy task, because the Chinese compositors of the 京華 were entirely unacquainted with diacritical marks etc. The French press of the Pei T'ang, which printed Professor Weller's index, is much more efficient.~~

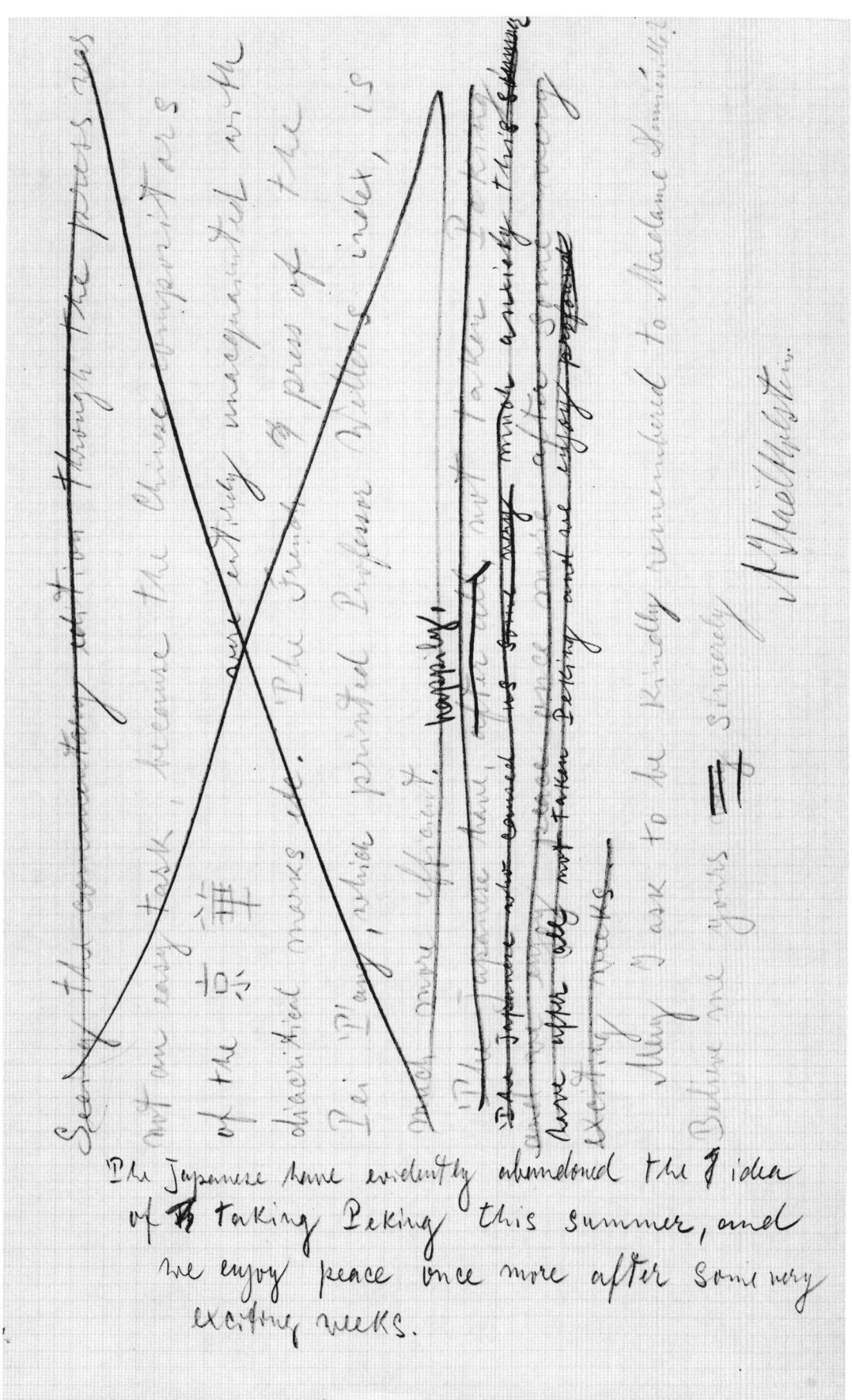

~~The Japanese have, after all happily, not taken Peking and we enjoy peace once more after some very exciting weeks.~~

~~The Japanese who caused us some very much anxiety this summer have after all not taken Peking and we enjoy profound~~

May I ask to be kindly remembered to Madame Sommerville?

Believe me yours ~~very~~ sincerely

A. Staël-Holstein.

The Japanese have evidently abandoned the ~~f~~ idea of ~~t~~ taking Peking this summer, and we enjoy peace once more after some very exciting weeks.

Dear Mr. des Rotours

I am very sorry that I was at the last moment prevented from carrying out my intention of seeing you off at the station when you ~~were leaving~~ left Peking about a month ago. It is such a pity you have gone away. You were one of the very few people with scientific interests in Peking and I enjoyed our meetings enormously. I have got some new ~~bud~~ Buddhas recently and regret very much that I cannot submit them to your expert judgment. When you left you were kind enough to say that you would try and get me a copy of ~~Cor~~ the late M. Cordier's lithographed Tibetan grammar. May I remind you of your obliging promise? I have several ~~Tibeto~~ students of classical Tibetan in my class now and possess no grammar at all. I think that Cordier's grammar is by far the best of all existing books on the subject and I would be <u>so</u> grateful to you for getting me a copy. Hoping to see you soon back again at Peking I remain yours most sincerely AStaëlHolstein.

Peking October 2nd 1922

Dear Professor Sirén,

Unfortunately I am busy tomorrow morning. But I shall call at your hotel on Wednesday at 10 a.m.

Yours sincerely

Tsing Hua Yuan,
d. 13. August 1929.

Sehr verehrter Baron Staël Holstein,

Gestern bei meiner Rückkehr aus den Bergen fand ich Ihre Sendung vor. Es ist wirklich sehr liebenswürdig, daß Sie sich meines beiläufig geäußerten Wunsches erinnert haben; nehmen Sie inzwischen meinen verbindlichsten Dank!
Anfang nächsten Monats werde ich mir erlauben Sie aufzusuchen.

Mit freundl. Empfehlungen

Ihr sehr ergebener

G. Ecke.

Peiping, ~~Peking,~~ June 7th 1936.

To the editor of the Harvard Journal of Asiatic Studies.

Dear Sir, I have with many thanks received the reprints of my article, and I beg to enclose a cheque for eleven dollars and ten cents, the amount of your bill dated April 22nd 1936. ~~I have received~~ ~~The re-prints of my article with many thanks. I have with many thanks received your~~ In his letter dated March 29th 1936 Professor Elisséeff, (who may have already left Cambridge on his usual trip to France) says that if I have other articles to give you for your journal, they will be welcome. I shall be very grateful to you, if you will publish my article entitled "Avalokita and Apalokita" in one of the forthcoming numbers of the journal. I am sending you the manuscript (ninety three pages) under separate cover. May I ask for the favour of a deferred telegram? ~~from you?~~ ~~If you~~ Please telegraph the one word "yes" if you intend publishing my article in one of the forthcoming numbers of the journal. If I find the word "no" in your telegram, I shall understand that my paper will not appear in the Harvard Journal of Asiatic Studies. I venture to ask for telegraphic advice, because I am very anxious to see the article, on which I have spent much time and energy, published. ~~[illegible]~~ I naturally prefer the Harvard Journal of Asiatic Studies, but I know of other periodicals, which would ~~publish~~ accept my paper. ~~If my article~~ In case my article should be published by the Harvard Journal of Asiatic Studies, I shall ask for one hundred extra-reprints.

Yours sincerely

A. Staël-Holstein.

My address for telegrams is: Stael Amexco Peiping.

Registered A.R.

Manuscript for print

To

the Editor of the Harvard Journal of Asiatic Stu[dies]

Boylston Hall

Cambridge Mass

U.S. of America

[...]報紙

[...]VING FORM

交通部電報局

TELEGRAPH OFFICE

MINISTRY OF COMMUNICATIONS

[...]M CPD 1B[...]	備註 Service Instructions:	VIA CGRA					來報號數 TELEGRAM NO. 15
[...]E 3 22	流水號數 RUNNING XB16	報類 CLASS	發報局名 OFFICE FROM CAMBRIDGE MASS				派送員 BY:
[...]員 LIU	原來號數 ORIGINAL NO. AC201	字數 WORDS 6		日期 DATE 30	時刻 TIME 147P		

LC STAEL AMEXCO PEIPING

YES

ELISSEEFF

注意：如有查詢事項請帶此紙

Note: Any enquiry respecting this telegram, please produce this form.

請閱背面

[...]

THE UNIVERSITY
HONGKONG.

Dec. 1. 1917.

Dear Baron Staël,

When are you coming here? I hope that the troubles in Russia have not caused you to alter your plans. The weather in Hongkong is very pleasant, although we have left off our summer clothes, it is still quite warm.

I am looking forward
to having you here as
my guest some time &
hope that I shall not
be disappointed.

Yours sincerely

Eliot

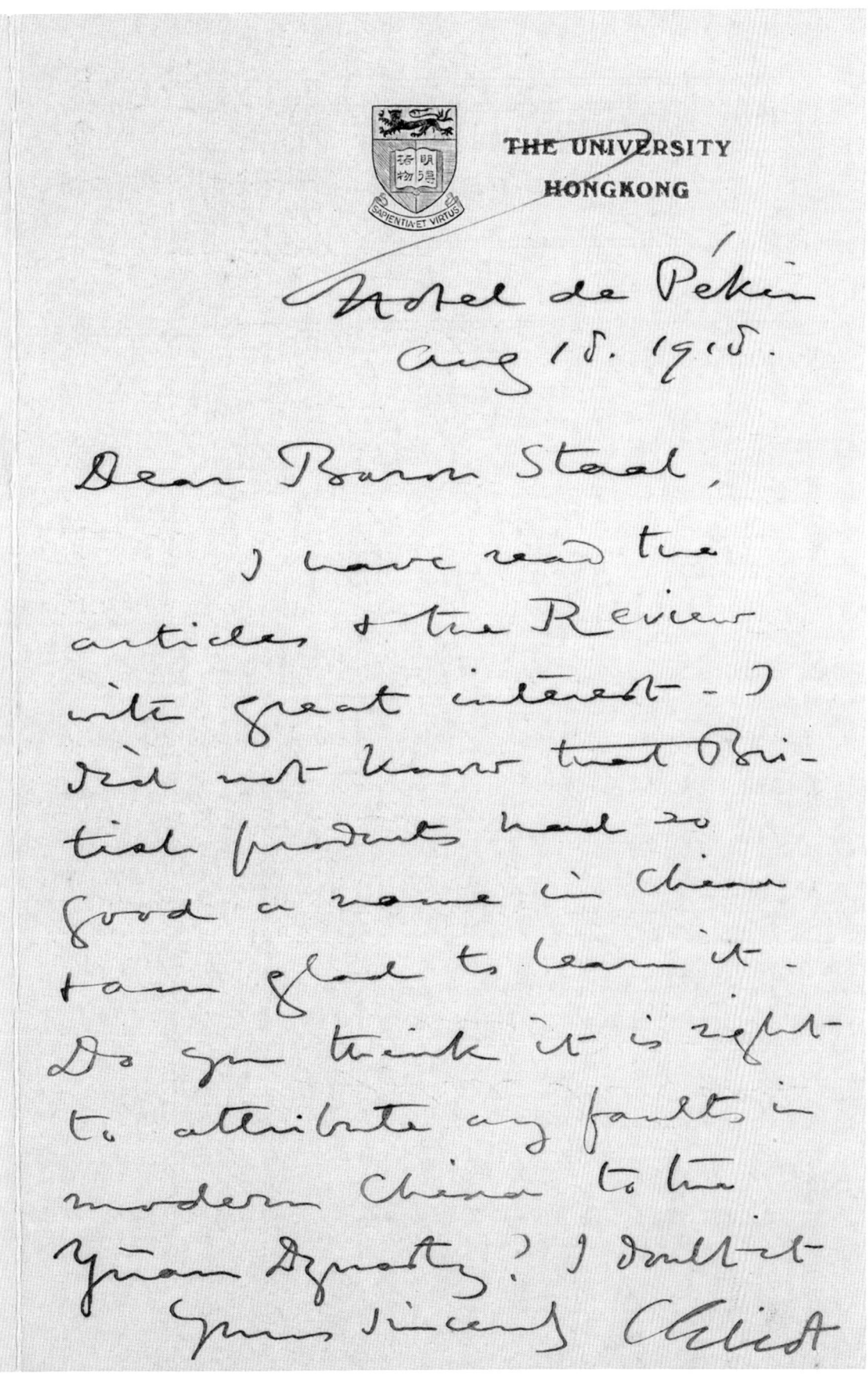

~~THE UNIVERSITY~~
~~HONGKONG~~

Hotel de Pékin
Aug 18. 1918.

Dear Baron Staël,

I have read the articles & the Review with great interest — I did not know that British products had so good a name in China & am glad to learn it. Do you think it is right to attribute any faults in modern China to the Yüan Dynasty? I doubt it.

Yours sincerely
C Eliot

GRAND HOTEL DE PÉKIN

TEL. ADDRESS: "GRAND HOTEL," PEKING — **PEKING** — CODE: A.B.C. 5TH EDITION

北京飯店

PEI-TCHING-FAN-TIEN

TELEPHONE No. 581 & 2250 TUNG-CHU

Peking, ... 191 ....

Thursday

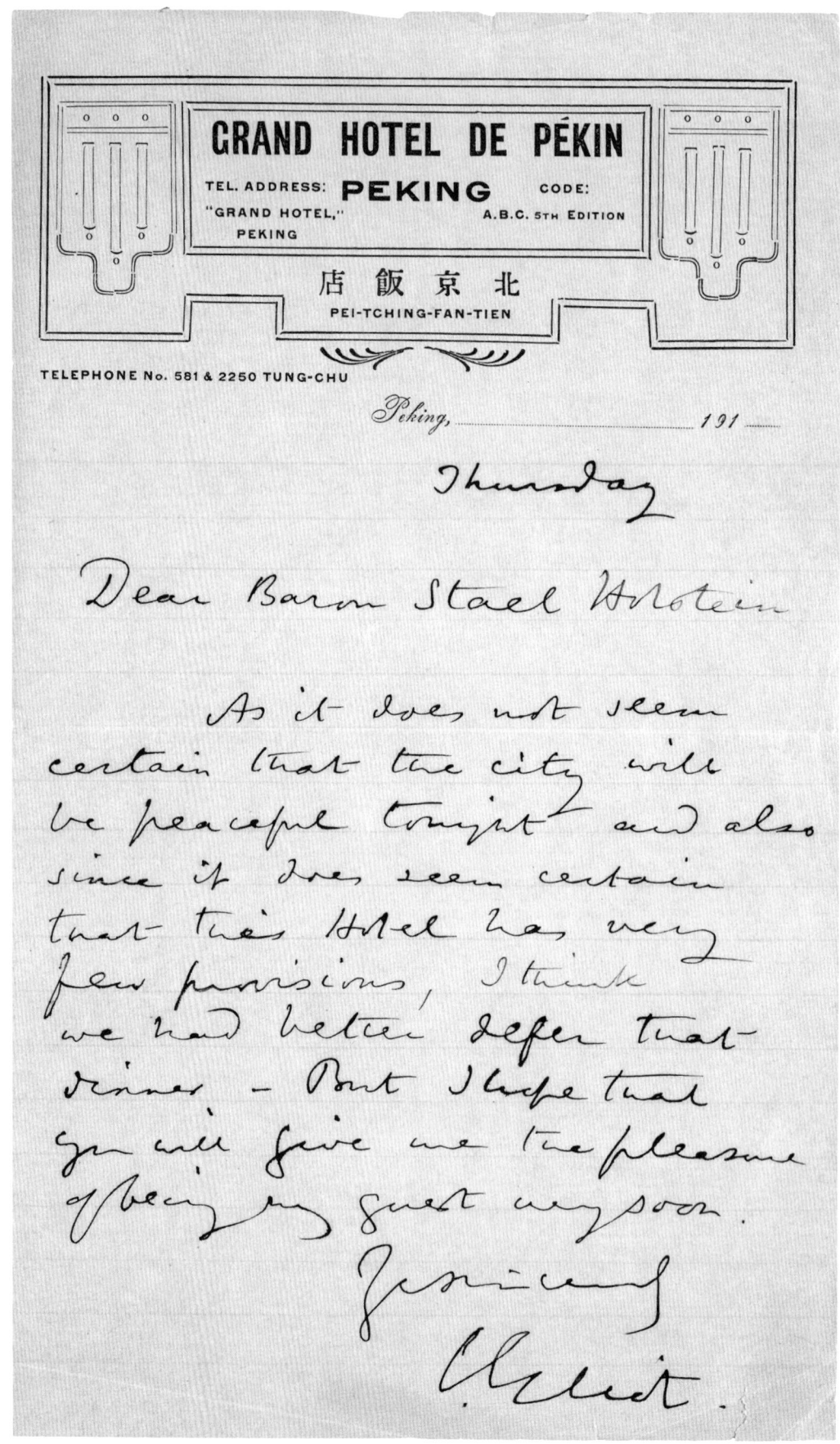

Dear Baron Stael Holstein

As it does not seem certain that the city will be peaceful tonight and also since it does seem certain that this Hotel has very few provisions, I think we had better defer that dinner — But I hope that you will give me the pleasure of being my guest very soon.

Yours sincerely

C. Eliot.

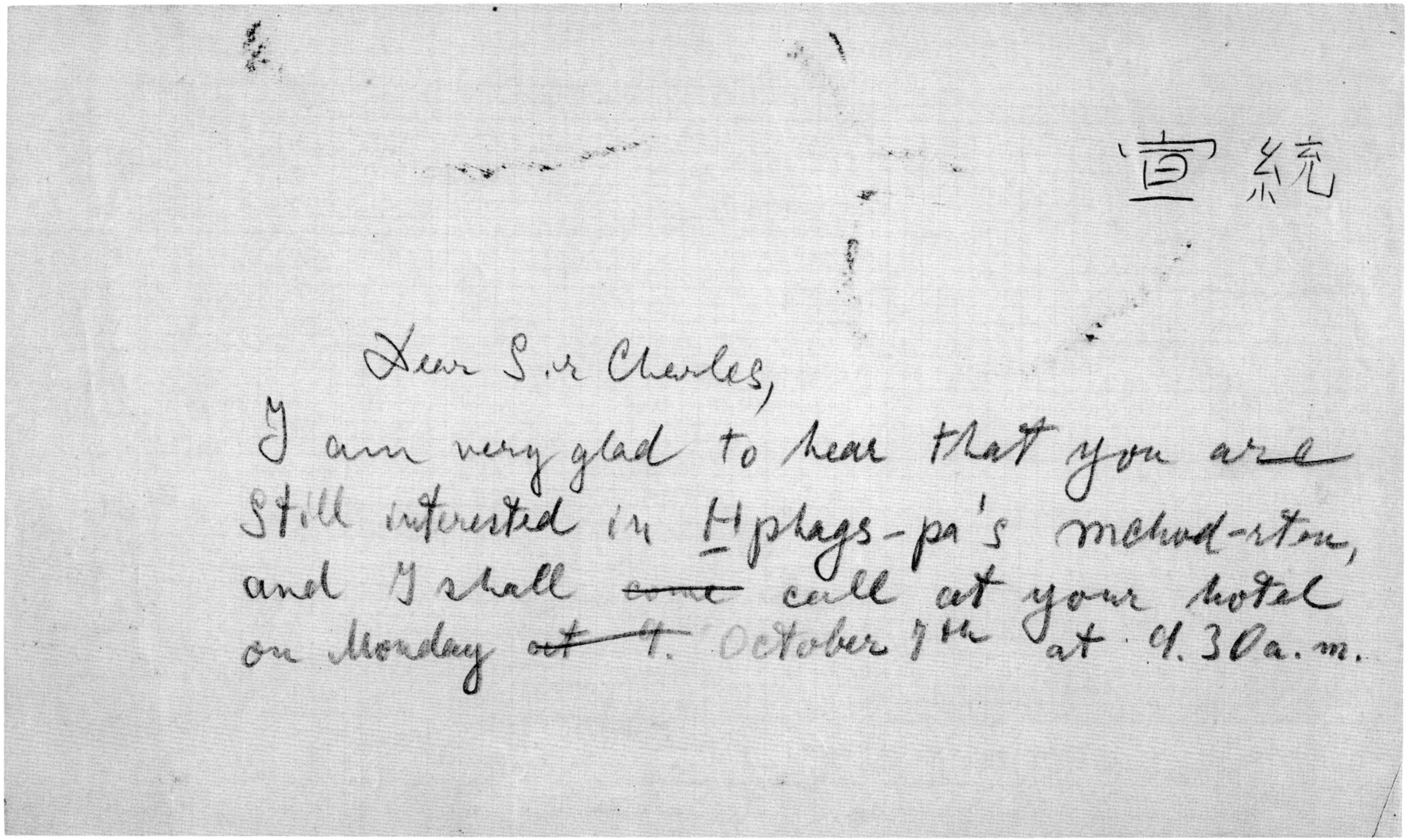

宣統

Dear Sir Charles,

I am very glad to hear that you are still interested in Hphags-pa's mchod-rten, and I shall ~~come~~ call at your hotel on Monday ~~at 9.~~ October 7th at 9.30 a.m.

BRITISH EMBASSY,
TOKYO.

Sept. 13. 1920

Dear Baron Staël.

Many thanks for your letter & the list of books. Some of them I have already but others are new to me.

I send you with this a copy of the Avadāna Cataka and hope that you will find it useful – as I have an opportunity of sending it to our Legation

today, I think that
it will be safer to send
it there than to address
it to the Club.

I am afraid that
I have not got any cata-
logue of ~~English~~ oriental
books published in England
which would be of any use
to you. If you look at
the list of new books
under the heading Ori-
ental which comes at

the End of the Literary Supplement to the Times, you will see what little there is to be seen, but very often weeks pass without any books being mentioned under this heading. The Lit. Supplement comes out every week & is sure to be in the Peking Club.

Yours sincerely

Eliot

BRITISH EMBASSY,
TOKYO.

Oct. 23. 1920.

Dear Baron Staël Holstein,

I have made a note that I sent the Avadāna-śataka to you on Sept 14. So long has elapsed since then, & I have not heard from you, that I begin to fear it may not have reached you safely — But if you have already acknowledged the receipt, don't trouble to write again

Yours sincerely

C Eliot.

Kyoto

BRITISH EMBASSY,
TOKIO.

March 10. 1921.

Dear Baron Staal,

Many thanks for your letter & the Avadānaçataka duly received. I hope that you found the latter useful.

I have not been able to examine very deeply the questions raised by the Kharavela inscription — Primâ facie, the new date for the Buddha's death now proposed seems plausible — From the point of view of Buddhist literature it does not seem to present any special difficulties.

I have at last received the whole of my book in proof from the publishers in London but some time must elapse before I can get through the necessary work of correcting such a mass and, as for some reason they rarely publish books in England in summer, I suppose it will have to wait for the autumn.

Where can we get the

Kāçyapaparivarta which
you say is being published
in Shanghai? I should be
very much obliged if you
could help me to obtain a
copy.

I am at Kyoto on
my way to Formosa where
I hope to spend a few weeks
& return to Tokyo in April.

Yours sincerely
Eliot

BRITISH EMBASSY
TOKIO

Dec. 17. 1921

Dear Baron Staël Holstein,

I deferred answering your letter until I had seen Takakusu. He says that he & his colleagues are under the impression that all essential points relating to their cooperation in the new Buddhist dictionary have been settled and that they are only awaiting the arrival of M. Sylvain Lévi, who is due here next February, to settle some matters of detail.

Perhaps I ought to tell you confidentially that though Professor Takakusu is the most unselfish & courteous of men, the Pali Text Society have found him terribly unbusinesslike, if judged by our coarse western standard.

£ I am sending you the Śikshâsamuccaya & the Mahâyânasûtrâlamkâra

in another parcel addressed
to the Club and am very glad
if I can be of any assistance
to you in the preparation of
your work -

My own book has at
last appeared, but it looks
to me very large & dull -
with best wishes for 1922

Yours sincerely

C Eliot

July 23. 1922

Dear Baron Staël Holstein

Many thanks for the Sutra Mahāyānasūtrālankāra duly received.

Have you seen Bendall & Rouse's translation of the Çikṣāsamuccaya which has recently appeared in England? If you would like it, I shall be happy to send it to you.

I did think of going

to Peking in May, because
I had to go to western
Japan to see the Prince
of Wales off & was comparatively near China – But
I could not manage it &
I am afraid that I am
not likely to be able to
manage it this year – I
am thinking of making a
tour in the opposite direction, ~~to~~ viz in the Hokkaido.

Yours sincerely

Eliot

Dear Sir Charles,

Many thanks for your kind note and for ~~your~~ offering me the loan of Bendall and Rouse's translation of the Çikṣāsamuccaya. I already possess the latter work and so there is no need for me to trouble you about it. As to the ~~[illegible]~~ Sanskrit text I hope you do not mind my keeping it a little longer. My edition of the Kāçyapaparivarta progresses very slowly. They cannot print more than thirty pages at a time because ~~they~~ their supply of ~~[illegible]~~ characters with diacritical marks (ṅ, ṛ, ṝ etc) is limited. So far ~~only~~ 105 pages only have been printed. I am very much disgusted with the printers, because of their stinginess. For a few dollars they could make sufficient type for a hundred or more pages but they will not do it. I am reading now Asaṅga's Sūtrālaṃkāra with the Commentaries of Sthiramati and of Asvabhāva (Cordier, ~~Cat~~ Catalogue du fonds Tibétain etc, ~~page~~ Vol. III pages 375 and 376) With the aid of these commentaries I can prove ~~what I believed~~ always that Lévi has completely misunderstood many passages. ~~For instance~~ ~~the words~~ e.g. the ~~[illegible]~~ words na ca svārtha eva pareṣūpadiçyamānaḥ parārtho bhavitum arhati on page 4 of the ~~text~~ text ~~[illegible]~~ obviously mean: "when the svārtha is being taught to others it ~~does not~~ cannot be considered as the parārtha [on that account]". On the same page we find the words svārthe hi paro niyujya-māne; ~~he~~ svārtha eva prayujyate which mean "if another person is directed [by his teacher] towards the svārtha he will be occupied with the svārtha only!" ~~It~~

I cannot conceive why Lévi did not consult the Tibetan commentar~~y~~ies before publishing his translation.

I am reading your book with ~~great~~ much interest and with great admiration for the author's unique accomplishments.

With ~~the~~ my best wishes for the New Year I remain yours gratefully

AStaëlHolstein.

BRITISH EMBASSY,
TOKIO.

June 5. 1924.

Dear Baron Staël Holstein,

Many thanks for your paper, which I have read with great interest. I am looking forward to receiving the Kâçyapaparivarta and hope that you will keep the Çikṣâsammuccaya as long as you need. You say that you find a great difficulty in obtaining oriental books from Europe. Have you tried Luzac 46. Great Russell St, London W.C. 2

& Geuthner 13 rue Jacob
Paris VIme? I find that I
get all that I want from them,
even occasional Russian books
on Buddhism.

I shall be delighted to
see Rabindranath Tagore & his
friends. My only fear was that
political difficulties might make
a visit to the British Embassy disagreeable to them.

I hope to pay a visit to
Peking about the beginning of
August & trust that you will

be there. Of course I know that
it is one of the worst periods
of the year for going to North
China, but I am afraid that
I cannot manage to do it at
any other time.

Hoping to see you there
I remain,

Yours sincerely
Eliot

British Legation,
Peking.

Aug. 14. 1924

Dear Baron Stael Holstein,

I tried to find you at the Club yesterday but was not successful. At present I am stopping here with the Counsellor, Mr Hoare, but as soon as the Minister returns I shall be in the Legation House. Tomorrow I am going out to the Summer Palace to spend a few days with

Johnston -

I hope very much that you are in Peking & that we shall be able to meet before I leave, which will probably be on the 21st or soon after -

Yours sincerely

C Eliot

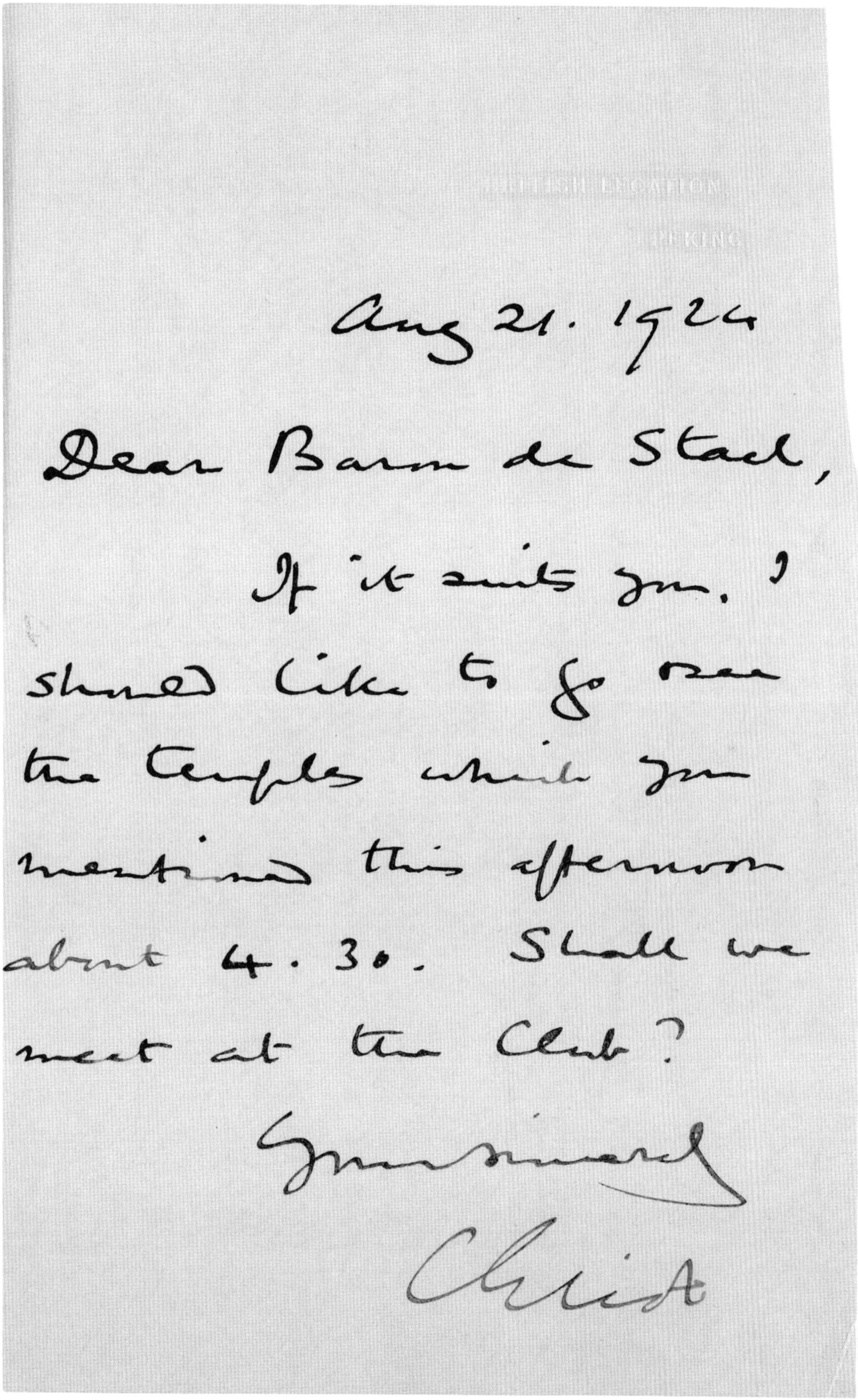

BRITISH LEGATION,
PEKING.

Aug 21. 1924

Dear Baron de Staël,

If it suits you, I should like to go see the temples which you mentioned this afternoon about 4.30. Shall we meet at the Club?

Yours sincerely

Clive

Dear Sir Charles, Many thanks for your kind note from Nara. 寍

~~My views I think there can be no doubt about~~

I think that the work which we now call the Kāçyapaparivarta is certainly the original Ratnakūṭa. ~~My view is confirmed~~ ~~by~~ My view ~~which was on~~ is not only supported by the arguments mentioned on pages VI, ~~and~~ XV (Sthiramati surely ~~[illegible]~~ regarded our Text as the entire and only Ratnakūṭasūtra) and XVI of my preface, ~~which, though partly "ex silentio", are which are not very strong,~~ but also by other considerations.

In the fourth chapter of the 歷代三寶紀 (Nanjio No 1504) as well as in the first chapter of the 開元釋教錄 (Nanjio No 1485) 大寶積經 pure and simple is given as one of the names of our particular Sūtra.

Our Sūtra is furthermore called 刪 (Pao dan [illegible] chuan da pao chi ching) the original single volume Mahāratnakūṭasūtra in an ancient note added to the ~~comment~~ Chinese translation of Sthiramati's Commentary. Comp. the Taisho Tripitaka Vol. 26, page 211, and Vol. 11, page 631 of the same edition.

~~I shall~~ ~~I hope I shall prove the point to the satisfaction of my readers in the Introduction to my translation.~~

I think Ganapati seems to be quite an important divinity in Lamaism. Comp. Grünwedel, Buddh. Mythologie, page 55 ([illegible], four hands). Among the 500 "Buddhas" of Snarthan (page 3) there is a red (dmar) Ganapati with 12 hands. In a newly discovered Lamaistic iconographical work also a drawing of the red 12 handed Ganapati is found. His Chinese name is given there as 紅部落王金剛 [Raktaganapativajra]; 部落 is originally a transcription of the Turkish word Bulag meaning "a crowd", but has been quite adopted into the Chinese language.

In the Peking Palace collection of Lamaistic divinities I have found two inscribed statuettes of elephant headed gods, photographs of which I enclose. I do not know the Sanscrit or Tibetan equivalent of the name Lung Yü x T'ien. I have never seen, or heard of, any representations of Ganapati in purely Chinese temples, and I am very much interested in your discovery; what characters are used in representing his name in Japan?

~~Dear Sir Charles,~~

~~Many thanks for your kind note from Nara.~~

The other day a leading member of the group who have so far financed my Sino-Indian Research Institute (comp. the ~~enclosed~~ ~~offprint~~ preface which I enclose) came to see me and said that the subsidy for the year ending on June 30th 1928 was not at all assured ~~the~~ unless a ~~some~~ printed appreciation of my work (by some ~~a~~ well-known ~~scholar~~ authority) could be ~~submitted~~ shown to the benefactors. May I ask you to write a few lines on the desirability of editions like the one I have just published? I shall be very much obliged to you if you will. ~~do~~ ~~it soon (the year has already begun).~~ ~~It will~~ It does not matter where ~~the~~ the lines appear ~~you publish~~ ~~your short~~ ~~the~~ ~~appreciation~~, but I think some periodical published ~~appearing~~ in China (perhaps: The China Journal of Science & Arts, 8 Museum Road, Shanghai) ~~perhaps~~ ~~to~~ or Japan preferable, ~~to others, because~~ ~~they will publish the notice sooner than~~ ~~those~~ ~~European journals,~~ ~~and~~ as sending the manuscript ~~to~~ to Europe would take a very long time; there is "periculum in mora", because the year ending on June 30th 1928 has already begun.

(8)

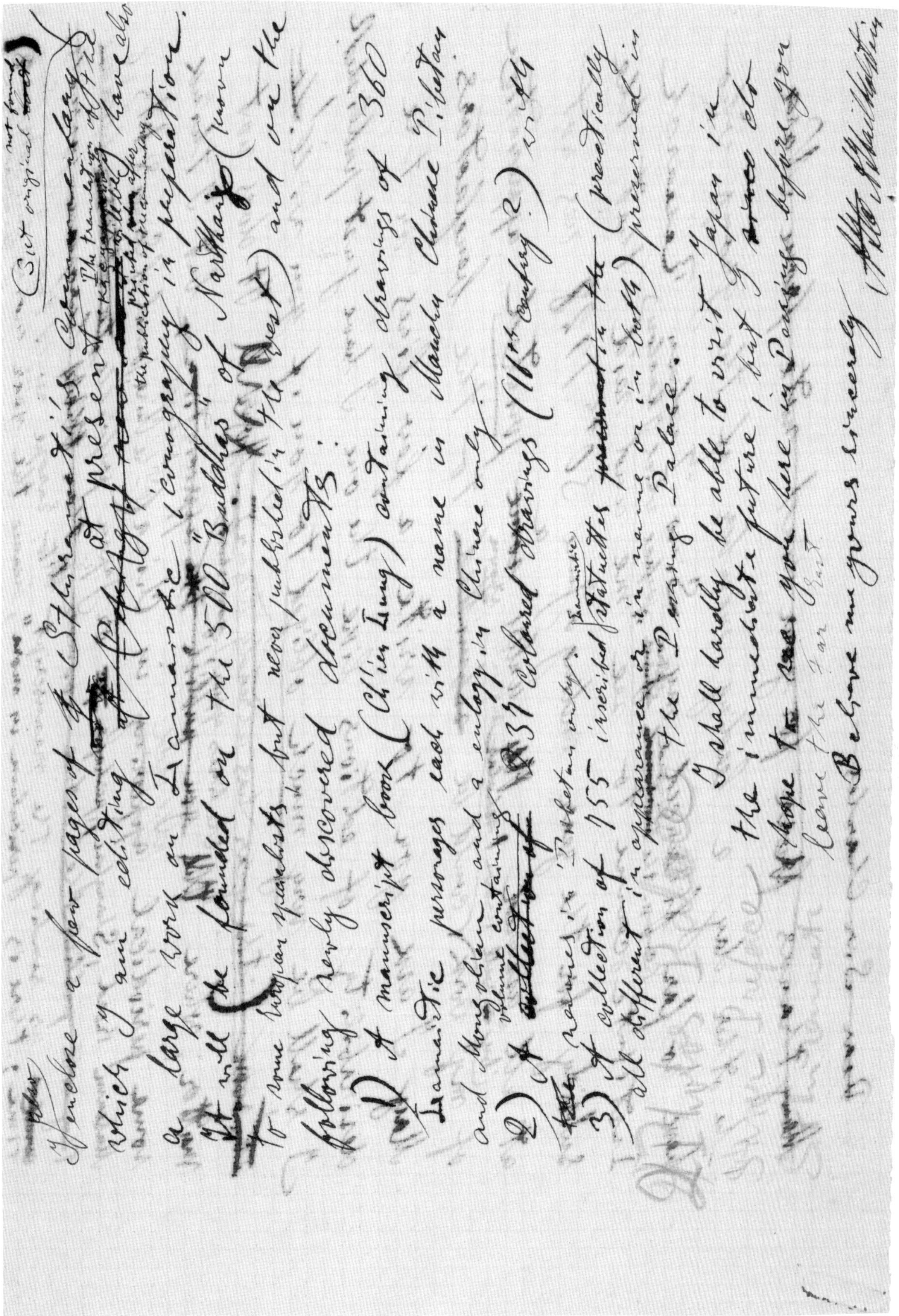

(See original ~~work~~ not found)

~~also~~

I enclose a few pages of ~~the~~ Sthiramati's ~~Commentary~~ which I am editing ~~at~~ at present ~~[illegible]~~ The translation of the Kāśyapaparivarta will be printed after the publication of the commentary. I have also a large work on Lamaistic iconography in preparation. ~~It~~ will be founded on the 500 "Buddhas" of Narthang (known to some European specialists, but never published in the West) and on the following newly discovered documents:

1) A manuscript book (Ch'ien Lung) containing drawings of 360 Lamaistic personages each with a name in Manchu Chinese Tibetan and Mongolian and a eulogy in Chinese only.

2) A volume containing ~~collection of~~ 37 coloured drawings (11th century?) with ~~the~~ names in Tibetan only.

3) A collection of 755 inscribed Lamaistic statuettes ~~preserved in the~~ (practically all different in appearance or in name or in both) preserved in the Peking Palace.

I shall hardly be able to visit Japan in the immediate future, but I ~~since~~ do hope ~~to see~~ you here in Peking before you leave the Far East.

Believe me yours sincerely

A. v. Staël-Holstein

THE
FUJIYA HOTEL
NATURAL HOT SPRINGS
MIYANOSHITA,
JAPAN.

TELEGRAPHIC ADDRESS "FUJIYA"

H. S. K. YAMAGUCHI
MANAGING DIRECTOR

Aug 30. 1927.

Dear Baron Staël Holstein,

I enclose herewith the reply from the Editor of the North China Branch of the R.A.S. from which you will see that any review which I might send would not appear till Sept. 1928. It is very unfortunate.

I have written at once to the Editor of the China Journal of Science & Arts to ask whether they will accept a review & hope that we may have better luck this time.

I am just leaving here for Korea & the Diamond Mountains. After about Sept 15

the best address for me will
be care of British ~~of~~ Consulate
General, Seoul (or, as the
Japanese call it Keijō).

In haste
Yours sincerely
Eliot

Dear Sir Charles,

Many thanks for your kind card and the welcome news concerning the China Journal. I have published ~~two books~~ in the Bibliotheca Buddhica:

No XII (Ṭišastvustik) (1910) and No XV (Kien-ch'ui-fan-tsan) (1913)

~~The first book contains a Buddhist sutra in the Turkish (Uighur) language with a German translation~~

In No XII which I published in collaboration with the late W. Radloff, ~~a Turkish (Uighur) translation of a~~ ~~for the of Buddhist sutra was t~~ a Buddhist sutra in the Turkish (Uighur) language appeared for the first time in Europe (with a German translation and notes).

In No XV, a Buddhist hymn by Açvaghoṣa and two other Sanskrit poems were edited in Chinese transliterations and in Tibetan translations, with reconstructions of the original Sanskrit texts and notes in Russian.

~~In addit~~ In 1900 I published a Sanskrit text (Karmapradīpa II)
with a German translation.

Registered A. R.

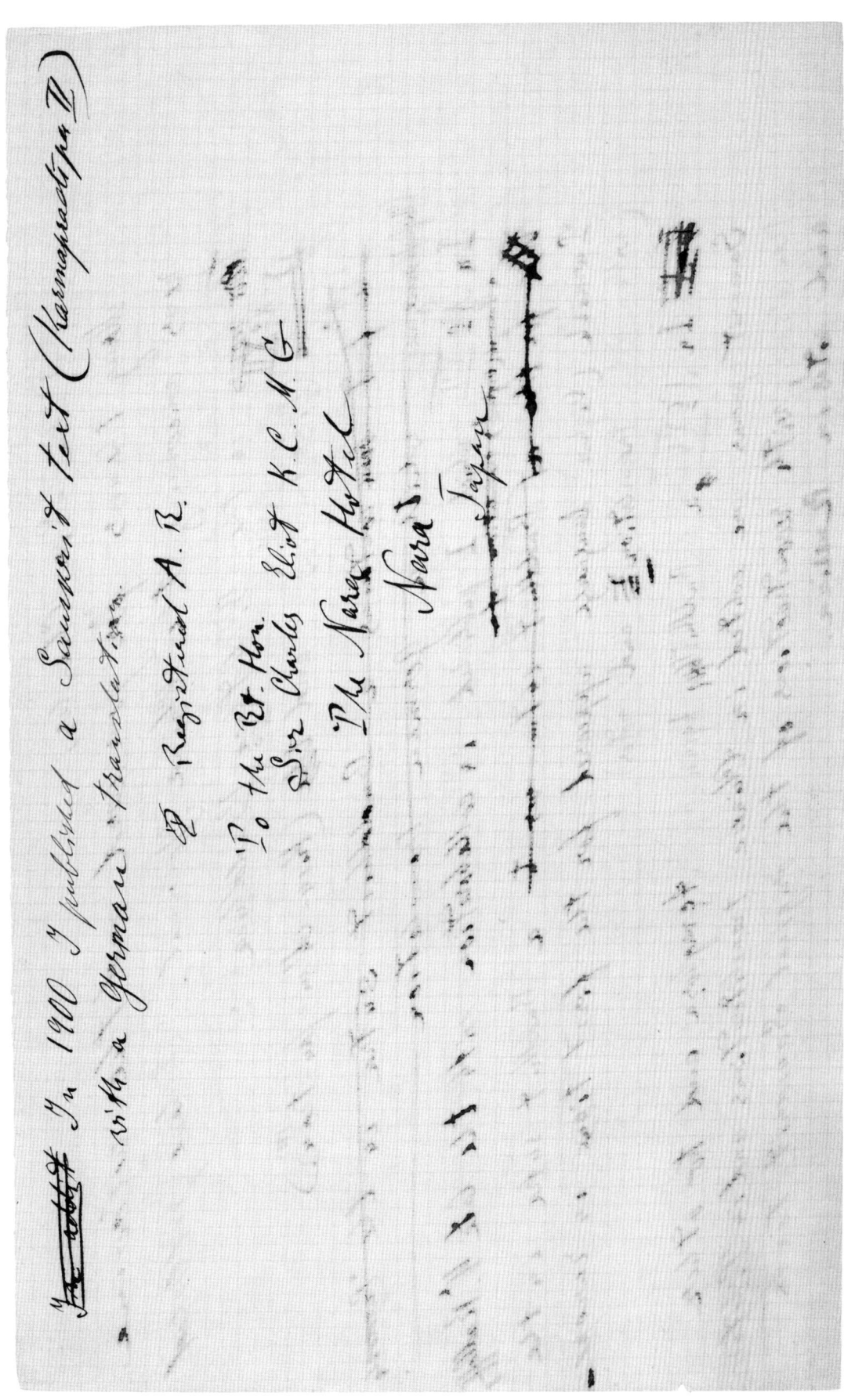

To the Rt. Hon.
Sir Charles Eliot K.C.M.G.
The Nara Hotel
Nara
Japan

In addition to those books I have published a considerable number of articles in various journals. ~~You~~ I think you possess most of ~~those~~ the later articles which appeared in the Far East in English and in French. ~~Of the~~ The earlier articles, ~~which were~~ most of which deal with the Pocharian question, ~~I do not possess any copies. They~~ appeared ~~[illegible]~~ in the years 1904–1914 in the following publications:

1) Journal of the Imperial Russian Geographical Society
2) Bulletin de l'Académie Impérial des Sciences de St. Pétersbourg
3) ~~Zapiski Imperatorskago Archeologicheskago Obshchestva~~ Journal of the Imperial Russian Archeological Society
4) Journal of the Royal Asiatic Society (London)
5) Sitzungsberichte der Königlich Preussischen Akademie der Wissenschaften.

I hope ~~if~~ that the card which the Bassompierres Madame de Varzée and myself sent you a few days ago. Believe me yours sincerely and gratefully Staël Holstein

THE NARA HOTEL.

GOVERNMENT RAILWAY HOTELS:
NARA HOTEL. SANYO HOTEL.
Nara Shimonoseki
JAPAN.

Cable Address: "HOTEL" NARA.
Telephone Nos. 153. & 166.

Nara, April 8 *192*8

Dear Baron Staël,

I am very glad that you like my review of your book & that it has been of some use - On the 26th of this month I leave for England & shall not be able to manage a visit to Peking. I greatly regret it, but I hope to return here in the Spring next year & perhaps I may have better luck then -

With all good wishes

Yours very sincerely

C. Eliot

My kindest regards to Madame de Warzée

THE TOR HOTEL, LTD.,
KOBE,
(JAPAN.)
A. MILDNER,
MANAGER

CABLE ADDRESS "TOR"
PHONE: FUKIAI 2153, 3153

KOBE, Feb. 9. 1930.

My dear Baron Staël,

I daresay that you remember visiting the Daibutsu of Nara with me not very long ago. The name of the image rather perplexes me. It is called Biru-shana — that is Vairocana — and also Roshana. The latter is the name used by the Japanese Chronicle — the Shoku-Nihongi — in describing the dedication — and also in the earliest translation of the Avatamsaka Sûtra (Nanjio no 87) whereas the later translation ~~uses~~ (Nanjio no 88) uses Birushana. Now what is this word Roshana? It is commonly said to be the Japanese equivalent of Locana, the Chinese pronunciation being Lu-shê-na. But on investigating the matter I cannot find Locana anywhere in Sanskrit works. The Dharma-Sangraha gives Locanâ as the name of a goddess, but neither in dictionaries nor in the index of any Sanskrit work that I have been able to consult, does the masculine form Locana appear as the name of a Buddha. Can you tell me of any place where it is to be found in Sanskrit?

Failing any instance of its use in Sanskrit being forthcoming, it seems simplest to explain Roshana as an abbreviation and in Japan the Shingon and Kegon (Avatamsaka) sects do hold that the two names are synonyms — On the other hand the Tendai sect distinguish Roshana & Birushana as equivalent to the Sambhogakáya and Dharmakáya respectively. In China, I am told, one often sees a triad of images representing Pí-lu-chê-na, Lu-shê-na and the Buddha — That looks as if Locana were a distinct being. I shall be greatly indebted to you if your great learning enables you to tell me anything about the use of the name in Sanskrit.

As Nara is rather cold at this time of year, I have removed to Kobe for a short time but hope to go back in March — I wish that you would come again and pay another & longer visit.

With best wishes & hoping that we may meet soon,

I remain

Yours very sincerely

C. Eliot.

Dear Sir Charles,

~~I remember~~ I do indeed remember our ~~visit to~~ inspecting the Daibutsu ~~in~~ last May, but I am sorry to say that I have not found any Buddha bearing the Skt name Locana and that I have never seen statues of ~~seen that~~ ~~[illegible]~~ ~~any~~ the trinity you mention (~~[illegible]~~ ~~Birushana~~ Vairocana, Locana and Çākyamuni). I have, however, asked one of my assistants to make enquiries and I shall write ~~to~~ you again ~~when~~ as soon as I get the results of his investigations. The enclosed note has been written by another Chinese assistant. I intend going to Japan towards the end of July and hope very much that we will meet (Miyanoshita ~~or~~ Chuzenji) there.

Believe me yours sincerely

THE NARA HOTEL
NARA, JAPAN

Tel. Nos. 153, 166, 262, NARA.
Cable Address "HOTEL" NARA.

March 22. 1930.

Dear Baron Staël-Holstein,

Many thanks for your letter of the 10th March which I have just received on returning to Nara for the Spring. It is very good of you to have taken so much trouble about Locana but please do not worry about the matter any more for I think it is pretty plain that Roshana (Lu-shê-na) is only another and shorter way of pronouncing Vairocana. Still, the T'ien-t'ai (as your assistant admits in the memorandum which you enclose) do distinguish the two as names for the Sambhoga kāya and Dharmakāya respectively & it is odd that they should have treated the two ~~names~~ as separate if they are merely variations of one word.

Reichelt in his "Truth & tradition in Chinese Buddhism" speaks several times of a Trinity composed of Vairocana, Locana, and Śākya-muni and even describes how the two former may be distinguished by the position of the hands. His book can hardly be ranked very high as a critical account of Chinese Buddhism but I should have thought that he would have been accurate in quoting facts like the above. But perhaps he is referring to T'ien-t'ai temples.

I look forward with great pleasure to meeting you in Japan in the summer. I am thinking myself of going to Karuizawa in late July & August & should like to persuade you

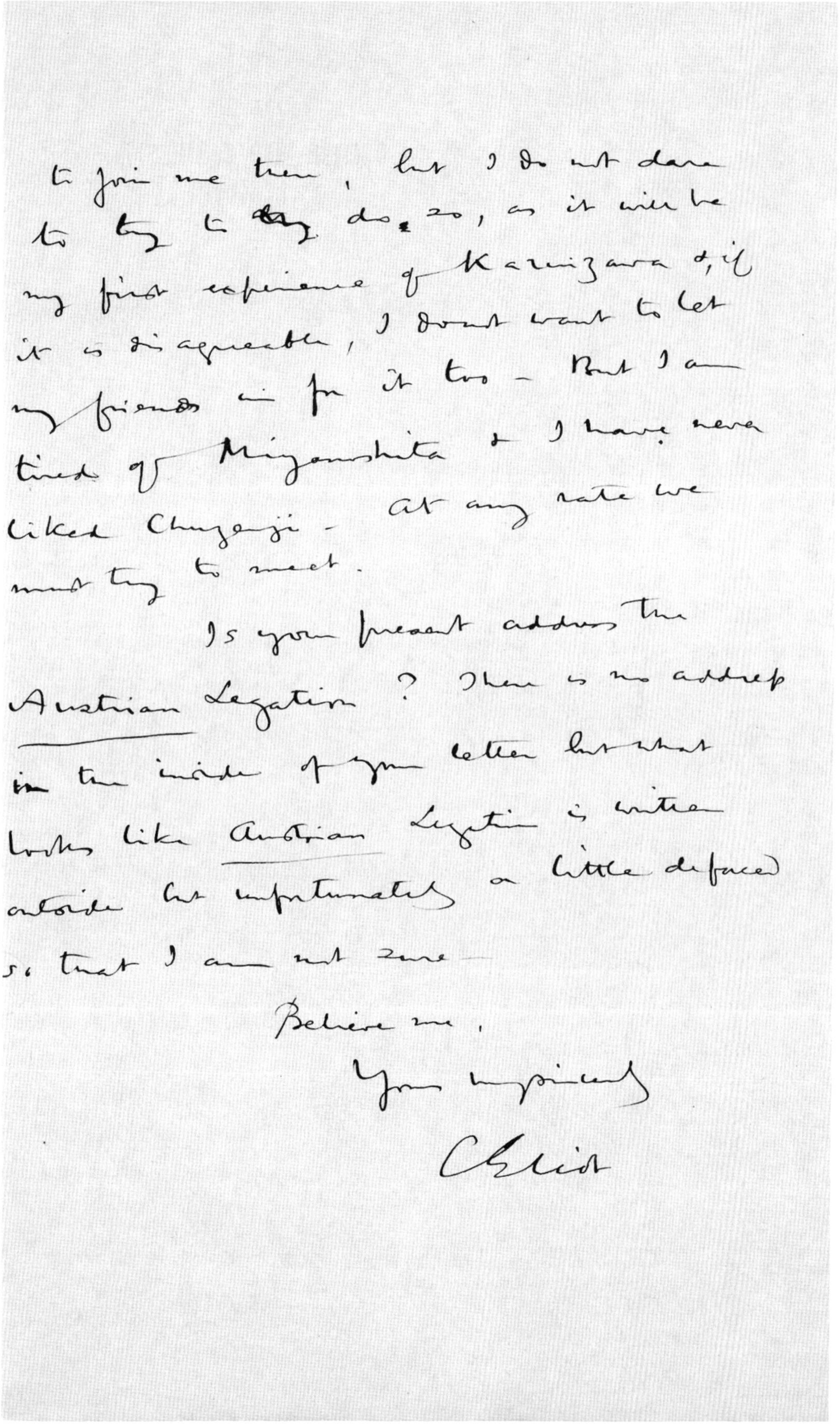

to join me there, but I do not dare
to try to ~~try~~ do so, as it will be
my first experience of Karuizawa &, if
it is disagreeable, I don't want to let
my friends in for it too – But I am
tired of Miyanoshita & I have never
liked Chuzenji – at any rate we
must try to meet.

Is your present address the
Austrian Legation? There is no address
in the inside of your letter but what
looks like Austrian Legation is written
outside but unfortunately a little defaced
so that I am not sure –

Believe me,

Yours sincerely

C Eliot

BRITISH HIGH COMMISSION,
VLADIVOSTOK.

Baron A. de Staël-Holstein informs me that he is a candidate for the Professorship of Sanskrit which is to be founded in the University of Peking and I have very great pleasure in warmly recommending him for the post. Though I cannot speak from personal experience of his work as a teacher, I can testify to his knowledge of Sanskrit and to his enthusiasm for the language & its literature, and I have no doubt that he is a most competent instructor.

Besides, his qualifications speak for themselves. He is a Ph. D. of Halle and has been assistant Professor of Sanskrit in the University of Petrograd since 1909.

There is however a special reason why the University should select Baron Stael for the new post. He has long been occupied with historical & linguistic researches into certain phases of the history of India & of Buddhism which are closely connected with the relations formerly existing

between India, Tibet &
China. His treatises on
these interesting and difficult questions (published
in the Bibliotheca Buddhica
& elsewhere) testify to his
great learning & his ability
as an expositor. He came
to Peking in order to prose-
cute these studies & to
gain a more thorough ac-
quaintance with Chinese,
Tibetan & Mongol transla-
tions from Sanskrit. By
electing him the University
of Peking would not only
obtain a most competent

Sanskrit scholar, but also one who has specially devoted himself to those branches of Indian literature & history which concern China & who is likely to add distinction to the University by publishing works of great interest & value to oriental scholars.

C. Eliot.

British High Commissioner for Siberia:
Principal of the University of Hong Kong.
Formerly Principal & Lecturer in Sanskrit at the University of Sheffield.

~~dass sie ihm aber nicht auf lange vor Schaden~~
~~gereicht mir, dass die fortgesetzten Seit~~
es, dass der Sanskrit-Index nicht abgeschlossen ist,
denn sie benötigen die Typen, welche nun schon
1½ Jahre im Satz festliegen. Wollen Sie die Güte
haben, mir in einem ganz billigen Telegramm (diese
Art von Telegrammen heisst ~~auf~~ auf Englisch "deferred telegrams") mitzu-
theilen, wann wir die Korrekturbogen hier in Peking erwarten dürfen. ~~etwa~~
~~So~~ Meine ~~telegraphische~~ Telegramm-Adresse ist: Stael Amexco Peking,
und ich schlage vor, dass Sie mir ~~etwa~~ das folgende ~~solch ein~~ ohne Unterschrift Telegramm
schicken: Stael Amexco Peking ~~Dezember~~ November. ~~[illegible]~~ Aus solch einem
Telegramm werde ich ersehen, dass wir die Korrektur~~bogen~~ des Sanskrit-
Index hier in Peking im November 1935 erwarten dürfen. Pankratoff ~~hat er ist von~~
~~der Sowjets hat Peking verlassen~~ hat Peking verlassen und wird wohl nie wieder im Institut arbeiten.
Die Korrekturbogen des ganzen tibetischen Index haben Sie hoffentlich inzwischen erhalten. ~~Meine Frau und~~
~~ich sendet Ihnen~~ Bitte empfehlen Sie mich Ihrer Frau Gemahlin. Meine Frau und ich senden
Ihnen viele herzliche Grüsse. Ihr ergebener A. Staël-Holstein.

Beiliegend ein auf zehn Reichsmark lautender
Scheck für das Telegramm.

Пекинъ 20го Февраля 1935 г.

Многоуважаемый Сергѣй Григорьевичъ,

Кончина профессора Woods'а меня очень огорчила, и я написалъ объ этомъ вдовѣ его и декану Chase.

~~Объ О на~~ Объ изданіи Vajracchedikā однако я не рѣшаюсь писать старымъ друзьямъ покойнаго ученаго ~~въ настоящее время~~ такъ скоро послѣ его смерти, и поэтому обращаюсь къ Вамъ ~~съ просьбою поговорить съ кѣмъ нужно объ этомъ дѣлѣ и когда~~ съ просьбою дискретно узнать, ~~что~~ [illegible] ~~что сдѣлали и что гдѣ находятся~~ гдѣ сейчас находятся мои ~~рукописи~~ когда-то (съ 1930 г.) готовые къ печати рукописи Vajracchedikā (~~тибетск~~ (санскритскій текстъ, тибетскій текстъ, ~~и~~ ~~полностью~~ шесть китайскихъ версій), введеніе и примѣчанія). ~~Для меня весьма~~

Въ 1930 г. я ~~просилъ, чтобы~~ думалъ, что ~~мною рукопись~~
~~изданіе~~, составленное мною въ сотрудничествѣ
~~съ Б. И. Панкратовымъ~~ съ разными ассистентами
(Б. И. Панкратовымъ и т. д.) изданіе ~~было~~ будетъ немедлен-
но напечатано. Въ этомъ я ошибся. Оказалось
что покойный проф. Woods хотѣлъ участвовать
~~въ этомъ изданіи, но какъ онъ себѣ пред-~~
~~ставлялъ это участіе я такъ и никогда~~
(Я раньше думалъ, что онъ хотѣлъ лишь перевести (не издать) Vajracchedikā на основаніи собранныхъ мною матеріаловъ.)
не узналъ. ~~Изъ его послѣднихъ~~ Въ своемъ
послѣднемъ письмѣ (отъ 4го ~~дек~~ декабря 1934 г.) онъ пишетъ
мнѣ ~~о~~ нѣсколько словъ о Vajracchedikā и

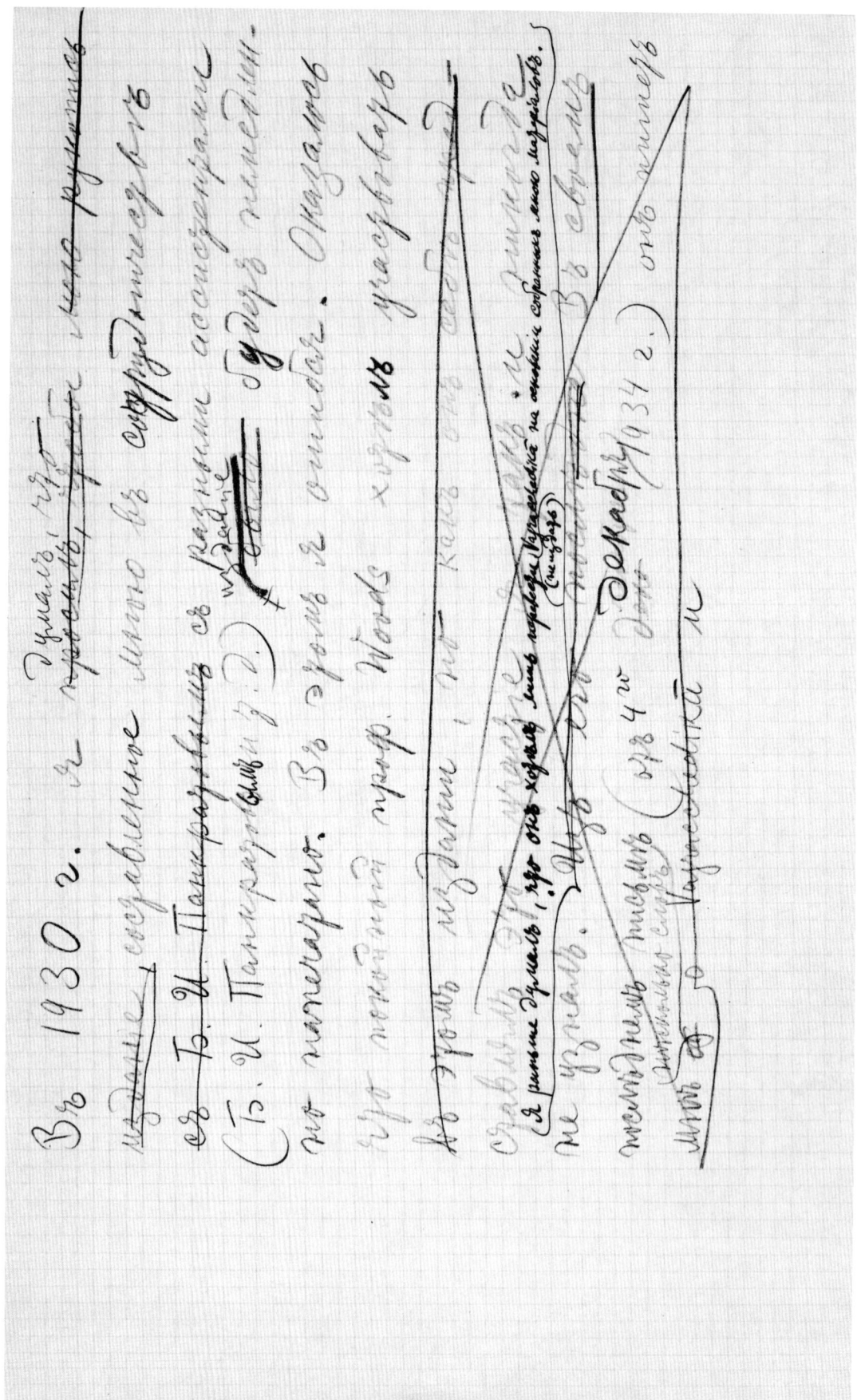

~~последнемъ письмѣ онъ опять говоритъ о томъ~~

въ ~~этомъ~~ изданіи. ~~и~~ Вследствіе этого

[полученная деканомъ Chase еще въ 1930 г., До сихъ поръ]

моя рукопись, осталась неиспользованной. ~~Въ~~

~~своемъ последнемъ письмѣ~~ Изъ последняго письма

[отъ 4го Декабря 1934 г.]

проф. Woods (письмо написано по-англійски, но

конечно рукой: In alter Treue James H. Woods)

явствуетъ, что проф. Woods отказался отъ

Vajracchedikā. ~~Онъ намеренъ~~ Упомянувъ объ этомъ

изданіи онъ говоритъ: But now I am making

other plans .... I ~~am~~ [have been] attempting to collect

instances from Buddhist books of the causes and the cure

for disintegration of consciousness...... Perhaps you have a string

of passages up your sleeve that will illumine my path for me.

~~Самое~~ Самымъ лучшимъ рѣшеніемъ вопроса объ изданіи Vajracchedikā было бы слѣдующее: рукопись возвращаемая ~~мнѣ~~ мнѣ въ Пекинъ съ разрѣшеніемъ напечатать изданіе Vajracchedikā въ Пекинѣ. Такимъ образомъ опасность, что моя рукопись будетъ когда-нибудь напечатана безъ всякихъ измѣненій въ Америкѣ, будетъ устранена. ~~Крупныя измѣненія~~ Я говорю объ опасности, потому что ~~я сам~~ ввиду вновь поступившихъ свѣдѣній ~~нѣк~~ нѣкоторыя измѣненія въ текстахъ являются необходимыми. Здѣшніе французскіе монахи (Лазаристы) (какъ китайскіе, ... такъ и другіе тексты) очень хорошо напечатаютъ Vajracchedikā и возьмутъ гораздо дешевле ~~чѣмъ~~ любой иностранной типографіи. ~~Было бы жаль если мы не~~

Если не удастся найти мою рукопись въ бумагахъ профессора Woods, то я легко могу возстановить изданіе изъ имѣющихся у меня черновиковъ.

~~Пожалуйста передайте поклонъ Вашей супругѣ.~~

~~Искренно преданный Вамъ~~

А. Сталь

Мнѣ кажется, что не слѣдуетъ пока говорить съ американцами о Vajracchedikā. Лучше подождать еще нѣсколько мѣсяцевъ. Пишу Вамъ теперь лишь потому, что боюсь возможнаго въ концѣ концовъ опубликованія моей нѣсколько устарѣвшей рукописи въ Америкѣ. ~~Нѣсколько лѣтъ~~ ~~два года~~ нѣсколько лѣтъ тому назадъ въ Америкѣ (по недоразумѣнію) была напечатана моя устарѣвшая статья въ то же самое время, когда въ Китаѣ вышла исправленная версія той же статьи.

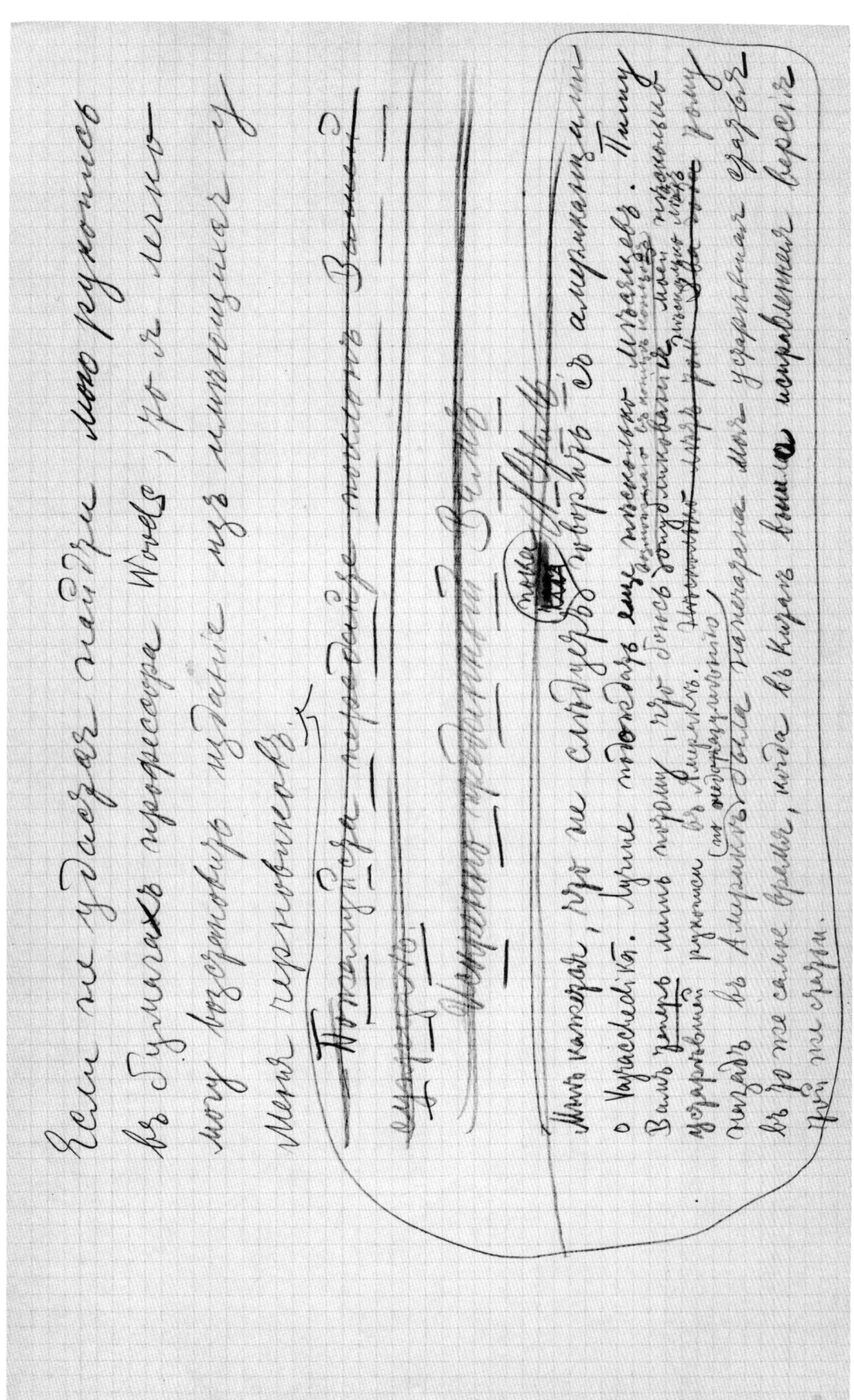

P.S.

Въ моемъ оффиціальномъ письмѣ я забылъ упомянуть о томъ, что я ~~конечно~~ отъ китайцевъ за чтеніе лекцій и т. д. никакой платы не получаю. ~~[illegible]~~ ~~От~~ Я состою лишь почетнымъ профессоромъ національнаго университета и членомъ-корреспондентомъ академіи и ~~другихъ~~ ~~учрежденій~~

An Elisséeff abgeschr & datiert 27.2.35 (1)

In 1934 I have been chiefly occupied with the history of the Tibetan Kanjur and with the study of certain (ancient Sanskrit) texts, which ~~about a thou~~ have been transliterated ~~not~~ (not translated) with Chinese characters.

Until quite recently the (A.D. 1700 Kanjur described by Laufer in) ~~Imperial copy of the Kanjur of the Asiatic Museum was supposed to be~~ 1909 was supposed to be the ~~mos~~ earliest ~~Tibetan~~ Kanjur published (~~Peking~~) under the auspices of the Ch'ing Emperors. I think I have proved in a paper printed ~~I have discovered two or a number of~~ in 1934 (on a Peking edition of the Tibetan Kanjur which seems to (incompletely) be unknown in the West) ~~that~~ at least one earlier Ch'ing version of the Tibetan Kanjur existed. ~~and that~~

(2)

~~that the a Kangur set discovered by myself~~
~~in Peking represents~~
~~A number of~~ Several works included in the
version described by Laufer ~~represent~~ (dated A.D. 1692)
are absent from the Kangur set discovered by
myself in Peking. Furthermore a

(3)

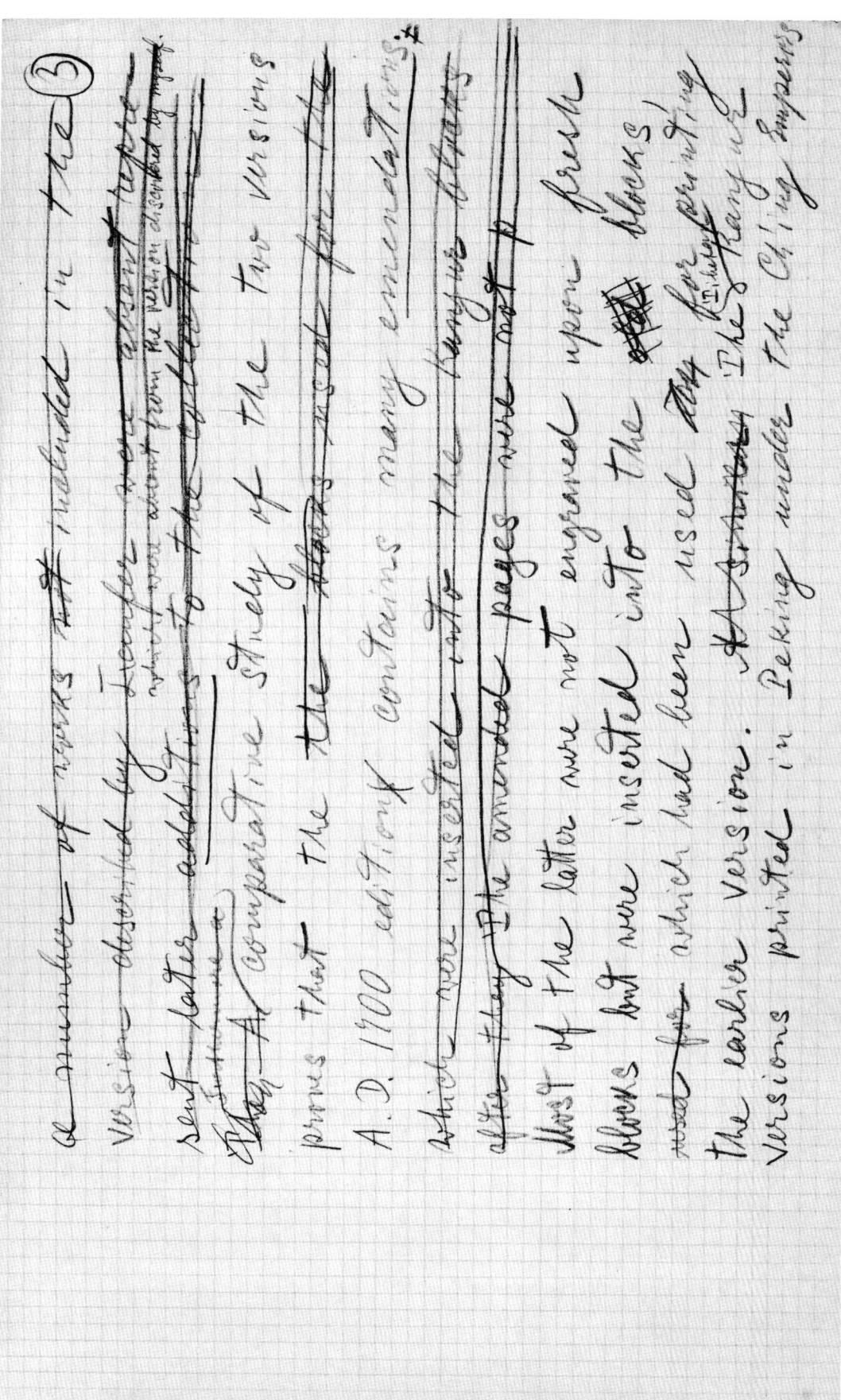

~~a number of works not included in the version described by Laufer were absent repre-~~
~~sent later additions to the collection~~ ~~which were absent from the version discovered by myself.~~

~~They~~ A comparative study of the two versions proves that the ~~the blocks used for the~~ A.D. 1700 edition✗ contains many emendations.✗ ~~which were inserted into the Kanjur blocks after they The amended pages were not p~~

Most of the latter were not engraved upon fresh blocks but were inserted into the ~~old~~ blocks, ~~used for~~ which had been used ~~for~~ for printing the earlier version. ~~A A similar~~ The Tibetan Kanjur versions printed in Peking under the Ch'ing Emperors

(4)

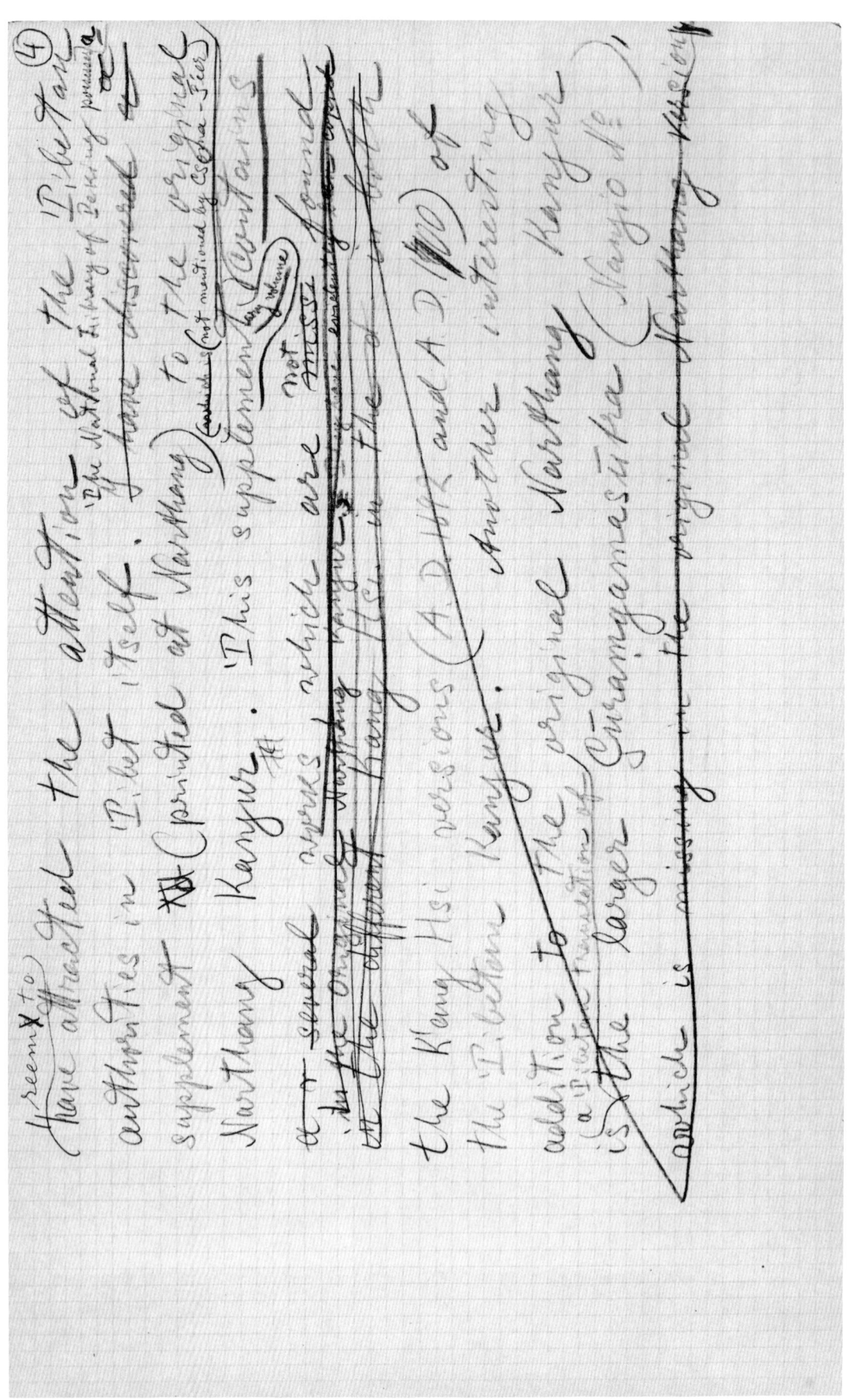

(seem ~~s~~ to) ~~have attracted~~ the attention ~~of~~ the Tibetan authorities in Tibet itself. The National Library of Peking possesses a ~~I have discovered a~~ supplement ~~XX~~ (printed at Narthang) to the original (~~which is~~) (not mentioned by Csoma-Feer) Narthang Kanjur. This supplement (very voluminous) contains ~~a or several~~ works, which are not ~~miss~~ found ~~in the original Narthang Kanjur; they have evidently been copied~~ ~~in the different Kang Hsi in the or in both~~ the K'ang Hsi versions (A.D. 1692 and A.D. 1700) of the Tibetan Kanjur. Another interesting addition to the original Narthang Kanjur is (a Tibetan translation of) the larger Śūramgamasūtra (Nanjio No.), ~~which is missing in the original Narthang version~~

(5)

~~The~~ in the original Narthang ~~Kanjur~~ edition, and some ~~(or all)~~ of them have evidently been copied from the ~~Ch'ing~~ Peking versions of the Kanjur.

Another interesting addition to the original Narthang Kanjur is a Tibetan translation of the larger Çūramgamasūtra (Nanjio № 446). That the Tibetan ~~Çūramgam~~ version of Nanjio № 446, ~~was which~~ did ~~is missing is not mentioned by Cs Csoma-Feer,~~ ~~was did~~ not belong to the original Narthang Kanjur is proved by the fact that only ~~one~~ the later version of the Narthang Kanjur Dkarchags (tables of contents) mentions it (I have ~~you~~ examined both versions of the Dkarchag). ~~this later Dkarchag the paragraph referring to the Tibetan version of Nanjio № has certainly been~~

(6)

~~added at a added after the completion~~

~~The fact that the~~ The title page of the Narthang volume containing the Tibetan version of Nanjio No. 446 shows the Imperial dragon pattern and suggests that this additional volume has something to do with the rulers of China. The fact that the volume is entitled rgyal pos mdzad pa ~~…~~ etc., made by [order of] the Emperor, ~~…~~ ~~owes the same~~ ~~confirms~~ supports the hypothesis, ~~which~~ which is finally ~~…~~ confirmed by a set of eight block-printed volumes, which I ~~lately~~ have discovered at the Yung Ho Kung monastery in Peking. These volumes contain four versions (Chinese, Manchu, Mongol and Tibetan) of Nanjio No. 446. An Imperial introduction

(7)

[A.D. 1763]

dated ~~A.D. 1763~~ (Ch'ien Lung 28) to the eight volumes states that the Sanskrit original of the sūtra (Nanjio № 446) ~~was~~ as well as ~~the~~ an ancient ~~original~~ Tibetan translation of it were lost during the reign of ~~the~~ king ~~Lang Darma~~ glan dar ma. ~~the eny king~~ of Tibet, ~~and~~ an enemy of Buddhism. The introduction goes on to say that ~~this new Tibetan translation has been m~~ the sūtra, of which only a Chinese translation was left, had "now" been translated from Chinese into Manchu from Manchu into Mongolian and from Mongolian into Tibetan. ~~Most Chine~~ Many Chinese and Japanese writers believe that the

8

sūtra never existed in Sanskrit and that its Chinese version is ~~this~~ an original Chinese composition ~~I have not~~ (not a translation). I am ~~very much~~ greatly interested in this question and have ~~much~~ already spent ~~much~~ much time in ~~studying~~ examining the four versions with the help of Mr. Pankratoff and a number of other friends, but ~~it will take a long time before my studies of the larger Çūramgama sūtra will~~ I shall have to study the problem for many more months before being able to publish my results. For the present I have

(9)

interrupted my studies of ~~the Tibetan~~ Buddhist literary history and laid aside a number of other unfinished treatises in order to continue my ~~studies~~ investigations of the ancient ~~to~~ Indo-Chinese transliterations, which seem to interest my Chinese colleagues of the National University and of the Chinese Academy of Sciences more than the problems mentioned above.*

* ~~The Chinese philologians are~~ * During my stay at Cambridge Mass. it was repeatedly pointed out to me that ~~I ... helping the Chinese scholars in their researches would be my most important task~~ I should try and help the Chinese scholars in their researches. I feel that I can assist them in ~~....~~ fixing the pronounciation of some characters at certain ~~periods~~ past epochs. Many Chinese scholars know how to handle the Fan Ch'ieh dictionaries but very few of them can find their way through the maze of Indian and Tibetan books, which ~~...~~ ~~must be consulted by should certainly not be neglected by~~ the careful phonetician cannot afford to neglect.

(10)

Among my unfinished articles is a paper giving a new explanation of the name Avalokita, the
translation of an edict addressed by the Emperor
Ch'ien Lung to the king of Nepal (in Tibetan
and Manchu only, no Chinese text), ~~[illegible]~~
a note on the history of the burning lens
in India (comp. Laufer, T'oung Pao, 1915, pages 562-563), a note on a comparatively ~~an~~ ancient
Tibetan ~~pamphlet~~ booklet on the use of tobacco, and a
~~[illegible]~~ description of a ~~unique~~ series of about sixty
portraits representing ~~this~~ all the spiritual ancestors
of the VIII Dalailamas (not 25 only). I have bought This unique ~~the~~ series (dating from
the XVIII century) here, but I cannot publish it, because
~~certain books which I have ordered from India and~~

(11)

I ~~cannot~~ am unable to get in Peking a certain Tibetan book, ~~here~~, which
contains a detailed history of each of the ~~sixty~~ odd per-
sonages (which include a rabbit and a bird). ~~here~~ I have repeatedly written to India and
to Tibet for that book, but it has not arrived yet.
~~yet. A number The publication of several Several other little discoveries of mine of mine~~
~~will have also have~~ which might interest ~~the~~
some western philologians, ~~will have to~~
~~yet.~~ Besides the documents mentioned above there
are several other little discoveries, which I hope
to publish after having seen my paper "on
~~the certain transliterations~~ certain Sanskrit formulas
transliterated with Chinese characters by ~~by the famous~~ Hsüan Tsang" through
the press.

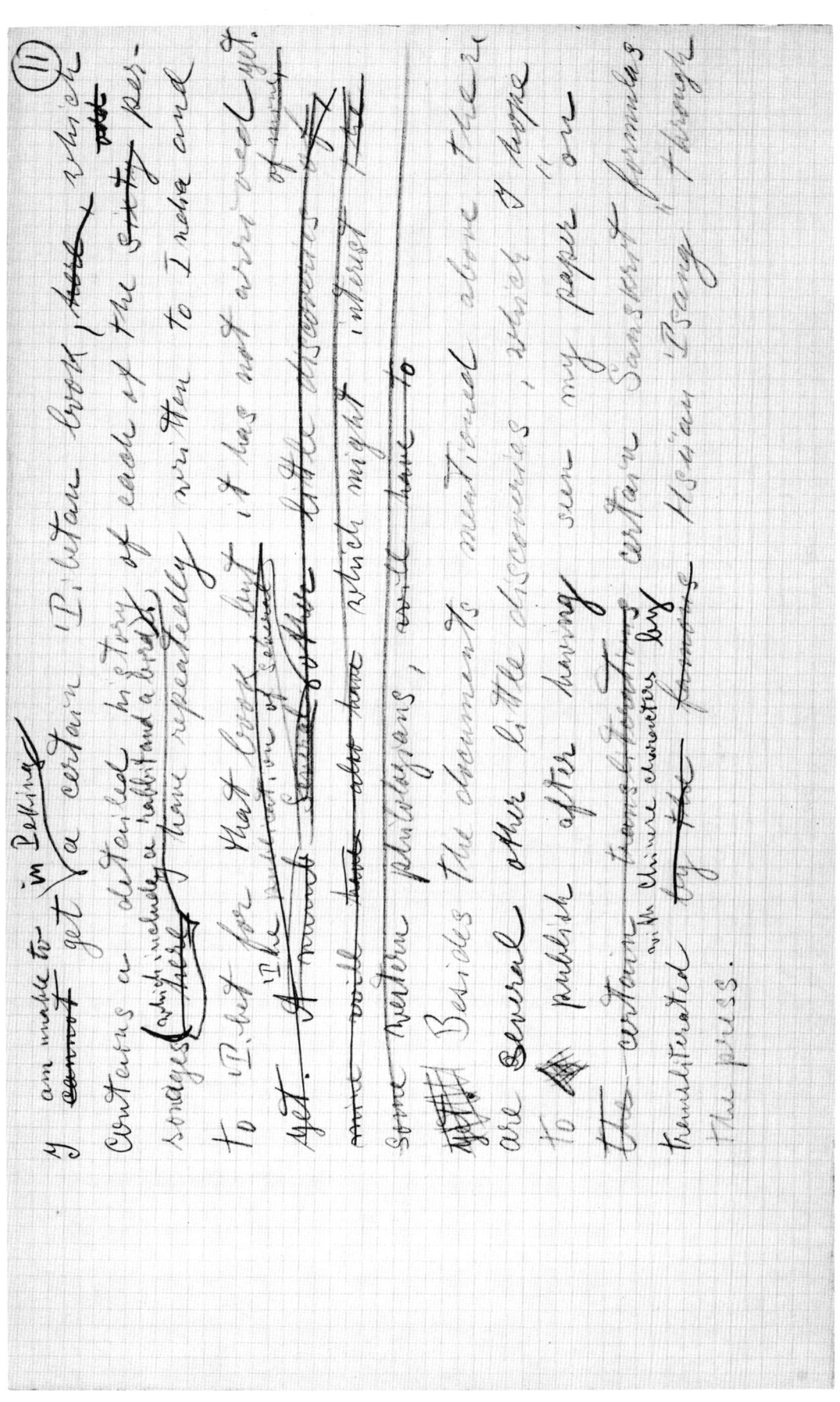

(12)

Hsüan Tsang as well as the other ~~The~~ Chinese translators
~~not long ago. The Dha~~ ~~The Chinese translators~~
~~of Indian ... S~~ of Sanskrit Buddhist books had
a very definite religious interest in transliterating
the Dhāraṇīs as correctly as possible because
~~they believed~~ the view that a mispronounced Dhāraṇī,
instead of helping the worshipper, ~~would~~ was (and is)
~~spell disaster for him~~ ~~meant~~ means disaster ~~In trans~~
a generally accepted ~~dogma~~ Buddhist dogma.
~~literating the names, on which~~

13

Many Indian and Central Asian names, which occur in Hsüan Tsang's Hsi Yü Chi, ~~cannot~~ could not so far be reconstructed satisfactorily because the exact phonetic value attached by the Chinese author to the characters used in ~~the~~ transliterating the names ~~as remained~~ was unknown. The phonetic value of some of these characters can undoubtedly be fixed by comparing ~~the~~ certain Dharaṇīs as transliterated by Hsüan Tsang with the original Indian Dhāraṇīs as preserved in a strictly phonetic alphabet by the ~~Kanjur~~ compilers of the Kanjur. I have collected all the Dhāraṇīs transliterated by Hsüan Tsang and

(14)

I am now comparing them with the Kanjur versions of the same Dhāraṇīs. I think that this ~~method~~ system is more likely to lead to ~~sat~~ satisfactory results than the ~~system~~ method ~~used by most other by~~ hitherto used by most writers on the subject, who ~~manipul mostly manipulate with names only~~ either entirely disregard the Dhāraṇīs ~~or fail to compare the Chine~~ or found their conclusions upon ~~mistaken~~ imperfect reconstructions of them. ~~I have tried~~ I think I have ~~I~~ succeeded in correcting some such ~~mistakes~~ imperfect reconstructions in a paper (also printed in 1934), which I sent you ~~not long ago. Our Lama (Phalos lotan gesrab)~~

(15)

not long ago. Our Lama ('Phags ldan çes rab) copies the Kanjur texts for me, and Mr. Ku the Chinese transliterations. Mr. 'Têng, ~~whom you have met~~ also in 193¾ examines the Chinese Buddhist ~~texts~~ books ~~looking for~~ ~~F~~ and has prepared a complete list of all the Dhāraṇīs (not only those transliterated by Hsüan 'Tsang) preserved in the 'Taishō 'Tripiṭaka. He has also made an index of all the characters treated by Karlgren in his Analytic Dictionary and in the Phonologie Chinoise.

(16)

I intend analysing the transliterations ascribed to the most important translators (Kumārajīva, I Ching etc.) one by one and fixing the phonetic values of the characters used in their transliterations. The phonetic values ~~which~~ inferred from the transliterations I hope to compare with the phonetic values deduced by Karlgren mostly from the Fan Ch'ieh dictionaries. In some cases

(17)

~~I intend taking all the [the most important] transliterators one by (Kumārajīva, I Ching etc.) one by one and comparing the ≠ phonetic values of the characters attributed by used by~~ ~~which~~ the various [ancient] authors must have attached ~~to the characters with the phonetic values noted by Karlgren~~. ~~In some cases~~ the [Dhāraṇīs] ~~the transliterations~~ strikingly confirm Karlgren's results. The character 墮, for instance, which was ~~rg~~ read 'd'uâ in ancient Chinese according to Karlgren (No 1009), stands for dhva (in dhvaja, the banner) in a transliteration dating from the VIII century (Comp. Taishō Trip. XI, 37a 14). But in many other cases the transliterated Dhāraṇīs ~~show~~ seem to show that Karlgren ~~was~~ [is] wrong in his reconstruction of ancient Chinese.

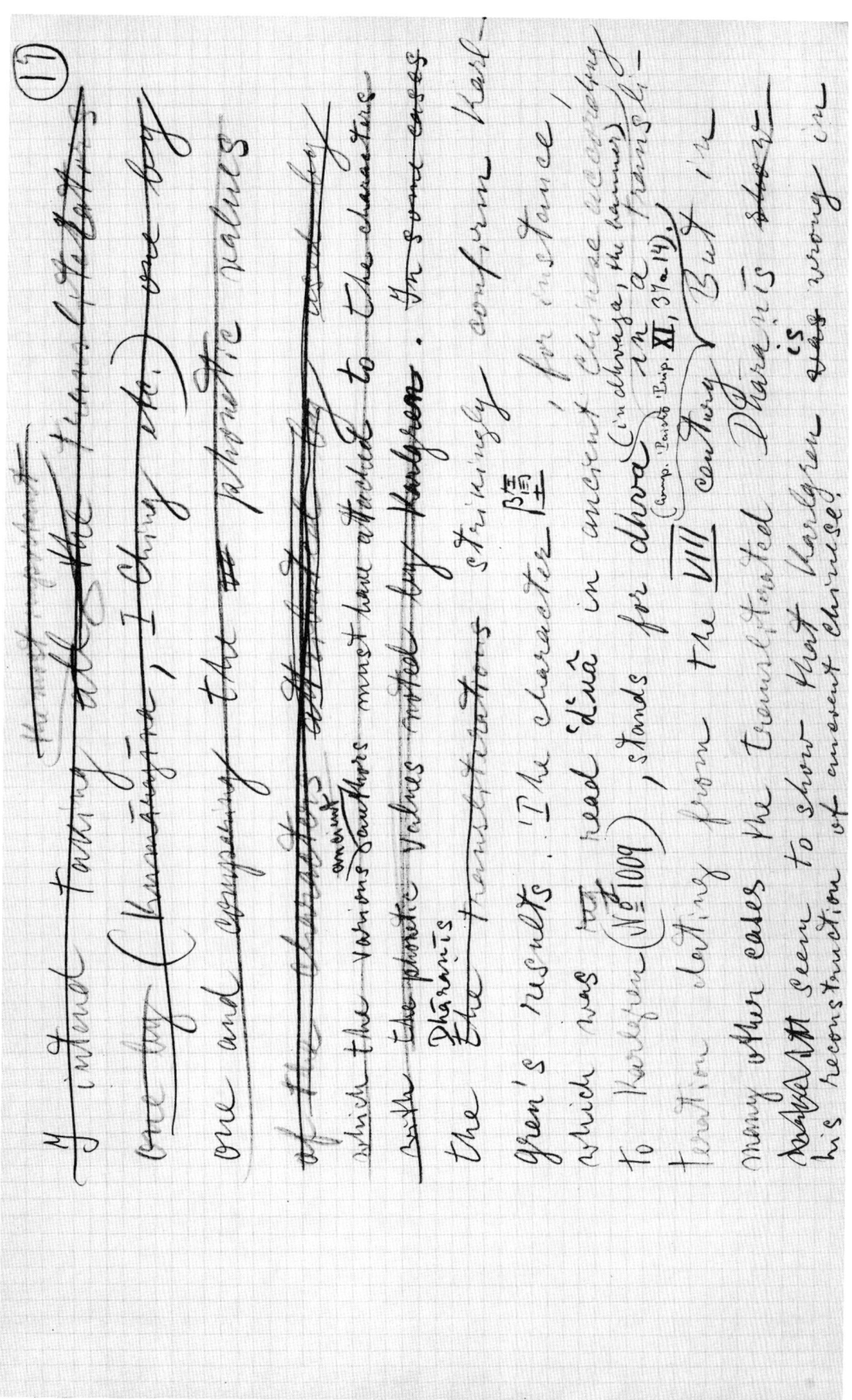

(18)

The character 曩 for instance ~~seems~~ to stands for ~~Skt.~~ na (never ~~not~~ for Skt. na plus nasal as far as I know) in very many ~~for nang or nan, nai etc.)~~ ~~in all most~~ ancient Dhāraṇīs ~~and~~ but its ancient Chinese reading according to Karlgren's (№ 188) is ~~nang~~ ᶜnâng. I think that the transcribed Dhāraṇīs should be ~~systematically studied and exploited in the~~ ~~and that~~ studied more systematically than has been done heretofore. ~~and that the various epochs to which the transliterators belong should~~

Mr. Pankratoff is also interested in ~~Chinese ancient~~ phonetics and possesses an important collection of ancient Chinese-Mongolian vocabularies, ~~which represent or~~ which contain valuable material for the history of both languages, but ~~the~~ his

(19)

analysis of these documents is not yet ready for ~~print~~. An other treatise by Mr. Pankratoff, however, is quite finished, and ~~Before me~~ I have a ~~ma~~ type-written (18 pages) of it before me. ~~manuscript before me, which~~ The manuscript contains an annotated translation of Ch'ien Lung's ~~famous~~ polyglot Yung Ho Kung inscription, and ~~which~~ I venture to hope that you ~~you that~~ will allow me to print ~~it~~ in the Parerga Pekingensia. A facsimile of this ~~This~~ particular polyglot (Manchu Mongol Tibetan and Chinese) inscription has been published by ~~Laufer~~ Franke and ~~Franke~~ Laufer (Epigraphische Denkmäler aus China, Berlin 1914), but no westerner has, as far as ~~I~~ we know, ever translated it. Several years ago I sent a type-written copy of

(20)

the introduction to Mr. Pankratoff's Dagurian grammar ~~(in E)~~ to Cambridge, ~~and the~~
where it was approved. Shall we continue printing the grammar (only a few
pages of it have been printed so far), or shall
~~we give it up?~~ we send the whole grammar
to you for approval? ~~Mr. Poppe's~~ We are
not certain as to whether the grammar is
worth printing or not, because ~~Mr. Poppe has~~
a few months after Mr. Pankratoff had
finished his work, Mr. Poppe's Dagurian grammar
~~appears~~ (in Russian) appeared. It should however
be noted that Mr. Pankratoff's work is written in English

(21)

and furthermore that the dialect described
by Mr. Poppe ~~is~~ differs from the
dialect treated ~~described~~ by Mr. Pankratoff.
The latter is of great assistance to me
because he knows the Mongol language (which I ignore)
very well and keeps on excellent terms ~~is acquainted~~ with all
the leading Lamas of Peking. This enables
me to obtain much useful information about Lamaism, ~~and~~
~~and kindred subjects~~
and to get hold of many books ~~etc.~~ unknown
in the West. Not long ago ~~Only the other day~~ Mr. Pankratoff
brought me a short history of the spiritual ancestors
of the Grand Lamas of Peking (Lcan skya Hutukhtu).

(the block-printed booklet) 22

The work is composed in Tibetan, but ~~it~~ contains a Sanskrit version (made in the XVIII century) in addition to the Tibetan original. ~~In the introduction to~~ In my edition of the commentary to the Kāçyapaparivarta and in ~~the majority~~ nearly all the articles, which I have published in Peking, I have had occasion to thank Mr. Pankratoff for ~~[illegible]~~ the valuable information ~~which I owe to him~~. I received from him. ~~[illegible]~~ It is also ~~Mr. Pankratoff~~ due to Mr. Pankratoff that my articles are comparatively well printed. ~~He does not speak any French but he manages to~~ He often goes to the Lazarist Press, talks with the

(23)

French directors as well as with the Chinese type-setters, and sees to it that my instructions are carried out.

Another very important source of information is Professor ~~Tschen Yin~~ Ki Y. K. Tschen, who has never been paid by myself or by the Sino-Indian Institute, but who ~~has~~ has regularly ~~attended~~ attended my Indo-Tibeto-Chinese ~~cou~~ privatissimum (3-4 hours weekly) ever since 1926, with the exception of the year 1928-1929, which I spent (in America.) ~~in America. He has studied in America~~ ~~an (Harvard) and in Europe, but~~

(24)

He is regarded as one of the greatest living sinologues by the Chinese and has ~~acquired~~ ~~an~~ become well acquainted with western methods during his years of study in America (Harvard) and Europe.

~~Anothe~~ Mr. T. W. T'ien (a research student ~~of~~ and former instructor of Tsinghua University) is a very good ~~pupil~~ beginner. ~~Heh~~ ~~T~~ ~~Tea~~ ~~Teaching him Sanskrit is~~ Even the teaching of elementary Sanskrit becomes a pleasure when one ~~finds~~ has to deal with ~~so enthusiastic~~ a pupil, who is as gifted and as full of enthusiasm as Mr. T'ien. The latter has an excellent knowledge of Chinese Buddhism ~~and~~ as well as of some European languages, including ancient Greek.

(25)

~~which~~ This enables him to progress ~~still~~ much faster than most of my ~~other~~ former Chinese pupils.

I have quite lately again examined Mr. Budde. ~~He~~ He is unfortunately not very much interested in Buddhism, but his knowledge of Chinese characters seems to be excellent.

26

I have worked more in 1934 than in most previous years. This is partly due to the fact that ~~as~~ the state of my health does not allow me to do much else. ~~On account of~~ Owing to the seriousness of my stomach trouble, ~~the~~ during the acute stage of which I had to spend about a month in the hospital, I ~~cannot~~ have become ~~also~~ (entirely) unable to travel* and could not leave Peking during the ~~summer~~ hot season. Therefore I continued my Indo-Tibeto-Chinese privatissim~~a~~um (as well as my researches) all through the summer of 1934.

*The extremely rigorous régime which I must observe in order ~~to keep passably well~~ (not to fall seriously ill again) is only possible at home or in the hospital ~~(out of~~ (to keep out of which is my chief concern).

HARVARD-YENCHING INSTITUTE

17 BOYLSTON HALL
CAMBRIDGE, MASSACHUSETTS

March 28, 1935

Dear Colleague:-

Thank you very much for your very interesting report in regard to the activity of the Sino-Indian Institute in China. I was much pleased to read your pages on the Kanjur studies, especially on your transliteration of the Dharanis, which gives such interesting results in the field of ancient Chinese phonetics. I was also most pleased to know about Mr. Pankratoff's activities and of his interest in phonetics.

Your words concerning Mr. T'ien confirmed what I always say to my colleagues, that a good knowledge of Greek makes it easier for a student to learn other languages.

Thank you very much for the interest that you take in Mr. Bodde. I was glad to know that his knowledge of Chinese characters seems to be excellent, but I think it is a pity that he has not much interest in Buddhism, because it is easier to understand later Chinese philosophy especially if you have a good knowledge of Buddhistic philosophical systems.

I was very sorry to learn that the state of your health is not good and that you have such serious trouble with your stomach. I hope that it is better now and that you will be able to have a rest this summer.

Concerning activities here, you may perhaps have heard that I am trying my best to arrange the studies in a scholarly way, remembering how well they were carried on by our faculty in St. Petersburg, where I had the pleasure of teaching with you. Mr. Mei, who has been lecturing in advanced Chinese courses, will return to Nanking at the end of this academic year and will be here no more. Mr. Ware is teaching mostly Chinese language courses. He will leave this country in May for China, will spend some days in Shanghai, and then go to Nanking; he also intends to visit Hangchow and then to go to Peiping. I hope that you will have the opportunity of seeing him and, when he calls on you, he will give you all the details about our activities here and our difficulties caused by the severe curtailing of income. Dr. Gardner has delivered a course of lectures on Chinese history and a very interesting introductory course mostly on bibliography, which enables the students to know what has been done by such scholars as Chavannes, Maspero, Pelliot, Karlgren, and others. I have heard from some of his pupils that the amount of information he is giving them on bibliography is amazing. I hope

2

that, as a result of this course, American scholars will not repeat the well-known story about the dream of the Emperor Ming, which was so harshly criticised by Maspero, or that in regard to the date of the arrival of Boddhidharma in China, on which Pelliot published his important article.

You have, perhaps, heard from Mr. Greene that we are to start this fall a periodical that is to have the name Harvard Journal of Asiatic Studies. The first number will be in memory of Professor Woods and will be published in November of this year. I shall be very glad to have you as a regular contributor to the journal, and I hope that you will not refuse to send us an article for this first volume, which will be larger than a regular publication. We should like to have the article by the middle of September. I will send you an official letter concerning this publication, but I am now asking you to be so kind as to request the Chinese scholars who will be able to contribute to this volume in memory of Professor Woods to send us some articles. The article can be in English, French or German. If it is in Chinese, we shall have to translate it here.

At the last meeting of the Trustees, a small amount of money was voted to start the preliminary work of preparing a Chinese-English dictionary. Professor Hung has kindly consented to allow us to make use of his staff at Yenching University during the summer months, when two or three dictionaries will be cut and pasted on cards. As you can imagine, it is a tremendous piece of work, and it will take a long time to get it into definite shape, but the work should be done because all the dictionaries which we have now are very incomplete and absolutely unreliable.

I am sending you, under separate cover, my last publication on Chinese bronzes, which is merely an assembling of some problems about which I took notes during the bronze exhibition in Paris in the spring of 1934.

Wishing you good health, I remain

Yours very sincerely,

George Elisséeff

Director

Prof. A. von Stael-Holstein,
Sino-Indian Institute,
ex-Austrian Legation,
Peiping, China.

HARVARD-YENCHING INSTITUTE

17 BOYLSTON HALL
CAMBRIDGE, MASSACHUSETTS

24 марта 1935

Многоуважаемый
Александръ Августовичъ,

спасибо большое за Ваше милое письмо, за Вашъ интересный отчетъ и за любезную присылку Вашей статьи относительно транслитерации китайскими иероглифами санскритскихъ дарани. Какъ только я получилъ Ваше письмо я навелъ справки о Вашей рукописи Vajracchedikā. Она находится въ квартирѣ покойнаго профессора Woods и его вдова обѣщала ее передать намъ въ ближайшие три дня. Какъ только Ваша рукопись будетъ здѣсь я ее отправлю Вамъ въ Пекинъ. Я очень радъ, что могу оказать Вамъ эту услугу, такъ какъ чувствую себя виноватымъ за долгое молчание. Я плохой корреспондентъ, но знаю, что всему есть предѣлъ и поэтому надѣюсь, что Вы великодушно извините мое неписание.

Въ моихъ объяснительныхъ запискахъ, которые я присоединилъ къ бюджету я упомянулъ, что Вы не только управляете Вашимъ институтомъ, но помогаете китайцамъ въ ихъ научныхъ изысканiяхъ и читаете лекцiи безвозмездно.

Въ моемъ англiйскомъ письмѣ я пишу Вамъ относительно нашего новаго журнала. Много было разговора о томъ какъ его назвать, наконецъ рѣшили окрестить его Harvard Journal of Asiatic Studies, чтобы можно было печатать статьи о буддизмѣ, о средней Азiи и обо всемъ что касается Asia Major. Первый №: будетъ посвященъ памяти профессора Woods. Мнѣ бы хотѣлось чтобы этотъ первый номеръ былъ исключительно хорошимъ и солиднымъ и я надѣюся, что друзья и коллеги покойнаго пришлютъ мнѣ достаточно статей, чтобы выпустить томъ страницъ въ триста. Я Вамъ буду очень обязанъ если Вы попросите китайскихъ ученыхъ, которые его знали написать что-нибудь – тема безразлична, не нужно чтобы статья была непремѣнно о буддизмѣ. Я напишу, конечно, Creel'ю который кажется зналъ покойнаго профессора Woods.

Вести занятія здѣсь не легко, студенты не такъ хорошо подготовлены какъ въ Европѣ и много не знаютъ потому что лишены классическаго образованія. Я стараюсь имъ многое объяснить во время лекцій, что лишь косвенно имѣетъ отношеніе къ китайскому или японскому, и на это уходитъ много времени. У меня 5 студентовъ слушаютъ японскій и 6, японскую исторію, на лекціяхъ по китайскому у меня всего 2. Года черезъ три занятія совсѣмъ наладятся и я надѣюсь, что студентовъ будетъ больше.

Trustees сильно урѣзали бюджетъ, сокративъ число стипендій (fellowships) и собираются усилить политику экономіи это, конечно, затрудняетъ научную дѣятельность и я думаю, что пока на время придется отказаться отъ изданія монографій.

Въ іюнѣ я уѣзжаю на лѣто въ Парижъ, потому что будущее лѣто придется сидѣть здѣсь изъ за 300 лѣтія университета.

Вѣра Петровна и я шлемъ нашъ сердечный привѣтъ Ольгѣ Владимировнѣ и Вамъ. Мы часто вспоминаемъ чудесные дни проведенные въ Вашемъ гостепріимномъ домѣ въ Пекинѣ.

Отъ всей души желаю Вамъ здоровья и всего наилучшаго.

Крѣпко жму руку.

Искренне преданный Вамъ

С. Елисеевъ

Am 11. April 1935 abgeschickt.

Dear Professor Elisséeff,

Mr. R. S. Greene asked me a few days ago to write to you about Dr. Creel. The latter has attended my privatissim~~um~~a for some ~~months and I had the impression that~~ months, but he is not doing so at present, ~~because his because I the study of the I An Yang bone inscriptions occupies all his time~~ because his purely Chinese studies occupy all his time. I ~~am~~ have not ~~acquainted with~~ studied Dr. Creel's writings, and I ~~cannot am not~~ am entirely incompetent to discuss his proficiency in Chinese. ~~All I can do~~ Consequently

all I can do is to report to you what
~~I hear~~ I ~~have~~ have heard from others. Dr. Creel is
~~con~~ regarded as ~~an~~ a good ~~expert in~~ Chinese historian
~~history by~~ by ~~B~~ some of the best native
scholars, and they believe that he would
make an excellent ~~teacher~~ professor of Chinese history in ~~America~~ any University.
His ~~st~~ interpretations of the bone inscriptions
are also attracting the attention of many
Chinese investigators. I hope that he will
be able to continue his studies.

Believe me yours sincerely

A. Staël-Holstein.

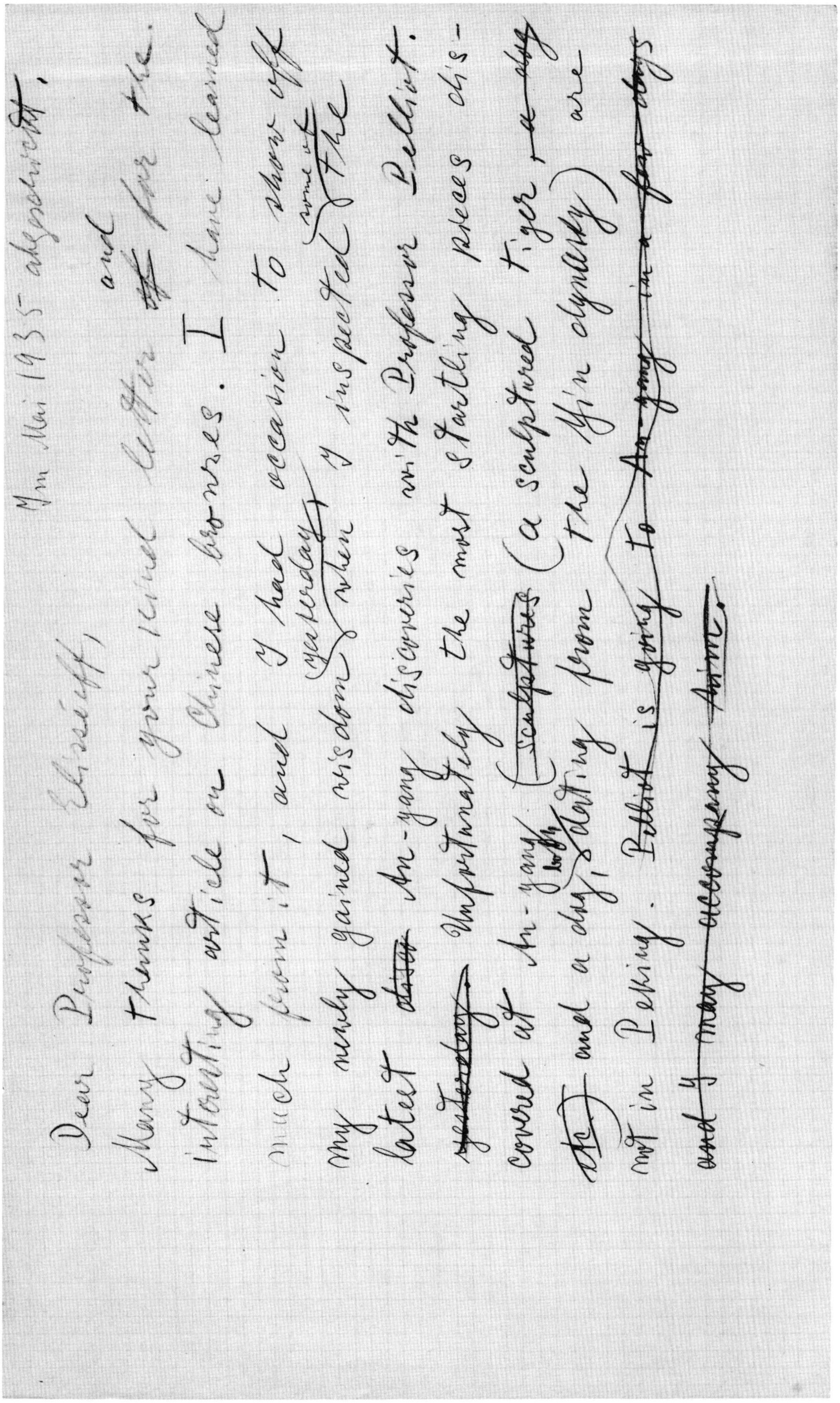

Im Mai 1935 abgeschickt.

Dear Professor Elisséeff,

Many thanks for your kind letter ~~of~~ and for the interesting article on Chinese bronzes. I have learned much from it, and I had occasion to show off my newly gained wisdom yesterday, when I inspected some of the latest ~~discr~~ An-yang discoveries with Professor Pelliot. ~~yesterday.~~ Unfortunately the most startling pieces discovered at An-yang ~~(sculptures~~ (a sculptured tiger~~, a dog etc.)~~ and a dog, both dating from the Yin dynasty) are not in Peking. ~~Pelliot is going to An-yang in a few days and I may accompany him.~~

I am happy
~~I am~~ ~~very~~ ~~much interested in pleased~~ to know
that you are working so successfully at Harvard
and that you ~~are introducing~~ are being guided
by the experiences gained in ~~#~~ the St. Petersburg
faculty. ~~# The years~~, It is I always remember the years, during which we both
belonged to that ~~famous body~~ learned body, ~~belong to my~~
~~most cherished memories.~~ with the greatest pleasure.

~~Dear Professor Elisseeff,~~

~~Many thanks for your kind letter.~~ I am very glad to hear that you are interested in my ~~printed~~ phonetic ~~studies~~ investigations, and ~~I your sa~~ that you want me to ~~con-tribute articles of my own to the Harvard Orient Asiatic~~ become a regular contributor to the Harvard Journal of Asiatic Studies. I hope ~~to dispatch my fi~~ that my first article (for the Woods Memorial Volume) will reach you about the middle of September and that it will be ~~accompanied by~~ a number of contributions by ~~Chinese scholars~~ friends of the late Professor J. H. Woods: Dr S. Hu ~~Shih~~, ~~and~~ Professor Y. K. Tschen ~~(陳~~ (this is how he transcribes his ~~—~~ family name: 陳) and Professor

'I'ang have definitely promised to let me have their articles before the 15th of August. I have also written to Professor Y. R. Chao, who I believe that resides at Nanking, asking him for a contribution. Professor Y. R. Chao has been teaching Chinese at Harvard.

May I ask to be kindly remembered to Vera Petrovna? My wife ~~and~~ sends you her heartiest greetings.

Believe me yours sincerely and gratefully

A. Staël-Holstein.

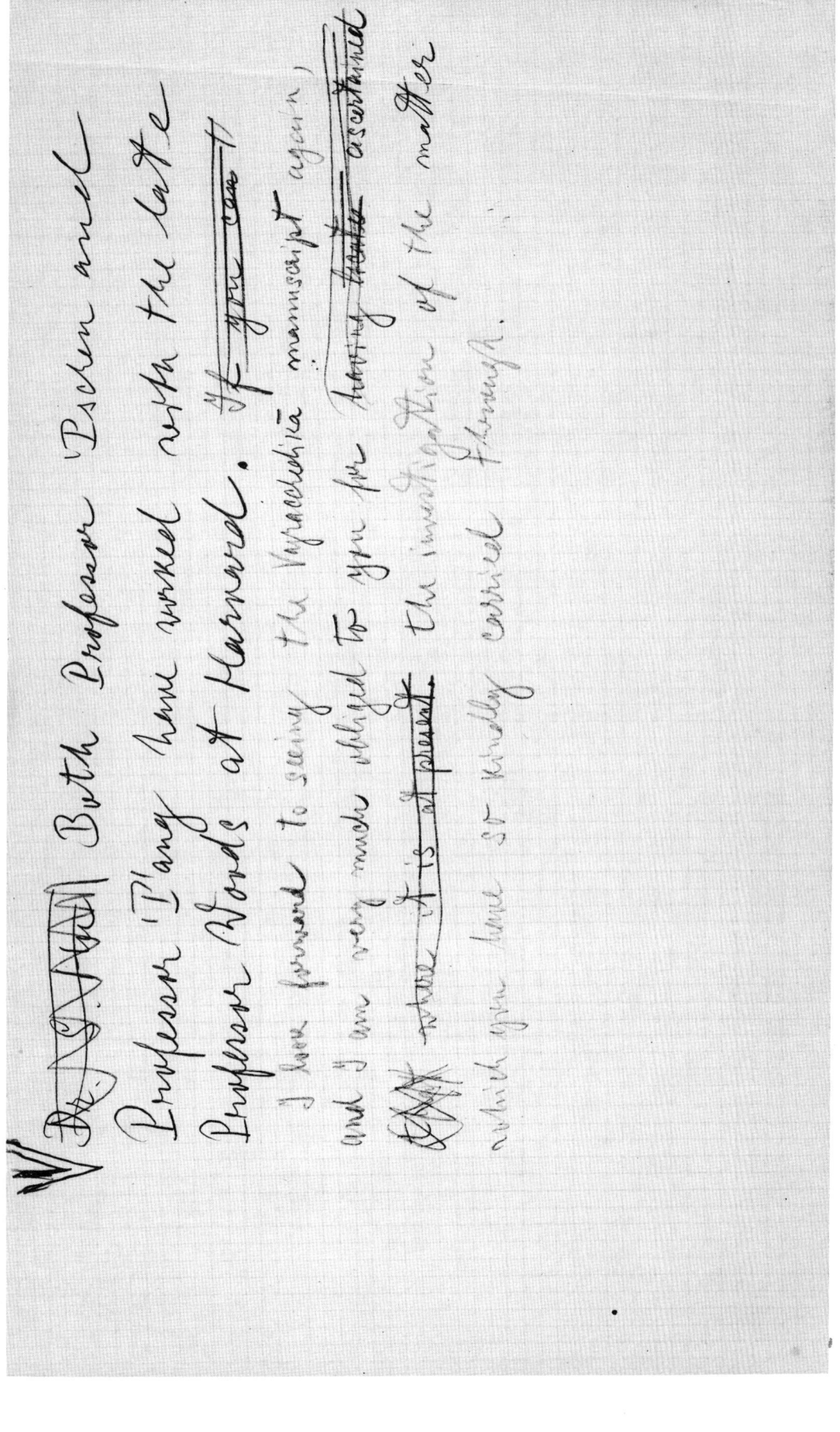

~~Dr. S. [illegible]~~ Both Professor 'Pschen and Professor 'P'ang have worked with the late Professor Woods at Harvard. ~~If you can~~

I look forward to seeing the Vajracchedikā manuscript again, and I am very much obliged to you for ~~having [illegible] ascertained~~ ~~[illegible] where it is at present.~~ the investigation of the matter which you have so kindly carried through.

HARVARD-YENCHING INSTITUTE

17 BOYLSTON HALL
CAMBRIDGE, MASSACHUSETTS

June 13, 1935

Dear Professor von Stael-Holstein:-

Thank you very much for your kind letter of May 12th. I am very grateful for your willingness to write an article for the Woods memorial volume and also to send us the articles of your Chinese colleagues. I hope that Mr. Chao, who is in Nanking and who was the first Chinese professor at Harvard, will send something for the volume.

I trust that your manuscript which Dr. Ware took with him is now in your possession and that you have heard from him all details about our life and activity here. I was glad to know that you met Professor Pelliot and that you had the pleasure of inspecting with him the latest An Yang discoveries. Dr. Ware has told you, probably, of our plan to bring out from China our Kanjur and Tanjur and of the suggestions which were given to us by Professor G. G. Wilson. The articles in the newspapers here are quite alarming about the North China region and it may be difficult to carry out Dr. Ware's proposal to you in regard to the sending of these valuable books.

Dean Chase asked me to answer the letter which he received from you a long time ago. As you may know, our budget was reduced 18% and especially the publication funds were drastically cut, so that it will be impossible for us to publish your fifteen Tibetan pictures. I spoke to Mr. Warner, and he suggested to me that Probstain, who is the editor in London and whom you doubtless know, is the man to interest in such a publication, and some of the young curators of the British Museum might write the explanation for this Jatakamala publication.

I am leaving here the 20th of June and shall be in Paris during July and the beginning of September. If you need your photographs or if I can do anything for this publication in Europe, let me know by writing to my Parision address: 75 Boulevard Pereire, Paris XVII. If you would like to have your photographs returned, please write to Miss Bayley, at this address, who will do the necessary.

With best wishes from Mrs. Elisséeff and myself to you and Mrs. von Stael-Holstein for a pleasant summer,

Sincerely yours,

Serge Elisséeff
Director

Prof. A. von Stael-Holstein,
ex-Austrian Legation,
Peiping, China.

Peking, September 29th 1935.

Dear Professor Elisséeff,

During the year 34/35 I received fourteen thousand (14000.00) Mexican dollars from the Treasurer of Yenching University. I used five hundred and thirty five (535.00) ~~dollars~~ Mexican dollars* ~~for paying for the printing of~~ for printing volume I of the Harvard Sino-Indian Series, four thousand (4000.00) Mexican dollars for representation, eight thousand five hundred and eighty six Mexican dollars and thirty one cents (8586.31) for paying my assistants (Lama Mgon-po, Mr. Pankratoff, Dr. Liebenthal, Mr. Pêng, Lama 'Phags-ldan-ges-rab, and Mr. Ku),

* See my letter (accompanied by a photographic reproduction of the receipt) to Dean Chase dated October 24th 1934, and Dean Chase's reply dated December 10th 1934.

and eight hundred ~~forty eig~~ seventy eight Mexican dollars and sixty nine cents (878.69) for buying, binding, storing, and shipping books.* Photographic reproductions of the receipts of my assistants and of the receipts connected with the buying, binding, storing and shipping of books are found on pages — below.

Believe me yours sincerely and ~~gratef~~ gratefully

A. Staël-Holstein.

* I kept the Kanjur and the Tanjur belonging to the Harvard-Yenching Institute in a strong-room ~~at~~ the bank, and I ~~sent~~ shipped one hundred copies of volume I of the Harvard Sino-Indian Series to the Harvard University Press. See Dean Chase's letter to myself dated August 23rd 1934.

HARVARD-YENCHING INSTITUTE

17 BOYLSTON HALL
CAMBRIDGE, MASSACHUSETTS

October 19, 1935

Dear Professor von Stael-Holstein:-

This morning I received from Hanoi the book review of the different publications of the Harvard Sino-Indian Series written by Gaspardone and published in the Bulletin of the French school in Hanoi. They asked me to give it to Mr. Friedrich Weller, but, since I do not know his address and presume that you do, will you please be so kind as to forward these two pages to him.

Dr. Ware, who is now back with us here, has told me about his visit to Peking and of the agreable time that he spent in your house. I was very glad to hear that the work is going on so efficiently, and I hope that the strict diet you are on is helping your health and that you are better this autumn.

I was in Paris this summer and there saw Professor Sylvain Lévi and all the other French orientalists. Just two days before leaving, I had a meeting with Professor Pelliot, who gave me interesting details about the Chinese archaeological excavations. The month of August I spent in Portugal working in the archives of Lisbon, where the reports of the Jesuits sent from China and Japan in the sixteenth century are preserved. At the end of September, we started our academic year here, and my colleagues and I have the impression that there is more interest in Far Eastern studies. Dr. Ware and Mr. Gardner have about eight students in Chinese and I have five students and three auditors in my first-year Japanese language course.

In November we shall have the Trustees' meeting, and I will state to them that I consider that it is better for the work of the Sino-Indian Institute that you should remain in Peking rather than come here. I hope that you also prefer to continue your work in Peking and not come here for one or two semesters.

Mrs. Elisséeff joins me in sending Mrs. von Stael-Holstein and yourself our kindest regards.

Sincerely yours,

S. Elisséeff

Director

Professor von Stael-Holstein,
ex-Austrian Legation,
Peiping, China.

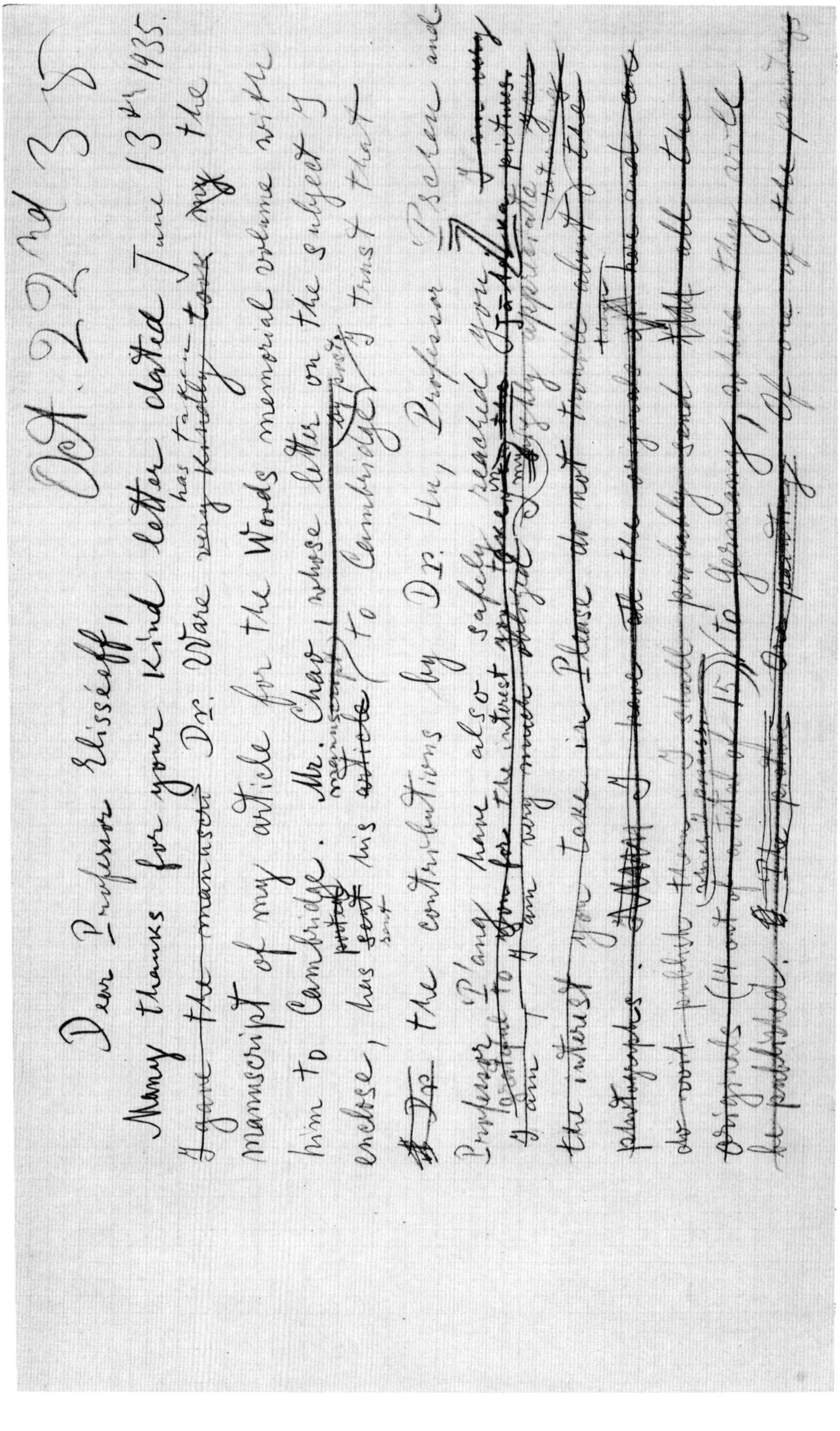

Oct. 22nd 38

Dear Professor Elisséeff,

Many thanks for your kind letter dated June 13th 1935. ~~I gave the manuscr~~ Dr. Ware ~~very kindly took~~ has taken ~~my~~ the manuscript of my article for the Woods memorial volume with him to Cambridge. Mr. Chao, whose letter on the subject I enclose, has ~~posted~~ ~~sent~~ sent his ~~article~~ manuscript to Cambridge by post. I trust that ~~Dr.~~ the contributions by Dr. Hu, Professor Pschan and Professor P'ang have also safely reached you. ~~I am very grateful to you for the interest you take in the Jātaka pictures. I am very much obliged I highly appreciate your returning the interest you take in Please do not trouble about the photographs. I have all the originals of them here and can do without publish them. I shall probably send all the originals (14 out of a total of 15) when I publish, to Germany, where they will be published. The picture One painting~~, ~~Of one of the paintings~~

I am very grateful to you for having sent me the Vajracchedikā-manuscript. ~~[illegible]~~ I had spent much time in compiling it 5–6 years ago, and I also had prepared a commentary of the Vajracchedikā (~~Chinese~~ Tibetan-Chinese) for the press. Both the text and the commentary could, however, not be published, because I did not know what was happening ~~with~~ to the text manuscript, which I had sent to America. Thanks to your kind intervention I shall now be able to publish ~~both~~ the text ~~(Sanskrit- & Tibetan-Chinese)~~ as well as the commentary here in Peking, and ~~I think I shall~~ it will be possible

~~be able~~ to do so without asking the Harvard-Yenching Institute for any contribution in addition to the ordinary appropriation of the Sino-Indian Institute. My Chinese friends do consider a polyglot edition of the Vajracchedikā (one Sanskrit text one Tibetan text and six Chinese versions) as a desideratum and have frequently asked me during the last 5-6 years quite when it was going to appear.

The Catholic University of Peking is starting a journal this autumn, which Dr. Biallas, the editor, hopes will become a second T'oung Pao. I have been asked to become a member of the editing committee, and to contribute an article to one of the first numbers. At present I am writing that article. In the Bulletin of the National Library of Peking I am publishing chronological tables for the years 1027-1986 (the first sixteen Tibetan cycles) giving the Tibetan cyclical designations with the corresponding Chinese and Christian dates (these tables are sous presse at present, and I enclose two sample pages from the latest proof sheets). I am publishing the chronological tables at the express demand of a number of Chinese scholars, who declare that the Tibetan ~~modes~~ methods of reckoning time ~~is~~ are extremely puzzling to them.

~~The Chine My Chinese friends, Besides these projects which~~ My former assistant, Professor Weller of Leipzig, has compiled a Sino-Soghdian index to the Dirghanakhasutra, and I intend publishing it in the 3rd volume of the Harvard Sino-Indian Series. I enclose the last three pages (from the first set of proof-sheets) for your inspection. ~~I hope that you have had a pleasant Summer in France~~ My family spent the hot season at ~~Pa-ta~~ Pa-ta-chu, but I remained at Peking most of the time.

With best wishes from ~~[illegible]~~ my wife and myself to you and Mrs. Elisséeff I remain yours sincerely

A. Staël-Holstein

Since Dr. Ware's departure, whose company we enjoyed here for a couple of months, no American orientalists seem to have come to Peking

According to an arrangement long ago approved by the Cambridge Mass. authorities that volume will consist of small articles. One of these small articles (by myself) has already been printed. Its title is:

The Sino-Indian Institute is constantly being visited by European scholars. During the last few months we have seen Professor Duyvendak, Sir Charles Bell and Dr. Fr. Rosen (former President of the Deutsche Morgenländische Gesellschaft) and others here.

HARVARD-YENCHING INSTITUTE

17 BOYLSTON HALL
CAMBRIDGE, MASSACHUSETTS

December 11, 1935

Dear Professor von Stael-Holstein:-

Thank you very much for your letter dated October 22, 1935, in which you gave me a general idea of the activities of the Sino-Indian Institute as well as of your own scientific work. I reported this information to the Trustees at their last meeting on Monday, November 18th and told them that I considered that your presence in Peiping is indispensable. They agreed with me, and the question of asking you to come here was abandoned.

Thank you very much for your article for the Woods memorial volume which Dr. Ware brought to this country. We have also received an article from Mr. Chao, but I have received nothing from Dr. Hu Shih. Have you heard from him as to whether he intends to come here for the Tercentenary? I understood from Mr. Greene that he never answers letters, and I should like to know whether we are to have the pleasure of having him in Cambridge. You probably know that Pelliot will be here for the occasion.

You have probably heard the sad news of the death of Professor Sylvain Lévi in Paris.

The volume of Demiéville and Ecke on the Pagodas of Zayton has finally been published, and the Harvard Press will send you shortly a copy of the book.

Wishing you and Mrs. von Stael-Holstein a Happy New Year, I remain

Yours sincerely,

Serge Elisséeff
Director

Professor von Stael-Holstein,
ex-Austrian Legation,
Peiping, China.

Peking January 28th 1936.

Dear Professor Elisséeff,

Ever since I received your letter dated December 11th 1935 I have tried to see Dr. Hu about the article ~~in order to ask him about his article for the Woods Memorial Volume~~ as well as about his trip to Cambridge in 1936. ~~About a week~~ But he is still in Shanghai, although Yuan T'ung Li

I am sorry to hear that Dr. Hu's article for the Woods Memorial Volume has not arrived at Cambridge.

told me ~~about~~ a fortnight ago that he was expected here "in a day or two". When I telephoned to Dr. Hu's house this morning I ~~received the same statement was given~~ the same information was given me. ~~I shall~~ As soon as he returns I shall ~~interview~~ see him ~~about the art~~ and ~~let ye~~ write to you again.

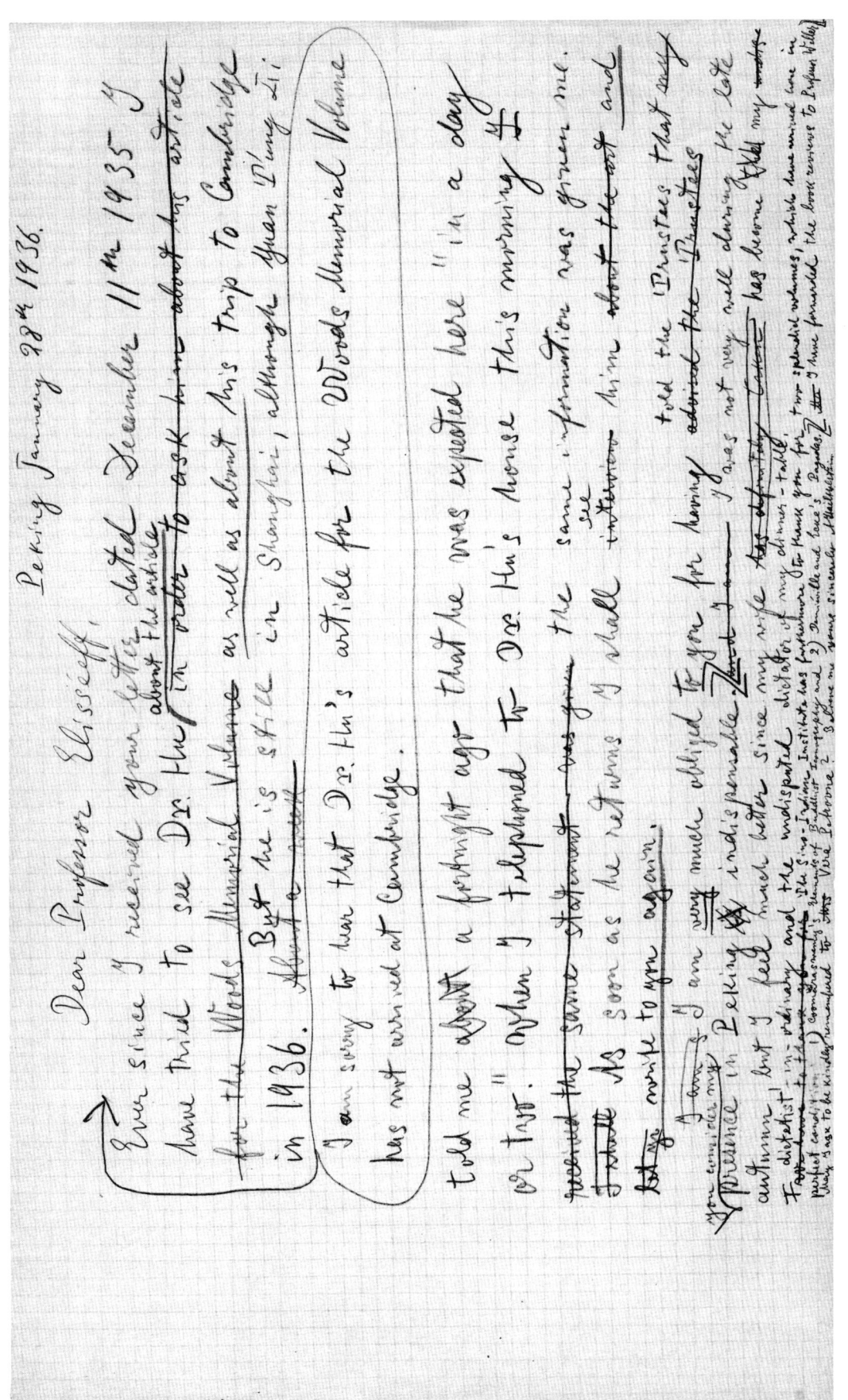

~~I am g~~ I am very much obliged to you for having ~~advised the Trustees~~ told the Trustees that ~~my~~ you consider my presence in Peking ~~as~~ indispensable. ~~and I am~~ I was not very well during the late autumn, but I feel much better since my wife ~~has definitely taken~~ has become ~~the~~ my ~~undis~~ dietetist-in-ordinary and the undisputed dictator of my dinner-table. ~~I have to thank you for~~ The Sino-Indian Institute has furthermore to thank you for two splendid volumes, which have arrived here in perfect condition: 1) Coomaraswamy's Elements of Buddhist Iconography and 2) Demiéville and Ecke's Pagodas. ~~the~~ I have forwarded the book reviews to Professor Weller. May I ask to be kindly remembered to ~~Mrs~~ Vera Petrovna? Believe me yours sincerely A. Staël Holstein

HARVARD-YENCHING INSTITUTE

HARVARD JOURNAL OF ASIATIC STUDIES
S. ELISSÉEFF, EDITOR

17 BOYLSTON HALL
CAMBRIDGE, MASSACHUSETTS

26 февраля 1936.

Дорогой Александръ Августовичъ,

спасибо за Ваше письмо отъ 28-го января и за Ваши хлопоты о статьѣ D-r Ху Ши. Мы къ сожалѣнію не могли дольше ждать. Выпускъ перваго номера нашего журнала уже и безъ этого сильно задержался. Сегодня я сдалъ въ печать всѣ рукописи и типографія обѣщала намъ всё сдѣлать черезъ три недѣли; такъ что къ первому апрѣлю номеръ долженъ быть готовъ. Всего мнѣ удалось собрать около 15 статей и номеръ будетъ около 150 страницъ. Второй номеръ предполагаемъ выпустить въ іюлѣ, третій въ ноябрѣ и четвертый въ январѣ. Харвардскій университетъ пригласилъ Dr. Ху Ши пріѣхать на 300-лѣтіе университета, но кажется до сихъ поръ не получилъ отъ него отвѣта.

Я очень радъ, что могъ услужить Вамъ убѣдивъ нашихъ „trustees", что для научной работы Вамъ важнѣе быть въ Пекинѣ, чѣмъ здѣсь, и что Вашъ отъѣздъ нарушитъ начавшуюся работу, а у насъ здѣсь нѣтъ никого, кто былъ бы подготовленъ быть Вашимъ слушателемъ.

Книга Coomaraswamy мнѣ не очень по душѣ, я ужасно не люблю когда сравниваютъ отдѣльныя христіанскія понятія съ буддійскими философскими понятіями. Это ничего не даетъ и вноситъ какое-то ложное чувство, будто между ними есть что-то общее. Книга Demiéville и Ecke очень интересная, но къ сожалѣнію иллюстрацій размѣщены такъ несуразно, что мѣстами страницы сложены такъ, что сгибъ листа проходитъ черезъ середину репродукцій.

Сердечный привѣтъ Ольгѣ Владиміровнѣ и Вамъ отъ Вѣры Петровны и меня.

Искренне преданный Вамъ

Сергѣй Елисеев

"Z" means: new paragraph.

Peking, February 27th 1936.

Dear Professor Elisséeff,

Dr. Hu has returned from the South, and, (in accordance with your instructions) I have asked him about his article for the ~~J~~ Harvard Journal of Asiatic ~~Oriental~~ Studies as well as about his proposed visit to America. He regrets very much that, on account of the pressure of official business, he has not yet been able to write ~~keep his promise~~ the article and to send you his manuscript, which was to be printed ~~appear~~ in the first (Woods Memorial) volume of the Journal. He hopes, however, to contribute a paper ~~on~~ to some of the later volumes of it. Dr. Hu has received the invitation to the Harvard tercentenary and will certainly attend the jubilee in September 1936. Z

(2)

During the last twelve months ~~##~~ I have continued my efforts to preserve as much as possible of the fast vanishing archaeological material connected with ~~##~~ the history of Buddhism (Lamaism and Foism) in North China. I have bought some ~~of the~~ ~~voitures~~ statuettes, pictures, documents etc. and have had many other ~~photographed~~ objects photographed in order to ~~preserve~~ perpetuate at least the memory of them for ~~future~~ the ~~specialists~~ ~~public~~ those interested in the history of religions. The Chinese authorities have but a very limited interest in Buddhist antiquities and do not take any effective measures in order ~~to prevent the sale of objects, which have no great~~ ~~show no obvious~~ ~~artistic merit, to the tourists, who carry constantly break up artist important series and carry The latter have mostly no regard for~~

to prevent the sale of such objects to the tourists, who without any regard ~~to~~ for the ~~st purpose~~ religious significance of the statuettes etc. carry them away to their distant homes as mere

③

curios. The objects lose a great deal of their value by being thus exported because the series (to which they belonged) are frequently broken up and the designations, under which they were known, do not always accompany them to their new homes. ⊕ I try to preserve the complete series and note the designations as well as the purposes, for which the objects were used. ~~In this way~~ I possess ~~I have~~ a large collection ⊕ of annotated originals and of photographs, ~~which~~ ~~[illegible]~~ and the collection, which has been inspected by many ~~specialists~~ American and European specialists ⊕, contains a considerable number of unica. Z

I continue my Sino-Indian privatissima (3-4 hours a week) ~~, but~~ ~~all~~ through ~~(throughout?)~~ the year (I interrupted them for about a month only last summer), and # the preparatory work which they demand ~~require~~ (the ~~anal~~ detailed analysis of the Sanskrit originals ~~as~~ as well as of the Chinese and Tibetan translations of certain Buddhist texts) occupies a considerable part of my time. ~~[illegible]~~ My class for beginners in Sanskrit (2 hours a week)

(4)

requires much less preparation. I do not lecture any more at the National University of Peking, but ~~receive my~~ teach my pupils at the Sino-Indian Institute. One of them (Mr. Chu) has been recommended to me by Professor Porter of Yenching and the other ~~one~~ (Mr. Ku) by Mr. Yüan, the director of the National Library. ~~Both of them are industrious and~~ Both Mr. Chu and Mr. Ku, (who are university graduates,) ~~are fairly industrious and Mr. Ku especially promises to become a good philologist. His knowledge of~~ ~~He knows~~ ~~German and French in addition to Chinese and English. Mr. Chu knows only English and Chinese and English.~~
have a fair knowledge of Chinese Buddhist literature and promise to become good Sino-Indian philologists. I can not say as much of the ~~students~~ (majority of beginners in Sanskrit,) whom I used to teach at the National University of Peking, ~~has become made~~ They were all undergraduates and had so many weekly lectures (up to thirty and more) to attend that they ~~could not devote enough time to~~

(5)

could not spare the time necessary for the proper preparation of their Sanskrit lessons at home. ~~The pupils, whom I taught privately, have to~~ Some of my private pupils, (Messrs. Yü and Lin) on the other hand, are making good progress. Two of them ~~are~~ ⊕ at present successfully continuing their studies at Paris under Pelliot, Baxot, ~~and~~ Demiéville etc, while Mr. T'ien is with ~~the~~ Professor Pavolini at Florence. It has been my ambition for many years to found a Sino-Indian school in China, and I ~~hope that~~ believe that, thanks to the munificence of the Harvard-Yenching Institute, my hope ~~is will be realised by~~ is being realised. Z

In addition to the two papers, which I sent you not long ago ("The Emperor Ch'ien Lung and the larger Sūramgamasūtra" and "On the sexagenary cycle of the Tibetans"), I have ~~the~~ lately written a number of short treatises, which will soon appear in print. My ~~edition~~ polyglot edition ~~of five pages of which I enclose, is now~~ of the Vajracchedikā, five pages (proof sheets) of which I am sending to you ~~enclose for your~~

(7)

~~inspection,~~ is intended to form ~~a~~ volume IV of the Harvard Sino-Indian Series. I have somewhat amended the Tibetan text of my manuscript, which you so kindly sent to me ~~##~~ last summer, and I hope that the ~~introduction, the~~ whole edition (with the introduction and the notes) will be printed before long. The entire manuscript of the commentary ~~of~~ the Vajracchedikā which I intend publishing as volume V of the Harvard Sino-Indian Series is ready for print. The Sanskrit original of the commentary is lost, and my edition will contain the Tibetan and Chinese translations only.

~~Vol~~ Mr. Pankratoff's Dagurian grammar, which was to ~~form vol~~ appear as volume VI of the ~~Sino-Indian~~ Harvard Sino-Indian Series has been practically ready ~~for print~~ for a long time, but we were not sure whether it ~~~~ was worth printing in view of the fact that Professor Poppe has not long ago published ~~~~ (in Russian) a grammar of the Dagurian language. When we submitted Mr. ~~When we consulted Professor Pelliot, who was here last summer, he told us that Mr. Pankratoff's grammar should certainly be printed, adding that we were at liberty to quote his words~~

(8)

Pankratoff's manuscript to Professor Pelliot, who was here last summer, he examined it carefully and told us that it should certainly be printed, adding that we were at liberty to quote his words wherever we liked. ~~I regret~~ I do not, unfortunately, know, when Mr. Pankratoff's grammar will be printed. The author, whose lungs were never strong, is in a Crimean sanatorium at present.

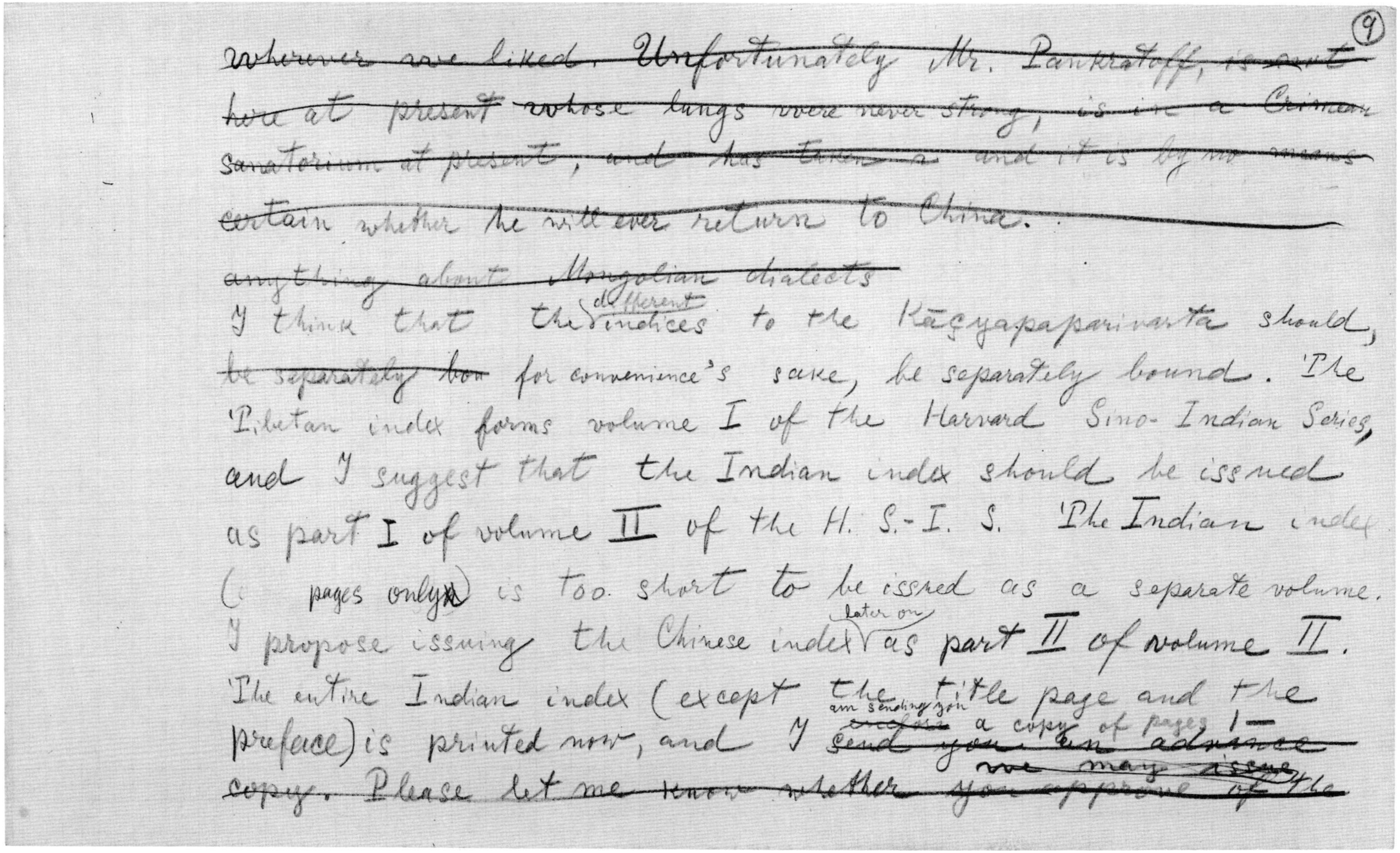

(9)

~~wherever we liked. Unfortunately Mr. Pankratoff, is not here at present whose lungs were never strong, is in a Crimean sanatorium at present, and has taken a and it is by no means certain whether he will ever return to China.~~

~~anything about Mongolian dialects~~

I think that the different indices to the Kāçyapaparivarta should, ~~be separately bou~~ for convenience's sake, be separately bound. The Tibetan index forms volume I of the Harvard Sino-Indian Series, and I suggest that the Indian index should be issued as part I of volume II of the H. S.-I. S. The Indian index (pages only) is too short to be issued as a separate volume. I propose issuing the Chinese index later on as part II of volume II. The entire Indian index (except the title page and the preface) is printed now, and I am sending you ~~enclose~~ a copy of pages 1— ~~send you an advance copy. Please let me know whether you approve of the~~ ~~we may issue~~

(10)

as well as proof sheets of the title page and of the preface. Please let me know whether we may ~~print~~ ~~as part I of volume II~~ issue part I of volume II as it is.

The first 20 pages of volume III of the Harvard Sino-Indian Series ("Parerga Pekingensia") contain an article "On a Peking edition of the Tibetan Kanjur which seems to be unknown in the West" by myself and are already printed. Professor Weller's Index to is intended to follow my article and I am sending you under seperate cover a copy of my article ~~and~~ as well as proof sheets of Professor Weller's Soghdian index. The pagination ~~of Professor~~ on the proof sheets is provisionary. I do not know how long the ~~preface~~ preface to the Soghdian index will be.

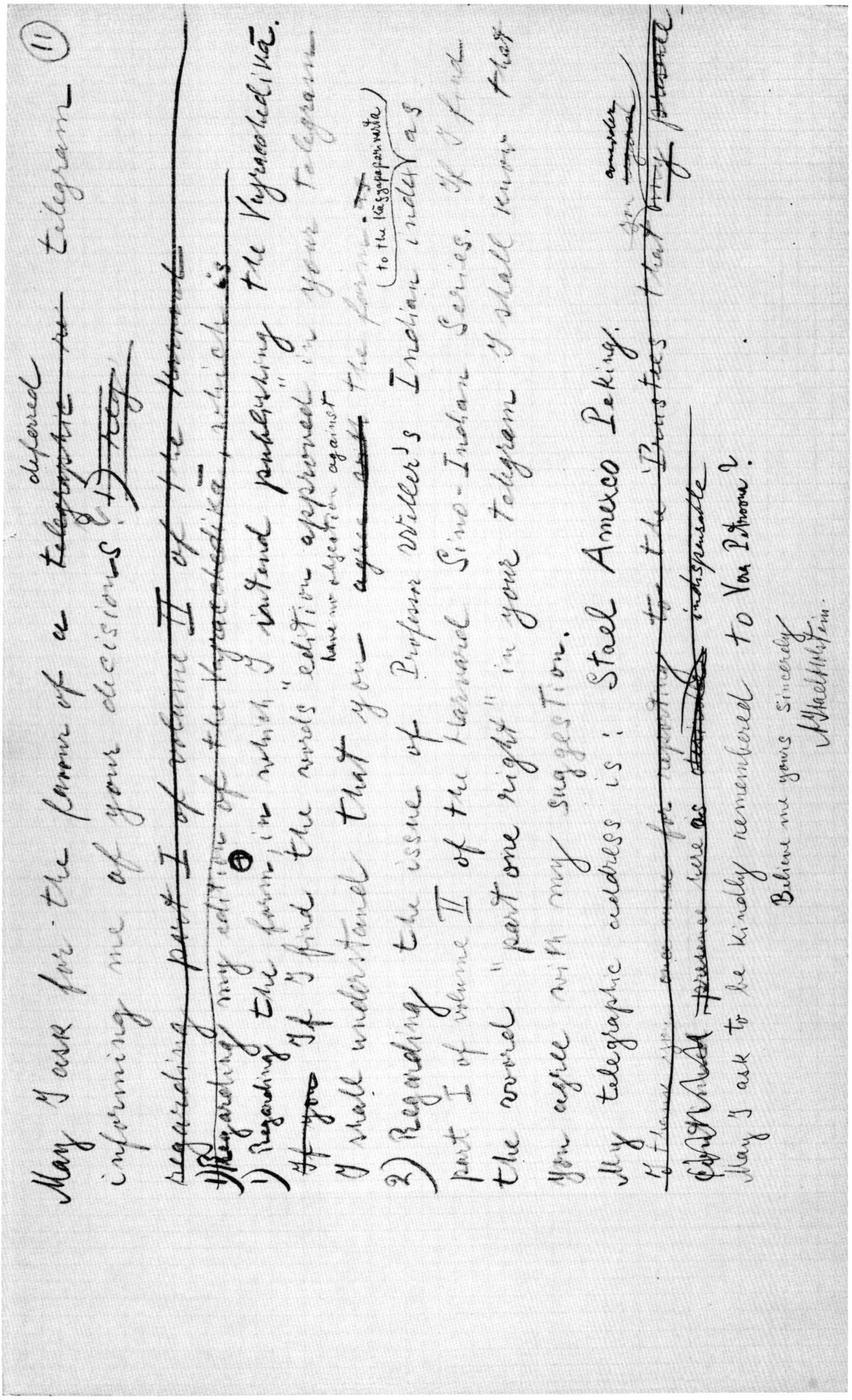

(11)

May I ask for the favour of a deferred telegram informing me of your decisions?

1) Regarding the form, in which I intend publishing the Vajracchedikā. If I find the words "edition approved" in your telegram I shall understand that you have no objection against the form.

2) Regarding the issue of Professor Weller's Indian index (to the Kāçyapaparivarta) as part I of volume II of the Harvard Sino-Indian Series. If I find the word "part one right" in your telegram I shall know that you agree with my suggestion.

My telegraphic address is: Stael Amexco Peking.

May I ask to be kindly remembered to Vera Petrovna?

Believe me yours sincerely

A. Staël-Holstein.

Note ③ [illegible]

~~[illegible]~~ I have ~~paid~~ not been authorized to use ~~the f~~ any of the funds of the Sino-Indian Institute for the purchase of statuettes etc. or for photographs ~~Said~~ I have ~~paid for~~ myself paid for the objects forming the collection.

Note (3) Lomes

~~Each complete serie~~ Complete series and properly annotated single pieces (which find their way into) ~~exported to~~ western <u>museums</u> represent, of course, gains rather than losses to science. ~~as well as to Chinese~~

Note ③ specialists

On ~~#~~ Sunday February 23rd 1936 Mme Pascalis, ~~who is publishing~~ a former pupil of the Ecole du Louvre, whose catalogue of the Lamaistic collection of the Ecole Française d'Extrême-Orient is being printed at present, lunched with us and inspected my collection. She arrived here with a letter of introduction from Mr. Victor Goloubev.

Note ⑤ Bacot

In a letter dated February 9th 1936 M. Bacot ~~expresses his be~~ says: "Il [M. Yü] fera faire de grands progrès à la bibliographie du Tibet."

Note only

Since 1932/33 the annual appropriation of the Sino-Indian Institute, which used to amount to 26 thousand Mex. dollars, has been reduced to 14 thousand Mex. dollars. Unless a further unexpected reduction should upset my plans, I think that I shall be able to pay for the printing of volumes IV and V out of the funds of the Sino-Indian Institute without asking for any additional subvention. In accordance with an agreement arrived at in 1934, one half of the cost of printing volumes II and III will be paid by the Sino-Indian Institute and the other half by the Cambridge authorities of the Harvard-Yenching Institute. Comp. Dean Chase's letter addressed to me on August 13th 1934.

Note (11) form

~~I intend Unless you~~ If the Cambridge authorities ~~have no object do agree with have~~ raise no objection, I shall ~~print~~ have the Vajracchedikā printed in the same way as my ~~which has had quite "a good press" in England Germany, Holland etc.~~ Kāśyapaparivarta text edition. ~~has been done.~~ I omit the Chinese ~~marks~~ punctuation marks for the reasons explained on page XX of my introduction to the edition of the commentary to the Kāśyapaparivarta, which has had as good a press in England Germany ~~Holland~~ etc. as the text edition. I venture to ask for a telegraphic reply, because the "Imprimerie des Lazaristes", on account of its limited supply of type, ~~is rather anxious wants to~~ wants to get through with volume IV as soon as possible. ~~, on~~

HARVARD-YENCHING INSTITUTE

17 BOYLSTON HALL
CAMBRIDGE, MASSACHUSETTS

March 24, 1936

Dear Professor von Stael-Holstein:-

Thank you very much for your letter of February 27th, which I received two days ago, as well as for your article and the proofs of the index to the Indian text of the Kacyapaparivarta.

I am also grateful for the trouble you took in regard to Dr. Hu Shih's article for the Harvard Journal of Asiatic Studies. I have never met Dr. Hu and shall be very glad to make his acquaintance when he comes to the Tercentenary of Harvard University.

Your lines about the disappearance of archaeological material connected with the history of Buddhism reminds me of what I recall about the first ten years of the Meiji period, when the Japanese had no interest in their antiquities and sold one of the most important and beautiful pagodas to a merchant, who intended to burn it so as to collect the metallic parts of the building. You must now have quite an important private collection of antiquities concerning Chinese religions.

I was also much interested to read the statement in regard to your teaching of Sanskrit and about your pupils who are in France and in Italy. I am quite sure that in a few years China will have Sino-Indian scholars, thanks to you.

Will you be so kind as to let me know how much you will need for the publication of Volumes 2 and 3 of the Sino-Indian Institute Series, half of the cost of which this Institute has agreed to subvention.

I was glad to hear about the publication of the Vajracchedikā and to receive proof sheets. You have probably received my cablegram reading:

"Edition approved. Part one right,"

and you know that I agree with you concerning the Kacyapaparivarta Indian index. It is too short to be published as a separate volume and it can probably be edited unbound so as to be bound later with the Chinese index, which, as you suggest, will form part two of the second volume. In regard to the pagination, will it not be wise to continue it so that the two parts will form one volume?

Professor von Stael-Holstein, 2

I was very sorry to learn that Mr. Pankratoff's health is not good and that he is in the Crimea. I think that there is no objection to publishing his Dagurian grammar even if there is a Russian grammar of the same kind by Professor Poppe, since, as I understand from your letter, his grammar is written in English and there are not many people who can read Russian.

I saw the last proof of your article in regard to Emperor Ch'ien Lung and the larger Sūramgama Sutra. The plates are well printed and the text looks good.

The Woods memorial volume will appear, as planned, on April first, and we will send you a copy with the additional reprints which you asked us to have made for you. If you have other articles to give us for our journal, they will be welcome and we shall be glad to publish them.

Sincerely yours,

S. Elisséeff

Director

Professor von Stael-Holstein,
Sino-Indian Institute,
ex-Austrian Legation,
Peiping, China.

Дорогой Александръ Августовичъ,

ещё разъ спасибо за Ваше письмо и за вложенную приписку, очень счастливъ, что могъ услужить Вамъ, убѣдивъ нашихъ „trustees" въ необходимости Вашего пребыванія въ Пекинѣ. Какъ Вы себя чувствуете и какъ Ваше общее состояніе? Надѣюсь, что суровый діэтическій режимъ оказалъ улучшеніе.

Сердечный привѣтъ отъ Вѣры Петровны и меня Ольгѣ Владиміровнѣ и Вамъ.

Искренне Вашъ

С. Елисеевъ

HARVARD-YENCHING INSTITUTE

17 BOYLSTON HALL
CAMBRIDGE, MASSACHUSETTS

30 іюня 1936.

Дорогой Александръ Августовичъ,

сегодня утромъ получилъ Ваше письмо и Вашу статью для журнала, которую мы, конечно, съ большой благодарностью приняли и съ большимъ удовольствіемъ напечатаемъ въ сентябрьскомъ, т. е. ноябрьскомъ, номерѣ нашего журнала. Я всегда охотно буду печатать всё эти Ваши присылки и журналъ нашъ всегда въ Вашемъ распоряженіи. На дняхъ Вамъ должно быть выслали второй номеръ журнала, который только что вышелъ, и который, по моему, интереснѣе перваго, но это, конечно, дѣло вкуса. Для третьяго номера у насъ имѣется уже статья Mlle [illegible] на какую-то тибетскую тему, но содержанія сейчасъ не помню, остальныя статьи еще точно не знаю какія.

Какъ поживаетъ Ольга Владиміровна? и какъ Ваши милые дѣти? Какъ Ваше здоровье, дорогой Александръ Августовичъ? Надѣюсь, что японская "экспансія" не слишкомъ нарушаетъ мирное теченіе жизни посольскаго квартала въ Пекинѣ и Вы можете спокойно работать, не тревожась о томъ, что творится кругомъ. Если судить по здѣшнимъ газетамъ, то жизнь въ Пекинѣ должна быть сейчасъ не изъ пріятныхъ, и въ связи съ событіями на югѣ Китая, многія отношенія должны еще больше обостриться.

Мнѣ въ этомъ году, по случаю трехсотлѣтія Харварда, предложили читать курсъ по исторіи Японіи въ "лѣтней школѣ" и я должен былъ остаться въ Кэмбриджѣ, что не слишкомъ весело. Вѣра Петровна уѣхала въ серединѣ апрѣля въ Парижъ къ сыновьямъ. Писала мнѣ, что таможенная забастовка прошла довольно безобидно и что послѣ того, что мы видѣли въ Россіи, она ни одинъ день не безпокоилась, видя что французскій "bon sens" не допуститъ никакихъ эксцессовъ. О томъ, что будетъ во Франціи въ данный моментъ, конечно, сейчасъ сказать очень трудно. Но я слышалъ отъ многихъ, что коммунисты отнюдь не пользуются большимъ успѣхомъ у большинства рабочихъ, которые обладаютъ небольшой собственностью, небольшими сбереженіями и терять этого не желаютъ.

21 іюля Вѣра Петровна и мои оба сына пріѣзжаютъ въ Нью-Йоркъ и должно быть до конца октября мальчики пробудутъ съ нами, а потомъ вернутся въ Парижъ къ началу занятій. Такъ какъ я считаю, что только во Франціи и въ Германіи существуютъ подлинные университеты, гдѣ студенты хорошо подготовлены и могутъ самостоятельно работать, а не выучивать наизусть, что они записали во время лекцій.

Вы должно быть слышали, что "trustees", во время апрѣльскаго засѣданія, постановили послать меня на 9 мѣсяцевъ въ Китай. Мы съ Вѣрой Петровной должно быть уѣдемъ изъ Америки въ послѣднихъ числахъ декабря 1936 и въ серединѣ января 1937 будемъ въ Шанхаѣ, откуда проѣдемъ на югъ въ Foochow, для инспекціи тамошняго университета, а потомъ въ Кантонъ, откуда мы проѣдемъ поѣздомъ и частью на аэропланѣ черезъ Ханькоу въ Chengtu, гдѣ мы пробудемъ должно быть около шести недѣль. Потомъ нужно будетъ заѣхать въ Нанкинъ, въ Цзинань и наконецъ пріѣдемъ въ Пекинъ, это должно быть будетъ раннимъ лѣтомъ. Это предполагаемый планъ, который можетъ не осуществиться, если военно-политическія событія въ Китаѣ примутъ угрожающія формы.
Я буду очень счастливъ повидать Ольгу Владиміровну и Васъ и поговорить съ Вами о Харвардскихъ и Харвардъ-Яньцзинскихъ дѣлахъ, за эти послѣдніе два года многое мнѣ стало яснѣе и понятнѣе.

Прошу передать мой нижайшій поклонъ Вашей супругѣ.

Съ сердечнымъ привѣтомъ

искренне Вашъ

СЕлисеевъ

Mitte Juli 36 abgesch.

Dear Professor Elisséeff,

I am very glad to learn that you will publish my article entitled "Avalokita and Apalokita" in one of the forthcoming numbers of the Harvard Journal of Asiatic Studies, and I ~~[illegible] you~~ highly appreciate the fact that you ~~informed me of~~ sent me a cable ~~[illegible]~~ in reply to my enquiry.

~~I am afraid that I have not yet answered~~

I think that the printing of the volumes ~~[illegible]~~ 2 and 3 of the Harvard Sino-Indian Series will cost ~~[illegible]~~ about two thousand fivehundred Peking dollars. ~~Your share~~ The ~~share, which the~~ Cambridge authorities agreed to pay ~~for these volumes will consequently amount~~ to ~~ab.~~ one half of the cost of these volumes (comp. your letter dated March 24th 1936).

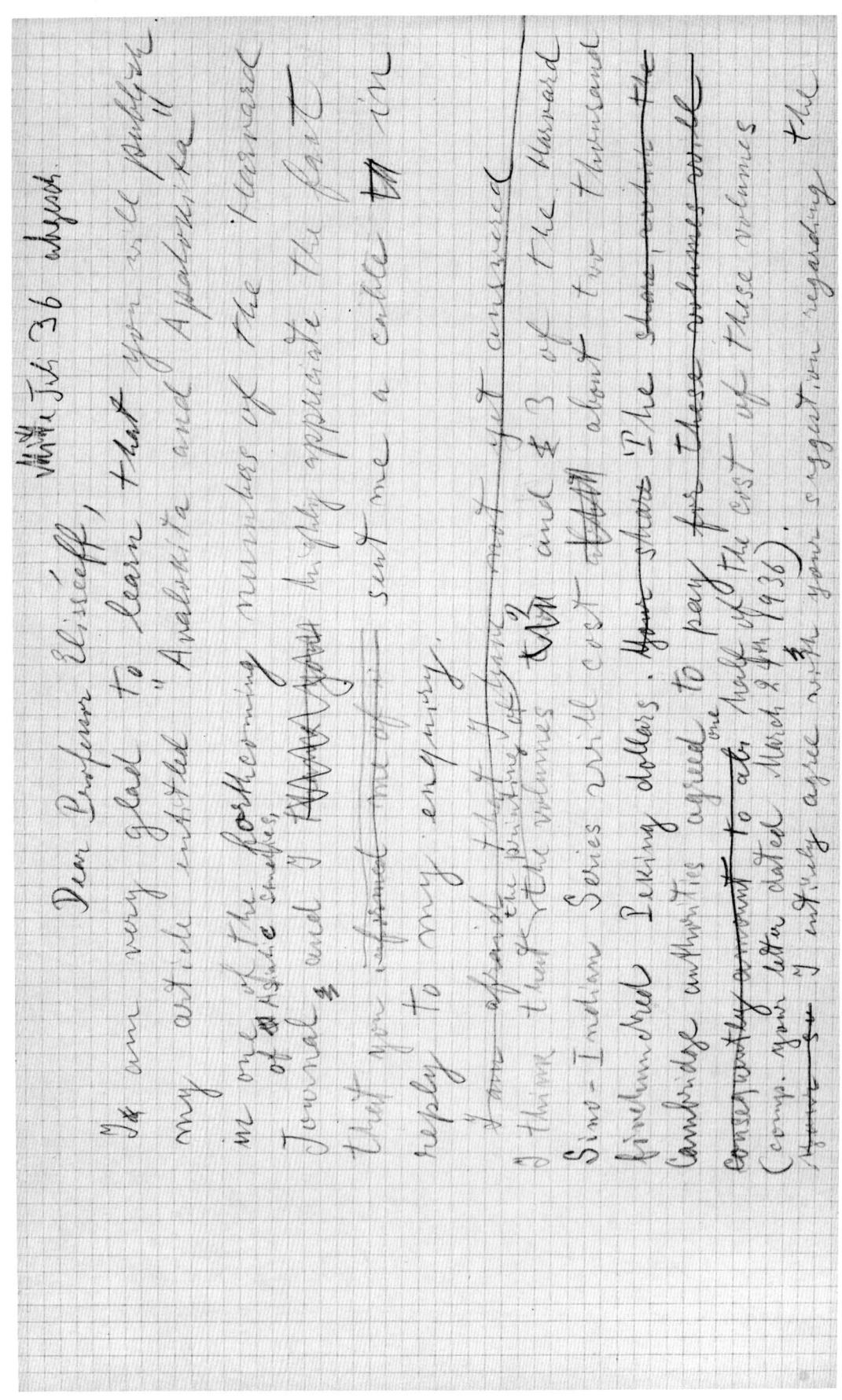

~~Your su~~ I entirely agree with your suggestion regarding the pagination of volume 2 of the Harvard Sino-Indian Series.

In the letter, which Dr. Erwin von Zach (Gang Kadji 39, Weltevreden, Java) ~~writes~~ addressed to me on June 23rd 1936, the following passage occurs:

~~I have~~ In my reply I have told Dr. von Zach, that ~~I have forwarded~~ his request has been forwarded to your address ~~and asked you to let him know, whether you have any use for his services.~~ that you will probably let him know, whether you want him to collaborate in the compilation of the dictionary or not.

It is very kind of you to enquire after my health. For the last six months I have been practically free from pain, but I still must refrain rigorously from drink and ~~from every kind of interesting~~ the dishes, which I am allowed to enjoy are extremely limited in number.

~~food (including the zakooski, which I love)~~. Under these circumstances I cannot accept any invitations and would cut an extremely poor figure at the forthcoming jubilee celebrations at Cambridge. Please tell the President and Fellows that I ~~[illegible]~~ send them my respectful congratulations on the occasion of the Harvard 'Tercentenary', and that I regret ~~that~~ my inability to express my wishes personally. ~~wishes cannot be expressed personally.~~ Whenever I open a dictionary I remember ~~the Harvard Yenching Institute,~~ Cambridge Mass., which has paid for ~~most of~~ many all the books I use, and whenever I sit down to a meal [illegible] I am conscious of the fact that I ~~am [illegible] obliged to~~ my American friends for what I eat as well as for what I eat ~~[illegible]~~ with.*

~~Dear~~ May I ask to be kindly remembered to Vera Petrovna? My wife sends you her compliments. Believe me yours sincerely AStaëlHolstein.

* My excellent false teeth were made ~~at the Harvard~~ by members of the Harvard Dental Faculty, over which ~~seven years ago~~ Dr. Miner presided in 1929.

HARVARD-YENCHING INSTITUTE

17 BOYLSTON HALL
CAMBRIDGE, MASSACHUSETTS

August 13, 1936

Dear Professor Stael-Holstein:-

Thank you very much for your letter of July 15th. We have already sent your article to the printer, and it will appear in our November number.

I will write to Dr. von Zach, but I do not think that we can use him for the work on our dictionary, because it is always difficult to do such work by correspondence with a person who lives as far away as the Dutch East Indies are from Cambridge.

I will transmit your congratulations to the President on the occasion of the Harvard Tercentenary.

We have had a summer school session here, and Dr. Boodberg, from California, lectured on Chinese history and the relations of China with the Central Asiatic nomads. Mr. Paine, from the Boston Museum of Fine Arts, lectured on Japanese art, and I delivered a course on Japanese history.

At the beginning of September, we shall have all the outstanding scholars from the whole world here, who will come to the Tercentenary, and I am quite eager to meet them.

I am already planning my trip to China, and shall probably be in Shanghai at the beginning of the year, going from there to Foochow, then to Canton and Hankow. From Hankow, I intend to fly to Szechuan, and then go to Nanking and, via Tsinan, to Peking, where I hope to see you and Mrs. von Stael-Holstein.

Wishing you good health during the hot summer in Peking, and asking you to remember me to Mrs. von Stael-Holstein, I remain

Sincerely yours,

S. Elisséeff

Director

Professor A. von Stael-Holstein,
Sino-Indian Institute,
ex-Austrian Legation,
Peiping, China.

HARVARD-YENCHING INSTITUTE

17 BOYLSTON HALL
CAMBRIDGE, MASSACHUSETTS

December 1, 1936

Dear Colleague:-

Thank you very much for your financial report, which I presented to the Trustees at their meeting on November 9th. I reminded them that I had already received your report on your activities in February.

Your leave of absence was probably delayed by the Harvard University office because of the Tercentenary festivities, but I hope that you have now received it.

Trusting that your health is much improved and that you are continuing your work in Peiping, I remain

Sincerely yours,

S. Elisséeff

Director

Professor A. von Stael-Holstein,
Sino-Indian Institute,
ex-Austrian Legation,
Peiping, China.

HARVARD-YENCHING INSTITUTE

17 BOYLSTON HALL
CAMBRIDGE, MASSACHUSETTS

1 декабря 1936 года

Многоуважаемый
Александр Августович,

Давно собирался Вам черкнуть, но последнее время было много всякой административной работы. Конец октября и начало ноября прошли в подготовке к собранию наших „trustees", потом нужно было просмотреть черновики протокола заседания. Кроме этого мне нужно было приготовиться к лекціям, которыя я должен был прочесть в Колумбійском университете. С 17-го по 21-е ноября я провел в Нью-Йорке и прочитал шесть лекцій на разныя темы. Теперь я снова в Кэмбридже и усиленно привожу в порядок все административныя дела, чтобы во время моего отсутствія все шло мирно и безмятежно. Выход последнего номера нашего журнала немного задержался, потому что после прочтения последних корректур нам нужно было еще составить указатель. Типографія обещала выпустить этот последній номер (№ 3 и № 4 вместе) в ближайшие дни. С будущаго года мы начнем второй том, таким образом каждый том будет соответствовать календарному году.

Мы с Верой Петровной уезжаем отсюда из Кэмбриджа 18го декабря и 25го декабря сядем на пароход в Сан Франциско. 11го января мы приедем в Шанхай, где пробудем дня три не больше и затем поедем в Фучоу, где останемся недели две, оттуда поедем в Кантон, где останемся до середины февраля и по вновь открытой железной дороге поедем в Ханькоу, а оттуда вверх по Янцзыцзяну в Ичанг, где, наверно, будет сесть на аэроплан и лететь в Чэнду. Март и апрель мы проведем в Сычуани и в начале мая будем в Куньмине, откуда по другому будет заехать в Гуйлинь и только в начале июня мы попадем в Пекин. Вот такие планы. Буду очень рад побеседовать с Вами о наших академических делах. Сердечный привет от Веры Петровны и меня Ольге Владимировне и Вам.

Искренне уважающий Вас

Ваш Сергей Елисеев

paper will not appear in the Harvard Journal of Asiatic Studies. I venture to ask for telegraphic advice, because I am very anxious to see the article, on which I have spent much time and energy, published. ~~The~~ I naturally prefer the Harvard Journal of Asiatic Studies, but I know of other periodicals, which would ~~publish~~ accept my paper. ~~If my article~~ In case my article should be published by the Harvard Journal of Asiatic Studies, I shall ask for one hundred extra-reprints.

Yours sincerely
A. Staël Holstein.

My address for Telegrams is: Stael Amexco Peiping.

Registered A.R.
Manuscript for print
To
the Editor of the Harvard Journal of Asiatic Stu[dies]
Boylston Hall
Cambridge Mass
U.S. of America

報 紙
[RECE]IVING FORM

交通部電報局
TELEGRAPH OFFICE
MINISTRY OF COMMUNICATIONS

[FR]OM GPD 19	備註 Service Instructions:	VIA CGRA					來報號數 TELEGRAM NO. 15
3 22	流水號數 RUNNING	XB16	報類 CLASS		發報局名 OFFICE FROM	CAMBRIDGE MASS	派送員 BY:
LIU	原來號數 ORIGINAL NO.	AC201	字數 WORDS	6	日期 DATE 30	時刻 TIME 147P	

LC STAEL AMEXCO PEIPING

YES

ELISSEEFF

注意：如有查詢事項請帶此紙
Note: Any enquiry regarding this telegram, please produce this form.

請閱背面
See Back

THE METROPOLITAN MUSEUM OF ART
NEW YORK

DEPARTMENT OF EDUCATIONAL WORK

September 29, 1928

Baron de Staël-Holstein
The Fogg Art Museum
Harvard University
Cambridge, Massachusetts

My dear Baron:

I am so sorry that my letter of June 5 did not reach you. I had understood from Mr. Sachs that you were to be here through February and therefore wrote asking that you speak for us at four o'clock on February 16. As you have noted in the folder, the other dates have been filled, and since large numbers of these folders go out, it is very difficult to inform the public that changes have been made.

Is there not a possibility that your stay might be prolonged to the 16th of February? We should like very much to have you among our speakers. Of course, there is the possibility of some speaker announced for November or December failing me, in which case I should be delighted to ask you to fill in--yet this is not really satisfactory.

I hope that when you are next in New York you will let me know, that I may discuss with you the possibility of a lecture here.

Sincerely yours,

Huger Elliott
Huger Elliott
Director of Educational Work

THE METROPOLITAN MUSEUM OF ART
NEW YORK

DEPARTMENT OF EDUCATIONAL WORK

October 31, 1928

Baron de Staël-Holstein
The Fogg Art Museum
Harvard University
Cambridge, Massachusetts

My dear Baron:

Is there any chance that you may still be in the United States on February 16, which as you remember is the date I have been saving in the hope that we may have the pleasure of having you speak to our regular audiences?

Should this not be feasible, could you lecture for us at four o'clock on Friday, December 14? Mr. Priest, our Curator of Far Eastern Art, hopes that you will be willing to speak on The Temples in the Gardens of Compassion and Peace--if I am correct in the title. May I announce you for that day and subject? And will you telegraph me, collect, as the time is short and I want to give as wide publicity as possible to the fact that you are to lecture for us?

We offer an honorarium of one hundred dollars and expenses to our lecturers. I understand from Mr. Priest that you have lantern slides showing your discoveries in the Gardens.

Sincerely yours,

Huger Elliott

Huger Elliott
Director of Educational Work

THE METROPOLITAN MUSEUM OF ART
NEW YORK

DEPARTMENT OF EDUCATIONAL WORK

November 2, 1928

Baron de Staël-Holstein
The Fogg Art Museum
Harvard University
Cambridge, Massachusetts

My dear Baron:

Thank you for replying so promptly to my letter and for consenting to give the talk suggested by Mr. Priest.

I trust that when you are next in New York I may have the pleasure of seeing you.

Sincerely yours,

Huger Elliott
Huger Elliott
Director of Educational Work

THE METROPOLITAN MUSEUM OF ART
NEW YORK

DEPARTMENT OF EDUCATIONAL WORK

December 18, 1928

Baron de Staël-Holstein
Fogg Art Museum
Harvard University
Cambridge, Massachusetts

My dear Baron:

I find that I have done something which I should not have done in allowing you to take with you the lantern slides made in the Museum for use by you in your delightful talk last Friday. They had not been properly labeled. Furthermore, I learn from Mr. Priest that you wish to purchase a group of these for your own use.

May I ask you to return the entire group to me and indicate by means of the numbers which appear on the slides those of which you wish to have copies made? I will then have the duplicates made and sent to you as soon as possible. The enclosed booklet will give you the terms on which these may be purchased.

I am still regretting that so few were able to get to your interesting talk. And please don't forget to let me have your expense account as soon as possible.

Sincerely yours,

Huger Elliott
Huger Elliott
Director of Educational Work

AMBASSADE DE RUSSIE
TOKIO

Tokio 1/14 Septembre 1917

Mon cher Baron

Je viens de recevoir 70 yens de M. Elisséeff qui me prie de Vous les transmettre de la part de M. Rosenberg. Avant de Vous les envoyer je voulais Vous demander ce que Vous préférez que je fasse – je pourrais Vous les faire

parvenir par un chèque de la
Yokohama Specie Bank ou peut-être
auriez Vous préféré que je les verse
à Votre compte courant chez Schet
Frazar ou ailleurs, - dont en
attendant Vos dispositions je garde
cet argent chez moi. - Que dites Vous
des derniers événements chez nous ?
On s'est dit si souvent que ça n'aurait

pas pu être plus mauvais, mais
il paraît que nous ne sommes pas
encore arrivés à la péripétie décisive. –
J'ai bien regretté de Vous avoir vu
si peu à Votre passage au Japon –
nous avons encore du beau temps et
demain je vais pour la dernière fois
à Kamakura chez Kronpensky qui
rentre ici lundi. – Nous avons deux

nouveaux membres de l'Ambassade
M. Ramming (lettre) qui remplace
Vaskevitch - il fait l'impression
d'un homme correct et bien élevé -
on ne peut pas dire la même chose
de son aide M. Plettner.

Mille choses - cher Baron -
rappelez moi au bon souvenir de
Кудашевъ, Hoyer et Kaindr,

Votre [illegible]

AMBASSADE DE RUSSIE
TOKIO

26 IX / 9 X 27

Mon cher Baron

Il y a de cela quelque temps que je Vous ai écrit pour Vous demander ce que je dois faire avec les 70 yens que [illegible] m'a remis pour Vous de la part de Mr. Rosenberg. N'ayant pas eu de réponse de Vous je pense que

peut-être ma lettre ou peut-être la
Vôtre n'est pas parvenue à sa destina-
tion. Je répète donc ma question car
je ne veux pas que Vous ayez des pertes
à cause du mauvais cours des yens
en Chine et je Vous serais reconnaissant
si Vous vouliez bien me donner Vos
ordres dans cette affaire - je pourrais
par exemple les verser à Votre compte

chez Sch. et Frazar ou ailleurs. –
Si Vous avez un moment de libre
écrivez moi donc ce qu'on dit à Pékin
de la nomination d'Abrik. Libes et
qui est candidat pour le poste de
Ugrave? Je ne serais pas mécontent
d'y aller, mais aussi je n'aime pas
faire des démarches dans ce sens,
mais j'aurais bien voulu savoir
de qui il est question. Wexman veut

P.S. Ne me nommez pas comme source pour les nouvelles des nominations → en cas qu'on n'en parle pas encore.

partir le 21 pour Pétrograd et ensuite Téhéran - je ne l'envie pas, le pauvre. -

J'ai vu Mazot ici et j'apprends que les Ahlfelds sont de retour - dites leur, je vous prie, bien des choses de ma part et aussi à Hoyer qui a été si gentil pour moi.

Donc, je vous prie, une petite réponse.

Votre

Weber.

LA LÉGATION DE DANEMARK

le 16 Novembre 1917
Pékin

Cher Baron !

— Voulez-vous nous faire le plaisir et venir dîner chez nous en petit comité Jeudi le 22 Nov. à 8.15.

— Espérant une réponse favorable, je vous prie,

Cher Baron, de croire
à l'expression de mes
sentiments très sym-
pathiques.

Mary Ahlefeldt L.

Pékin, le 3 avril 1918

SWEDISH LEGATION

Monsieur le Baron,

Je regrette vivement qu'il m'est impossible de Vous accompagner demain dans Votre tour dans la campagne. Mais après-demain, jeudi, j'aurai du temps, si Vous en avez.

Croyez, Monsieur le Baron, à mes sentiments

les plus distingués

Sten Konow

Pékin, le 6 juillet 1928

Légation de France
en Chine

Cher Monsieur de Staël,

Voulez-vous nous faire à ma femme et à moi-même le très grand plaisir de venir déjeuner à la maison lundi prochain 9 juillet à 1 heure.

Comptant sur une bonne réponse, je vous prie d'agréer, cher Monsieur de Staël, l'expression de mes sentiments les meilleurs.

[illegible]

AMBASSADE DE BELGIQUE,
WASHINGTON, D.C.

Princess de Ligne has received your kind letter of April fifteenth and will be very pleased to have you come to tea on Wednesday, April seventeenth, at five o'clock.

Washington, April 15th, 1929.

Légation de France
en Chine

Le 16 Juin 1924.

Mon cher Staël

Je vous envoie avec ce mot un petit souvenir pour vous et pour votre fiancée & j'y joins mes meilleurs souhaits pour vous deux en attendant de vous les renouveler demain

Bien amicalement votre

D de Martel

Washington, D.C., den 25. Januar 1933.

Lieber Baron Stael !

Es war sehr nett von Ihnen, unserer zu Neujahr zu gedenken. Sie befinden sich ja jetzt an einem der Brennpunkte der Weltgeschichte; hoffentlich werden Sie dadurch nicht in Ihrer benei=denswerten Forscherruhe gestört werden.

In der Hoffnung, dass es Ihnen persönlich gut geht und dass Sie über kurz oder lang wieder einmal hier durchkommen, senden meine Frau und ich Ihnen die herzlichsten Grüsse und Wünsche,

Stets Ihr

Prittwitz

LÉGATION DE BELGIQUE
EN CHINE

PÉKIN, LE 31 juillet 1934

Cher Baron,

J'ai vivement regretté de ne pas vous avoir rencontré ce matin.

Je me permettrai demain soir vers 6 heures de vous présenter Mr. le Dr Bommer Conservateur des Musées Royaux de Belgique qui s'intéresse à vos belles peintures. Mr Bommer connaît Mr de Lavallée-Poussin et les sinologues belges.

Bien merci et cordialement votre

R Gérard

JAPANESE LEGATION
PEKING.

September 29.

Dear Baron de Holstein,

With this, please find your passport duly visaed, and also a letter addressed to the Japanese authorities in general to whom it may concern asking ~~you~~ them for rendering you

facilities in regard
to your journey, especially
in connection with
the quarantine.

I am sorry to
hear that this
Legation charged
you $1 the last
time. I have had
your passport
visaed free of
charge by the

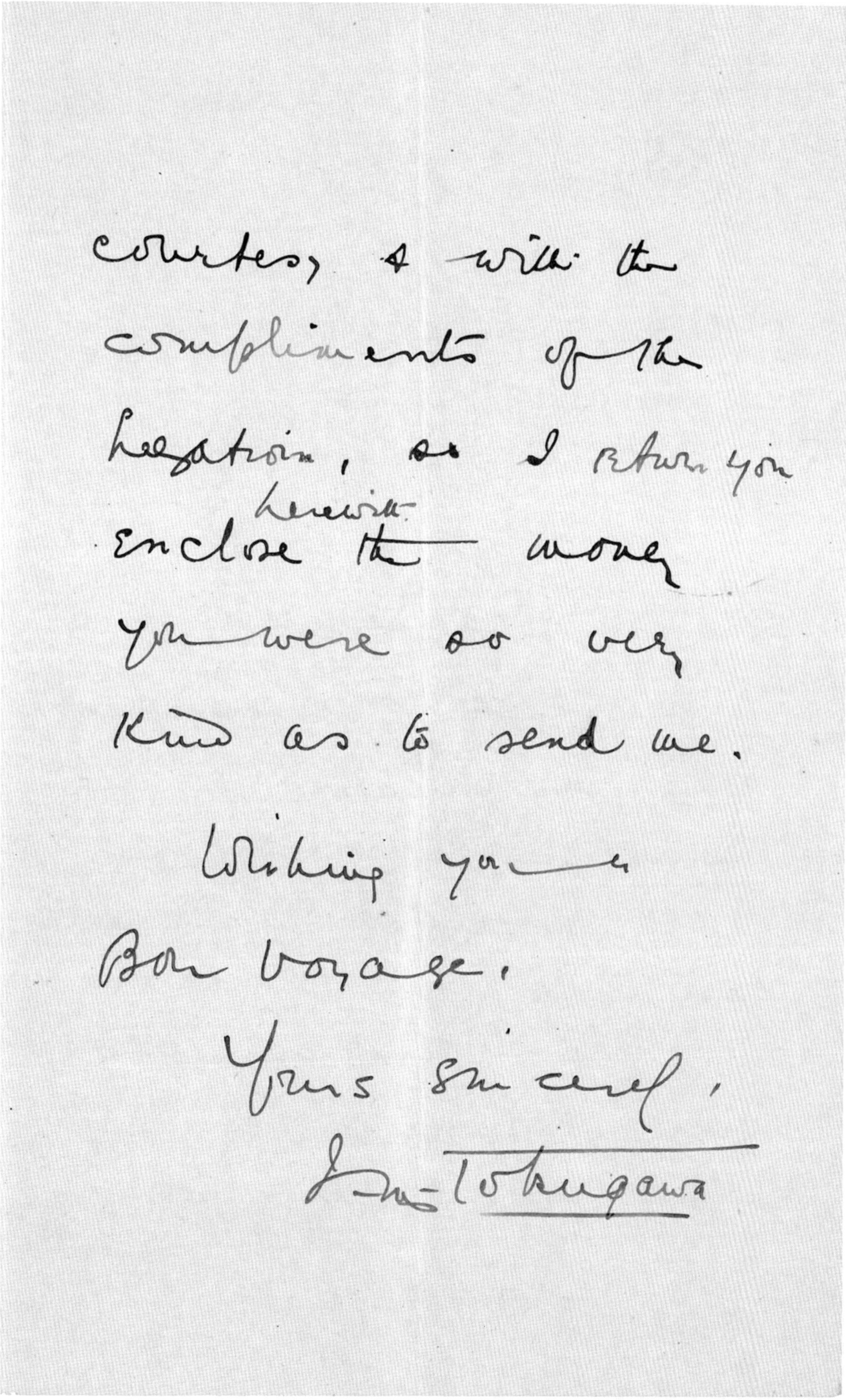

courtesy, & with the
compliments of the
Legation, as I return you
herewith
enclose the money
you were so very
kind as to send me.

Wishing you a
Bon voyage.

Yours sincerely,
[illegible] Tokugawa

LE MINISTRE DE RUSSIE
BANGKOK

Ce mercredi

Cher Baron,

J'ai déjà prié Lutsachevitz de vous transmettre qu'à mon grand regret je ne pourrais pas disposer de ma soirée de demain pour aller avec vous et Yakovlev au théâtre chinois et que je priais de fixer un autre jour. J'espère que ce changement ne contrecarre pas vos

plans et que vous ne m'
en voudrez pas trop de
vous faire faux bond.
Peut-être que nous pourrions
remettre la partie à dimanche
?
J'écris dans ce sens à
Yakovleff et vous prierais
d'avoir la grande bonté
de diriger mon boy chez
lui. (Il connait le sia-
mois mais ne sait pas le
lire. Donnez lui votre
médaille, je tâcherai de
la déchiffrer).
Croyez, cher Baron, avec
toutes mes excuses, à mes
meilleurs sentiments
[illegible]

LÉGATION DE RUSSIE
À PÉKIN.

Дорогой Баронъ —

Ledger просилъ васъ
передать, что они, т.е. Durazzo,
онъ и Toussaint расчитыва-
ютъ очень на васъ на
поездку съ ними. Поездъ
отходитъ въ 9 часовъ и билетъ
нужно брать до ст. пересекаю-
щей Лунъ-хайскую ж.д. Будетъ
специальный вагонъ и

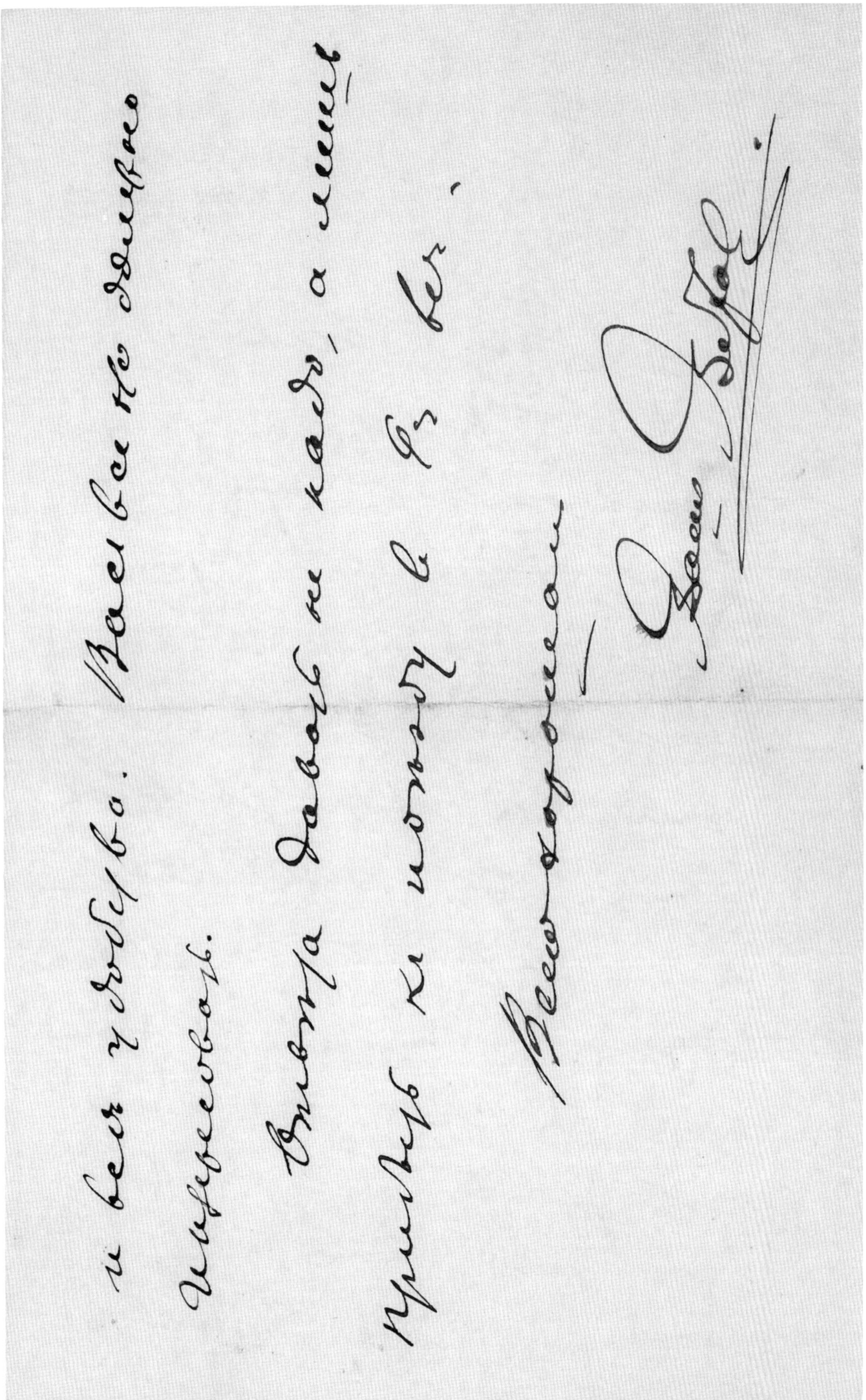
и всей удобство. Вас всё-таки должно
интересовать.

Ответа давать не надо, а лишь
привезть к поезду в 9ч веч.

Весь хорошим

Ваш [illegible]

BRITISH LEGATION,
PEKING.

My dear Baron,

Thank you very much indeed for the delightful New Year's Greetings — it is truly perfect to have one of your own pamphlets on which to send them — a delightful idea. Thank you again, and I likewise wish you all the very best for the New Year.

Yours sincerely,

[illegible]

10 Ta Yang Yi Pin Htg.
Peiping. Aug 24, '33.

Dear Baron,

I take the liberty of enclosing copy of a letter I have just written to Dr. Stuart which explains, more fully than I could do this afternoon, the anomalous situation in which I now find myself.

With best wishes,

John King Fairbank

Copy

10 Ta Yang Yi Pin Hutung,

Peiping. Aug. 24,'33.

Dear Dr. Stuart,

In continuation of our conversation this afternoon at the station, I should like to explain my present situation in somewhat more detail.

On learning in May that it was not possible, at that time, to grant new fellowships under the Harvard-Yenching Institute, I at once saw Prof. Porter and Mr. Roger Greene, and on their advice applied to all the local educational institutions which might desire my services as a teacher during the coming academic year. I had already thought of the possibility of teaching at the Customs College a course on the History of the Service, which is the precise subject of my research, and had taken certain measures to that end. Toward the end of May I learned that a new course, on the History of the Service, had been added to the curriculum of the College; I applied for the position and shall be lecturing there twice a week during the coming academic year. The Catholic University were unable to decide upon the appointment of teachers until some time later in the summer, and I have not heard from them in regard to the application which I filed. Peita had no openings for me, and Pingta none for either Mrs. Fairbank or myself unless we could teach in Chinese or Russian. At this point Prof. T.F.Tsiang of Tsing Hua, whom I came to China with the general intention of studying under whenever I might be able, and to whom as editor of the Chinese Social and Political Science

Review I had recently submitted an article, intimated that there might be an opening for me under the Economics Dept. at Tsing Hua. Subsequently I was offered the opportunity to teach three courses there,- the History of the Customs Service, the Renaissance and Reformation, and Modern Economic History,- and naturally accepted with alacrity.

Dean Chase's letter of July 25 informs me that a fellowship of $800 as a Harvard-Yenching Fellow for the coming academic year will be offered me by vote of a certain committee which will meet in September. I wrote him earlier in this month as to the teaching obligations which I have contracted,and I have now replied to his letter of July 25 to the general effect that since I cannot well break contracts already made for the coming academic year, I can hardly engage in full time research during that period, nor accept a subsidy for that purpose; that the fact of my teaching five hours a week in the subject of my research, and continuing Chinese with a teacher one hour a day, can hardly be adduced as adequate reason for accepting even a smaller subsidy; but that at the same time I should much prefer, if I am to receive support from any institution, to receive it in the future from the Harvard-Yenching Institute rather than from the Guggenheim Foundation, whose blanks I have received, or the General Education Board, whose blanks were sent me at Dean Chase's request, or any of the other organizations of a similar nature to whom I have applied for application forms. In view of these considerations, I have suggested to Dean Chase that the important consideration from my point of view is that of funds for the year beginning July 1,1934; and I have asked him accordingly if it might be possible either to postpone my acceptance of the fellowship he mentions until such time as I could make proper use of it, with the hope also that the amount of the stipend could be increased, or to accept the fellowship for $800 now, with the proviso that only nominal payments be made under it for the first three quarters of the year and a sum of $600 or $700 be given me about July 1 next.

In this way it is my hope that complete rejection of the grant may be avoided, just as acceptance of it in toto is obviously impossible.

Yours sincerely,

J.K.Fairbank.

北平國立清華大學
NATIONAL TSING HUA UNIVERSITY
PEIPING. CHINA

10 Ta Yang Yi Pin Hutung
Peiping. Oct 10, 1934.

Dear Baron von Stael,

I venture to enclose copy of a memorandum on the training of young Americans like myself in the field of Chinese Studies, which I drew up last summer as a digest of the problem as it seems to be viewed by myself and most of the young men I know here.

The practical suggestion at the end is not necessarily practicable, and is put forward to raise issues only.

If you should be able to find time to look it over, I should much appreciate any comment. But I trust you will not go far out of your way to do so.

Mrs Fairbank and I had an excellent summer in Shansi. We are taking a short trip to Hongkong next month to see old consular records. Hoping to see you before then, -

Yours sincerely,

John King Fairbank

SUGGESTIONS REGARDING THE TRAINING OF

AMERICAN STUDENTS FOR RESEARCH IN CHINESE STUDIES.

The following suggestions are a product of personal experience and observation, and numerous discussions with fellow students, during the past two years. Since first drafting this paper, I have come to doubt the entire practicability of the proposal for a General Examination. But the issues raised still appear to be fundamental, and a student's point of view on them may be of some use.

The Student's Objective. Nearly all workers in Chinese Studies have a much larger field to cover than Chinese Language and Literature, because they must be versed in a general field of knowledge, and keep up on it, at the same time that they work on Chinese materials. No doubt in all fields a division may be made between the general principles, technique, or background, on the one hand, and the particular local languages, cultures, or circumstances connected with the research student's subject of study, on the other: the student applies his general training to the particular materials on which he is working.

In the case of Chinese Studies, difficulty arises because of the more than average amount of time needed to master the language which is the key to the materials upon which the student must work. Further difficulty arises because the field is comparatively uncharted. Under these circumstances, more than the usual amount of pressure is put upon the student, if he is to keep up to the standards achieved in Western studies.

This problem may be illustrated by reference to the field of Modern Chinese History, in which the ideal requirements are probably no greater than in other fields such as art or philosophy.

1) In the first place, students of Modern Chinese History must be fundamentally students of History, rather than of the Chinese Language. They must possess the training and knowledge necessary for intelligent historical research, -- as much grounding as possible in the fields of economics, government, and international law, a lively and sustained interest in those fields, as well as in the field of general history. If they do not, their research will lack breadth and vitality, and their interpretation of historical fact may be based on antiquated assumptions.

2) Students of Modern Chinese History must have a knowledge and appreciation of the long flow of Chinese Civilization and culture before the modern period, -- as deep an understanding as possible of Chinese philosophical and legal ideas, political and economic institutions, social customs, fine arts, and general historical development. They should possess some of the currency of allusion, reference, and illustration used in Chinese literature. Such a background is to be gained partly through books in Western languages, partly through reading in Chinese, and partly through first hand experience in China.

- 2 -

3) As their chief tool, students of Modern Chinese History must have a grasp of the Chinese Language sufficient for all purposes connected with their professional work. At the very least, they should a) be able to converse freely in the mandarin dialect about, first, the practical matters of every day life, and, second, the subject of their research; b) be able to read the newspapers and periodicals which form the vehicle of contemporary Chinese thought and opinion; c) be able to read the documents, source materials, and reference works with which their research is concerned; d) be able to read anything which may be written by Chinese scholars in their field or about their subject.

4) Students of Modern Chinese History may find it often advisable to approach their subject through the study of Modern Chinese Foreign Relations, because the materials for the latter are at present more accessible and better organized, because these Chinese materials can be checked or amplified by foreign materials, and so definitive results may be expected sooner than in domestic history. But in such case further linguistic tools will be necessary to the student, - Japanese and Russian, - Spanish, Portugues, and Dutch, besides the usual French and German. In any case, students merely of Chinese domestic history should have access to works which have been or will be written in Japanese and Russian, whether or not they take up the International History of the Far East as related to China. The possible linguistic burden is overwhelming.

Equally extensive ideal requirements could no doubt be outlined for any other subject in the Chinese field. Students attempting to meet requirements of this magnitude, - in other words, students in the general field of Chinese Studies, - face a typical problem, - the problem of mastering Chinese as well as the background of their particular subject.

This puts a premium on time. They can approximate an ideal training in proportion as they can use their time to the fullest advantage, and with the greatest efficiency.

While this situation is now common to all branches of scholarship, it is particularly bothersome in the field of Chinese Studies because little or no system has been achieved for the guidance of students. Research workers using Chinese must not only expend more energy than workers using less difficult languages, if they are to achieve equally high standards of scholarship; they must also decide for themselves where and how to apply their energy. They must find an effective answer to what may be called the Problem of Procedure.

The Problem of Procedure. This is the problem of What to do Next. In this new and uncharted field, students must evaluate the relative importance of the various aspects of their training. They must determine the order in which different disciplines should be taken up, and the extent to which each should be pursued. For instance, should the beginning student concentrate for five years entirely on the spoken language? Should he plunge immediately into his special field? Should he begin by reading the Four Books? Or should he do all three, - pai hua, wen li, and special field, - at the same time in varying proportions? A student seeking light on this one question can collect advice as varied as the experience of the advisers, who usually recommend doing what they did.

Will a student get more understanding of Chinese civilization by reading foreign books about China, or by reading a selection of Chinese texts? Or if both, in what proportion? Should he take frequent trips into the country, or stick closely to his characters?

How, in short, should the student who is spending from three to five years in China apportion his time?

__Necessary Considerations in Seeking a Solution.__ This Problem of Procedure, which includes both the problem of What to study, and the problem of When to study it, is faced by every worker in the field of Chinese Studies. What is said below applies certainly to students of Modern Chinese History, and presumably to students in many other fields as well.

A satisfactory solution of the problem, in the last analysis, must be worked out by each student for himself, depending on his individual circumstances and temperament. But there are at least three general considerations which should be pertinent in the case of most American students: account must be taken of 1) the Ph.D. requirement in America, 2) the individualism usually manifest among students of Chinese, and the wide variety of their personal circumstances, 3) the possibility of advising and guiding them according to a general plan, to secure a certain minimum of all round development and prevent the evils of a narrow specialization.

__Evils of the Ph.D. Requirement.__ The coming generation of American students of Chinese civilization may be expected to pursue something like the following program: 1) they will take their B.A. degrees in American universities and become graduate students, beginning Chinese then if they have not already done so; 2) as graduate students they may take an M.A., begin a doctoral dissertation, or complete one; but sooner or later they will come to China, probably to Peiping, for a more concentrated study of Chinese.

Because the culture and civilization of China are so radically different, it is self-evident that American students should live and study in China before they reach the point of writing about it. Because the language is difficult, and can be studied with more ease and concentration in China, they

- 4 -

should come to this country as soon as possible after graduation.

But if these students expect later to teach in American universities, they must follow the rules laid down for the mass production of guaranteed intellect, and eventually secure a Ph.D.

Thus they face a dilemma.

If they finish a Ph.D. before coming to China, they must do so either by studying the language and using it under extremely adverse circumstances, or by delaying their serious attack upon the language. If they spend three to five years in China beginning the language, they will have to begin a Ph.D. on their return, and so will have delayed their worldly advancement. Bright young men should not be expected to delay their attack upon either the language or the Ph.D.

From the ambitious student's point of view, it may be preferable to work on both at once. But here also adifficulty arises, - at least for students of Modern Chinese History; the sources in western languages are at present so unexplored, so valuable (e.g. the N.C. Herald), and so much easier to work upon, that the student writing a doctorate from both foreign and Chinese sources may find himself sacrificing his progress in Chinese to the progress of his thesis.

If the Ph.D. requirement is to be applied to students of Chinese in the same degree as it is now applied to students in other fields, young men may be discouraged from entering the Chinese field. Judging men by the quantity of their output, - the widely disclaimed but commonly accepted standard, - will put the worker in Chinese Studies at a disadvantage which the richness of the field may not make up for, in the eyes of a beginning student. Even with a Ph.D. students using Chinese may not be very productive.

Standards like the Ph.D. are necessary and desirable. But students using oriental languages cannot be expected to attain it as soon as students using European languages. Yet it seems unjust to penalize the former because they attempt the more difficult task.

Unfortunately this is what happens to students of Chinese. The Social Science Research Council is not interested in students who are still working for their Ph.D. The American Council of Learned Societies will make no grants "to assist in the fulfilment of requirements for any academic degree". Of course these regulations were originally meant to apply to students using European languages. If they are applied to students who must master Chinese before writing their doctorate, their effect is to limit the amount of support available for Chinese Studies, - since most students will master Chinese, if at all, by coming to China on fellowships, with Ph.D.s yet to do.

- 5 -

Difficulty of a General Plan for all Students. A second consideration affecting the Problem of Procedure arises from the individualism manifested by students of Chinese. The apparent difficulties and exotic charm of sinology attract to the field men of decided individuality, who are usually either very determined gentlemen, or at least have a penchant for being different from their fellows. As a group they could not easily be brought to conform to a general plan of procedure or study. Nor are their individual circumstances sufficiently similar to allow it. Some have wives and doctorates, some have one but not the other, some have neither. Their fields of study very widely. Regimentation would be impossible. In the expanding state of sinology at present, it would be decidedly stultifying.

But all students of things Chinese are on a common ground in two respects: 1) they must have a knowledge of the language; 2) they must have an understanding of Chinese civilization. Some progress in both is essential to students of all ages or degrees of attainment, in all fields and all manner of circumstances. These two realms of knowledge are closely connected and constitute, as it were, the two ruts of a single road.

How far can and should students travel together on this main road before branching off?

It is at this point, I believe, that constructive work may now be done: by establishing in Peiping a General Course or Examination System, to consist of a suggested curriculum, which students may follow if they wish, and on which they may be examined from time to time, with the object of aiding them to acquire, in the most efficient and comprehensive manner, a certain minimum background of knowledge regarding the Chinese Language and Chinese Civilization. This proposal is made as a starting point for discussion of the question. The following details likewise are made as specific as possible in the hope of crystalliying opinion on the practical problems involved.

A General Course: the time it should occupy. The time which the average student could spend upon such a course of study would be arbitrarily limited by circumstance. 1) The student will plan to return eventually to America. He cannot afford to spend more than four or five years away from the spot where appointments are made and where his own generation is getting into its stride. 2) The student cannot expect to be supported for a longer length of time by the institutions which may send him to China. 3) During the latter part of his stay in China, he is certain to wish to begin upon the vocabulary and materials of his special field. Consequently the equivalent of three years fulltime study would, from the student's point of view, be the maximum time which he would like to put upon preparatory work of a purely general sort.

- 6 -

Division of this time.

1) All students who intend to study some aspect of Chinese Civilization should be expected to devote the equivalent of one full year to the reading of a general bibliography on China. These books might be in western languages (e.g. the Middle Kingdom), in translation (e.g. Legge), or in simple Chinese (e.g. the San Tzu Ching). Taken together they should deal with all aspects of Chinese history, art, literature, etc, etc, etc, and give the student a general outline of these subjects, and a realization of their divisions, problems, and extent.

2) All students who intend to use Chinese in research should be expected to devote the equivalent of two full years to elementary language study, quite aside from the special vocabulary and reference works of their special field. Two years is not sufficient for a student's preparation to do research. But all students could profitably spend two years time on a general course, before leaving the main road. In that length of time they could get a rudimentary spoken vocabulary, 3-4000 characters, an acquaintance with wen li style, and experience in the use of dictionaries and the technique of study. They would not have a knowledge of Chinese, but in two years they could get a foundation to build upon, and an idea of how to go about their further study.

At least one third of this preparatory period should be devoted to studying the Civilization rather than the Language because of the fact that, in studying and interpreting things Chinese, American students will need understanding as much as reading ability. The former is no less difficult to acquire than the latter. Because the assumptions implicit in Chinese action are not always the same as those in the West, understanding of them cannot be taken for granted. Students of Modern Chinese History, for instance, can interpret their facts correctly only if they understand the tacit assumptions underlying the thoughts of the Chinese actors. Background is particularly desirable in the case of students of Modern Chinese History. But it is no less true that students of the ancient past can learn about it by studying the recent past, especially in a country where the past still exists.

A General Course: the administration of it.
I. Peiping the logical center.

How rapidly the facilities for studying Chinese in American universities will develop, and how strongly the sinological training of American students in America is advocated, - I do not know. The training of American students in European centers may also be advocated. But theoretically a strong argument may be advanced for studying the Civilization of China in the place where it is, and the language in the place where it lives. Study in China, even allowing for transportation costs, is still as feasible financially as study at home or in Europe. In China, for many and obvious reasons, Peiping is the natural center for study. It might remain so even in the event of political changes.

- 7 -

II. the administration should be flexible. Logically, one should produce oaks from acorns, acquire a reading knowledge of a language and then use it. But psychologically, any student with initiative enough to study Chinese wants to attack his special field as soon as possible. He wants to plunge it, get over his depth, and so learn to swim. His progress in the Chinese language as a whole, after a certain point, becomes too slow or too uninteresting to satisfy him, and may be discouraging. He is tempted to begin on his special vocabulary, in which at first he can get quicker results. He freely admits that a broad foundation is desirable and in fact essential in the end. Unfortunately, after he becomes involved and absorbed in the work of his special field, he may never find time to go back and build it up.

As a compromise between student and pedagogue, any student taking a general course of the sort here proposed should be free to follow any order of study which suits him. On completing the course he should be expected to have done the equivalent of three years work. But he should be allowed to spread this work over five years, or compress it if possible into two, and pursue other lines of work at the same time.

III. there should be no residence or time requirements. Naturally, most students coming to China will have done a certain amount of reading and language study, and perhaps taken degrees, before they come. The extent to which they will have done the work suggested as part of a General Course will vary considerably among individuals. For this reason, any student who wants to should be allowed to take the examinations, without regard for the length of time he has studied, where he has studied, or how long he has been in China.

The Content of a General Course.

I. Chinese Civilization:

A. Reading Lists:

- to be drawn up by a committee of qualified scholars
- to be arranged according to subjects
- to include all the important or definitive works on these subjects,
  - divided into those that should merely be known about
  - and those recommended for careful reading

- 8 -

- these lists to be distributed gratis and without formality to all persons asking for them

B. Examinations:

- to be correlated with the Reading Lists
- to be drawn up and supervised by an individual or a committee on the spot in Peiping
- to be divided into sections according to subjects and parts of subjects
- the questions on any subject to be set separately if desired
- and at any time the student wishes, subject to the convenience of the examiners
- the individual or committee conducting the examinations to have no other formal duties than to set questions orally or in writing and grade the candidate
- these examiners to receive a nominal fee, or none at all, for their time
- applicants for examination to submit a brief statement indicating why they believe themselves prepared to pass an examination
- but to pay no fees whatever
- successful candidates to receive a simple form of certificate indicating the examinations which they have passed and their standing.

II. Chinese Language:

A. Curriculum:

- also to be drawn up by a qualified committee
- and to be distributed in the same way
- also to be divided into subjects, - e.g. the recognition or writing of characters; study of pai hua texts, wen li texts, newspapers, etc.; simple conversation, etc.
- under each subject, textbooks and materials to be recommended specifically,

- 9 -

- and methods of study to be suggested
- as well as an order of study
- but no "set books" or required work

B. Examinations:

- also to be administered by an individual or a committee, presumably the same persons as those concerned with the examinations mentioned above
- separate examinations to be set for each subject of those just mentioned
- periodic as well as final examinations to be arranged in each subject: e.g. an examination on 2000 characters, another on 4000; an examination on simple wen li, another on more complicated wen li
- students to be examined on application, to receive no supervision and pay no fees, as in the case of I. A above.
- the certificate above mentioned to be given only for proficiency and knowledge in both branches of the course.

The Administering Agency. It is obvious that the above course, consisting of suggested subjects and materials for study, and examinations, but not involving any sort of instruction or supervision, would not need to be administered by an institution. In fact the administration of such a course would involve so much adaptation to constantly changing circumstances that it might be a demoralising hindrance to any institution charged with the administration of it.

On the other hand, students desirous of completing the work suggested for such a General Course, might well make use on their own account of the facilities offered by institutions in Peiping. They might take work as they pleased at the College of Chinese Studies, Yenching University, and elsewhere, as has been the general practice among students in the past.

To arrange for the drawing up of the Reading Lists and Curriculum, some representative agency, such as the Committee for the Promotion of Chinese Studies in America, should be found. They would have to guide them the curricula worked out by the

- 10 -

College of Chinese Studies, the office of the United States Military Attache, etc., etc. But they would have to modify and consolidate all such curriculaX in order to adapt them to the needs of academic students, who intend to pursue research and probably teaching, rather than missionary work, army intelligence work, or the like.

To arrange for the setting and reading of the Examinations, an agency of some sort would have to be found in Peiping, presumably a committee, the membership of which might change, but one member of which should be a permanent chairman. On this one individual would fall the burden and responsibility of management. He would have to possess unusual qualifications, in order to make the scheme succeed: he should be a resident in Peiping, able to give a certain amount of his time, possessed of the necessary breadth of background and knowledge to direct the examining policy, and gifted with tact.

In addition to arranging for examinations, this individual should be ready to advise any students who might come to him for advice; and he should also keep a record of Chinese teachers or scholars qualified to help foreign students in various fields of study. A sum of money should be found to cover his clerical expenses, and something more; but this would be the only expense involved, necessarily, in the program outlined above.

<u>The Value of this Proposal: I. Scholarship.</u> From the point of view of scholarly standards and breadth of viewpoint, the completion at one time or another of such a General Course as that outlined above should certainly enlarge the background of the average American student who comes to Peiping to do his real preparation for research. Fellowships usually stimulate the student to concentrate upon his special field; studying for a General Course of the type outlined should afford him opportunity to branch out.

<u>II. The Student.</u> From the point of view of the student, such a course as that outlined might be of great practical and psychological value.

Practically, it might help to solve the Problem of Procedure, assist the student in determining his best next step, and so increase his efficiency. It might also give the student a valuable acquaintance with the content of other parts of the Chinese field, and so facilitate the correlation of his special material with pertinent material elsewhere.

Psychologically, a General Course and Examinations would give the beginning student a series of concrete objectives. American activists need objectives. Once embarked on the sea of Chinese Studies, they desire to reach a port. To do so they must set a definite course, but since they are at the same time learning to navigate, they have no assurance that their course is the proper one. The knowledge is disconcerting. A definite and attainable program, in which the student could put his confidence, and a series of objectives such as examinations, on which the student could concentrate and by attaining which he could measure his progress, would be of the greatest help.

Missionary workers, consular students, and military attaches have such a series of objectives. But so far nothing has been worked out for academic students. I believe the latter have suffered as a result.

III. Sinology. From the point of view of the sinological curriculum in America, the establishment in Peiping of a curriculum of the sort outlined might be a profitable experiment, through which something could be learned of the procedure and materials that should eventually be used for American students in the United States. In this way a General Course in Peiping might be worth supporting, even if the facilities for Chinese Studies in America should so increase as to make it unnecessary after a few years.

IV. the Ph.D. If the Examinations for the General Course outlined above were developed to a sufficiently high standard and received proper support, it might eventually be possible to induce American institutions to accept the certificate given for the General Course as a mark of attainment equivalent to the passing of a General Examination for the Ph.D. in America.

No doubt if the General Course suggested were accepted by some institutions, it would not be accepted by certain others, on the grounds that the latter institutions desired a still higher standard. But cooperation between a group of institutions, - a rare phenomenon, - might eventually be got. If so, it would then have become possible for an American student to attack both the Chinese Language and his General Examination for the Ph. D. at the same time.

Steps to be taken.

1) Working out of the Reading Lists and Curriculum mentioned.

2) Discovery of an individual capable of administering the course in Peiping, - a scholar, a diplomat, undogmatic, sympathetic, able to help students and yet leave them alone.

- 12 -

3) Enlistment of the cooperation of institutions granting fellowships, which might urge the recipients of fellowships to cooperate in the testing out of an experimental curriculum, and for that purpose take the examinations, voluntarily, and not as a condition of holding their fellowships.

4) Discovery of a sum of money to cover the clerical expenses and salary, if any, of the administrator in Peiping.

John King Fairbank

Peiping, June 1934.

3 HSI-CHIAO HUTUNG

PEKING, CHINA

November 5, 1924.

Dear Baron von Holstein:

Have you any information concerning the details of organization of the Pali Text Society of India? How large a grant do they receive from the Indian Government? Are quarters provided for them by the Government? What rate of pay do they give to translators? These and any other details would be most useful to me at the present time and I shall feel greatly obliged if you can furnish me with any information which you have.

Yours sincerely,

John C. Ferguson

PEKING, CHINA

June 13, 1925.

Dear Baron Von Holstein:

My friend, Honorable Wang Yung-pao, formerly Chinese Minister to Japan, is carrying on an extensive literary investigation of the philology of Chinese dialects. This brings him into constant difficulty as to the transliteration of religious names derived from Sanskrit. He asked me recently if there was any Sanskrit scholar in Peking and I told him of you and your pupil. He has expressed the desire to call on you and I shall be glad to arrange an hour some day when it is convenient for you.

Yours sincerely,

John C. Ferguson

華文學校

NORTH CHINA UNION LANGUAGE SCHOOL
COOPERATING WITH
CALIFORNIA COLLEGE IN CHINA
PEIPING (PEKING) CHINA

March 21, 1932

Baron von Stael-Holstein,
Ex-Austrian Legation,
Peiping.

Dear Baron Stael-Holstein:

Dr. Pettus has sent me a copy of a report which Dr. Hogan has made concerning the organization and work of the School. In this report Dr. Hogan has given a brief survey of the needs of the Library which is of great interest and importance. I have requested Dr. Pettus to allow me to circulate this report to the Friends of the Library and he has kindly allowed me to do so. Herewith I am sending you a copy for your information and consideration.

Yours sincerely,

John C. Ferguson

Chairman

ÉCOLE FRANÇAISE
D'EXTRÊME-ORIENT

N° 2263

GOUVERNEMENT GÉNÉRAL DE L'INDOCHINE

Hanoi, le 3I Octobre I928

P. I.
Le Directeur/de l'École Française d'Extrême-Orient

à Monsieur le Directeur du Sino-indian
Researches Institute, Pi-kouan h'ou-tong,
Pékin.

Monsieur le Directeur,

J'ai l'honneur de vous demander s'il ne vous serait pas possible d'offrir à l'Ecole française d'Extrême-Orient un exemplaire de votre "Comparative Calendar for Chinese, European and Mohammedan history" publié en I926. Nous ne possédons pas cet ouvrage, et nous hésitons à en faire l'acquisition, étant donné les relations d'échange qui existent entre nos deux institutions.

Veuillez agréer, Monsieur le Directeur, avec mes remerciements anticipés, l'expression de ma considération distinguée.

Finot

Monsieur le Directeur,

J'aimerais beaucoup étudier le "Comparative Calendar for Chinese, European and Mohammedan history" mentionné dans votre lettre du 31 octobre 1928 (№ 2263). Voulez-vous avoir la bonté de m'indiquer, où je pourrais acheter cet ouvrage? ~~[illegible]~~ Mes assistants et moi, réunis au "Sino-Indian Research Institute" n'ont pas eu les moyens de ~~faire paraître~~ lancer des publications pendant ces dernières années faute de subventions régulières. Pour les mois ~~8~~ septembre-décembre 1927, par exemple, nous n'avons reçu que des promesses. ~~Pour cette époque nous n'avons, [illegible] jusqu'ici~~ Aucun de nos protecteur ne nous a envoyé, jusqu'ici, de l'argent pour cette époque. Notre futur est assuré par la libéralité de l'Université de Harvard, mais nous n'avons pas pu nous débarasser de nombreuses dettes.

Veuillez agréer, Monsieur le Directeur, l'expression de ma haute considération.

A. Staël-Holstein.

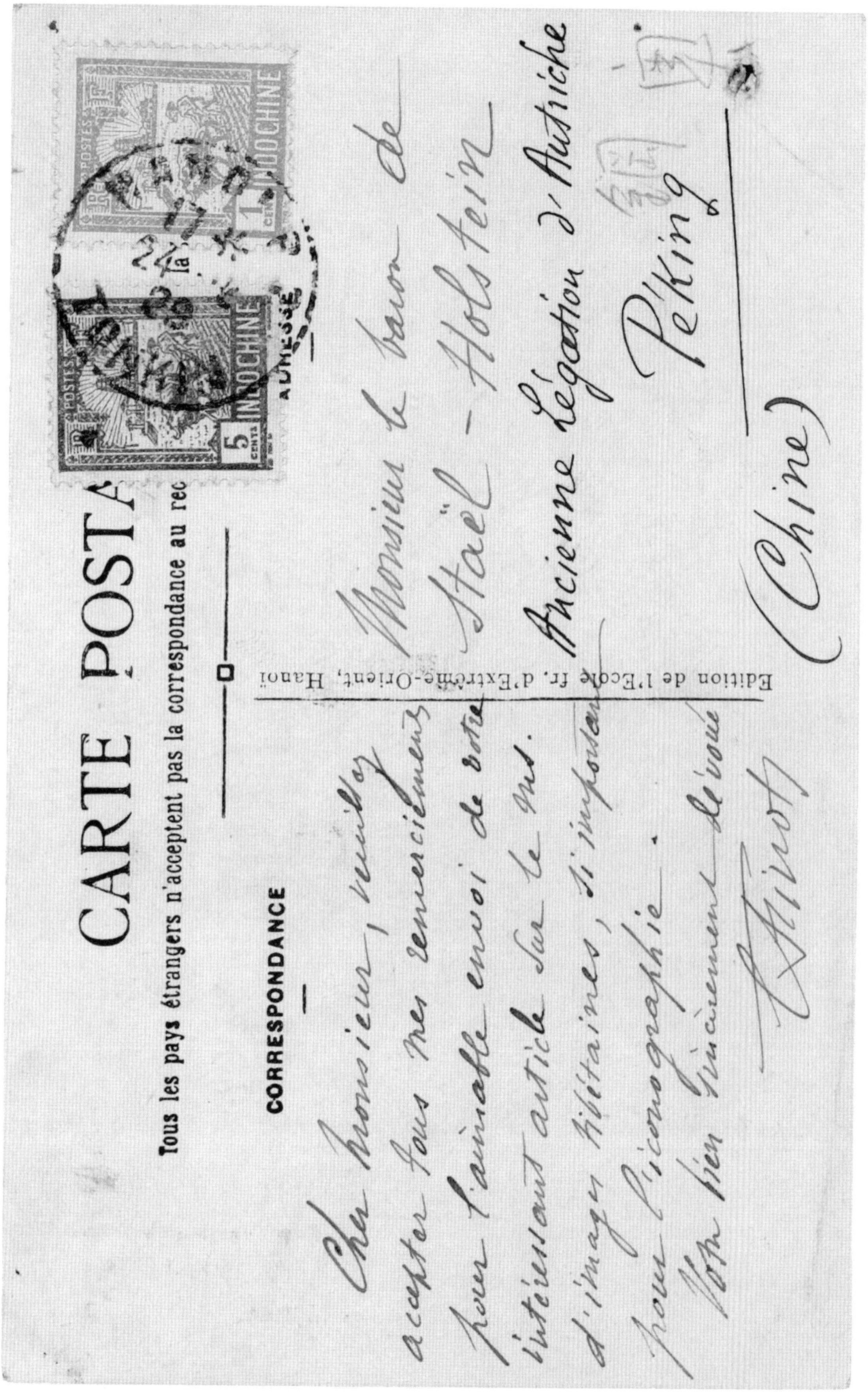
CARTE POSTA[LE]

Tous les pays étrangers n'acceptent pas la correspondance au rec[to]

CORRESPONDANCE

Cher Monsieur, veuillez accepter tous mes remerciements pour l'aimable envoi de votre intéressant article sur le ms. d'images tibétaines, si important pour l'iconographie.

Votre bien sincèrement dévoué

Finot

Edition de l'Ecole fr. d'Extrême-Orient, Hanoi

ADRESSE

Monsieur le baron de Staël-Holstein

Ancienne Légation d'Autriche

Péking

(Chine)

Hochverehrter Herr Doctor,

Meine Frau [struck out] hat seit dem November keine einzige Einladung angenommen, und kann zu ihrem grössten Bedauern am Donnerstag (den 15. Mai) nicht bei Ihnen speisen. Ich nehme aber Ihre freundliche Einladung für meine Person mit dem grössten Dank an.

Mit den besten Grüssen

Ihr ergebener A. Stael Holstein.

Hochverehrte gnädige Frau

Ihre gütige Einladung nehme ich mit dem besten Dank an und werde am Dienstag den 20. Mai um 1.15 bei Ihnen erscheinen.

Es küsst Ihnen die Hand Ihr Ihnen ganz ergebener

A. Stael Holstein

Chère Baronne,

Comme c'est aimable de votre part de m'envoyer le cadre. Je vous le renvoie ci-joint avec tous mes remerciements.

Veuillez croire, chère Baronne, à l'expression de mes sentiments très sincèrement dévoués.

Dear Mr. Fu,

I tried to invite you personally this morning and went first to the Pei Hai where they told me that you were lecturing at the National University. When I arrived at the University I learned that you had just left, and I tried to telephone to your private house, but found that you were not in.

Will you, please, give me the honour of your company at dinner tomorrow (Thursday, March 22th) night at 8 o'clock? A German sinologue Dr. Fuchs has promised to come. The dinner will take place at my house in the former Austrian Legation. Hoping very much to see you tomorrow I remain

Yours sincerely
A. Staël Holstein.

Peiping, April 3rd 1932

Dear Dr. Fu,

I am very much obliged to you for your letter and for the rare distinction which the Academia Sinica has conferred upon me. ~~I highly ap I am immensely proud of~~ I highly appreciate the honour and shall try to prove a worthy research fellow.

I also received with many thanks the copy of Kovalevsky's dictionary which you so kindly ~~sent me~~ presented to me. ~~I am very glad that I possess a complete and which will That valuable work is indeed a~~ I greatly value the volumes of which I never before possessed a complete set.

Believe me yours sincerely and gratefully

Dear Dr. Brown,

One of the Sanscrit formulas which we find on the boards is the following: Namah sattvanam samyaksambuddhanam ("Adoration to the wholly enlightened beings"). The formula Om Manipadme Hum, which we ~~have already~~ discussed before, also occurs. There is, as far as I can see, nothing of special interest on the boards. I am sorry to say that I ~~could~~ have not been able to discover any Indian or Tibetan characters on ~~the~~ your photo which I enclose.

Believe me yours sincerely

Former Austrian Legation Peking March 17th 1935.

Dear Dr. Fu,

~~I am [illegible]~~ I shall be so pleased if you will ~~come and~~ dine with me here tomorrow (Monday, March 18th) at 8 p.m. It will be a stag-party in honour of Dr. Hedin, who has promised to come.

Believe me yours sincerely

A. Staël Holstein.

Black tie.

Peking May 14th/1935.

Dear Professor Fu,

I am awfully sorry to say that I ~~must~~ cannot ~~I ask you to excuse~~ dine with you on Saturday. ~~I must leave I am leaving Peking today as~~ I ~~am going~~ must go to Shanghai etc. ~~on Tuesday~~ on private ~~bus~~ business) today and shall not be back for some weeks.

I enjoyed the An-yang bronzes which you so kindly showed us on Saturday very much, and I thank you once more for your invitation.

Believe me yours very sincerely

A. Staël Holstein.

Peking, April 8th 1936.

My dear Dr. Fu,

I am very much obliged to you for sending me the beautifully bound volume, which you published on the occasion of Mr. Ts'ai's 65th birthday. (It contains a great mass of ~~material~~ fine valuable insights, which ~~is entirely~~ are quite new to me.) I also highly appreciate the fact that the misprints in my short contribution to the volume have been duly corrected.

Believe me yours very sincerely

AStaëlHolstein.

Austrian Legation, Peking, April 28 th 1936

Dear Dr. Fu,

I am greatly in need of a work, which cannot be found in the Peking libraries: Julius Jolly's [Indische] Medizin, which appeared in the ~~Gr~~ Grundriss der Indo-arischen Philologie (und Altertumskunde) (Encyclopaedia of Indo-Aryan Research) in 1901. I want to consult Jolly's work before sending an article, which I am writing for the ~~Jour~~ Harvard Journal of Asiatic Studies, to America, and I venture to ask you to lend me the book, which you ~~posses~~ (IHP) possess, according to the Union Catalogue, for a week or two.

Believe me yours sincerely

A. Staël-Holstein

4645

來報紙 RECEIVING　　中國電報局　　本局號數 JOURNAL NO.

THE CHINESE TELEGRAPH ADMINISTRATION

PEKING VIA NORTHERN 局 OFFICE　　34

由 From	CFO 17/6	附註 —REMARKS—	交 To
時刻 Time	11 點 H 24 分 M	NORTHERN	時刻 Time 點 H 分 M
簽名 By	K A I		簽名 By

原來號數 TELEGRAM NO.	R34	等第 CLASS		字數 WORDS	8				
發報局 Office from	SHANGHAI	日期 Date	17	點 H	11	分 M	40M		

BARON STAEL

PEPING

VIELE HERZLICHE GLUECKWUSNSCHE

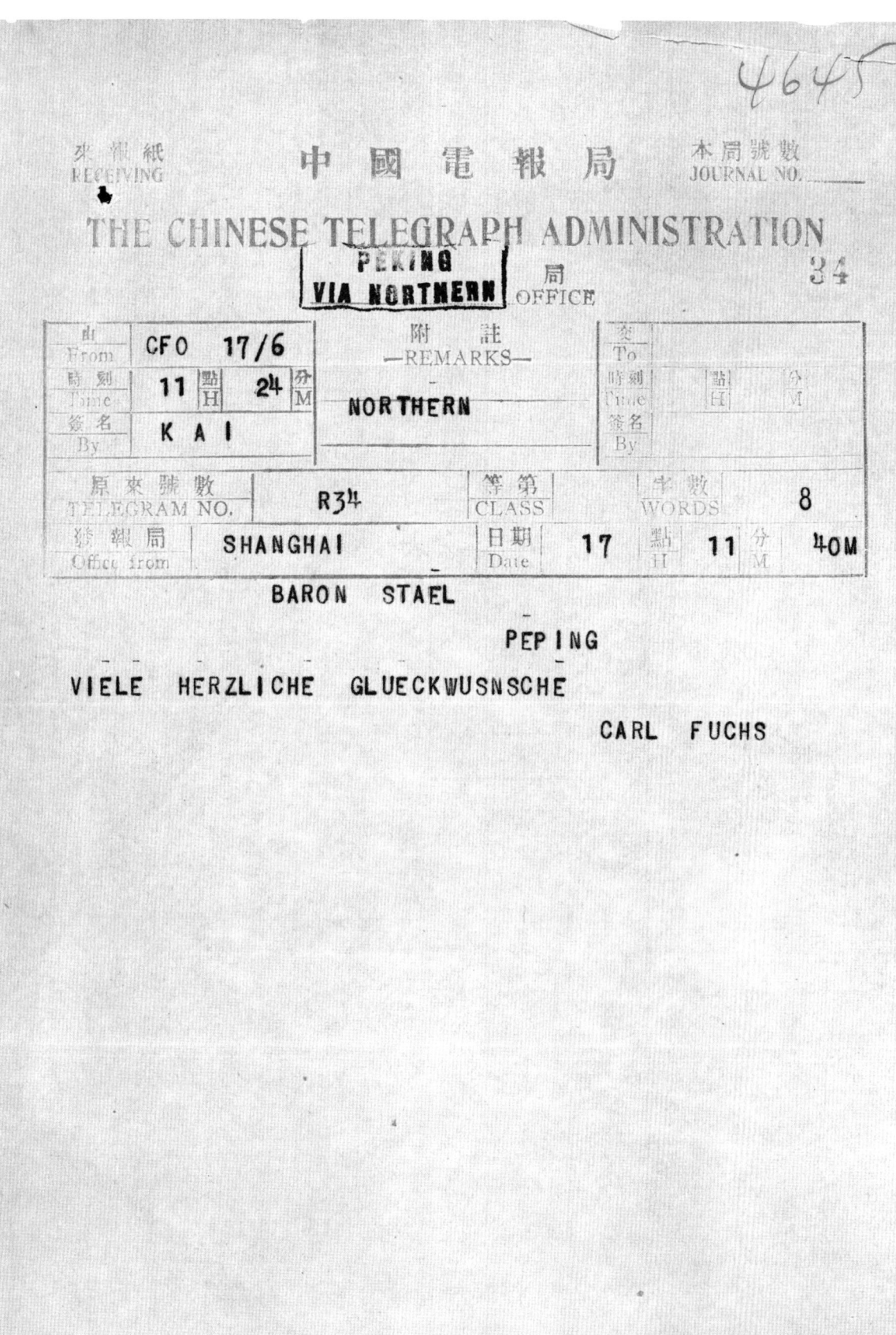

CARL FUCHS

Mukden, den
27. XII. 29.

Sehr verehrter Herr Baron!

Erst neuerdings wieder vernahm ich von Ihnen etwas, als Dr. Betrsing hier durchkam. Die Bemühungen um Ihr Institut scheinen guten Erfolg gehabt zu haben, und ich wünsche Ihnen diesen auch weiterhin. Bereiten Sie z. Z. neue Publicationen vor? Gibt es sonst viel Interessantes aus dem wissensch. Pekinger Leben zu melden? Ich sitze hier abseits vom grossen Betriebe in meinem Bau und bestelle meinen Acker weiter. Eine kl. buddh. Arbeit erscheint demnächst; neben anderen kl. Themen arbeite ich jetzt an der Übersetzung von 慧超, 往五天竺國傳殘卷. — Soeben beendige ich eine kleine mandschurische bibliographische Arbeit über Specialphrasen-Wörterbücher 成語字典; (– Sammlungen)

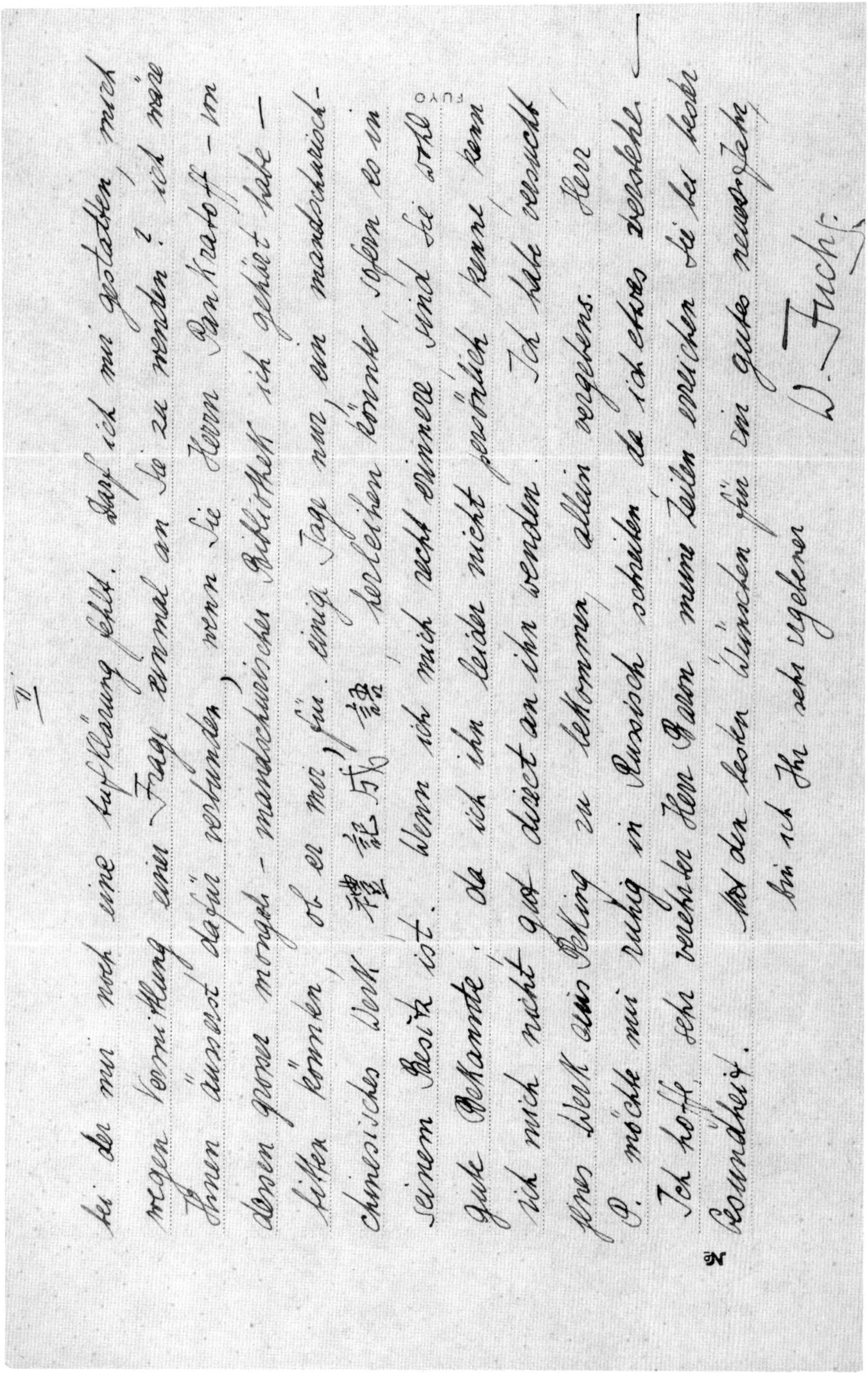

II

bei der mir noch eine Aufklärung fehlt. Darf ich mir gestatten, mich wegen Vermittlung einer Frage einmal an Sie zu wenden? Ich wäre Ihnen äusserst dafür verbunden, wenn Sie Herrn Pankratoff – von dessen grosser mongol.-mandschurischer Bibliothek ich gehört habe – bitten könnten, ob er mir, für einige Tage nur, ein mandschurisch-chinesisches Werk 禮記成語 herleihen könnte, sofern es in seinem Besitz ist. Wenn ich mich recht erinnere, sind Sie wohl gute Bekannte; da ich ihn leider nicht persönlich kenne, kann ich mich nicht gut direct an ihn wenden. Ich habe versucht jenes Werk aus Peking zu bekommen, allein vergebens. Herr P. möchte mir ruhig in Russisch schreiben, da ich etwas verstehe. —

Ich hoffe, sehr verehrter Herr Baron, meine Zeilen erreichen Sie bei bester Gesundheit. Mit den besten Wünschen für ein gutes neues Jahr

bin ich Ihr sehr ergebener

W. Fuchs.

Mukden, den 28. II. 31.

Sehr verehrter Herr Baron!

Bei meinem letzten Aufenthalt in Peking erwähnten Sie mir gegenüber etwas vom Geschick des 108. Bandes des mandjur. Tripitakas; dieser Band ist wohl nicht erschienen, wenn ich mich nicht irre? Dürfte ich Sie wohl bitten, mir einige Worte darüber mitzuteilen?

Im Katalog der Staatsrat-Bibliothek, dem 內閣大庫檔冊目錄, ed. im 玉簡齋叢書, Sammlung 1, von Lo Chen-yü, fand ich zufällig 2 Schriften über die Gurkha: auf p. 8a ein 廓爾喀恭頌歌詞, auf p. 11: 廓爾喀番表. Die Bibliothek dürfte ja jetzt zerstreut sein, aber vielleicht findet sich etwas in Ch'ing-hua oder bei Herrn Yüan.

Zugleich erlaube ich mir, Ihnen einen kleinen Aufsatz zum mandjur. Tripitaka zu übersenden.

Mit den besten Grüssen,

ergebenst

Ihr W. Fuchs.

中國文化經濟協會
NATIONAL COUNCIL
OF THE
CHINESE CULTURAL & ECONOMIC INSTITUTE

OFFICE OF THE EXECUTIVE SECRETARY

FU LU CHU, CHUNGHAI, PEIPING.

January 25, 1932

Dr. Stael Holstein,
Austrian Legation,
Peiping.

Dear Dr. Holstein:

It was my great pleasure to have a talk with you last week. I am happy to say that I like to see you again in the near future.

Dr. J. Leighton Stuart would be happy to have an interview with you Wednesday afternoon, if you could be free from previous engagement. Hope you will drop me a few lines in comfirming this appointment.

With my personal best regards to you.

Sincerely yours,

Philip Fugh

Philip Fugh

中國文化經濟協會
NATIONAL COUNCIL
OF THE
CHINESE CULTURAL & ECONOMIC INSTITUTE
FU LU CHU, CHUNGHAI, PEIPING, CHINA.

February 11, 1932

Dr. Stael Holstein,
Austrian Legation,
Local.

Dear Dr. Holstein:

May I have the honour to inform you that at the request of the Presidents Mr. Hsung Hsi-ling and Dr. J. Leighton Stuart, you are kindly invited to be present at the first meeting of the Society of Friends of the Palace Museum, sharply at half past two in the afternoon of February 15, (next Monday) 1932, at Fu Lu Chu, Chunghai.

As the Society has been newly organized under your respective sponsorship, your valuable consultation and advice will be earnestly sought for its advancement and public service.

Hope that nothing will prevent you from attending this important meeting.

Sincerely yours,

Philip Fugh

Philip Fugh
Secretary of
Society of Friends of Palace Museum

Philip Fugh,
20 Chuan Ta Hutung,
Hsi Szu Pailo,
Peiping, China.

Thursday afternoon-

My dear Dr. Steal Holstein,

It has been sometimes since our last visit, but the delightful hours we spent together will always gives me a happy memory. It was a greatest pleasure to hear your voice through the telephone on the other day, but sorry that the previous engagement made it necessary for me to attend without having the pleasure with you.

I hope you realize how much you have established in my admirations and I am looking forward with the keenest interest to see you again <u>before</u> very long.

With my personal warmest regards, I am

Very sincerely yours,

Philip Fugh

崇內江擦胡同十號
電話東局一三九六

CHINA
ARTS AND HANDICRAFT.

華藝月刊

Illustrated Monthly for Friends of Arts, Collectors and Dealers.

15. Hsia Kung Fu.
~~10 Chiang Tsa Hutung~~ XXXXXXXXXXX

Telephone XXXXX 184 E.

Peking 12th January 1932.

Baron A. von Stael-Holstein,
Ex-Austrian Legation,
Peiping.

Dear Baron,

referring to our conversation of two weeks ago I take the liberty to remind you of the contributing article on Tibetan Arts which you had the kindness to promise me for one of the next issues of our new magazine "China Arts and Handicraft", of which I am now Chairman and Editor in Chief. Kindly let me know the exact title of such article at an early date.- The sudden illness of our former editor, Mr. H.von Hellfeld is not going to affect the existance of the magazine, new arrangements having been made for its regular continuation.

Awaiting the favour of your reply, I am,

very sincerely yours,

H. K. Fung

H. K. Fung,
Chairman and Editor in Chief.

Dear Dr. Fung,

Some months ago you very kindly ~~asked me to write some give you~~ gave me this leaf ~~these pages~~ from your album. ~~and asked me to write for a spe for some~~ Please excuse me for keeping them (which I wrote on one of the pages) for such a long time. The ~~sent~~ Sanscrit sentence reads: Anityo batāyaṃ kāyaḥ karmaiva tu na kṣīyate, and means: This body, ~~hélas~~ alas, is impermanent, but the deed (karma) never perishes.

Believe me yours sincerely

AStaëlHolstein

। अनित्यो बतायं कायः कर्मैव तु न क्षीयते ।

AStaëlHolstein

Peking, May 22nd 1932.

Santiniketan
Bengal India.
18.8.31

To.

Baron A. Von Stël. Holstein
Ph. D. M. Litt.
and Mr. Phang.

Sir:

I am very very sorry not to write to you any letter since I had the misfortune to depart from you both. I hope you have not forgotten me.

Since I left china I had been ~~was~~ touring over many countries and gathering experiences. I was in Kasmir ~~a~~ and Lasa too.

Last year I worked in the library of the Asiatic society of Bengal, and this year I work in the research department of this place under Principal V. Bhattacharya whom you perhaps know. I prepared a catlogue of Pali-canonical works for the use of the Tibetan Lamas and sent it to Dalai Lama.

When I was with you you asked me to stay and work in your library and the institution for Buddhistic research, which you have started in cooperation with some American universities. I could not abide by your request then as I had to return to India soon.

Now I again propose to

visit China before long. So will you please let me know whether I will be of any use to you and your institution. I will be highly obliged if you both can kindly take me to my original place of 1928.

Thanking you both in anticipation of a favourable reply

I am Yours
Sincerely.

T. S. Geshe Lama.

खुंहैगुन

३०-११-३१

प्रियमित्रा होलास्थन, फंदराब,

नमस्ते! अहं बुद्धस्य कृपाभ्य महा-भारत-देशात् महा-चिन-देशे आगत। आनंदः जातः।

अहं इदातीं कुशलं अस्मि। अद्य मम बहु कर्तव्यं अस्ति। अतः तव गुरुशालं आगन्तुं न शक्नोमि।

श्वः अहं तव समीपं आगामि-ष्यामि।

सर्व अत्र कुशलं अस्ति। तव सदैव कुशलं इच्छामि।

तव मित्रः

गेशे लामा

Chateau de Glanville
the 15th September

Dear Baron de Staël-Holstein

Did I ever write to thank you for the translation of the inscription on the iron tablet with silver inlay? — I am generally most methodical about my letters, as soon as I reply. I either destroy the letter or, if, later in years there is something which I wish to keep, I put the date answered & file it among my letters to keep.

On your letter before me with its kind translation, I find no date and I am shocked at myself. Please accept now my sincere thanks and for your ne-

The trip across America was terrifically hot — In fact, up to the date of sailing, it was almost unbearable and would have been so had we not been invited into the country on a beautiful lake. My friends had a steam yacht and when it was unbearable we went on the water.

When I arrived in Paris, it was also hot but I live in a big old-fashioned flat, as you know, and it was possible to be comfortable.

In Chicago I spent an afternoon with Laufer in the Field Museum and afterward we had tea together. We spoke of you and he seemed to think it very an impor-

tant his disagreement with you about a word which
I am, I fear forgotten — was it „Turkhan"? He
said it was purely question of accent and that
as he had lived in the part of Asia where the
word was used, he knew the proper accent (so
he thinks) which made the meaning different.
He has not an attractive personality and still
speaks English with a strong German accent —
isn't it strange? But he has entirely broken with
Germany and says he is in the black books of all
the German savants.

I received a letter from Prof. Foucher who has
left India and has been sent by the French
Government to Persia for a year.

Prof. Sylvain Levi is leaving in October for
India to open Rabindra-nath Tagore's university
at Bholpur — M. Pelliot is going to America for the
reunion of all the Asiatic Societies. So Paris will
be abandoned this ~~year~~ autumn.

I am not yet sure what or where I shall
go but I shall not remain during the winter.

M. Crane has been in Paris and dined
with me just before I came to this enchanting
old Louis XIII chateau — surrounded by a moat
and full of delightful memories — for my
friend is one of my oldest friends in France.

Mr Crane, as you probably know, succeeded
in crossing Asia and Siberia into Russia after
having been stopped at Chita and sent back for
24 hours. He had many gruesome tales to tell

He said there were no more hotels either at Moscow or Petrograd – He remained in his car. Lenine is more guarded than the Tzars and he claims that the peasants call him "the Tzar Lenine"!

I have just heard that a charming friend of mine whom you perhaps knew in Petrograd, princess Vera Lapoukine – Demidoff – was atrociously murdered a few months ago near Kieff – And another, who has just escaped being executed, is at Riga – when will it all end?

I was very sorry to learn of the death of poor M. Boppe. How dreadful for his poor wife, so far away from France!

When you see General Mather will you kindly ask him if he received my thanks for his photo which I was so delighted to have! I am sending you the two photos I took of you and our Dutch friends (I cannot for the moment remember their name!)

Hoping these will find you and all my Peking friends well

I am Very sincerely yours

Alice Getty

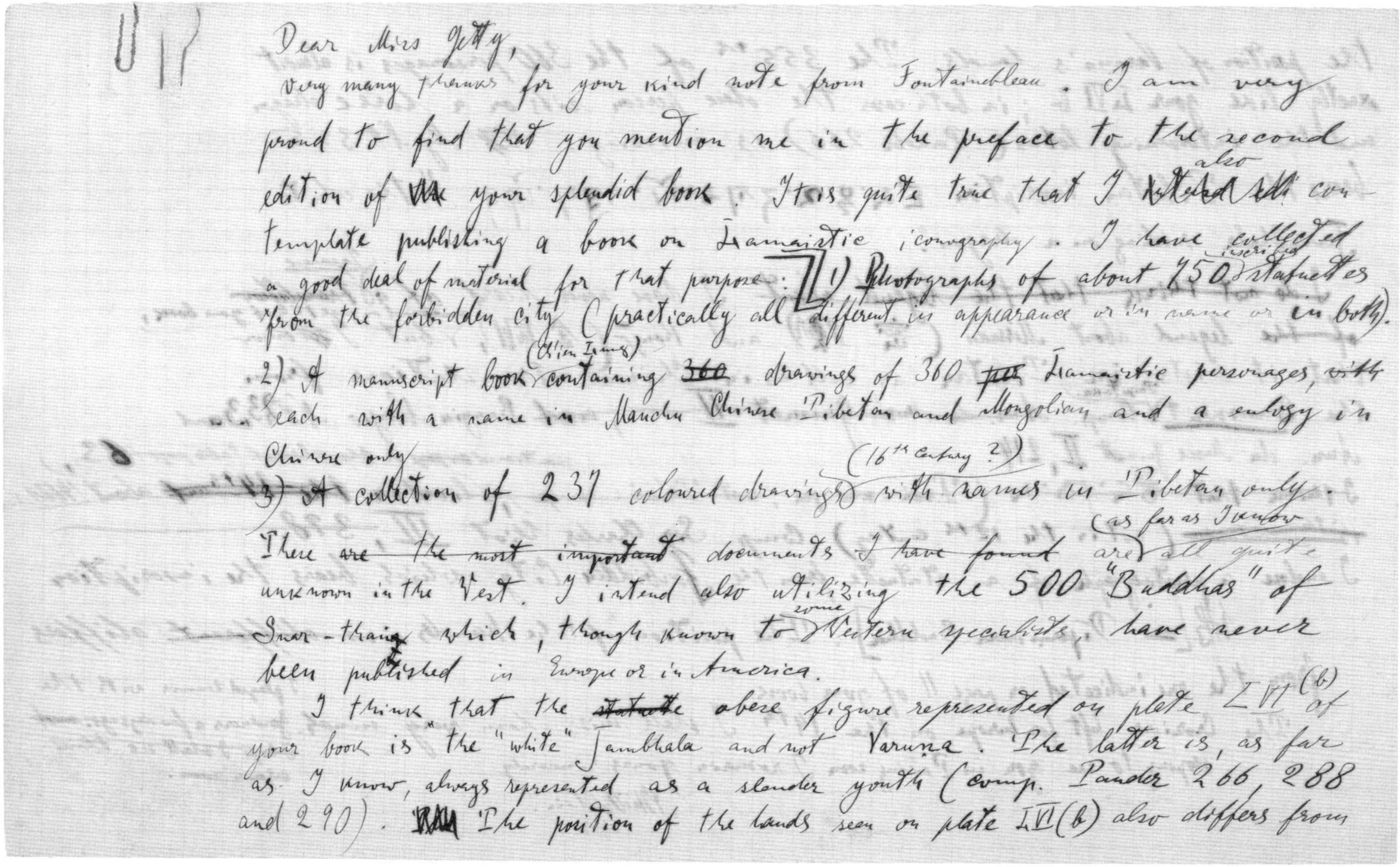

Dear Miss Getty,
very many thanks for your kind note from Fontainebleau. I am very proud to find that you mention me in the preface to the second edition of ~~the~~ your splendid book. It is quite true that I ~~intend~~ also con-template publishing a book on Lamaistic iconography. I have collected a good deal of material for that purpose: 1) Photographs of about 750 inscribed statuettes from the forbidden city (practically all different in appearance or in name or in both).
2) A manuscript book (Ch'ien Lung) containing ~~360~~ drawings of 360 Lamaistic personages, each with a name in Manchu Chinese Tibetan and Mongolian and a eulogy in Chinese only
3) A collection of 237 coloured drawings (16th century?) with names in Tibetan only.
These ~~are the most important~~ documents ~~I have found~~ are (as far as I know) ~~all~~ quite unknown in the West. I intend also utilizing the 500 "Buddhas" of Snar-thang which, though known to some Western specialists, have never been published in Europe or in America.
I think that the ~~statue~~ above figure represented on plate LVI (b) of your book is the "white" Jambhala and not Varuṇa. The latter is, as far as I know, always represented as a slender youth (comp. Pander 266, 288 and 290). ~~The~~ The position of the hands seen on plate LVI (b) also differs from

the position of Varuna's hands. The 355th of the 360 personages is almost exactly like your LVI b; in both cases the obese person sits on a horse dragon and the intervening lotus (Pander 266) is missing. ~~[illegible]~~ My No 355 bears the Tibetan inscription [illegible] "the white Jambhala riding on a dragon".

~~I do not think that the legend about~~ I have never heard of a Japanese ~~Translation of the~~ legend about Missaku (密跡) and Kongō (金剛), mentioned on page 152 of your book, but I know that it exists in Tibetan as well as in Chinese translations from the Sanskrit Tripitaka. Comp. ~~Ann. du Musée Guimet II~~, ~~and~~ Bunyiu Nanjio No 233 and Ann. du Musée Guimet II, 214.

~~(mentioned on page in the chronol. table page 163,)~~

~~I think that [illegible] (Tson-kha-pa, not Ts'oi-ka-pa), lived in the 14th and about 1400 A.D. 15th centuries (not in the 12th century) Comp. Sir Charles Eliot III, 398.~~

I enclose a photograph of a statuette from the Forbidden City which bears the inscription 佛 [= Dipamkara Buddha]. The position of the hands ~~is different~~ differs from the one indicated on page 11 of your book.

The Croziers left for Europe on the 14th I shall miss them very much. I played tennis with the Gardners a few days ago. ~~and I hope I shall see them again soon.~~

Hoping to see you in Peking soon I remain yours sincerely

A. Staël-Holstein.

Taianfu

Dear Baron

We were very sorry not to see you before leaving — we thought you might be coming to see us off? I wanted to thank you personally for the most interesting data you sent me. It is a great help to know that one can say this assemblage belongs to the Garbhakośa maṇḍala —

I have come up against the Seven Star deities on the way up to Tai shan. Of course, the priest knew nothing. But I am sending you two ~~titles~~ of books he uses for the ceremonies — He claimed that they contained "all about" them (He probably only reads a verse or two at the ceremonies) — and today in a temple, I got another title.

If these books can be procured, & if you know of someone who could translate for me the passages relating to the Seven Stars, will you not let me know at Shanghai (Astor House) where I shall be until the 26th, how much it will all come to and I will send you on the amount —

We had a superb day & sunset at on Tai Shan and a ~~fine~~ day to come down — a wonderful & most successful trip — & what a view from on top! —

Tomorrow we go to Chefoo & then to Soochow — none of these places have I ever seen before —

This is just a hurried note — a sleepy note (for we were up this a.m. extremely early) to thank you for giving yourself so much trouble to let me know about Amitayus — and my joy at learning that my theory can be worked out with an authority behind it —. But I hope to find still more and more ancient appeari— —

Best of greetings from us both

Very sincerely yours

Alice Getty

after Shanghai
Poste Restante
Saigon
and then
75 av. des Champs Elysées
Paris